STERLIN
Test Pre

AP

U.S. History

Complete Content Review

5th edition

Customer Satisfaction Guarantee

Your feedback is important because we strive to provide the highest quality educational materials. Email us comments or suggestions.

info@sterling–prep.com

We reply to emails – check your spam folder

5 4 3 2 1

ISBN-13: 979-8-8855720-7-1

Sterling Education materials are available at quantity discounts.

Contact info@sterling–prep.com

Sterling Test Prep
6 Liberty Square #11
Boston, MA 02109

© 2024 Sterling Education

Published by Sterling Education

 Printed in the U.S.A.

STERLING
Test Prep

Thousands of students use our study materials to achieve high AP scores.

Scoring well on AP exams is essential to earn placement credits and admission into competitive colleges, positioning you for success. Understanding the material, extracting and analyzing information, and distinguishing between similar answer choices are more effective than mere memorization. With this book, you will master AP U.S. History content and develop the ability to apply your knowledge on test day to achieve a high score.

This study guide provides thorough coverage of topics tested on AP U.S. History. This book is clearly presented and systematically organized to review essential facts and historical events. From the founding of the United States of America to the present-day political and societal challenges, this targeted preparation guide is perfect for learning about the history of America and its democracy.

Learn about influential historical figures and important events that established the foundations of America, the meaning and significance of social movements, and how each important historical event shaped the country's political development and cultural heritage.

Highly qualified history teachers, scholars, and researchers prepared this learning material to build knowledge and skills for understanding American history. Our test preparation experts structured the content to match the current College Board curriculum for targeted and effective learning.

Using this book will significantly improve your AP U.S. History score!

240309akp

Featured on

Advanced Placement (AP) prep books by Sterling Test Prep

Biology Practice Questions

Biology Review

Physics 1 Practice Questions

Physics 1 Review

Physics 2 Practice Questions

Physics 2 Review

Environmental Science

Psychology

United States History

World History

European History

U.S. Government and Politics

Comparative Government and Politics

Human Geography

Visit our Amazon store

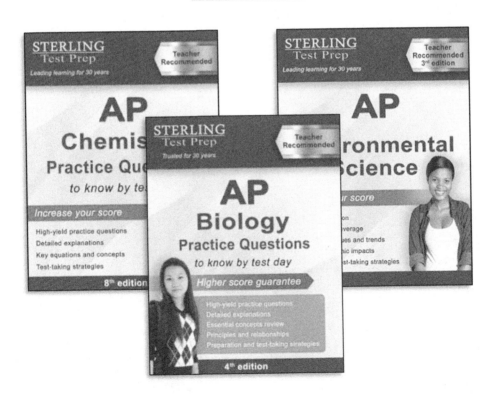

If you benefited from this book, we would appreciate if you left a review on Amazon so others can learn from your input. Reviews help us understand our customers' needs and experiences while keeping our commitment to quality.

Table of Contents

Table of Contents (*continued*)

PERIOD 1: PRE-COLUMBIAN PERIOD TO 1789 (*continued*)

Table of Contents (*continued*)

Table of Contents (*continued*)

Table of Contents *(continued)*

Table of Contents *(continued)*

Table of Contents (*continued*)

PERIOD 1

Pre-Columbian Period to 1789

Political History: Pre-Columbian Period to 1789

European exploration sought wealth, power, and Christian converts

From the 8th to the 15th centuries, the Christian kingdoms of the Iberian Peninsula sought to drive out the Moors, Muslims from North Africa who had conquered most of the peninsula in the early years of Islam. The gradual *Reconquista*, or Reconquest, was not complete until 1492.

In 1479, two Spanish monarchs, King Ferdinand of Aragon (1452-1516) and Queen Isabella of Castile (1479-1555), married and united their kingdoms. Thirteen years later, their armies expelled the Muslims from their last stronghold.

The *Reconquista* was not a mere political conflict but a crusade driven by a devotion to the Christian religion and hatred of infidels. Whereas Iberian Muslim rulers offered Christians and Jews considerable religious freedom, the Christian rulers sought to use an intolerant Christianity to unite their subjects and vanquish a common enemy.

Reconquista fighters saw themselves as obviously superior to enemies who rejected Christ and developed rules of war reflective of this view. These rules made it legal to enslave any conquered people. As soon as the *Reconquista* was complete, Muslims and Jews faced a choice of conversion or expulsion from Spanish lands.

The *Reconquista* nourished religious devotion, a markedly militaristic mindset, and a romantic understanding of war. Spanish fighters, especially the Castilians who were to conquer the Americas, also had roots in an agricultural society where personal relationships, reputation, and honor were the critical elements in determining a man's worth. At the same time, materialistic motives were apparent as well.

As the Spanish kings frequently lacked the funds to finance military actions, military leaders would risk their own money, securing, in turn, rights to conquered land and a share of the spoils. These pre-existing notions of simultaneously seeking monetary reward, divine favor, and a glorious reputation in romantically inspired military adventures made the conquistadors a perfect fit for their demanding roles of conquerors of a New World across the enormous ocean and of people they saw as savages and heathens. They were prepared for an adventure, and Admiral Columbus's voyages (1492, 1493, 1498, 1502) gave them one.

After centuries of relative isolation, the Crusades had brought Europeans into contact with eastern cultures again. Temporarily recapturing the Holy Land allowed them to gain familiarity with the abundance of spices, silk, jewels, gold, and other goods flowing from China, India, and other parts of Asia beyond the Middle East.

Unfortunately, South and East Asia were thousands of miles away, across deserts, mountain ranges, and lands where both the climate and the inhabitants were inhospitable. The long and treacherous journey from the East made spices and other goods expensive when they reached the West.

Columbus, underestimating the distance to the Indies (Asia), proposed to open new sources of wealth and glory by sailing westward rather than following the route around Africa that the Portuguese were exploring. In 1492, his persistent lobbying finally resulted in funding for his expedition. Ferdinand and Isabella did not have complete faith in Columbus, but they realized that the potential benefits and costs were relatively low.

Upon arrival, Columbus was disappointed by the people he found. Although friendly and peaceful, they did not have any of the vast riches Marco Polo and other travelers had written about. Indeed, they did not know how to work metals and had no weapons other than simple spears. The main problem Columbus faced was profitability, derived from his deficient understanding of geography. Ultimately, he considered the islands part of the Indies, thinking that Hispaniola was Japan and Cuba the Asian mainland.

The landing of Columbus, c. 1492

However, it was apparent that the abundant ports and cities he had heard about were nowhere to be found and that none of the people he met had any contact with the Great Khan of the Mongols. Admiral Columbus (1451-1506) had hoped to ally with the Khan against the Muslims as part of a farfetched scheme to use profits from the new possessions to reconquer Jerusalem. It had been prophesized that the reconquest of Jerusalem would bring about the Second Coming of Christ.

The fortress and trading post system that the Portuguese had set up on the coast of Africa was not a realistic option for the Caribbean either. Trading posts would only be helpful if there were a sizeable trade, but there was no indication of such an enterprise. While the colonies served primarily as sources of wealth and power, they continued to be imbued with a religious purpose. In the Latin American colonies, the preaching orders of the Roman Catholic church—Franciscans, Dominicans, and Jesuits—played vital roles.

Friars participated in most expeditions, and conquest and conversion often went hand in hand (though with questionable success). Within ten years of Cortés landing in Mexico, one Franciscan friar claimed to have personally converted more than 200,000 Indians to Christianity.

Spanish explorers: thanksgiving before the image of the Virgin

Jesuits were most prominent in these activities, and the order was established as a special operations force of the Counter-Reformation. In Brazil, the Jesuits pushed European settlement inland as they pressed farther up the rivers to create new, tightly-knit frontier settlements of Christian Indians isolated from the sinfulness of the conquistadors. In Paraguay, their settlements were so numerous and successful that it almost appeared to be a separate country. The territory had its army and about 100,000 Indians under Jesuit tutelage.

Early contact with indigenous peoples in Africa and the Americas

Establishing contact with the Indians shocked Christian Europeans: the indigenous people of the Americas did not appear in the Bible or the other primary source of authoritative knowledge, the writings of the ancient Greeks and Romans. At the outset, it was not even clear whether or not the Indians should be considered human. From the perspective of Christian Europe, this would require the Indians to have the ability to reason and a soul that could be saved from eternal suffering through conversion to true faith. Once the pope had declared that Indians were human, the Spanish began to recognize their humanity. They saw them as a part of the united community of God and recognized that they had certain rights.

Europeans, generally, and the colonists especially had few qualms about subjecting American Indians and Africans to harsh discipline and hard work or taking away other peoples' lands or humanity. Before the second half of the 18th century, the only major exception was the dissent of some highly articulate Spanish friars and theologians. Dominican friars on Hispaniola had come to convert the heathen but witnessed death and destruction on an unprecedented scale.

Primarily because of diseases the Europeans brought, with the added effect of violence and forced labor, the population of Hispaniola dropped from maybe several million in 1492 to less than 30,000 twenty years later. One day in 1511, Antonio de Montesinos (1475-1540) gave the first sermon on the treatment of the native peoples: *"Tell me, by what right of justice do you keep these Indians in cruel and horrible servitude? On what authority have you waged a detestable war against these people, who dwelt quietly and peacefully on their own lands? . . . Are these not men? Have they not rational souls? Are you not bound to love them as you love yourselves?"*

The colonists were outraged by this attack, but the Dominicans continued to question the legality and morality of the colonial enterprise and forced a protracted debate among lawyers and theologians in Spain. The Dominican theologian Francisco de Vitoria used the medieval conception of natural law to demonstrate that Indians were rational beings with rights to life, liberty, safety, and property, which could not be abridged by the pope or by the king of Spain. His writings went far toward creating a foundation for international law and suggesting all human beings' fundamental equality and dignity.

The most famous defender of Indian rights was Bartolomé de Las Casas (1484-1566), formerly a priest who owned former Indian lands worked by forced Indian labor. He experienced a crisis of conscience in 1514, became a Dominican friar, and spent most of his life working for better treatment of the Indians. Las Casas argued that the European purpose in the New World should be peaceful conversion.

In 1550-1551, he argued the case of the Indians at a hearing in Valladolid, Spain, debating for several months about the legal and theological aspects of colonization and empire. His primary opponent was the scholar Juan Ginés de Sepúlveda, who argued the Aristotelian point that the civilized had every right to rule over barbarians.

Las Casas and his supporters had some influence on the development of Spanish colonial law. Most of the time, the protections guaranteed to Indians and Africans existed only on paper. Because he tended to exaggerate, Las Casas was also used to propagate the so-called "Black Legend," the idea that Spanish rule was more cruel and unjust than that of the other colonial powers. It would be difficult to argue that the other powers of the 16th and 17th centuries were significantly better.

Spanish explorers raising a memorial cross

Diverse patterns of colonization

European colonial powers, including England, Spain, France, and the Netherlands, had some shared goals for the colonizing process. However, the substantial differences in the cultures of these countries and the variety of environments encountered in the New World led to a remarkable difference in the patterns and outcomes of imperial ventures. Governments' divergent considerations and purposes played a significant role in creating differences in how countries administered and ruled the distant lands they claimed.

For example, the Spanish government was far more involved in governing its colonies than England. The Spanish central control model led to different development trajectories than the English's mostly hands-off approach. The land and its natural resources also greatly affected development trajectories; areas suitable for growing export commodities, like sugar and tobacco, imported large numbers of enslaved people, while areas characterized by more mixed agriculture evolved differently.

In some of the following areas, the economy became significantly more diversified, allowing the development of crafts, commerce, and small-scale manufacturing. Other factors, including warfare, laws, religion, disease, racial sentiments, gender roles, and relations between colonists and Indians, made a difference and ensured that the American colonies—despite their commonalities—became a mosaic of social, economic, and cultural patterns.

Cultivation of tobacco at Jamestown, c. 1610

Spanish, French, Dutch, and British colonization models

One of the most significant differences between the colonial powers was the difference in cultural perceptions of economic development or, more simply, the meaning of making money. To the Spanish elite, comprised of the monarchy, nobility, and the church, which dominated society and stamped their cultural values on the process of colonization, it was ultimately titles, honor, luxury, and the glory of God that mattered.

There was no glory in working hard or accumulating capital; money was supposed to be spent on luxuries and leisure or, even more prudently, on conquests, wars, and the conversion of heathens. They sought wealth primarily through extracting mineral resources or demanding tribute and labor from native populations and placed little emphasis on economic development in the sense of modernization or progress.

The Spanish were aristocratic and pre-capitalist, and despite the manifestations of their greed, they valued money as a means to an end rather than an end in itself. Admiral Christopher Columbus (1451-1506) died, despite his noteworthy nautical achievements and vast wealth, feeling unrecognized as an administrator and religious pioneer.

Christopher Columbus (1451-1506)

In the 1770s, the Spanish sent explorers into California, and by 1776, they had established San Francisco. The fierce resistance of the Yuma Indians closed the overland route to California from the 1780s to the mid-19th century, forcing colonists to arrive by sea. Nevertheless, the Spanish established over twenty settlements along the coast from San Diego to San Francisco. There was virtually no white settlement in the interior.

The mission towns, located about a day's ride apart, were usually manned by a couple of friars and a handful of soldiers. The labor in the settlements was done by Indians who were either forced or persuaded to join the missions and hunted down if they tried to run away. The Indians were treated as slaves, even though they were not enslaved people in a legal sense.

Eventually, the missions claimed vast lands—as much as one million acres per settlement. Soldiers and ambitious colonists received huge land grants virtually for free, and even foreigners could be granted lands if they became Spanish and Catholic.

Mission Indians of Southern California, c. 1780

The Dutch mostly tried to gain independence from Spain between 1568 and 1648. They had a very different culture and a different order of priorities. In the 17th century, the Netherlands became the world leader in shipping, commerce, and finance. The government was a federal republic where merchants were profoundly influential, and colonial ventures were directed by joint-stock companies rather than the Crown.

These joint-stock companies had armies and navies and utilized force whenever necessary to secure profits, but capital gains rather than glory or honor were usually the aim. Over time, their primarily commercial orientation and impressive financial savvy were not enough to protect their leading position in the world economy, as other militarily stronger nations surpassed them.

The British colonies were unusual because the government exercised very little control over their development compared to other colonial powers. The colonies were created almost haphazardly for economic, religious, and political reasons. There was little or no uniform administration, and the colonists in America grew accustomed to having rights and privileges relatively independent from the Crown.

The North American colonies were generally seen as unattractive because they did not bring immediate profits from high-value commodities like gold, silver, or sugar. Those already rich and powerful saw little reason to waste their time or energy on these projects. Instead, they became opportunities for middle-class or lower-class Europeans who wanted to improve their status, become rich, or create religious utopias.

The cultural development of these colonies was heavily influenced by the beliefs and customs of the immigrants who arrived. Puritans in England, Germans in Pennsylvania, and Scottish Highlanders in the North Carolina hinterland brought unique behaviors and lifestyles that remained influential despite the necessary adaptations to the New World environment and the colonial system.

Settlers in North Carolina, c. 1653

With the decline of Spanish power in the 17th century, France emerged as the most significant power on the European continent. France's power depended on the government's ability to extract soldiers and taxes from a large population to fight large-scale and expensive wars. The French government discouraged mass emigration to the colonies and was reluctant to use scarce resources and manpower to defend American settlements.

Canada and Louisiana seemed to have few natural resources that could be easily exploited, and efforts to develop these areas tended to be halfhearted. The French were more concerned with Haiti, which promised to be a major supplier of highly demanded sugar.

Competition over resources led to conflicts

As the power of Spain began to decline in the early 17th century, the Dutch, who were fighting for their independence from Spain, began to challenge Spanish hegemony in the Americas. France and England followed suit. Due to the continuing decline of Spain and the eventual defeat of the Dutch in several wars with the English, the rivalry between France and Britain eventually became the central conflict in 18th-century North America. The colonial powers also had Indian allies who played essential roles. In many cases, the Indians favored the more accommodating and less land-hungry French and Spanish rather than the increasingly populous and aggressive English colonies.

Between 1688 and 1748, the colonial powers were embroiled in three major wars that could arguably be classified as world wars. The first was King William's War (1688–1697), known as the Nine Years' War in Europe, which was fought to prevent France, the primary power on the continent, from becoming too dominant. In North America, the war was fought for different purposes, as the French were few and seemingly weak there, trying to hold on to vast territorial claims on the Hudson Bay region and the St. Lawrence and Mississippi Rivers with a minimal settler population.

The French inflicted numerous defeats on the English colonists, partially because of the effective combination of French, colonial, and allied Indian troops. The French were also victorious in North America because the English government prioritized the West Indian colonies, as the profits from the sugar islands made them more valuable.

The arrival of the Indian allies at the French camp

Queen Anne's War (1702–1713) was also part of a more massive European conflict, the War of the Spanish Succession. Again, the goal was to limit the power of France, as a member of the French monarchy inherited the throne in Spain. This meant the British had to battle Spanish and French forces in the Americas. Once again, the British clashed with the French and their allies to the north, but this time with greater success.

France was forced to cede Nova Scotia, Newfoundland, and the Hudson Bay region by the war's end. Meanwhile, Spanish Florida had been completely devastated by the brutal raids of the British and their Indian allies, inflicting so much death and destruction that the Spanish colony never quite recovered.

A generation later, two other wars erupted in the Americas, and once again, they were intertwined with a European conflict, the War of the Austrian Succession. In the War of Jenkins' Ear (1739-48), the main issue was the British monopoly on the slave trade to the Spanish colonies. Much of this war played out in South and Central America and the Caribbean, but in 1742, Spanish forces invaded Georgia. After this attack was repelled, the North American theater was relatively calm.

By 1744, King George's War (1744-1748) had broken out with renewed fighting between the French and the British. The British forces captured the Fortress of Louisbourg in Nova Scotia, but this did not prevent French forces and their Indian allies from raiding frontier areas. The British settlements north of Albany had to be abandoned entirely until the war ended in 1748. The colonists in New York, and especially those in Massachusetts, suffered massive casualties during this war and were incensed when the peace treaty traded Louisbourg for a town in India.

European conflicts brought political instability in North America

Early modern Europe was a dangerous and violent place with numerous long, brutal wars. The continual conflicts between the great powers did not only occur at home but spread to include lengthy, costly, and destructive colonial wars.

For example, the Spanish settlements in Florida were often attacked by English and French forces and their respective Indian allies. So much death, destruction, and enslavement ensured that by the early 18th century, the whole area was almost devoid of people. Other Spanish colonies faced fierce Indian uprisings, such as the Pueblo Rebellion of 1680 and the Pima Revolt of 1751.

The 17th-century Beaver Wars, also known as the Iroquois Wars, were a series of wars between the Iroquois tribes, supported by the Dutch and English, and the Algonquian tribes, supported by the French. The imperialist Iroquois sought to extend their domains and control the fur trade in the Great Lakes region, expanding from their eastern strongholds into new, western lands. In wars increasingly marked by extreme brutality, the Iroquois enlarged their empire and destroyed or displaced many of the other Indian tribes.

As enemy groupings disintegrated and fled to the west and south, large swaths of land in the Great Lakes region and the Ohio Valley became virtually depopulated. This strengthened the hand of England in colonial North America and even facilitated the settlement of this area by white Americans in the early United States.

The 18th-century Chickasaw Wars, although ostensibly a conflict between Indian tribes, had similar beneficial effects on British interests. The Choctaws, acting as proxies of the French in Louisiana, sought to defeat the Chickasaws. The Chickasaws were allied with the English and threatened French communications and trade along the Mississippi River. French efforts to wage European-style campaigns with heavy artillery proved futile, as did the decades-long Choctaw harassment consisting of raids, ambush attacks, and failed sieges.

Colonial governance of late 17th century

The move from autonomy or neglect to stricter control by the royal government was mainly tied to trade policies. The British Empire was set up to follow a mercantilistic model of political economy, which in practice meant a desire to control or even monopolize both exports to and imports from the American colonies, regulating and often limiting the colonies' trade with other countries or even with other colonies within the empire.

The Navigation Acts specified that shipping to and from Britain and the colonies could only be handled by English ships, an effort to deprive the Dutch of their maritime supremacy. Eventually, Americans were barred from producing finished iron goods—everything was to be imported from Britain.

In 1686, the royal government attempted centralization by revoking the old charters of the northeastern colonies and introducing a new administrative structure, the Dominion of New England. The government became concerned that the northern colonies began deviating from mercantilism by developing their trade and manufacturing, competing with the home country. The proposal was intended to impose a system more like the Spanish colonies in the Americas. However, this structure collapsed only three years later in the wake of the so-called Glorious Revolution in England. More generally, mercantilist policies were unsuccessful in preventing the development of a mixed economy of agriculture, commerce, and manufacturing in the colonies or in convincing the colonists that their role was simply to make the home country rich.

One of the main reasons why mercantilism remained less than capable was a lack of sincere efforts to enforce the laws on the books. Instead, Britain preferred to look the other way and continued to allow the colonies to develop by the wishes of local white men with property. The government was so concerned with their rivalry with the French that they thought it would be imprudent to alienate the colonists, especially as the French were often more successful in recruiting Indian allies than the British.

Colonial autonomy and imperial authority

As the British colonies grew in population and productivity, the home government became more interested in their development. Whereas the colonies emerged from various commercial ventures, idealistic projects, and personal ambitions and practiced considerable autonomy in the early years, the government now tried to impose its authority on the American subjects of the Crown. Many proprietary colonies became royal colonies with royal governors who wielded considerable power that tended to increase over time.

The colonies typically had two other organs of government: the council appointed by the Crown and the assembly elected by voters. Although the power of the assembly was limited in some ways, it had the paramount prerogative of controlling taxation. Agents of the assemblies also cooperated with the British Board of Trade, which wielded much power in colonial matters. Through measured protests against overzealous governors, the colonists were usually able to maintain considerable autonomy without engaging in outright conflict with the British government.

One example of the government's efforts to standardize legislation and impose imperial control on colonial matters it had long neglected was the *Debt Recovery Act* of 1732. This law introduced uniformity throughout the empire in treating people who could not pay their debts. It stipulated that houses and enslaved people should be treated as equivalent to land in the collection of debts, meaning that enslaved people, buildings, and real estate could be sold at auction if debtors could not satisfy their creditors otherwise.

In Virginia, the assembly called the House of Burgesses, passed a new law in the 1740s to counteract this law, making it more difficult for British merchants to collect on the debts of the influential Virginia planters.

The *Hat Act*, also passed in 1732, was a more direct attempt to extend mercantilism using precise regulations to limit colonial manufacturing to avoid any undesirable competition for manufacturers back in Britain. The *Hat Act* not only limited the number of hats that American hatters could make, sell, or export; it even specified how many workers and apprentices hatmakers could employ. The point of this legislation was to force colonists to buy more expensive hats imported from Britain, which consequently fostered much resentment of a seemingly arbitrary power play on the side of the Crown.

Britain's attempts at more imperial control

When the war with France ended in 1763, Britain was left with enormous debts incurred in protecting the colonies and conquering Lower Canada. Part of the reason for the proclamation limiting white settlement on the continent was the cost of administration and war connected with expansion.

In addition to limiting costs, the government also wanted to increase revenue. The British sought to accomplish this by making the collection of existing duties more effective and imposing new duties on the colonies. Part of the rationale was that Americans should pay for their defense. However, many colonists argued that without any French threat, there was little need for a standing army of British soldiers in the colonies.

The 1764 *Sugar Act* imposed duties on molasses and other goods, which were still indirect or external taxes. The 1765 *Stamp Act* was a direct or internal tax on many kinds of printed materials. Although the British argued that the level of taxation was relatively low, the colonists protested because they were not represented in Parliament. They believed that as English subjects, they could not be taxed without representation and pointed out that they also paid local taxes, which contributed significantly to the war effort.

Reading the Stamp Act, c. 1765

Opponents of taxation without representation formed the Sons of Liberty and worked to make the new laws challenging to enforce. Parliament meanwhile argued that the colonies technically were mere corporations subject to British authority, and the government considered the interests of the American colonists in a kind of virtual representation. In 1766, Parliament repealed the *Stamp Act* while sticking to the principle that Britain had every right to legislate for the colonies.

The following year, a new set of laws, the Townshend Acts, were passed to impose duties on a variety of goods and to follow up on existing trade regulations. These laws were met with new protests and boycotts, and tensions escalated, especially in Boston, where riots ensued when the authorities seized a smuggler's vessel.

In 1770, a mob confronted British soldiers, resulting in five deaths. Although the soldiers involved in the shooting were acquitted, the incident became known as the Boston Massacre and added to the outrage of many colonial dissidents. Later that year, all the taxes were withdrawn except a tax on tea. Despite the concessions of the government, tensions continued to mount. Between 1772 and 1774, disgruntled community leaders in the thirteen colonies formed the *Committees of Correspondence* to coordinate activities and provide information against what they considered to be the outrages of the government in Britain.

The *Tea Act*, passed by the British Parliament in 1773, was intended to ensure that the East India Company could sell its tea in the American colonies at a lower price than colonial merchants and smugglers with access to Dutch tea. The opposition was widespread since the Act harmed the interests of many American merchants and smugglers while also violating the principle of no taxation without representation. The *Boston Tea Party* resulted from this opposition to the new legislation.

The response to the *Boston Tea Party* was the introduction of four new laws: the Coercive Acts. Known among Patriots as the Intolerable Acts, they altered the Massachusetts charter, changed rules regarding the trials and quartering of British soldiers serving in the colonies, and shut down the port of Boston until the vast sums destroyed by the Tea Party had been compensated. Another new law extended the territory of Quebec to include the land beyond the Appalachians, thus limiting the thirteen colonies' opportunities for westward expansion.

The government saw these acts as a way of making an example out of Massachusetts, but many Patriots saw them as arbitrary and tyrannical. Corresponding committees began to function as shadow governments, and Patriots in Massachusetts formed the Massachusetts Provincial Congress and started training military recruits for battle against the British authorities. Eventually, the Continental Congress was formed, calling for a general boycott of British imports.

Colonial independence movement

Starting in the mid-1760s, some colonists expressed severe concerns about British rule in America. They rejected Parliament's authority to tax the colonies since they were not represented in Parliament. They also resisted British efforts to collect duties and impose new laws that they perceived detrimental to their economic well-being and political autonomy.

After the Boston Tea Party (December 16, 1773) and the British response (known collectively as the *Coercive* or *Intolerable Acts*) colonial subjects divided into Loyalists, who supported the Crown and Patriots, who felt that loyalty to the Crown was no longer possible.

By 1775, fighting broke out between Patriots and British soldiers in Massachusetts, and the conflict between the colonies and the metropole (colonial power) escalated into a full-fledged war. Representatives of the thirteen colonies declared independence from Britain in 1776, claiming that King George III (1738-1820; 1760-1820) had become a tyrant and no longer had any right to rule in America. These United States Founding Fathers espoused ideologies of republicanism and classical liberalism and insisted on a new understanding of social relations based on equality.

Boston Tea Party, throwing tea overboard, December 16, 1773

Ideas and arguments over individual rights

The leaders among both Patriots and Loyalists were typically educated men who owned property. For example, many of the leaders of the Revolution were prominent planters from the South, especially Virginia. Loyalists were often well-connected, with close ties to British trade, finance, and official life. Wealthy merchants, fur traders, government officials, and people associated with these groups were often Loyalists.

Although many colonial elite men were Patriots, the primary support for colonial protests came from backcountry farmers, artisans, and shopkeepers. Even common laborers could make their support for the revolution known, sometimes in rowdy mob actions.

Women also contributed to the resistance against Britain. They did their share by boycotting British imports, supporting Patriot soldiers, and spying on the enemy. Mercy Otis Warren (1728-1814) used literature to attack the Loyalists and organized meetings in her home. At the same time, many women were Loyalists and worked to secure British victory.

On either side, everyday activities became infused with political meaning. Patriot women were forced to relearn spinning and weaving skills to avoid buying British textiles. The thinking behind the Revolution was heavily influenced by certain strains in English thought, especially that of liberals like John Locke (1632-1704) and republicans like James Harrington (1611-1677).

Mercy Otis Warren, c. 1814

Philosopher John Locke believed that all men were born free and equal and that the origin of the legitimate government could only be a social contract where citizens retained some God-given rights such as life, liberty, and property. The government should be limited in its activities and rely on the consent of the governed while protecting their natural rights. American Patriots also believed that governments, whether at a state or federal level, should rely on checks and balances to ensure that no branch of government got the upper hand, a way of thinking influenced by the French Enlightenment thinker Montesquieu (1689-1755).

Even though Montesquieu had used the English system of government as an example of a suitably mixed constitution with an appropriate balance of powers, the American Founding Fathers were skeptical of monarchy and aristocracy in the British tradition. In the tradition of Harrington and other Republicans, they viewed the British government with high suspicion, focusing on the corruption of the royal court and the dangers of standing armies and public debts.

One of the most prominent prerevolutionary writers was John Dickinson (1732-1808), who authored the *Letters from a Pennsylvania Farmer* (1767-1768) in response to the Townshend Acts. Dickinson exemplifies another line of thinking about colonial politics and governance, not influenced by liberalism, republicanism, or the Enlightenment. Instead, Dickinson was a constitutionalist with a legal background.

As a lawyer and property owner, Dickinson argued that there could be no legitimate taxation without representation and that there could not be such a thing as "virtual representation." He fully acknowledged the British right to control and regulate trade, to impose import and export duties, and even to rig the whole system in favor of British merchants. In Dickinson's view, the principle that property owners had to be involved in the political process before paying taxes was inviolable.

In breaking with the established rule of tradition and monarchy, the founders who penned the Declaration of Independence wanted to go beyond the ancient rights of Englishmen and the existing constitution. They made the natural rights of men to life, liberty, and the pursuit of happiness a new foundation of political legitimacy.

They explained that when a government such as the British threatened these rights, the inhabitants of the colonies had every right to resist and even overthrow the authorities. Rather than conceiving rights as something dependent on a given political system, Jefferson, the principal author of the Declaration, considered these rights natural and "unalienable" and insisted that any legitimate political system must be set up to preserve those rights.

American Revolutionary War

The American Revolutionary War (1775-1783) was a military conflict between the thirteen British colonies in North America and Great Britain. It began on April 19, 1775, when British troops attempted to seize military supplies stored by the colonists in Lexington and Concord, Massachusetts. This led to a series of fights between British troops and colonial militiamen, and by the summer of 1776, the rebels were waging a full-scale war for their independence.

The 1783 victory of the United States was not a foregone conclusion, given the considerable human and financial resources available to the vast British Empire. At the high point, the royal army had almost 80,000 troops, whereas Washington only had 20,000 under his command. However, taking the colonies against many inhabitants' will was very difficult. The areas involved were vast, and it was difficult for the British to control rural areas or even protect Loyalists from the wrath of the Patriots.

The commander in chief of the Continental Army during the Revolutionary War was George Washington (1732-1799). He led the colonial forces to victory and became a national hero. Washington's military strategy was to avoid large-scale battles with the British and instead focus on disrupting their supply lines and communication networks.

General George Washington, c. 1776

Even though the Loyalists formed a significant minority among the colonists, they were rarely utilized by the British generals and were often mistrusted. This contributed to the failure to win the hearts and minds of a large population that did not take a clear standpoint at the outset of the conflict. Similarly, the British promise of freedom to enslaved people who would fight for the Crown helped recruit some soldiers seeking emancipation but alienated the influential planters in the South.

The Americans had the advantage of being more familiar with the land than British regulars and German mercenaries. They also learned tactics from the Indian wars that made it possible to keep an insurgency going, disappearing into the woods after quick ambush-style attacks. Washington mostly avoided big battles, which made it impossible for the British to inflict a decisive defeat on his army.

Most importantly, France, Spain, and the Netherlands intervened in the war on the rebels' side. The French especially spent enormous sums of money supplying the war effort and contributed soldiers and naval support. The involvement of other maritime powers also forced Britain to shift its focus to the defense of other colonies, including the lucrative sugar islands in the Caribbean.

Another crucial factor was the support of many, if not most, colonists for the revolution. Thousands of ordinary people were committed to the cause and its ideology. They were willing to risk their lives or otherwise sacrifice for the cause. They became motivated and engaged by the many high-profile conflicts in the years preceding the American War of Independence. They participated in town meetings, Sons of Liberty protests, and more violent forms of agitation. During the Revolutionary War, as many as 400,000 Americans took up arms against what they considered a tyrannical government.

The *American Revolutionary War* was fought over eight years and ended with the *Treaty of Paris*, signed on September 3, 1783, by representatives of King George III and representatives of the United States. The treaty officially ended the war and recognized the thirteen colonies as an independent, sovereign nation.

Native American interests after the Revolutionary War

The Revolutionary War offered stark alternatives to the Indian tribes as they typically had to choose between land-hungry colonists eager to settle their lands or a distant British government with a mixed track record.

In general, the colonists' victory did not bode well for the Indians as the British government gave up its claims to the Indian Reserve west of the Appalachian Mountains, essentially leaving it as spoils of victory for the Americans. The Iroquois Confederacy, long a powerful united force with strong ties to Britain, was torn apart as some of the constituent tribes supported the revolutionaries, and others remained loyal to Britain. Iroquois and Cherokee offensives against the Patriots had already been met by ferocious counteroffensives employing scorched earth tactics.

While the British had been decisively defeated at Yorktown, there had not been any similar event to end the war between the newly formed United States and the Indians of the Northwest. Since those tribes were not party to the Treaty of Paris that officially ended the war, they refused to accept American rights to the region. The British occupied the forts in the region and provided the Indians with weapons and gunpowder in exchange for furs.

The new American government nevertheless made provisions for taking over the land and distributing it among white settlers. The Land Ordinance of 1785 and the Northwestern Ordinance of 1787 outlined the rules of this process, but both Indians and settlers often refused to follow these rules. As a result, tensions mounted, and violence was common.

As early as 1785, the Western Confederacy was forming to unite the Indians in the region against white encroachment. Among the many tribes involved were the Huron, the Shawnee, and the Miami. Raids against white settlements became familiar and were sporadically met by military action. In 1790–1791, allied Indian forces led by Little Turtle and other war chiefs inflicted devastating losses on American military expeditions, including the troops of Arthur St. Clair. St. Clair, the governor of the Northwest Territory, lost more than 600 men and 200 civilian followers in one battle.

After this setback, the American government changed its strategy for military operations against the Indians. Instead of relying on local militias, General Anthony Wayne built a legion of well-prepared soldiers. He finally handed the United States a decisive victory over the Western Confederacy at the 1794 Battle of Fallen Timbers. Shortly after, the war ended with a treaty in which the Indians recognized American sovereignty in the Old Northwest and surrendered massive tracts of land in Ohio and Indiana.

Political history – summary of the period

European expansion into the Western Hemisphere caused intense social/religious, political, and economic competition in Europe and the promotion of empire-building. European exploration and conquest were fueled by a desire for new sources of wealth, increased power and status, and converts to Christianity.

European overseas expansion and sustained contacts with Africans and American Indians dramatically altered European views of social, political, and economic relationships among and between white and nonwhite peoples.

With little experience dealing with people different from themselves, Spanish and Portuguese explorers poorly understood the native peoples they encountered in the Americas. This led to debates over how American Indians should be treated and how "civilized" these groups were compared to European standards.

Differences in imperial goals, cultures, and the North American environments that different empires confronted led Europeans to develop diverse colonization patterns. Seventeenth-century Spanish, French, Dutch, and British colonizers embraced different social and economic goals, cultural assumptions, and folkways, resulting in varied models of colonization.

Competition over resources between European rivals led to conflict within and between North American colonial possessions and American Indians. Conflicts in Europe spread to North America as French, Dutch, British, and Spanish colonies allied, traded with, and armed American Indian groups, leading to continuing political instability.

Late 17th-century efforts to integrate Britain's colonies into a coherent, hierarchical, imperial structure and pursue mercantilist economic aims met with limited success, due mainly to varied forms of colonial resistance and conflicts with American Indian groups and were followed by nearly a half-century of the British government's relative indifference to colonial governance. Britain's desire to maintain a viable North American empire in the face of growing internal challenges and external competition inspired efforts to strengthen its imperial control, stimulating increasing resistance from colonists who had grown accustomed to a considerable measure of autonomy.

Great Britain's massive debt from the Seven Years' War resulted in renewed efforts to consolidate imperial control over North American markets, taxes, and political institutions—actions that were supported by some colonists but resisted by others.

During and after the imperial struggles of the mid-18th century, new pressures began to unite the British colonies against perceived and real constraints on their economic activities and political rights, sparking a colonial independence movement and war with Britain. This movement was fueled by established colonial elites and grassroots movements that included newly mobilized laborers, artisans, and women and rested on arguments over the rights of British subjects, the rights of the individual, and the ideas of the Enlightenment.

Despite considerable loyalist opposition and Great Britain's overwhelming military and financial advantages, the patriot cause succeeded because of the colonists' greater familiarity with the land, their resilient military and political leadership, their ideological commitment, and their support from European allies.

During and after the colonial war for independence, tribes attempted to forge advantageous political alliances with one another and with European powers to protect their interests, limit migration of white settlers, and maintain their tribal lands.

Notes for active learning

Notes for active learning

Economic History: Pre-Columbian Period to 1789

Agriculture and economies of native populations

Indians in the Southwest (present-day Arizona, New Mexico, and surrounding areas) made a living from agriculture for thousands of years before the Europeans arrived. They mainly grew maize (corn), introduced from Mesoamerica around 2,100 B.C. Various sedentary cultures developed in this arid region, relying on irrigation and other techniques to collect and conserve the water needed for agriculture. Maize cultivation spread quickly across the Southwest's drylands, possibly carried along by migrant agriculturalists heading north from Mexico. Despite the rapid diffusion rate, maize did not immediately become the primary source of nutrition for the hunter-gatherers who already lived there. Instead, they incorporated maize farming into their wide selection of food sources, trying, as foragers usually do, to limit the risk that the failure of one food source might have catastrophic consequences. At first, maize was only a minor component of their diet and way of life.

Before the dawn of agriculture, bands of hunters and gatherers tended to be small. Except for exceptional circumstances, such as an essential ritual or a task that required extensive collaboration, their groups typically consisted of only ten to fifty people. Only over time did the role of maize expand, allowing for more extensive and sedentary settlements. Hunting and gathering remained important, but the productivity of agriculture allowed populations of 2,000 or more to congregate in one community. Other Indians lived in smaller settlements of a few hundred people or continued to live in tiny groups dispersed across the region. Among the Ancestral Puebloans (the best-known farming society of the prehistoric Southwest), settlements eventually became so large that the actual fields could be some distance from the tillers' dwellings. Even though this could be a disadvantage, joining to pool food and other resources and protect and defend the community was highly advantageous.

However, the forces of centralization and dispersal never reached a stable equilibrium. Instead, farming conditions and environmental changes caused communities to enter cycles of abandonment and regeneration. The intensive agriculture of the Pueblos ultimately proved unsustainable when sustained droughts began to occur in the 12th century. Droughts resulted in widespread famine, and many significant settlements were left behind as the Pueblos sought new lands and ways to survive. The traditional centers of population and civilization experienced an irreversible decline.

In the Pacific Northwest, abundant fish in the rivers and along the coastline allowed for an unusual phenomenon: the development of complex, settled communities among peoples who remained hunters and gatherers. Upon their arrival, European explorers witnessed complex coastal societies unfamiliar with agriculture but still home to large villages and elaborate social hierarchies.

Pueblo girl winnowing beans

Northwestern Indians had large, durable houses and economies specialized enough to participate in wide-ranging trade networks. In the interior, some diverse Indian tribes retained the mobility and egalitarianism typical of hunter-gatherer groups. Other communities, especially along the Columbia and Fraser Rivers, lived sedentary lifestyles and exhibited wealth and social inequality. Among the latter peoples were the Chinook, who lived by the Columbia River (in present-day Washington and Oregon). They excelled at hunting elk and fishing salmon and mainly depended on the abundance of fish in the river. Their society was very stratified, with a minority of shamans, warriors, and traders who limited their contact with less privileged commoners who comprised most of the population.

They even prevented their children from playing with peers from less prestigious backgrounds. To mark their status, the Chinook would flatten the heads of infants to distinguish them and maintain their superiority over round-headed people. Since those without deliberately deformed heads could be enslaved, having a round head implied not only inferiority but servility as well. The Chinook picked up the practice of slavery from other tribes farther north.

In California, the Indians were not precisely farmers but engaged in horticultural practices to increase their access to food and medicinal plants. They employed these gardening practices in various environments, including forests, grasslands, and wetlands. They also used fire to facilitate the growth of crops (fertilizing the soil with ashes) and to reduce the risk of more massive, disastrous fires. Burning also prepared new areas for cultivation or allowed new, wild growth that would attract game. Even old, cultivated areas could be put to the torch to enable continued use, leading toward a more sedentary lifestyle.

Mobile lifestyles in the Great Basin and the western Great Plains

The high desert region between the Rocky Mountains and the Sierra Nevada is known as the Great Basin. It is an arid region, mostly poor in flora and fauna, but water is plentiful in some small areas, allowing some plants and animals opportunities to thrive. Overall, the land is unsuitable for farming, nor is there much game for hunting. Seemingly inhospitable, the land has been a site of human habitation for thousands of years.

In the Great Basin, Indians had to be highly mobile and knowledgeable to exploit the few ecological niches successfully, often spread dozens of miles apart, which allowed them to eke out a living. Their familiarity with local microenvironments was crucial to survival, as was the ability to utilize a wide range of wild plants as food and fiber—the Southern Paiute gathered seeds from more than forty species of grass.

In this unyielding environment, bands remained small, with no more than thirty people in the desert and maybe up to one hundred in slightly more forgiving areas. They were almost always on the move but knew of places near water sources that could be used to set up camp. Leadership was not authoritarian but a matter of leading by example, advising juniors in the band, and working towards consensus decisions that everyone could accept. At any rate, those who disagreed were free to leave. Membership in these small bands was quite fluid, although members were often closely related.

On the Great Plains east of the Rockies, some Indians farmed and lived a semi-sedentary lifestyle in small villages along the rivers. The main challenge to plains agriculture was that rainfall could be insufficient for raising maize. In the northern areas, the growing season was shorter as well. Consequently, the progress—or rather fluctuations—of agriculture on the plains followed trends in precipitation, conquering drier lands to the west in wetter periods and falling back toward the east when the threshold was not met. Some Indians lived in fortified villages of up to several hundred people along the Missouri River, raising corn, beans, and squash.

For most of those who lived on the plains, much depended on the bison. Even men engaged in farming would typically leave the village to follow the great buffalo between planting and harvest. The Indians used fire to engineer the grasslands where the bison thrived and tried to regulate the bison.

Before the Europeans brought horses and guns to the Americas, bison had to be hunted on foot, chased, and trapped in corridors and corrals where they could be killed or stampeded across high cliffs called buffalo jumps. This elaborate system of hunting large numbers of bison provided a considerable surplus that encouraged feasting and significant trade. This enabled some groups to maintain a nomadic hunter-gatherer lifestyle, exchanging meat and hides for corn from the farming villages.

Economy of the Northeast and the Atlantic Seaboard

The Eastern Woodland culture consisted of Indian tribes inhabiting the eastern United States and Canada. These woodlands stretched from the Atlantic Ocean to the Mississippi River and the Great Lakes and were favored with relatively moderate climates and ample precipitation. Across such a vast area, there was, of course, some variation regarding both climate and specific natural resource endowments. In general, conditions were suitable for hunting in the vast forests and farming along the numerous lakes and rivers.

There were, of course, differences in ways of life, including diet, housing, clothing, and modes of transportation. Nevertheless, the Indians of the woodlands lived in similar ways. Their societies were stratified and distinguished between chiefs, noblemen, and commoners. Intertribal disputes over land, the audacity of young men, and quests for revenge made brutal warfare a staple of everyday life. Fortified villages were a necessity.

Mostly, these Indians were farmers and deer hunters. They made bows and arrows, stone knives, clubs for hunting and war, and pottery and vessels made from wood and bark for cooking. The Iroquois, a confederation of northeastern Indian tribes in the Great Lakes region and the Northeast, were mainly farmers but combined agriculture with gardening, hunting, fishing, and foraging.

The Iroquois cultivated some plants, including pumpkin and tobacco, but their main crops—the "three sisters," a special providence from the Creator—were corn, beans, and squash. They knew how to combine these organisms in single plots where bean plants climbed the corn stalks, with the big leaves of the squash underneath keeping the soil moist and shaded, thus preventing the growth of weeds. This technique could keep the soil fertile for decades. When it eventually lost that fertility, the whole community would have to uproot and move. The Iroquois also knew how to conserve meat, fish, vegetables, and berries for the winter.

Iroquois dwellings

The success of the Iroquois adaptation to their productive environment enabled strong population growth. Large numbers of warriors provided the foundation for a culture of imperialist expansion, with frequent wars against the less sedentary Algonquian tribes in the surrounding areas.

Over time, Iroquois expansion was only halted by the Algonquian move toward farming, which raised their populations sufficiently to withstand the Iroquois onslaught. In southern New England, Algonquian tribes relied predominantly on slash-and-burn agriculture. They cleared fields by burning, farmed for a year or two, and then moved the village to a different location to repeat the process. Many Algonquians depended mainly on hunting, fishing, and gathering, especially in the Far North.

Algonquin Indian

The Algonquian economy continued to revolve around the seasonality of food resources. They lived in villages of a few hundred people belonging to the same clan. However, these villages often dissolved into smaller groups of people roaming around to sites where food was plentiful at a time of year. Later, these groups could join again in a new village or join with others in new ways. It was a flexible system adapted both to the availability of foodstuffs and the threat of war.

Economic changes driven by technology and trade

The exploration of the Americas was made possible in part by prior technological developments in Europe. The Spanish and Portuguese pioneered a vessel called the caravel, which made oceangoing exploration possible. These were relatively small, narrow, sturdy ships, often with two lateens (triangular) sails.

Their larger counterpart, the carrack, usually had a full rig: two square sails and one lateen sail. They were slower ships but harder to board and could carry more cargo. European navigators acquired the magnetic compass from the Muslims.

Caravel with oars

However, it was probably the Portuguese who first used mariner's quadrants to accurately measure the angle from the North Star (or the Southern Cross, in the Southern Hemisphere) and thus determine latitude, which was crucial in the unknown waters.

Accurately determining longitude was not possible. Navigators would generally try to follow a certain latitude from east to west and then estimate the ship's speed by observing the hull's movement and the hourglass. Having guessed the speed, they could guess their position, although with limited accuracy.

Oceangoing ships were so crucial in the new world economy that Europeans continued pursuing navigational technologies. By the 18th century, they developed octants that made the measurement of latitude even simpler and more accurate. Around the same time, astronomers developed a method for predicting the angular distance between the moon and other celestial bodies.

Using this technique, the navigator at sea could use a new device, a sextant, to measure the angle between the moon and a planet or star, calculate the time at which the moon and the celestial body would be at that angle, and then compare local time with the standardized time of the national observatory. Knowing the time difference between the two points allowed a precise determination of longitude. After millennia of navigation, seafarers could finally determine their vessel's exact position at any given time.

Portuguese galleons and carracks

Expanding European economic interests into new areas worldwide also led to innovations in business organizations. This was not so much the case with the Spanish and Portuguese, whose ambitions of honor, glory, and aristocratic leisure were, in a sense, feudal and medieval.

Later, Dutch and English colonial projects had more of a mercantile and capitalist flavor. Among the innovations they pioneered in response to the quest for colonial riches were two of the most important financial innovations of all time: the joint-stock company and the stock exchange.

The earliest joint-stock company in England was the Company of Merchant Adventurers to New Lands, chartered in 1553. More significant and vastly more wealthy and influential was the East India Company, granted a royal charter by Queen Elizabeth I in 1600. This charter gave the Company, as it became known, enormous trade privileges in India, effectively a temporary monopoly on trade between England and Indian ports. The Company went far beyond mere trading ventures, supporting its mercantile clout with veritable armies and navies. It eventually expanded its political power until it was mainly the government of a colonized subcontinent.

Similarly, the Dutch East India Company was a tremendously powerful political, military, and economic force. Starting in 1602, it issued shares that could be traded on the Amsterdam Stock Exchange. This brilliant financial innovation made it easy for joint-stock companies to attract investor capital since it became much easier to both buy and sell shares. The Dutch East India Company was arguably the world's first modern corporation. It was allowed to operate with limited liability, meaning that investors could only lose what they had invested and were not liable for any further debts incurred by the company.

Henry Hudson (1565-1611) sailed on the river that now bears his name on behalf of the Dutch East India Company, and his explorations led to the establishment of New Netherland (present-day New York). Eventually, Dutch interests in the Americas would be pursued by a separate Dutch West India Company. However, before that time, the joint-stock Virginia Company established in England in 1606 had already established a settlement at Jamestown.

Henry Hudson, c. 1610

New crops and livestock effects on native populations

When the Europeans arrived in the New World, wheat, barley, and rice did not grow there, nor were corn, potatoes, and sweet potatoes found in Europe and Asia. The Americas had few domesticated animals: llamas and alpacas, dogs, guinea pigs, and some fowl species. There were no horses, cattle, sheep, or goats. The Columbian Exchange would change all this and transform the environment on each continent.

The exchange of crops affected people on both hemispheres. When corn made its way to China and potatoes to Ireland, the food supply increased and supported higher population levels. Similarly, wheat and cattle shaped the post-Columbian future of the Great Plains, the Texas grasslands, the Argentinian Pampas, and the Brazilian interior.

The introduction of horses proved a great opportunity and advantage to many Indians. Horseback riding created a new way of life, especially for the Plains Indians. It changed how people lived, interacted with their environments, and felt about themselves. With time, horses aided the Europeans in their ultimate quest to "pacify" or subdue the Indians. The Spanish had a famous equestrian tradition, one of the most successful horse cultures Eurasia had ever seen. After 1492, they used their skill as mounted combatants to conquer vast swaths of lands in the Americas. From Mexico, conquistadors also struck north into the American Southwest, continuing onto the Great Plains.

Even with the presence of Spanish equestrians, it took a long time before the use of horses spread to the indigenous population in North America. The Spanish in New Mexico knew their horse monopoly was vital to maintaining control in a vast and sparsely populated region.

Cayuse and his mount

The Indians began to ride horses, starting with the Pueblo uprising in 1680. After that, horse culture spread at breakneck speed. Trading and stealing horses from other tribes became a prominent activity among the Indians in the Southwest, the Great Plains, and the Great Basin. Fifty years after the Pueblo rebellion, horses became integrated into Indian culture as far away as the northern Rocky Mountains, and another fifty years later, horse culture became predominant throughout the Trans-Mississippi West. California also developed its version of the Spanish *vaquero*, or cowboy, with its way of training horses and a unique way of life.

Having horses allowed for a new way of life, partially by promoting more efficient hunting expeditions. Assaulting the bison was much less daunting from horseback than on foot. The horse facilitated long-distance trade and travel, opening the indigenous groups to new goods, impulses, and ideas. At the same time, horses again proved to have tremendous military consequences.

Early adoption of horses gave some tribes the advantage they needed to punish their enemies and expand their hunting lands, which forced the other tribes to exploit the reach and power of the horse to survive rapidly changing conditions. For some, the world seemed to have enormous potential when seen from horseback—endless possibilities on the horizon filled mounted warriors and huntsmen with a spirit of freedom, pride, and confidence.

Christopher Columbus brought the first cattle on his second voyage across the Atlantic to Hispaniola. The imported cattle reproduced rapidly, and soon imports were no longer needed. A generation later, Caribbean cattle were brought to Mexico and, within a few decades, had reached north into what is now Texas and south into Colombia and Venezuela.

The cattle adapted to this new ecological setting and roamed the verdant grasslands in vast herds. Wild cattle sometimes constituted a nuisance for Indian farmers, but the Indians soon found the cow very beneficial. Cattle provided meat, milk, tallow, hides, transportation, and a source of labor.

Even as the Indian population declined due to the smallpox scourge and other epidemics, there was a rapid increase in European livestock as cattle, sheep, and horses flourished on new farms or formerly unclaimed lands. In a way, the Indian population of Mexico, for example, was replaced by European livestock.

European influences on American Indian warfare

Trade was essential to relations between indigenous people and colonists in North America. The fur trade was especially crucial because furs were considered highly fashionable status symbols in Europe. In return for furs, European traders offered iron knives and axes, textiles, blankets, utensils, cookware, and jewelry that Indians could use to improve their standard of living or display their social status.

Over time, the Indians became dependent on these items and often preferred them to traditional goods that could be made with local resources and indigenous knowledge. Also, the traders introduced strong alcoholic beverages like rum and whiskey. Perhaps because many of the Indian tribes saw spiritual potential in a trance- or dream-like state, alcohol quickly became incredibly popular. Social problems arose consequently, and some colonies made attempts to prohibit the sale of alcohol to Indians. The high demand and correspondingly high profits made most of these laws ineffective.

The dependence on alcohol made several of the tribes dependent on furs, which in turn encouraged both ecological mismanagement and intermittent warfare with other tribes over hunting grounds. These wars were facilitated by and became bloodier due to another European trade good: firearms. The trade of weapons was on such a scale that the price of beaver pelts could be quoted in pistols or traded guns.

The French and English also supplied their Indian allies with firearms as part of their efforts to limit each other's influence. Their encouragement of wars for territory and hunting grounds increased the prevalence and scale of conflicts in colonial North America.

Trading with Indians

New American crops stimulated European population growth

Corn was not known in the Old World before the voyages of Columbus, but it quickly became a staple crop in the earliest stages of the Columbian Exchange. By 1630, Spain was heavily invested in the commercial production of corn, far surpassing the traditional subsistence farming in Mesoamerica.

Similarly, potatoes and sweet potatoes were unknown in Europe before the exploration of the Americas. The white potato came from the Andes Mountains in South America, where the indigenous people developed many varieties adapted to varying microenvironments. It eventually became a staple crop in Europe and was brought to North America by Scotch-Irish immigrants in the 18th century. The potato is a good source of many nutrients, and in many European locations, a plot of potatoes was much more productive in terms of calories than an equivalent plot of other food crops. The sweet potato also became an essential crop in Europe.

Peppers were grown in Central and South America. Spanish explorers took pepper seeds back to Spain as early as 1493, and the plants soon spread across Europe. Today, they are grown in tropical areas of Asia, Africa, and the Americas. Tomatoes also originated in the New World, specifically in the highlands of South America. They were brought to Mesoamerica in an intercolonial exchange, but also to Spain, where their use in new sauces earned the label "Spanish" cuisine.

The explorers also took peanuts back to Spain, where they were still grown. From Spain, traders and explorers took peanuts to Africa and Asia. Peanuts were brought to the southern part of North America along with the Africans who were shipped there as slaves.

Some Indians used cacao beans as currency, and Columbus took some to Europe as an example of American money. Cortés watched the Aztec court drinking chocolate, and eventually, this drink also became familiar and appreciated by European colonists. By the early 17th century, the drink was becoming popular in Europe itself, and later in that century, the first chocolate house was opened in England.

New crops from the Americas made the European diet more varied and sophisticated but also contributed significantly to population growth. This is especially true of corn and, even more importantly, potatoes. Incorporating potatoes into the European diet allowed higher food production and a form of insurance against catastrophic grain harvest failures that could result in misery and famine. The highly nutritious potatoes also strengthened the immune systems of Europeans suffering from debilitating diseases like dysentery, measles, and tuberculosis. The introduction of potatoes was accompanied by higher birth rates, lower mortality rates, and a rapid population rise in Europe and the United States.

New sources of precious metals and the European shift to capitalism

The abundance of gold and silver in the mountain ranges of the Americas revolutionized the European economy. In the 16th century alone, the supply of these precious metals multiplied by a factor of eight.

This flood of the new currency was so overwhelming that it tended to destabilize rather than strengthen the old order in Europe. However, this had certainly not been the intention of the Spanish monarchs. The feudal system, where land ownership was paramount, was challenged as money, a new measure of wealth, played more significantly.

The new money could be used to invest in new ventures in trading and manufacturing and was much more liquid and accessible than land. The feudal aristocracy in Spain, moored to the land by regulations that prevented them from participating in middle-class business activities, was left out as a new economic order emerged, where elites in other more dynamic and mercantilist countries came to the forefront. Since the Habsburg monarch Charles was both King of Spain and Emperor of the Holy Roman Empire (Germany and the surrounding areas), money spread quickly across Austria, Germany, Italy, the Netherlands, and Switzerland.

The wastefulness and warmongering of the Spanish kings meant that most of the bullion from America had to be devoted to paying off debts. On several occasions, the Crown was even forced to default on those debts, meaning that despite the enormous riches obtained in the Americas, Spain was virtually bankrupt. Rather than land, precious metals became the foundation of power and status. A new class of merchants and capitalists emerged, eventually dominating Europe and the world.

Even on the fringes of Europe, the Ottoman Empire, which controlled Turkey, the Balkans, and most of the Middle East and North Africa, was far from immune to the impact of American silver. The impact was suddenly felt in 1584 when the Ottoman currency fell precipitously amidst shocking price inflation. The currency fell to half of its former value and never regained its significance in world trade again.

Arguably, the influx of silver from the Americas did more to undermine the worldly power of the Islamic countries in the centuries that followed than any other factor. In fact, throughout the world, the new European wealth eroded the value of holdings in every other country in the Old World while allowing Europe to expand and form a Eurocentric world trade system. The silver of America made a world economy possible for the first time, as much of it was traded not only to the Ottomans but to the Chinese and East Indians as well. Eurasia's great civilizations were thus brought under the influence of American silver and its destabilizing effects. Europe's prosperity boomed, and its people wanted all the teas, silks, cotton, coffees, and spices that the rest of the world could offer in the new global economy.

Encomienda system

Since the Spanish needed the Indians as workers and payers of tax or tribute, they strove to uphold some aspects of Indian life to the extent that it served their own goals and did not contradict Spanish domination or the tenets of Christianity. Even in Mexico and Peru, where indigenous religion and clergy virtually disappeared, the traditional aristocracy remained, with the backing of Spanish colonial authorities. These noblemen served as middlemen, imposing tax and labor demands on the population at large.

By the middle of the 16th century, the taking of Indians (other than prisoners of war) as enslaved people became illegal in Spanish America. New forms of imposing labor and taxes had been introduced. So-called *encomienda* was granted to conquistadors and other members of the Spanish elite. These grants meant that Indians were "commended" to an authority figure who was supposed to offer protection in return for service and taxes.

Although the Inca and Aztec Empires demanded labor and tribute from their subjects, the new demands of the *encomenderos* who held Spanish grants were often excessive. At the same time, the responsibility for protection was too frequently neglected. Thus, the sense of reciprocity usually encountered in traditional Indian culture was often lost somewhere along the way.

Encomiendas covered the region from New Mexico in the North to Chile in the South, usually proving destructive to indigenous communities. Even the holders of grants were often troubled and disappointed by the performance of the *encomiendas*, especially as the Indian populations continued to decline.

The government in Spain also had concerns about the system, as they feared the establishment of a powerful aristocracy so far from their seat of authority. The institution was dismantled by limiting the ability of children to inherit *encomiendas* and prohibiting certain kinds of labor demands. *Encomiendas* remained in some areas of the empire but mostly in marginal areas. Instead of grants of people, land grants would form the new basis of wealth.

Meanwhile, the colonial government used royal officials to demand Indian labor and tax more directly. Indian communities were required to offer laborers to work on state projects, such as building churches and roads, or in labor gangs working in mines and on plantations. Thousands of Indians were recruited for this forced labor. Although they were paid a wage, they often encountered systemic abuse and work requirements that could have grave consequences both for individuals and the community. Some Indians decided to leave their communities to avoid taxes and forced labor, going to work for Spanish landowners or city dwellers instead. Uprooted Indians thus became mobile wage laborers for mines, farms, and urban enterprises.

Spanish and Portuguese importation of slave labor to the Americas

The Atlantic slave trade occurred across the Atlantic Ocean from the 16th to the 19th centuries. Most of those who came to the Americas through the brutal Middle Passage were from Central or West Africa, sold by other Africans to European traders who arrived at the many forts and trading posts established primarily for this purpose. The number of slaves was so high that more blacks than whites came to the Americas before the late 18th century.

Only about 5 percent of the enslaved people were taken to North America; the rest were brought mainly to South America (especially Brazil) and the islands of the Caribbean to work on plantations. They labored to produce coffee, tobacco, cocoa, and sugar for European consumers who held these new commodities in high esteem and could create new, pleasant lifestyles for themselves. The slaves grew cotton and rice, toiled in gold and silver mines, built houses, and cut timber. Some were skilled laborers, craftsmen, or domestic servants.

The first African slaves in the New World came from Europe rather than directly from Africa. In the early 16th century, they arrived on ships carrying various goods for sale rather than on dedicated slave ships. This was an extension of the existing Portuguese traffic in slaves, which had been carried on for decades before Columbus' first voyage.

Portuguese mariners grew accustomed to buying African slaves on the West African coast and taking them to the Atlantic islands or even to mainland Portugal, where enslaved Black people had become common in Lisbon and on some of the great estates.

The arrival of the first slave ship directly from Africa may not have come until 1526. By 1550, many transatlantic slave ships were headed for the Spanish colonies in the Caribbean, and the first slave vessels began to arrive on the Spanish Main. In this early period, many were sent to work in the mines, especially the gold mines on Hispaniola.

Since the Spanish did away with some of the more unsavory parts of the slave trade business, the Portuguese remained dominant. They also served their own needs for manpower, with the traffic to Brazil eventually accounting for almost half of the Atlantic slave trade. Starting around 1560, it was the demand for sugar in Europe and the corresponding demand for labor on Brazilian sugar plantations that drove this trade.

By 1630, Africans replaced the original Indian labor force operating Brazilian sugar mills, and these mills were producing almost all the sugar consumed in Europe. Later, sugarcane planting spread to islands in the Eastern Caribbean, rendering the sugar complex the central fact of life in many colonial societies, including possessions of the Spanish, Dutch, English, and French. The success of sugar, in turn, encouraged the significant westward expansion of slave systems across Latin America and the present-day United States.

Slave trade

While the demand for plantation commodities, the environment of the tropics, and European ideas about race and identity were significant determinants of how the slave trade developed, African agency was also a key factor. Both Europeans and Africans had long traditions of slavery, but unlike the Europeans, Africans did not use skin color to determine someone's eligibility for slavery. Instead, they often chose to make criminals, debtors, and prisoners of war into slaves. As the transatlantic slave trade expanded, some African wars were initiated with the specific purpose of enslaving people.

The merchants who sold slaves to the Europeans and the chiefs who supplied those merchants usually had strict criteria for who could be enslaved. As a consequence, the supply of slaves depended not only on whom plantation owners wanted to purchase but also on whom influential Africans wanted to sell. The victims of the slave trade were also able to exert agency at times. Slave rebellions occurred frequently, and the risk of such events probably increased costs to the point that it reduced the scope of the overall traffic.

Abundance of land and labor shortage flued the slave trade

One of the big problems confronting planters in the British colonies was that both white and Indian laborers had options and could be challenging to control. White indentured servants could run away and blend into the population or even band together and demand government intervention on their behalf. Easy access to land ownership in the colonies also made the idea of doing backbreaking, poorly paid work for others unappealing to Europeans. Similarly, if Indians were forced to do plantation labor, they could use their local knowledge and connections to disappear.

At the same time, Indians were very vulnerable to Old World diseases, while Europeans succumbed to malaria more easily than Africans. Thus, if Africans could be subjected to the harsh slave codes of the Caribbean, mainland planters could have a more reliable source of labor. This facilitated the export of tobacco from the Chesapeake area and rice from South Carolina, enriching a planter aristocracy at a tremendous human cost.

Depiction of a tobacco wharf in colonial America

The slave trade expanded rapidly to absorb the demand for new slaves to work on the plantations and farms and in the households and shops of whites in British North America. About 500,000 Africans were brought from Africa and the Caribbean to what is now the United States before the end of the transatlantic trade in 1807. This was only 6 percent of the total number of enslaved people brought from Africa to the Americas. Slaves on the North American mainland reproduced at much higher rates than elsewhere, which in turn led to the development of a sizable internal trade in enslaved people.

African slavery gradually replaced Indian labor

The decline in Indian populations encouraged a corresponding increase in the use of enslaved Africans to meet the labor requirements in the colonies. Enslaved Africans were with the Spanish from the very beginning and were even among Cortés's army as he went to conquer the Aztecs and occupy Tenochtitlán. Later, enslaved people were put to work farming sugar and rice in Mexican fields. The numbers were significantly smaller than in Brazil and Haiti, but the black population outnumbered the colony's Spanish settlers.

The Spanish colonies, which valued sugar plantations and gold and silver mines, often made widespread use of slave labor. This was the case in Cuba, Venezuela, Colombia, Peru, and Ecuador. In parts of Spanish America, where plantation agriculture and giant mines were not dominant, Africans were few and far between, although some enslaved people were engaged as craftsmen or house servants.

Portuguese Brazil was the world's leading sugar producer rather than the Spanish colonies. Unlike most agricultural produce, sugarcane had to be processed on the spot using expensive and sophisticated machinery. It was cut and pressed in a sugar mill, and the juice was then heated to make the sugar crystallize. In other words, sugar production combined farming and manufacturing, requiring unusual capital and labor.

The labor was also unusual because it was exceptionally strenuous and intense in the harvest season, and the mortality rates on the plantations were correspondingly high. Some free workers participated as skilled laborers or artisans but enslaved people did most of the work. In Brazil, African slaves soon constituted half of the total population.

Based on a single crop produced by slave labor, Brazil became the first great plantation colony and a model that other European nations would later follow in their Caribbean colonies. Ever since, despite the diversification of the economy, Brazilian society has continued to reflect its origins in plantation hierarchies and slavery. The white planter families emerged as a powerful and wealthy aristocracy taking control of local communities. They established connections with merchants and government officials to maintain their control of the flow of money and the use of force.

At the bottom of the social hierarchy were the enslaved people, who were treated merely as property. This harsh, unmerciful version of slavery was quite different from African circumstances where slaves, despite their low social status, were treated as human beings with individual dignity and, in many cases, included as part of the extended family. Enslaved Americans were subject to a new form of trade, where they were virtually interchangeable commodities. Most enslaved people only survived for a few years in the New World, but others replaced them with ships plying the triangular trade between the Americas, Europe, and Africa.

Differences in geography and climate led to agricultural diversification

The climate and natural resources of the British colonies affected settlement patterns and differences in long-term development trajectories. The climate made New England less vulnerable to infectious diseases, but winters could be severe, the growing season was relatively short, and the soil tended to be rocky. The abundant timber resources were helpful for the shipbuilding industry, supporting the growth of fisheries and seaborne commerce.

The Middle Colonies farther south had a milder climate and good soil for farming, which led to the development of prosperous agricultural communities. Grain, corn, and meat were sold to other colonies. Functional ports and the central location of these colonies allowed for the rise of merchants and artisans in the two biggest cities of the colonial era, Philadelphia and New York.

In the southern colonies, the warm climate allowed for a long growing season and the spread of plantations that grew export commodities. Virginia had a mix of plantations and family farms and mixed agriculture of cash commodities, food crops, and livestock. Planters dominated the tidewater areas, while the backcountry and the less favorable land found in North Carolina were settled mainly by small farmers. Subtropical South Carolina and Georgia resembled the Caribbean colonies more closely, strongly focusing on growing rice—and later indigo and cotton—using slave labor.

Savannah, from a print of 1741

The middle colonies, including New York, New Jersey, Pennsylvania, and Delaware, were more diverse regarding religion and ethnicity than New England, dominated by Puritans (c. the 1930s) from the low English country. The Netherlands and Sweden had tried to establish colonies in this region, and the vast tracts of fertile land soon attracted immigrants from Germany, France, Scotland, Ireland, and other places in Europe.

Some came as indentured servants but ended up as successful craftsmen or farmers. Pennsylvania, founded by Quakers, offered religious freedom to various sects and denominations, and New York offered citizenship to anyone who embraced Christianity. Quakers, Baptists, Methodists, Episcopalians, Lutherans, Amish, and Mennonites flocked to the middle colonies from other colonies and Europe.

Quaker woman preaching in New Amsterdam (Manhattan, NY)

The fertile soil allowed farmers in the middle colonies to grow a significant surplus of grains for export. Pennsylvania became the largest producer of food on the continent. The rivers of the area offered useful connections between port cities and a hinterland that supplied fur and lumber. These rivers also supplied energy for mills and other manufacturing enterprises.

The economy flourished, but not everyone benefited equally. In some areas, land ownership was controlled by the Dutch *patroons* and Englishmen favored by the Crown, and the riches of the cities tended to be concentrated among a few prosperous merchants. Although there was a sizable middle class of farmers, artisans, and shopkeepers, there was also a vast underclass of tenants, laborers, servants, and enslaved people.

While the economy of the middle colonies was diverse and encompassed hunting, trapping, fishing, farming, crafts, mining, metalworking, manufacturing, shipping, and trade, the Chesapeake colonies, Virginia and Maryland, relied greatly on tobacco. Large plantations were the centers of economic activity, to the detriment of urban development.

Planters brought in indentured servants and enslaved people to work the land, secured the best farmland and organized most of the shipping themselves. Population growth was slow, as there were limited opportunities for poor European immigrants, and the mortality rate was high due to widespread epidemics.

Colonial slave market in the 17th century

The rebellion of Nathaniel Bacon in 1676–1677 appealed to disempowered whites by attacking both Indians and local authorities in Virginia. However, it was soon struck down by the power of the Crown and the planter class. The rebellion was spurred by a decline in tobacco prices, which caused economic hardship. In the 18th century, Chesapeake farmers and planters chose to reduce their risk of failure by diversifying crops, and they began producing more grains, flax, and meat.

Heavy use of slave labor in the South

While the development of the British West Indies and the mainland colonies were intimately connected politically, culturally, and economically, the Caribbean islands had unique characteristics. Their intense focus on producing sugar and their dependence on trade for virtually everything else gave them little of the semblance of self-sufficiency found in some mainland colonies. The vast plantations worked by hundreds of slaves, often owned by wealthy men who did not even live on the islands, were another distinguishing characteristic.

Barbados, for example, had been founded as a tobacco-growing colony but soon shifted to sugar as competition from the Chesapeake colonies intensified. Slaves—and, at first, convict laborers from Ireland—cut down tropical forests of the island to grow sugarcane. Almost 400,000 enslaved people were brought in, but death rates were high, and many were resold in other American markets. Nevertheless, by the 18th century, blacks outnumbered whites by three to one – a relatively low ratio compared to many of the other colonies.

The colony of Carolina split into North and South Carolina in 1729, and it had its twin origins in the cultures of Barbados and the Virginia backcountry. The northern part of the colony, settled by Virginians, lacked land suitable for plantations and natural ports facilitating international trade.

The southern part became a colony in the Caribbean mold, featuring large plantations, a slave majority, and a monocultural focus after rice became the predominant crop early in the 18th century. South Carolina was also a center for trade in enslaved Indians. Eventually, the colony began efforts to attract European immigrants to the backcountry, partially as a defense against potential slave rebellions.

Carolina rice field

Georgia was established much later than the Carolinas. It had a stunted development due to the original prohibition of slavery in the colony. Only a few Europeans settled there before slavery became legal in 1749. For that reason, Georgia's early history was like that of North Carolina. With the advent of plantation slavery, Georgia was on its way to becoming like South Carolina and, by extension, the Caribbean possessions.

Economic growth, expanded social networks, and new labor systems

Since the main aims of colonization were to take control of land and resources and sell exports to Europe, the colonists had a pressing need for a labor force. Many workers were needed on the vast "new" lands to raise crops and livestock, labor in mines, mills, docks, shops, and workshops, or as craftsmen or servants. Because of this need, colonial elites worked tirelessly to find new labor sources, including both free and indentured immigrants, convicts, Indians, and Africans. Early labor forces were often a mix of African, Indian, and European workers. Where large plantations dominated, there was a tendency to rely almost exclusively on slaves of African descent eventually.

Scene on a plantation

These massive plantations in the South produced many of North America's leading export commodities, primarily tobacco, rice, and indigo. Also, the northern colonies exported wheat and wheat flour, corn, fish, livestock and horses, and some lumber and metal products. Foodstuffs were often sold to the planters on the Caribbean islands, where sugar was the dominant export, integrating the mainland colonies into the sugar economy.

The French colonies on the mainland exported little value except for large numbers of furs. New Spain (present-day Mexico and the southwestern United States) had an economy focused on mining. However, by the 18th century, silver exports were supplemented by other colonial exports like sugar, tobacco, cocoa, cotton, and dyes. The failure to distribute water resources equitably was a disaster for agriculture, which meant that the Indian population that provided most labor continued to decline.

European explorers, merchants, conquerors, and settlers initiated much of the activity that eventually linked the Atlantic World. However, other groups played essential roles as change agents. The creation of an Atlantic World contributed significantly to the creation of a world economy, promising great wealth for some, modest comforts for others, and devastation, ruin, and enslavement for many indigenous people of Africa and the Americas.

American precious metals allowed a more dynamic, freer economy in Europe, and colonial stimulants, like tobacco, sugar, and cocoa, promoted harder work and a culture of mass consumption, paving the way for the Industrial Revolution. Labor systems were transformed as Indians and Africans were exploited as slave labor, while European colonists could rise from subordinate positions to become independent farmers, traders, and craftsmen.

The Atlantic exchanges were not merely economic. The crossings of people, books, habits, and customs spread new ideas and beliefs, forcing colonizers and the colonized to adjust their views. Religious and political philosophies shaped how colonies were organized. Especially in some of the English colonies purposely established as New World utopias. At the same time, the European encounter with America led to a new understanding of the world, forcing intellectuals and scientists to reconsider the ancient writers and the Bible as infallible sources of authority. The discovery of new lands and peoples opened intellectual worlds and questioned old verities. Newly emboldened Europeans and Americans began revolutionizing the world through science, technology, and political transformation.

The labor systems of the New World drew upon the availability of conquered Indians and Africans who could be bought in the West African ports. European workers were also essential. Before 1700, most white immigrants came to the Americas as indentured servants rather than free men and women. Some were convicts, but most paid merely for the costly passage to the Americas with years of their lives. Like slaves, they received no wages but were provided with room, board, and simple clothing. They were not allowed to marry or have children, and their working conditions were often miserable. At the end of their contract, they were free to leave and use their acquired skills to secure their financial independence.

However, this solution to the problem of securing labor was not particularly satisfactory to the white elite or indentured servants. Similarly, using Indians as slaves became controversial in the Spanish possessions, and their death rates and tendency to escape made African slaves a relatively favorable alternative, especially for plantation owners who needed a large labor force to grow sugar and other staples.

Slavery did not become equally widespread in areas without plantation agriculture, suggesting the role of practical considerations in developing new labor systems. The success of plantation products, especially sugar and tobacco, increased the demand for workers and enabled the planters to invest in more land and enslaved people. The success of sugar and tobacco in Europe and slavery in the Americas were tightly entwined and interdependent.

Sugarcane cultivation

At the same time, the flow of sugar and tobacco stimulated European workers, enabling them to work harder and encouraging them to enter labor markets to make wages without which they could not procure colonial goods. While Africans and Indians became dependent on European wares, the Europeans grew dependent on colonial commodities. Consequently, entrepreneurs on both sides of the Atlantic made enormous profits.

Economic history – summary of the period

Before the arrival of Europeans, native populations in North America developed a wide variety of social, political, and economic structures based in part on interactions with the environment and each other. The spread of maize cultivation from present-day Mexico northward into the American Southwest and beyond supported economic development and social diversification among societies in these areas; a mix of foraging and hunting did the same for societies in the Northwest and areas of California.

Native societies responded to the lack of natural resources in the Great Basin and the Western Great Plains by developing mostly mobile lifestyles. In the Northeast and along the Atlantic Seaboard, some societies developed a mixed agricultural and hunter-gatherer economy that favored permanent villages.

The introduction of new crops and livestock by the Spanish had far-reaching effects on native settlement patterns and economic, social, and political development in the Western Hemisphere. By supplying American Indian allies with deadlier weapons and alcohol and by rewarding Indian military actions, Europeans helped increase the intensity and destructiveness of American Indian warfare.

Improvements in technology and more organized international trade methods helped change economies in Europe and the Americas. New crops from the Americas stimulated European population growth, while new sources of mineral wealth facilitated the European shift from feudalism to capitalism. In the economies of the Spanish colonies, Indian labor, used in the encomienda system to support plantation-based agriculture and extract precious metals and other resources, was gradually replaced by African slavery.

The abundance of land, a shortage of indentured servants, the lack of an effective means to enslave native peoples, and the growing European demand for colonial goods led to the emergence of the Atlantic slave trade. Spanish and Portuguese traders reached West Africa and partnered with some African groups to exploit local resources and recruit slave labor for the Americas.

Along with other environmental and geographical variations, including climate and natural resources, it has contributed to regional differences in what would become the British colonies. The demographically, religiously, and ethnically diverse middle colonies supported a flourishing export economy based on cereal crops. In contrast, the Chesapeake colonies and North Carolina relied on the cultivation of tobacco, a labor-intensive product based on white indentured servants and African chattel.

Colonies along the southernmost Atlantic coast and the British islands in the West Indies took advantage of long growing seasons by using slave labor to develop economies based on staple crops; in some cases, enslaved Africans constituted most of the population.

As the European nations competed in North America, their colonies focused on gaining new sources of labor and on producing and acquiring commodities valued in Europe. "Atlantic World" commercial, religious, philosophical, and political interactions among Europeans, Africans, and American native peoples stimulated economic growth, expanded social networks, and reshaped labor systems.

The growth of an Atlantic economy throughout the 18th century created a shared labor market and a full exchange of New World and European goods, as seen in the African slave trade and the shipment of products from the Americas.

Notes for active learning

Foreign Relations: Pre-Columbian Period to 1789

Spain–Britain rivalry to control the Western Hemisphere

The voyages of Columbus (1492, 1493, 1498, 1502) soon turned into a diplomatic issue. Columbus found the lands south of the Canary Islands (outside the northwesternmost part of Africa) and thus conceivably reserved for the Portuguese under the 1479 Treaty of Alcáçovas. Ferdinand and Isabella hurried to secure their claim by seeking support from the pope, who proposed a western boundary for Portuguese claims.

This eventually led to the Treaty of Tordesillas, signed in 1494, which divided Castilian and Portuguese claims along with a north-south line 370 leagues west of the Cape Verde Islands. This would eventually justify the Portuguese claim to Brazil and the Spanish claims elsewhere in the Americas, as the treaty formally divided the non-European world between Spain and Portugal.

Queen Isabella of Castile (left) and King Ferdinand V of Aragon (right)

However, as early as the peace treaty signed by France and Spain in 1559, the two parties agreed that attacks west of the Azores or south of the Tropic of Cancer should not be a reason for the war in Europe. In practice, all colonial areas were subject to continual warfare outside the customary rules of the declaration of war Christian ideas of "just war." Spain reserved the right to attack anyone trying to trade in the Caribbean, and the other nations reserved the right to attack and capture the Spanish treasure fleets. Outside Europe, anything was fair game. This principle became known as "no peace beyond the line."

The English started their American involvement as privateers and smugglers in the 16th century. After 1600, they set up several colonies on North America's mainland and the Caribbean, disregarding Spanish claims. In 1655, they even took Jamaica, a colony already set up by Spain.

In 1670, the Spanish finally faced reality and recognized the English settlements as legitimate. This ended the anarchic era of "no peace beyond the line," and it became possible to some extent to distinguish between pirates and lawful traders. This was not the end of piracy; on the contrary, the first half-century after 1670 is often considered the golden age of pirates and Buccaneers.

An example of the sometimes chaotic colonial rivalry between the European powers before 1670 was the early white settlement in Florida. The French established the first colonial outpost in 1564 specifically attacking Spanish treasure galleons sailing past. The following year, a Spanish expeditionary force was sent out to destroy the settlement, and the Spanish commander ordered summary executions of the surrendering Frenchmen.

A few years later, in 1573–1574, the Spanish government changed its policies toward the Americas, deciding that the church, rather than the military, should be the chief representative of the Crown in the Americas. Part of the rationale behind this new policy was that the missionaries would be less ruthless and exploitative in their dealings with the indigenous people.

The Franciscan missions in 17th-century Florida turned out to have hugely disruptive effects on the Indians. They now had to live in mission villages and become full-time farmers, incorporating European crops and animals into a new way of life. They were very vulnerable to the diseases brought by the colonists, resulting in many deaths and a steady population decline. Military assaults by English and French forces destroyed the population.

French and Dutch colonial efforts

The French sent numerous explorers to North America and made pioneering discoveries around the Great Lakes and the Mississippi Valley, founding settlements from Quebec and Montreal in the North to New Orleans and Baton Rouge in the South. However, peopling these settlements proved a tremendous challenge. The Company of New France (Canada) failed to bring the promised colonists across the Atlantic. The imposition of direct royal rule in 1660 did make a difference, but these areas could never compete with the English colonies regarding population.

Indians at a Hudson Bay Company trading post

Instead, they became dependent on friendly Indian tribes militarily, commercially, and regarding finding wives for French men. Indians who joined the settlements were legally accepted as French and, in principle, eligible to take up residence in France without any naturalization process. Despite the French efforts to invite Indian partners and allies, the lack of actual colonists gave France a severe disadvantage in the colonial rivalry with England.

After 1660, the competition between French and English colonists over the lucrative fur trade escalated. The English challenged the monopoly of the French by chartering the Hudson Bay Company, while at the same time, French and mixed-race individual traders also sought to circumvent regulations. Eventually, a system emerged where wealthy merchants in Montreal could send licensed traders far and wide to procure furs.

Most of the actual trapping continued by the Indians, and the fur trade played a significant part in the many wars between the Great Lakes tribes throughout this period. Thus, the European competition over the furs of beavers and other animals, due in significant part to the popularity of beaver hats across the Atlantic, severely destabilized a vast region in the Americas. The expansion of fur trading and exploration into the Mississippi Valley led to the foundation of the vast colony of Louisiana, stretching in parts the entire north-south length of the present-day United States and from the Rockies to the Appalachians.

The lack of easily accessible natural resources and the failure of the French government to provide the infrastructure, commercial facilities, and physical safety necessary to make the colony attractive for settlement meant that few Europeans chose to migrate there.

The Dutch in New Netherland (encompassing present-day New York and parts of the surrounding states) were also primarily interested in the fur trade. Like the French, they relied to a great extent on building alliances and trading with the local Algonquian and Iroquois tribes. The port of New Amsterdam, today's New York City, became a vital hub for exporting furs and other American commodities to Europe.

The Dutch West India Company tried to support colonization and population growth by granting vast tracts of land to so-called *patroons* who would, in turn, invite immigrants to become tenant farmers on their land, but this policy was only moderately successful. After the Anglo-Dutch wars of the 1660s–70s, New Netherland was ceded to the English.

The Dutch trading with the Indians

Colonial dissatisfaction with European powers

Colonial subjects were often dissatisfied with their European rulers, who saw the colonies primarily as a source of resources and revenues for the mother country. They especially complained about the distribution of lands and occasional failures to protect vulnerable settlements against European rivals or hostile indigenous people. Also, they often circumvented laws and taxation by smuggling goods from one colony to another, weakening the European powers' grip.

The fur trade is an essential example of this latter tendency because of its significance to Indians, colonists, and European governments. While governments tried to control the fur trade and introduce monopolies, widespread smuggling occurred in and between the English, French, and Dutch colonies. The same thing happened with tobacco from the Chesapeake colonies; it is sometimes suggested that the amount of tobacco smuggled was at least equal to the amount of tobacco exported through approved channels. Some settlements in the Caribbean were created with smuggling as their primary purpose.

European governments sought to limit the colonial production of commodities that could be made in the home country. In England, the 1699 *Wool Act* prohibited American colonies from exporting wool or yarn and cloth made from wool to Britain, and it also restricted trade in wool between the colonies. At other times, the governments would issue regulations that favored their colonies over those of their rivals or some colonies at the expense of others.

For example, the *Molasses Act* of 1733 favored planters in the British West Indies by taxing molasses imports from the colonies of other countries. This legislation favored sugar growers in the British colonies. The *Molasses Act* was very harmful to the interests of New England and the middle colonies since they had grown accustomed to buying less expensive molasses from French, Spanish, and Dutch possessions. This favoritism demonstrated that many British leaders considered the West Indian colonies more critical to the imperial economy than the mainland colonies.

Conflicts over French-Indian fur trade

Britain had been trying to tap into the fur trade in the French territories in North America since the 17th century. In the 1740s, tension intensified as traders from the British colonies crossed into the interior to trade with Indians in the Ohio Country, land which France claimed.

During King George's War, Britain imposed a moderately successful blockade on French trade to and from North America. As French traders lacked manufactured goods to purchase furs, British traders soon became dominant in the Ohio Valley. An expedition into this area, led by Pierre-Joseph Céloron, failed to reassert French dominance.

In the early 1750s, new French military and diplomatic expeditions were sent into the area in response to Indian recalcitrance and the British decision to assign lands in the West to an Ohio company. The French and Indian War began when George Washington, leading colonial troops and Indian allies, attacked a small scouting party under the leadership of Joseph Coulon de Jumonville.

By that time, the long-standing relationship between the Iroquois and the British became increasingly strained because of British claims to Indian lands. The Mohawk, one of the Iroquois tribes, declared the "Covenant Chain" broken, leading to the Albany Congress in 1754, where representatives from several colonies tried to establish some form of cooperation to improve relationships with the Indians.

Only the 1758 Treaty of Easton succeeded in satisfying the Iroquois and other tribes under their suzerainty by establishing the Allegheny Mountains as a boundary for white settlement. The Cherokees, long-standing allies of the British, revolted against the governments of Virginia and the Carolinas in 1758 after a long series of disappointments and misunderstandings. The Cherokees were not allies of the French but fought their war, drawing thousands of British soldiers away from the northern theater. This war lasted until 1761.

The French and Indian War and conflicts with American Indians

The French and Indian War (1754-1763) was the fourth in a series of conflicts between the British and the French in North America, all with significant participation by indigenous tribes. Before the war broke out, much of the territory claimed by the two European powers was effectively controlled by Indians: the Mi'kmaq and the Abenaki in what are now the borderlands between Canada and the eastern parts of the United States, the Iroquois along the Great Lakes and the Ohio River, Creeks, Choctaws and Cherokees in the South, Huron, Ojibwa and other tribes in the Northwest, and so on.

The French and Indian War got its name because many tribes sided with the French. French allies included most Algonquian peoples to the north and many other tribes in what the United States is now. In contrast, the leading Indian ally of the British was the Iroquois Confederacy. The Indians tended to favor the French because the much smaller French population constituted less of a threat to Indian livelihoods and behaved less aggressively toward Indian neighbors.

Some Indian tribes were eventually convinced to remain neutral, following the British promises that white settlement in the interior would be limited after the war. These promises would later lead to increased tension between the British government and the ambitious colonists who wanted to use these lands for their purposes. The continuing conflicts between Britain and France finally ended in a decisive British victory in the French and Indian War, forcing France to give up virtually all its possessions in North America.

First shot in the French and Indian War, May 27, 1754

At the end of the French and Indian War, the British took over the forts in the Great Lakes area, and the Ohio country surrendered and was abandoned by the French. The Indians in the region, especially those who allied with the French, were treated as conquered people with no say in the region's future development. This was true of the Algonquian tribes around the Great Lakes and the Huron, Illinois country tribes, such as the Miami and Kickapoo, and even some Ohio country tribes that signed the Treaty of Easton. Also, one of the Iroquois tribes, the Seneca, became unhappy with their alliance with the British.

Jeffrey Amherst, the British commander-in-chief in North America at the time, felt that the Indians were unlikely to resist the British without the support of the French. Consequently, he treated them with contempt, cut back on gift-giving and gunpowder sales, and left only very small garrisons to defend the forts. At the same time, a religious awakening broke out among the Indians, with the prophet Neolin urging indigenous people to avoid the bad habits and corrupting influence of Europeans altogether.

In 1763, when these tribes learned that France was prepared to give up their territorial claims in the region, widespread uprisings broke out, starting with the attack on Detroit by the Ottawa Chief Pontiac. The Indians failed to capture Fort Detroit and Fort Pitt (Pittsburgh) but took control of eight other forts in the next several months.

Pontiac's attack on Fort Detroit, July 31, 1763

Although the conflict only lasted until the following year and ended in diplomatic accommodation, the relationship between colonists and Indians reached a new low as massacres were perpetrated and hatred stoked on both sides.

The Royal Proclamation of 1763, reiterating the British government's commitment to keeping white settlement east of the mountains, had already been underway before Pontiac's Rebellion. The massive uprising created a new sense of urgency as officials scrambled to appease the Indians. The idea was to (at least temporarily) separate colonists in the East from Indians west of the Appalachians, establishing what was termed an Indian reserve.

Colonists now faced prohibitions against making private purchases of land west of the mountains; all land had to be purchased by the Crown after negotiations with indigenous leaders. Both speculators and prospective settlers among the colonists were disappointed with the proclamation. Some whites were already living beyond the boundaries established by the Crown. There was pressure on the British government to enter new negotiations with the Indians. In 1768, treaties with the Cherokee and Iroquois granted the colonists access to lands in what is now Kentucky and West Virginia.

Disputes over who should bear the costs of the lengthy French and Indian War and other matters that divided colonists and the imperial government brought new tensions into play. Brits and colonial Americans increasingly feared conspiracies on the other side, and the Crown's efforts to reassert control over the colonies after a long period of salutary neglect eventually prompted an armed rebellion and the Declaration of Independence (July 4, 1776) for the thirteen colonies.

International alliances of the newly formed United States of America

The significant breakthrough for American diplomacy was the alliance with France, which entered in 1778. Alliances with Spain and the Netherlands soon followed, turning the Revolutionary War into a significant international significance.

The efforts of Founding Fathers Benjamin Franklin (1706-1790), Thomas Jefferson (1743 to July 4, 1826), and John Adams (1735 to July 4, 1826) as diplomats were vital to international recognition of the United States and securing financial and military support for the war effort. In 1789, Jefferson became the first secretary of state under the new constitution. The need for coordinated and effective foreign policy was one of the reasons for creating a new constitution to replace the more decentralized Articles of Confederation.

The outbreak of the French Revolution in 1789 caused both international tensions and extensive debate within the United States. Many Americans hoped France would turn into a republic like the United States. France was a natural ally against the British monarchy. The revolution in France was considerably more radical than in America. It entailed so much violence and demanded such drastic changes that some Americans were frightened. A split occurred within the political elite, with Republicans taking the French side and Federalists supporting the British. President George Washington (1732-1799; 1789-1797) sought to maintain a balance and was very wary of entangling the United States in European affairs.

By 1793, Britain entered the international wars of revolutionary France. The United States remained neutral and signed a treaty with the British, strengthening commercial ties while securing the withdrawal of British forces from the forts in the Old Northwest. This treaty was designed by federalist leader Alexander Hamilton (c. 1755-1804) and vehemently opposed by the Jeffersonian Republicans.

Thomas Jefferson (left) and Alexander Hamilton (right)

While relations with Britain were improving, relations with France were increasingly hostile. The United States refused to make payments on its war debts, arguing that the debts were owed to the Kingdom of France and not to any Republican state. Consequently, France allowed privateers to begin seizing American ships. Since the United States did not have a navy, hundreds of ships were taken without any effective response.

By 1798, the Adams administration decided to seek congressional authorization to revive the Navy and the Marine Corps, break off all treaties with France, and fight the French navy. The so-called Quasi-War of 1798–1800 followed. The war consisted of a series of naval engagements, and by 1800, the activity of French privateers and warships along the American seaboard had declined significantly. Nevertheless, the Federalist administration of John Adams became increasingly popular due to the passage of the *Alien and Sedition Acts* (1798), introduced to silence dissenters and limit the rights of immigrants during the war.

Foreign relations – summary of the period

Spain sought to establish control over colonization in the Western Hemisphere and to convert or exploit the native population. The French and Dutch colonial efforts involved relatively few Europeans and used trade alliances and intermarriage with the American Indians to acquire furs and other products for export to Europe.

The goals and interests of European leaders sometimes diverged from those of colonial citizens, causing growing mistrust on both sides of the Atlantic, as settlers, especially in the English colonies, expressed dissatisfaction over territorial settlements, frontier defense, and other issues. English population growth and expansion into the interior disrupted existing French–Indian fur trade networks and caused Indian nations to shift alliances among the competing European powers.

Britain's victory over France in the imperial struggle for North America led to new conflicts among the British government, the North American colonists, and American Indians, culminating in the creation a new nation, the United States.

Throughout the second half of the 18th century, American Indian groups repeatedly evaluated and adjusted their alliances with Europeans, other tribes, and the new U.S. government. After the British defeat of the French, white–Indian conflicts continued to erupt as native groups sought both to continue trading with Europeans and to resist the encroachment of British colonists on traditional tribal lands. In response to domestic and international tensions, the new United States debated and formulated foreign policy initiatives and asserted an international presence.

Notes for active learning

Social History: Pre-Columbian Period to 1789

Columbian exchange

Millions of years ago, the supercontinent Pangaea was torn apart by continental drift, and North and South America were separated from Eurasia and Africa. The long journey of separation and divergence caused evolution to take different directions in the Old and the New World, leading to the emergence of unique indigenous cultures and ecosystems that had no counterparts across the ocean.

After 1492, humans began to reverse this process by establishing connections that transferred plants, animals, and microorganisms between Afro-Eurasia and the Americas. This transfer, the *Columbian Exchange*, represented a spectacular ecological reversal and a significant turning point in world history.

The concept of an *"Atlantic World"* describes the complex exchanges between Western Europe, West Africa, and the colonies in the Americas. In numerous areas, including the political, military, legal, and economic histories and this megaregion's demographic, social, cultural, and intellectual histories, national boundaries were transcended by international cross-cultural exchanges. The many connections between different points in the Atlantic World developed in a complicated web of exchanges that often transcended the scope of any national or colonial government's authority. The development of chattel slavery, religious awakenings, trade expansion, epidemics, environmental change, and even colonialism itself should be seen in this light.

Spanish explorers: Cortés, Coligni, de Soto and Verazzani

Thousands of ships carried millions of men and women, including explorers, soldiers, officials, traders, farmers, preachers, laborers, servants, and slaves from Europe and Africa to the Americas. They brought precious metals, agricultural commodities, furs, pioneers, and colonists, who may or may not have been successful, across the Atlantic. Every journey brought new encounters and reshaped the cultures of the Americas and the Old-World continents, connecting millions of lives in time and space.

Demographic and social changes following the arrival of Europeans

Before the Columbian Exchange, the peoples of Eurasia and the Americas differed in ways that would have spectacular effects once regular communication between the two hemispheres was established. Eurasian civilizations had more centers of high population density, kept a more comprehensive range of domesticated animals, and suffered from some infectious diseases unknown in the New World. Trade, migration, and war allowed these diseases to spread widely across Europe and Asia. Europeans developed resistance or immunity to smallpox and other epidemics as these diseases became endemic.

The Indians of the Americas had not had the same opportunity to develop natural immunity to many of the diseases prevalent in Europe. Deadly epidemics followed in the wake of European explorers, and once established, they were able to spread from one Indian population to the next without direct contact with whites. Microorganisms could travel in the other direction as well; it appears that the voyages of Columbus brought syphilis, a harrowing and deadly venereal disease, from the Americas to Europe. In general, the exchange of diseases was asymmetric and took a higher toll in the New World.

The rapid spread of smallpox in the Americas was one of the most devastating events of world history. It cost far more lives than all the wars and conquests initiated by the conquistadors and other European colonists, and a more significant proportion of the population died than in the Black Death, the catastrophic epidemic that hit Europe in the 14th century.

Only about 10 percent of indigenous populations survived the spread of smallpox and other epidemic diseases between the late 15th and the early 17th centuries. In some cases, entire cultures disappeared, and lands were laid waste, forever altering the demographic composition of two continents and facilitating the rapid establishment of European dominance.

Meeting of Cortés and Montezuma, November 8, 1519

In 1520, a group of Spaniards from the smallpox-ravaged island of Hispaniola (today divided between Haiti and the Dominican Republic) landed on the Mexican mainland. Another Spanish force defeated them under the leadership of Hernán Cortés, who had arrived in the previous year. One of his men contracted smallpox, and when his party set off for the Aztec capital, Tenochtitlán, they brought the deadly disease with them. The Spanish soldier eventually died, but smallpox had already spread to the Aztec population.

Having been forced to flee after an initial confrontation, Cortés returned in 1521 to find the large city devastated by disease and death. Large numbers had already perished, including most of the Aztec army. Unable to defend the capital properly, the Aztecs were easily defeated by Cortés and his Indian allies. The Spanish entered in triumph only to see streets covered in the dead and dying, as well as houses that had become tombs as all the inhabitants had passed away.

The Inca Empire was similarly overwhelmed and demoralized by the effects of smallpox. There, the disease arrived and wiped out the population even before the Spanish conquerors appeared. The efficient road system that tied the empire together also had the unfortunate effect of aiding the rapid spread of disease. Within months, the old emperor, his immediate successor, and most other persons of authority died.

Warring factions emerged in this power vacuum, and a young leader, Atahualpa, eventually came to power. After this brutal civil war had already destabilized and weakened the Inca, a small group of highly motivated Spaniards led by Francisco Pizarro was able to capture Atahualpa, take Cuzco (the capital), and swiftly establish Spanish authority over what had once been an impressive indigenous empire. Much of the Inca population succumbed to smallpox, and other European diseases led to devastation.

As the Europeans began to bring enslaved Africans to the Americas, they also brought yellow fever along. This disease was endemic in Africa, so many Africans were immune. This was not the case with those of European descent, who suffered high mortality rates in American yellow fever epidemics into the 19th century. Part of the reason the Europeans established their hegemony in the Americas centuries before they achieved the same result in Africa was the significant difference in the impact of the disease. Tropical diseases made Africa a "white man's grave," while in the Americas, conquest and control were made easy by the collapse of indigenous cultures in the face of shocking epidemics.

Early conquistadors and settlers were typically men. As they desired female companionship, intermarriage became common in Spanish America. This gave almost instantaneous rise to a mixed-race population called *mestizos,* which quickly became the numerically superior part of the population in many of the Spanish colonies. Some indigenous women were forced to become wives or concubines. Over time, the amount of European, Indian, and African "blood" a person possessed became one of the central organizing principles of Spanish American society, and a kind of hereditary caste system evolved.

Heroic defense of Cuzco

The racial hierarchy created by the Spanish elite assumed that people could be meaningfully classified according to racial and ethnic origins because these determined the differences between people. The caste system was more than a way of ascribing social status; it also had economic implications. Those who belonged to the lower end of the system met proportionally higher demands for taxes and tribute payments. Socioeconomic status largely corresponded with skin color, appearance, and family background.

Peninsulars (born and raised in the Iberian Peninsula, a Southwestern European landmass occupied by Spain and Portugal) held the most important government offices. They possessed much wealth, while darker skin and non-European ancestry entailed poverty, inferiority, and servitude. Being white allowed a person to claim status and respect, while people of color faced obstacles and prejudice. However, even whites born in the colonies faced discrimination by the Peninsulars, which eventually led the former group, known as *criollos*, to seek independence from the Latin American countries in the early 19th century.

Zambo was used to identify individuals of mixed African and Indian descent. Marriages and liaisons between Africans and Indians took place throughout the Spanish colonies and their borderlands. At times, groups of runaway slaves would mix with local Indian populations. In one unconquered region of present-day Ecuador, a group of shipwrecked enslaved people took control of an indigenous community. Another group revolted on a slave ship and wrecked it on the border between Honduras and Nicaragua, united with the local Miskito people. They eventually came to dominate society and engage in extensive slave raids.

Intercultural contact and conflicts between colonizers and natives

Indian trade with Europeans and access to European goods and technologies offered new lifestyles, status symbols, and ways of waging war. Better tools, weapons, and household goods were significant advantages that could tilt the balance of a preexisting rivalry between tribes in favor of those most closely connected to the white newcomers. These opportunities also induced indigenous people in French, English, and Dutch territories to increase their trapping activities, as furs were highly sought after in Europe.

For these reasons, Indians often thought it beneficial to maintain a working relationship with European settlers despite the disruptive effects of a disease, the introduction of new flora and fauna, and the outright expropriation of land. Thus, early colonial relations were often a mix of cooperation and intermittent conflict.

The rapid and continuous increase of the white population and the corresponding quest to control land and other natural resources inevitably created tensions that, at times, erupted into murder, massacre, skirmishes, and war. In the long run, Indian resistance tended to be futile, as wars typically ended in defeat and the surrender of rights and land. As white settlement moved beyond the coastline, conflicts intensified and multiplied as both Indian refugees and European colonists encountered and confronted the tribes of the interior.

There are many examples of the changes wrought by social contact. The Catawba people, once a formidable tribe in the Southeast, were so devastated by 18th-century smallpox epidemics that most of its members died, and the rest had to accept a settlement on a small reservation in South Carolina.

Similarly, the Huron tribes in present-day Ontario succumbed to epidemics in the 1630s. Then, in the 1640s, it came under attack by the Iroquois Confederacy, which was trying to secure control of new territories and replace members who died from European diseases. The Hurons were initially farmers drawn into the fur trade by their French allies; some joined the Iroquois, and others made desperate attempts to resettle in new lands. By that time, however, most of the Huron population had died.

Like the Hurons, who divided into traditional and pro-colonist factions at the time of their collapse, the Wampanoags ended up devastated by disease and war and failed to preserve much of their identity and culture, which had been challenged by contact with Massachusetts colonists. The Wampanoags, who eased the colonists' transition to America and are remembered in the celebration of Thanksgiving, initially forged peaceful relationships with the white settlers to access trade goods and win allies against their Indian enemies.

Eventually, the leader of the Wampanoags, King Philip (1638-1676), concluded that the influence of the colonists—especially the spread of Christianity and the hunger for land—was detrimental to the traditional Indian culture. King Philip initiated a bloody conflict with the English colonists (1675-1678). The consequences of the war mostly harmed the Wampanoags and allied tribes; despite heavy losses, the English successfully defended their settlements. Thousands of Indians were killed, died from disease, or were sold into slavery.

King Philip, or Metacomet

English colonization driven by land development

Unlike the Spanish quest for precious metals and the Dutch and French involvement in the fur trade, English colonization of the North American mainland sought to reproduce a European way of life by focusing on family farms. This was especially true of the northern colonies because the southern colonies featured slave-based plantation agriculture more closely resembling Caribbean models than anything seen in Europe.

Access to land and political and religious autonomy made these colonies attractive to immigrants, including couples, families, and single men and women. Heads of immigrant families could be rewarded with land grants. Others received grants directly from the Crown, bought or rented land, or simply chose to squat on land that had not yet been distributed to other white settlers.

The new landowners were often mobile and opportunistic, utilizing farmlands in an unsustainable way and then moving on to greener pastures when the soil was exhausted. The access to ample, fertile land made farming the most crucial activity in the English colonies, engaging most of the population until the 19th century. Also, English settlers engaged in shipping, shipbuilding, fishing, and trade.

The British hunger for farmland and other natural resources, combined with the lack of racial intermixing in these colonies, led to a pattern of frequent and often enduring hostilities between the colonists and the indigenous people. Although there were many examples of cooperation, peaceful trade, and even military alliances between whites and Indians, tensions were often persistent. They resulted in raids, plunder, retribution, and outright wars leading to conquests and massacres.

Part of the societal problem stemmed from different conceptions of land rights; the Indians generally believed that such rights only extended to specific uses of the land and its resources at a given time or season. The British equated landownership with absolute and unrestricted control of the land to the exclusion of others. The introduction of crops and domestic animals from Europe also disturbed existing ecological systems and challenged the Indian way of life.

Development of British-American slavery system

The sale of slaves to the British colonies in North America accounted for a tiny proportion of the transatlantic slave trade. At first, most enslaved people did not even arrive directly from Africa but rather from other colonies in the Caribbean. Even though African captives arrived in Virginia as early as 1619, the British system of slavery in the Americas developed on the islands during the first half of the 17th century.

Following the Brazilian model, these Caribbean colonies thrived by focusing on the production of sugar on large plantations where almost all the workers were enslaved Black people. Slaves became the majority on these islands; their rights were minimal, and their lives were often short.

The treatment of enslaved people differed significantly from the African tradition, where slaves were more commonly treated as inferior members of the family with the ability to gain their freedom after some years of service.

Slavery on the North American mainland was initially of a more complex and humane nature, with Africans sometimes treated more like indentured servants or at least as people who eventually might gain freedom for themselves or their children. The term "slave" was not used, and for some time, no laws specified the conditions of these workers.

However, as the availability of indentured servants from England declined and Africans became a more substantial proportion of the workforce, political leaders in the southern colonies took steps to ensure that the institution of slavery would secure a constant supply of laborers. They turned to the models of the Caribbean and sought to define slavery as a permanent situation where people would be treated as property for life.

In the northern colonies, which were unsuitable for plantation agriculture, slavery was less common. Maintaining enslaved people over the long northern winters made less sense as there was little farm work. Still, there were substantial numbers of enslaved people, especially in the cities, where they more typically performed household chores or worked in shops and workshops. Some historians argue that northern whites tended to enslave people as a status symbol rather than primarily to make a profit. The New England colonies were also heavily involved in slave trading, where there was much money to be made.

Emergence of racial concepts and beliefs

Three early modern developments were responsible for the entry of racial stereotypes into the European view of the world: the emergence of the transatlantic slave trade, the formation of social structures in colonies settled by Europeans, and the *Limpieza de Sangre* (i.e., purity of blood) on the Iberian Peninsula. The latter was indirectly linked to colonial development in the New World, while the first two were intimately connected with it.

Controversy exists regarding whether racial concepts already existed at the beginning of the slave trade. When Africans were sent to the New World as slaves, it may, in part, have been because they were already seen as inferior. The slave market system followed its logic and led to the development of concepts of race.

Dutch selling slaves to the Virginia planters

The rules of the new markets governed the establishment of the transatlantic slave trade. Besides, the Europeans usually did not enslave people themselves but instead purchased the enslaved people from other Africans or Arab intermediaries. In other words, they needed to build business relationships with African merchants and chiefs based on equality or at least some element of mutual recognition and respect. Nevertheless, the trade increasingly contributed to the perception that Africans in the New World were inferior.

The widespread use of enslaved Africans necessarily contributed to the racialized social structures of the New World. The structures usually preceded the explicit and elaborate justifications for their creation and maintenance. The social system of the Spanish Colonial Empire appeared to be organized strictly according to racial origins, with clear distinctions between whites, blacks, Indians, and intermediate categories.

However, this system was more rigid in theory than in practice, and some people could transcend racial boundaries and improve their position in society. As this shows, the racial elements of the system of social stratification did not necessarily indicate ubiquitous racism. Unlike later developments in the British colonies, the Spanish and Portuguese Colonial Empires allowed the intermingling of peoples and the crossing of racial lines rather than seeing the mixing of races as an abomination and a threat to society.

Domestic slave trade

British, Spanish, and French ideas of racial and cultural superiority

While slavery and the slave trade expanded, Europeans elaborated on racial ideas, which served to legitimize the unprecedented use of fellow humans in new and more brutal forms of slavery. Blacks were typically portrayed as not only inferior and savage but often as subhuman or a different species of humans altogether. These notions were thought to justify the introduction of chattel slavery, in which enslaved people were treated entirely as property.

Although these ideas evolved partially in response to economic developments, the English often associated blackness with wickedness and death even before interactions with the African continent became common. Historically, the English had fewer connections with Africa than Mediterranean peoples, such as the Spanish and the French, and their ideas about black people were often rooted in legends and outrageous tales about demons and monsters rather than personal interaction.

Power and ideology allowed slave masters control of slave families. Slave owners often preferred to purchase enslaved men, but since these were also in demand in the Caribbean, the mainland colonies ended up with a greater balance of women and men than elsewhere. Sometimes, slave women were brought in to provide companionship for enslaved men or, more strategically, to ensure the reproduction of the slave population.

In slavery, Africans saw their accustomed gender roles and kinship structures challenged or fundamentally changed. Men were forced to hoe the fields reserved for women in West Africa. Both men and women performed their work as part of the owner's commercial plan rather than to feed their families, to the extent that they were even allowed to have families. Although masters often encouraged procreation, they viewed enslaved people as property, meaning their rights as spouses and parents were severely limited or even non-existent.

African women, who saw the role of mother as the most important of all, experienced tremendous physical and mental anguish from constant demands that they not only bear children at regular intervals but return to the fields quickly after that. Furthermore, the pregnancies were often the result of rape by the master or someone else in the household. Obligations toward children limited opportunities to resist or attempt to escape, and the breakup of families was a common form of disciplinary action against enslaved people who were considered unruly.

Notions of superiority and inferiority also affected the relationships between white settlers and indigenous people. The New England Puritans, for example, believed that the Indians had been lured into settling in the New World by Satan, leading them away from God. When epidemics broke out among the Indians due to the introduction of European diseases, they took this as confirmation that God favored them and meant to punish the natives. Even brutal warfare and outright massacres were justified in the same way and seen as righteous actions in the name of the Lord.

Slave auction

In the 18th century, the difference in racial ideas between Spanish, French, and British colonizers persisted. The Spanish continued to rely on complex hierarchies of status and power where mixed-race individuals such as mulattoes and mestizos were viewed differently from blacks and Indians. A caste system gave each person a social status depending on their specific mix of European, African, and indigenous descent.

Such subtleties did not exist in the British colonies, where mulattoes were mostly the same as blacks, and mestizos were rare and lacked the special status of intermediaries between colonists and natives. In the French model, Indians and Métis could be "natural" subjects of France and part of that community. This reflected the lack of French settlement in New France and the corresponding dependence on Indian or mixed-race intermediaries in building commercial ties and brokering alliances.

French Métis

Race became extraordinarily important in the version of slavery that evolved in British North America. In other times and places, slaves and masters often came from the same racial background. This meant that some enslaved people could be freed and integrated into society on equal terms, but this was impossible in the colonies. There, slavery became intimately tied to differences in racial characteristics, leading to lasting segregation and inequality. Since enslaved Black people were "chattel," the law in practice defined white people as human beings and black people as things or property.

Racial hierarchy in British colonies

In the Spanish colonies, the intermixing of races had occurred since the beginning. It resulted in a complex but, to a certain extent, flexible status hierarchy based on skin color and birth. When the French and Dutch established colonies in the Americas, few Europeans were involved, especially few European women. As in the Spanish case, this led to widespread intermarriage, and mixed-race offspring could rise to prominent positions in colonial society. Louisiana law prohibited Catholics from marrying non-Catholics, but there were no restrictions based exclusively on race.

By contrast, some of the English colonies began to legislate against marriages between whites and slaves, and later between whites and any black or mulatto person. The Chesapeake planters were especially fearful of a coalition of white and black laborers and sought to ensure rigid separation of the races to discourage cooperation across color lines.

Rules against miscegenation extended to the northern colonies as well, especially since beliefs about race often were fused with religious sentiment. Massachusetts and Pennsylvania, with their strong religious foundations, had stringent rules against interracial sex and marriage. Free blacks or mulattoes who were caught having sex with whites could be sold into slavery.

Although intermarriage was frowned upon and often prohibited, interracial sex was nevertheless reasonably common, occurring both as everyday transgressions of community norms and as one aspect of masters' abuse of slaves in a slave society. However, being of mixed race did not qualify an individual for an intermediate status in British colonial society. On the contrary, most offspring of black-and-white unions were and remained slaves throughout the colonial period. As many as one in three black Americans living today have a male ancestor of European descent, mostly because of such liaisons between slave women and their owners.

African resistance to dehumanization of slavery

Despite the fear of violent retribution, slaves sometimes managed to demonstrate their agency by resisting slavery in various ways. These included "passive" acts of resistance: avoiding work, pretending to be sick, and ignoring the commands of masters and overseers. More direct forms of resistance included destroying equipment, organizing slowdowns, and even severe attempts to confront the power of owners, such as arson, large-scale sabotage, and murder.

Another way of resisting was by running away. Typically, running away was a negotiation tactic. Slaves hoped that by disappearing and avoiding their work if only briefly, they might convince their owners to improve the terms and conditions of their enslavement. Although enslavers, in principle, had full control over their property, the humanity and agency of the slaves forced them to bargain about the pace and amount of work to be completed and many other aspects of slaves' lives.

Some enslaved people also attempted to run away for good. Those who ran away had often served in roles that allowed them to leave the plantation occasionally, providing them with more familiarity with the outside world. In colonial times, they often headed to cities with a free black population or to swamps, forests, and other inhospitable areas where they would be challenging to find. If there were numerous runaways in an area, they sometimes managed to form Maroon communities, which helped them elude capture or even violently confront search parties.

The most dramatic form of resistance that slaveholders feared was rebellion or armed uprising. Such conspiracies and insurrections were more common on the Caribbean islands, where blacks often represented an overwhelming majority of the population and where large numbers of Africans with a common culture and language were sometimes brought in within a short period. However, they also occurred in both the northern and southern colonies on the North American mainland.

The most massive colonial uprising was the Stono Rebellion of 1739. On the mainland, rebellions were usually doomed from the outset. Reinforcements could always be brought in to subdue the slaves and execute anyone believed to have been involved. Also, slaveholders did their best to divide and conquer slave populations by differentiating between light and dark skin, house slaves and field slaves, plantation slaves, and family farm slaves. This prevented enslaved people from building the kind of cohesion and unity required to carry out mass uprisings.

Effects of revolutionary ideals on social fabric

Even in colonial times, white settlers were trickling through the mountain passes and into what is now Kentucky and Tennessee and deeper into the South and the Ohio Valley. The viability of their settlements was threatened by the Proclamation of 1763, by Spanish and French designs on the area, and by Indian resistance to their occupation of the land. These areas were characterized by instability, overlapping authority, conflicts, and cultural mixing. The brutality of military action and massacres, both during and after the Revolutionary War, also marked the hatred between peoples.

Large numbers of colonists in the British colonies were not of English origin but hailed from other parts of Europe. Thus, white culture in North America was diverse from the beginning. One crucial cultural influence was that of the Scotch-Irish Protestants from Northern Ireland. Many immigrants settled in western Pennsylvania and later traveled along the Appalachians into the southern backcountry.

Their emphasis on herding cattle and pigs and isolation, leisure, and hunting, rather than community, hard work, and farming, differentiated them from English colonists. They were also significantly different in their other habits and values, which, along with the deep class divide of Southern society, often led to conflict with other segments of the white population.

Differences between the coastal areas and the backcountry also prevailed in the North. Rural New England's economy was still based on subsistence agriculture after the Revolutionary War. When merchants and tax collectors began to demand that debts and taxes be paid in hard currency, many farmers in the hill country could not pay and ended up losing their land and other valuables.

Having secured independence from Britain, some Americans were eager to define their new national identity as Americans. Especially among the elite, many saw this as a necessary condition for building a united and cohesive nation across a vast geographical expanse. It was important that this new culture be republican and that American art and architecture have a distinctly republican flavor.

The image of George Washington became especially popular as Washington was considered the most celebrated American and a prime example of a virtuous republican citizen. His image appeared not only in paintings but also in engravings and on china. After his death, authors began to publish biographies of Washington.

Engraving of George Washington

In addition to visual artists and literary figures, American inventors, architects, scientists, and philosophers also contributed to the new American culture. Education was especially crucial in shaping a national, republican identity. In this case, education did not just mean schooling but, more generally, being exposed to art, culture, and knowledge in specific ways that promoted civic virtue.

The American Revolution altered women's lives as well as the lives of men. Many women oversaw the household and the family when the husband and other males left, and some adopted republican principles to demand greater equality for women. Abigail Adams (1744-1818) suggested that her husband, Founding Father John Adams, should "remember the ladies."

Abigail Adams, c. 1815

In general, the Revolution and the republican ideology underlying it suggested a critique of all authority, hierarchy, and traditional constraint, which encouraged women to take on new roles and have opinions. However, an essential role of women in revolutionary ideology was as mothers of virtuous male citizens.

Since women were primarily responsible for rearing, nurturing, and educating children, they needed the proper virtue and republican outlook. Academies were built to prepare American women for this role, which some historians call "republican motherhood." While extending women's rights, opportunities, and importance, this way of thinking also cemented the division of appropriate activities between men and women, emphasizing that the proper arena for a woman was the private sphere of the home.

Social history – summary of the period

European overseas expansion resulted in the Columbian Exchange, a series of interactions and adaptations among societies across the Atlantic. The arrival of Europeans in the Western Hemisphere in the 15th and 16th centuries triggered extensive demographic and social changes on both sides of the Atlantic. Spanish and Portuguese exploration and conquest of the Americas led to widespread deadly epidemics, the emergence of racially mixed populations, and a caste system defined by an intermixture among Spanish settlers, Africans, and Native Americans.

Continuing contact with Europeans increased the flow of trade goods and diseases into and out of native communities, stimulating cultural and demographic changes. European colonization in North America stimulated intercultural contact and intensified the conflict between groups of colonizers and native peoples. Unlike their European competitors, the English eventually sought to establish colonies based on agriculture, sending relatively large numbers of men and women to acquire land and populate their settlements while having a relatively hostile relationship with American Indians. The increasing political, economic, and cultural exchanges within the "Atlantic World" profoundly impacted the development of colonial societies in North America.

The British–American system of slavery developed out of the economic, demographic, and geographic characteristics of the British-controlled regions of the New World. Many Europeans developed a belief in white superiority to justify their subjugation of Africans and American Indians, using several different rationales. Reinforced by a strong belief in British racial and cultural superiority, the British system enslaved black people in perpetuity, altering African gender and kinship relationships in the colonies. It was one factor that led the British colonists into violent confrontations with native peoples.

The presence of slavery and the impact of colonial wars stimulated the growth of ideas on race in this Atlantic system, leading to the emergence of racial stereotyping and the development of strict racial categories among British colonists, which contrasted with Spanish and French acceptance of racial gradations.

Unlike Spanish, French, and Dutch colonies, which accepted intermarriage and cross-racial sexual unions with native peoples (and, in Spain's case, with enslaved Africans), English colonies attracted both males and females who rarely intermarried with either native peoples or Africans, leading to the development of a rigid racial hierarchy. Africans developed both overt and covert means to resist the dehumanizing aspects of slavery.

As regional distinctiveness among the British colonies diminished over time, they developed broadly similar patterns of culture, laws, institutions, and governance within the context of the British imperial system.

As migrants streamed westward from the British colonies along the Atlantic seaboard, interactions among groups that would continue under the independent United States resulted in resource competition, shifting alliances, and cultural blending. Migrants from within North America and around the world continued to launch new settlements in the West, creating new distinctive backcountry cultures and fueling social and ethnic tensions.

New voices for national identity challenged tendencies to cling to regional identities, contributing to the emergence of distinctly American cultural expressions. Enlightenment ideas and women's experiences in the independence movement promoted an ideal of "republican motherhood," which called on white women to maintain and teach republican values within the family and granted women new importance in political culture.

Notes for active learning

Intellectual and Cultural History: Pre-Columbian Period to 1789

Christianization of native populations

A primary justification for the Spanish conquest of the New World was the Christianization of the Indian population and its adoption of Spanish values and ways of life. An excellent example of the challenges involved in this program is New Mexico, founded in 1598 when Juan de Oñate, the scion of a wealthy mining family, established a colony in the upper Rio Grande Valley.

At the time, the Pueblo Indians in the area lived in villages called pueblos, and Franciscan missionaries built mission churches on the outskirts of these existing villages. By 1680, they established thirty missions and several religious stations in the region. The relationship between the Pueblo and the Spanish was always strained. As many as twenty thousand Pueblos converted to Christianity. The newly converted adopted Christian marriage and burials and participated in feast day processions and other rituals. While the Pueblos were baptized, attended church, and accepted communion, they continued to perform traditional religious ceremonies considered anathema by the Spanish.

Spaniards destroying Mexican idols

The Franciscan missionaries were frequently outraged by such transgressions. They would seek to punish indigenous beliefs and behaviors by desecrating shrines, destroying religious objects, and imposing corporal punishment on traditional religious leaders. At the same time, the Pueblos were forced to build new churches and to pay tribute to the *encomenderos,* who were supposed to offer military protection from warlike tribes in the region.

By the 1630s, the Pueblos erupted in rebellion against the Spanish colonizers and their assault on the Indian way of life. In the following decades, tensions continued to mount as epidemics, drought, poor harvests, and raids by the Apache and the Navajo negated the anticipated march to progress. In the 1670s, a missionary accused Indian villagers of witchcraft, and some Pueblos were executed or flogged. By the 1680s, Pueblo's discontent was unleashed in a rebellion of unprecedented scale and ferocity.

Led by a victim of religious persecution, the Indians sought to remove every trace of the European way of life. They killed their livestock, cut down their trees, and took river baths to wash away the effects of baptism. Many missionaries were killed, and the city of Santa Fe was laid to waste. Almost 400 people were killed in the uprising, and it took twelve years before the Spanish returned. By that time, some of the Pueblos welcomed the Spanish. They wanted the Spaniards to protect them against enemy raiders and regain the benefits of trading with the Europeans, who had access to goods that were not available. The Spanish also decided to reach a new understanding with the Pueblos.

The *encomienda* system was no more, and fewer labor demands were made. They granted land to the Pueblo villages and appointed an advocate to protect their rights and argue their cases in court. Even the Franciscans became more tolerant, avoiding the subject of traditional Pueblo ceremonies as long as they were performed in secret. The Spanish colonizers generally attempted to define norms and roles in the new colonial societies.

New notions of gender were constructed in the context of the Roman Catholic family and religious structure. Spanish women were seen as naturally more virtuous and valuable than others; their virginity was "protected," and a woman's adultery was punishable by death. Women of other races or mixed blood were seen as having exotic bodies. However, they could also be portrayed as innocent mothers and wives in the mold of the Virgin Mary; they were more typically regarded as highly sexual beings, seductive, and available for Spanish men. The Spanish sometimes married indigenous women and even more frequently had sexual relationships with them, often resulting in mixed-race offspring. Thus, many never became "proper" mothers and wives but rather mistresses raising illegitimate children. Latin American life had a strong flavor of patriarchy, a system women could only escape by joining a convent.

European influences on American Indian culture

Indian culture was forced to change by the advent of Europeans, simply by the force of disastrous epidemics and dramatic population decline. Later, the ways of the Europeans altered Indian practices at a deeper level. Indigenous people were encouraged to fight wars against each other to capture slaves for white buyers, and the goods they received in return, such as alcohol, caused not only cultural change but also dependence and social problems.

Indians were also encouraged to hunt animals such as deer for their pelts only rather than focusing on food needs. This led to the overhunting. Similarly, European land use put vast tracts under monoculture, eliminating other uses for the area and exhausting the soil. Thus, European influence tremendously impacted the Indian way of life.

At the same time, Indian culture also influenced the European colonists. This is especially true of the Spanish colonies, where widespread intermixing of races led to a parallel mixing of cultural, social, and economic values. The British settlers also adopted aspects of Indian culture, most importantly, the corn-raising system. Styles of artistic expression have also influenced both ways.

Colonial officials expressed considerable concern about their subjects "going native" by adopting Indian lifestyles, especially for whites who had been captured in raids or war. Long-time captives often refused to return to what the colonists considered civilized life instead of running away from settlements to rejoin their captors.

Pueblo cart

After the Pueblo Revolt, Spanish colonial officials used heavy-handed tactics to squelch new insurgencies, but their overall strategy was a higher accommodation of Indian culture. The activities of the Franciscan missionaries were restrained. The Pueblo could worship according to their tradition and perform their rituals. They were also granted land, and a Spanish lawyer was sent to serve their interests in courts of law. Similarly, after a joint Spanish and Pueblo forces were able to strike a decisive blow against nomadic Comanche raiders, finally, the colonial government in New Mexico sought peaceful coexistence rather than the destruction of the tribe.

The Spanish, supported by the bonded labor of the local Indians, expanded their mission settlements into California, providing opportunities for social mobility among enterprising soldiers and settlers that led to new cultural blending. Despite these opportunities, the number of migrants to California remained low. Consequently, the culture of the area was heavily influenced by the Indians. The dependence on local materials constrained even the architecture of the Spanish missions and artistic renderings in the churches show the influence of Indian styles.

In contrast, the English colonists often failed to accommodate native interests, primarily because the English were so numerous and so eager to secure new lands for farming and other activities. Their entrenched view of their superiority also made the English inclined to push their values and culture on neighboring peoples.

The "praying towns" instituted by the Puritans in New England were meant to convert Indians not only to Christianity but, more broadly, sought a full conversion to a European way of life. They insisted that Indians should be farmers rather than hunters and gatherers and should adjust their clothing, hairstyles, manners, and family relations to European norms. Women lost much of the stature and influence they previously possessed in traditional settings. This wholesale conversion to a new way of life was very different from the methods of the French Jesuits in Canada, who tolerated syncretism—a mix of Christian and native rituals and practices—in their conversion efforts.

African slaves tried to preserve their native culture

The Middle Passage, or the slave voyage to the Americas, was a traumatic experience for the slaves. After being captured, they could be branded, shackled, forced to walk long distances, and confined to dark dungeons for long periods even before they boarded ships where filth, disease, and abuse were the order of the day. Some chose to commit suicide either before or during the long journey to the Americas. Despite these traumas, Africans were able to preserve some of their culture, language, belief systems, traditions, and memories. Some even organized rebellions and took control of slave ships.

Differences between European cultures, as well as the various origins of the slaves in Africa and the environmental settings of the Americas, meant that slave societies differed considerably from each other, but there were many similarities as well. Every slave system differentiated between African-born enslaved people and American-born descendants. Status systems also evolved with hierarchies where free whites were at the top, slaves at the bottom, and free people of color, often mixed-race, held an intermediate position.

Color and "race" played a role in American slavery; it had not played in Africa. Slaveholders gave American-born slaves more opportunities to acquire skills and perform domestic duties, especially if they were mixed race—often a consequence of abuse or sexual relationships between slave women and male members of the slaveholding family. They were less likely to do the excruciatingly mindnumbing and backbreaking work in the fields and mines and more likely to be given their freedom by masters, a process of liberation called manumission.

This system, created by those who owned slaves, did not necessarily correspond with notions of status among the slaves themselves. Africans who had been nobles or fetish priests in their homelands sometimes continued to exercise authority, or at least influence, within the community of enslaved people. However, differences in origin, birth, and color did tend to split slave communities along racial and ethnic lines, which slaveholders usually saw as an advantage. They did not want enslaved people to be capable of collective actions.

In the Americas, Africans kept at least some features of their traditional cultures alive, whether in language, art, or traditional practices and beliefs. The exact level of continuity was very variable, depending on the extent to which members of the same tribe were transported together in sufficient numbers to obtain a critical mass. Ongoing connections between the Old World and the New also enabled slaves to maintain their culture over time.

Yoruba culture, for example, virtually flourished in northeastern Brazil due to the frequent trade contacts with the Bight of Benin. Members of the various Akan groups were predominant in Jamaica, while Ewes were plentiful in Haiti. Slaveholders could make efforts to obtain a mix of slaves from different ethnic groups, but the regular patterns of the slave trade often undermined such efforts.

Sugar plantation

Despite Africans' hopes of retaining their identities, the brutal facts of reality indicated that they had to adapt and change. They also had to be open to developing new forms of culture based on the heterogeneity of cultures on diverse plantations. Also, they had to bow down to the culture and manners of the enslavers so that the new Afro-American cultures reflected adaptions of African cultures to American realities. In this sense, the new cultures were dynamic and creative, but their development was, of course, by no means free or unfettered.

Religion was one crucial aspect of a culture where forced adaptation and creative syncretism occurred. The Spanish and Portuguese colonists and missionaries were eager to convert Africans to Catholicism, and some enslaved people became very devout Christians. They even organized in new Catholic fraternities divided by African origins. Still, beliefs and practices from Africa remained important and raised the ire of the Inquisition, which investigated paganism, heresy, and demonic deeds. Africans were frequently accused of witchcraft.

Africans continued to perform religious rituals rooted in African tradition in the English islands. These practices were called obeah, and those who served as ceremonial leaders had high status in the slave communities. Similarly, religions derived primarily from African sources, such as candomblé and Vodun, remain significant in Brazil and Haiti, respectively. They have survived centuries of attempted suppression.

Bringing beliefs and customs across the Atlantic was easier than bringing religious institutions. Without a class of clergy or religious specialists, aspects of religion were subject to change in a new and extremely challenging setting. Enslaved people often held Christian and traditional beliefs simultaneously or attempted a syncretic fusion of the two. For Muslim Africans, this was far more difficult. As late as the 19th century, a significant slave rebellion among Muslim slaves of Hausa and Yoruba origins targeted whites and infidel blacks.

Slave resistance and rebellions

While the drudgery, brutality, and isolation of plantation slavery certainly discouraged it, resistance and rebellion were nevertheless an essential feature of black history in the Americas. Wherever there were slaves, there were people evading work, running away, or even directly confronting owners and overseers.

From the outset in the early 16th century, slaves in Spanish America disrupted communications, plotted rebellions, and sought other ways to subvert or escape authority. Communities of runaways formed throughout the Americas, and such communities flourished, especially in Colombia, Venezuela, Brazil, and some Caribbean islands. Some of these communities became veritable towns or small kingdoms. For example, 17th-century Palmares (in Brazil) contained numerous villages and possibly as many as 10,000 inhabitants. This society of runaways was made up of African and American-born slaves, organized and led by Angolans. They successfully fought back against Portuguese and Dutch aggression for a century. Similarly, the "Maroons" of Jamaica managed not only to break away from their chains but also to be recognized as a virtually independent community.

Slave rebellions organized by African ethnic groups were a regular feature of life in the Caribbean and Brazil. In North America, where slave survival and reproduction rates were higher, and the American-born contingent correspondingly larger, such rebellions based on ethnic unity were more challenging to orchestrate. Nevertheless, more subtle forms of resistance were an essential part of slave existence in North America as well.

In Suriname, many runaways fought a protracted war against the authorities in the 18th century. Despite the brutal prosecution of the war by enslavers and the government, the war eventually came to a standstill, and the Maroons were able to create a separate society based on West African cultural forms fused with the ways of Europeans and Indians, a new and genuinely Afro-American culture. Today, many descendants of these runaways live in Suriname and French Guiana, maintaining some of their traditions, customs, and beliefs.

Puritans of the New England colonies

Both economic and religious factors motivated the founding of the New England colonies (Massachusetts, Connecticut, Rhode Island, and New Hampshire). Unlike the Spanish colonies—where missionaries set out to spread the religion of the home country—the New England colonies were settled by religious dissenters. They were mostly Puritans, who sought to purify the church at home but decided instead that they would have to create a new society across the Atlantic, taking on an "errand into the wilderness" to show the world a "city upon the hill," an ideal community for other Christians to observe and eventually emulate.

The Puritan settlement was remarkable in that many people—20,000 in the 1630s alone—arrived there when crossing the Atlantic was a significant endeavor regarding cost and safety, and the conditions in the promised land was very uncertain. Before long, they founded numerous towns and set up churches on their favored Congregationalist model, which allowed each church substantial autonomy in contrast to the Church of England. Attending church was mandatory, but only a select few, the "saints," were church members.

As Calvinists, the Puritans believed that every individual was predestined for either salvation or damnation, and they developed elaborate tests and procedures to ensure that only the former group was recognized as members of the church. This was important because Massachusetts was a theocratic society where only church members could vote in elections, individual morality was heavily regulated, and death or banishment from the colony could punish dissenting views.

One of those banished was Roger Williams, who considered religion a private matter, wanted to separate church and state and made church attendance voluntary. After being exiled, he founded Providence and was able to start a new colony in Rhode Island. Unlike the other New England colonies, Rhode Island became known as a land of religious freedom. Connecticut was more open to religious diversity among the Puritan colonies than Massachusetts, as it did not limit voting rights to church members.

Despite the hierarchical division of people based on religious factors, colonial New England was a relatively egalitarian society for its time. Most of the inhabitants lived on small farms where they produced much of what they needed for themselves. Their religious beliefs indicated that God had called them to do hard work and that material success was a sign of divine favor. For these reasons, the Puritans strove to improve their material lot and engaged in various crafts and trades. The colonial economy grew, and the average standard of living was quite high, even though New England crops such as barley, oats, and rye were also produced in Europe and not in high demand as exports. Growth was supported by active provincial and local governments that worked to improve the region's infrastructure and subsidized the building of mills and other early manufacturing works. The legal system was adapted to capitalist development by securing the sanctity of contracts and property rights. New England became famous for its entrepreneurial spirit.

Roger Williams building his house, c. 1636

Anglicization of the British colonies

Starting in the late 17th century, the diversity and novelty of the individual British colonies on the North American mainland began to disappear in some ways. Colonists adjusted to the climate and health risks and found ways to sustain growing populations with food. Families became more European in structure, and even warfare became more European, increasingly focused on colonial rivals rather than Indians. The Crown began to take a greater interest in the far-off colonies and imposed a more coherent legal and political structure on them. The colonies became increasingly anglicized, meaning they came to resemble England to a higher degree.

The colonies also became more cosmopolitan as more urbanization took place, and information from the Old and New Worlds could be gathered from pamphlets and newspapers due to the spread of print culture. This was less prevalent in the South, home of the slave plantations than in the North, home of colleges, seminaries, and law schools. The southern elite outwardly emulated the English elite, but their way of life was fundamentally different. At the same time, they were still dependent on their commercial ties with England.

Across the colonies, the dominant elites were beginning to depart from their original projects, utopian or not, and express admiration for the workings of the British system of government. Colonial intellectuals absorbed the discourse of leading British writers on politics, law, and religion. They saw themselves as British patriots and fought wars against the Spanish and French with remarkable enthusiasm and imperial fervor. European innovations inspired even the religious revivals in religious thought, and American thinkers familiarized themselves with the classical liberalism of John Locke and the great minds of the French and Scottish Enlightenment.

Ethnic and religious colonial diversification

Even before the influence of Enlightenment freethinkers, some colonies began to expand religious tolerance to welcome immigrants rather than try to create a new society where everyone shared the same beliefs, as had been the case most prominently in Massachusetts. Rhode Island was founded in explicit opposition to the Puritans' zeal for persecuting dissenters, and the foundation of Maryland also coincided with an articulation of principles of religious tolerance. The *Maryland Toleration Act* (1649) did not go as far as Rhode Island, as only Christians who believed in the Trinity were accepted. The primary purpose of religious toleration in Maryland was to secure a haven for English Catholics in the New World.

William Penn, c. 1718

In Pennsylvania, founder William Penn (1644-1718) allowed migrants of all faiths to settle. He and his fellow Quakers were convinced that people should find God in their own way, and unlike the other colonies, no official church was established in Pennsylvania. Penn believed religious toleration would ensure peace and prosperity in the new colony and invited persecuted groups to leave Europe behind and find freedom in the New World. However, religious freedom did not mean religious equality. Only Christians could participate in politics as voters or officeholders.

Enlightenment ideas of self-government and liberty

In addition to the long history of salutary neglect on the part of the Crown, leading to a long-standing tradition of self-government and relative autonomy in the colonies, colonial thinkers also applied Enlightenment ideas to the question of colonists' rights against the king. They were suspicious of authority and often embraced the notion of popular sovereignty—the people as the source of authority—proposed by John Locke.

Portrait of John Locke

Locke, writing in the late 17th century, believed that government resulted from a contract between the people and those in power, a social contract that created and maintained society. Unlike some previous writers, Locke held that such social contracts always had limits because some of the rights of the people, such as life and liberty, were "inalienable rights" and could not be given away.

The doctrine of the divine right of kings suggested that the monarch could not be subjected to any authority on Earth and answered only to God. According to this theory, the power came from God, and the people had no right to judge or depose the king, no matter how disappointed they might be with his decisions or how his representatives committed many travesties. Any attempt to do so would be turning away from God since the king ruled by God's grace.

In 18th-century America, the government was coming to be seen as something created by man rather than ordained by God. The king had no divine right to rule, and his role was to serve the people and preserve their liberties—not only in the home country but also in the colonies.

Resistance to perceived excesses on the part of the British government also drew on the ideology of republicanism. Republican thought, originating in the ancient world and the Renaissance, came to America through English Republicans. They saw the virtue of the citizenry rather than the king's judgment as the best guarantee for a prosperous and free commonwealth.

Republicans saw power as essentially corruptible and feared the tendency of all governments to culminate in tyranny unless vigilant citizens watched them. While placing a new emphasis on freedom and civic virtue, this line of thinking also instilled Republicans with a certain paranoia and a tendency to develop conspiracy theories.

According to American Republicans of the 18th century, politics must be a continuing struggle between freedom and power. Power must always be kept in check for the people to maintain their liberties because it would otherwise be prone to aggression and corruption. Therefore, a just and virtuous society depends on engaged citizens. In extreme cases, virtue would have to mean opposition and protest and an armed revolution against the ruling government. Every man of substance (i.e., property owner) should be able to carry arms if necessary to stave off the abuses of ambitious kings. Republicans were especially concerned about using military force and taxes as instruments of imperial aggrandizement.

The Great Awakening

In addition to the influence of new political ideas came the complicated religious situation in America. The colonies represented a variety of religious projects and a spirit of denominational competition. This, too, drew on a long tradition of questioning the authority of established churches and dissent in matters of thought and belief. This contributed to the general anti-authoritarian mindset of the mid-18th century, especially after the tremendous success of the evangelical Great Awakening.

The Great Awakening was an outburst of emotionally charged revivals across many of the British colonies in North America in the 1730s and 1740s. It broke away from the theological boundaries, social hierarchies, and traditional rituals of Protestant Christianity by introducing a new brand of much more individualistic and personal faith. This personal faith was based on stirring sermons, strongly felt belief, and a deep need for salvation and redemption, leading to further quests for introspection, moral improvement, and influential religious experiences. The Great Awakening had a lasting impact on religious affairs and stimulated new ways of thinking about politics and social issues.

Interior of Christ Church, Boston

Cultural and educational influences in British colonies

Colonization involved adaptation to a new environment, building new institutions, and creative transformations of cultural practices. The simple and, in many ways, different colonial societies of the 17th century became more complex and similar in the 18th century. Subject to many of the same regulations, political institutions, and laws, the colonies found commonalities they could eventually use to present a more united front against the British government. This happened despite the lack of real movement away from British culture and political thought in the colonies. Instead, the collective experience within the imperial system made understanding and cooperation possible.

One of the main reasons for cultural convergence was the spread of print culture. The printing presses in the colonies and materials imported from Britain supplied both literary and more popular written works in vast numbers at very reasonable prices. Poems, music sheets, chapbooks, and stories about robbers and pirates were exceedingly popular. At the same time, the rapid spread of literacy meant that colonial Americans were also reading about politics, history, and religion, coming together as a kind of unified reading public.

The educational system that taught people how to read also created a sense of uniformity despite significant differences between the colonies. Education was especially valued in New England, as the Puritans saw illiteracy and ignorance as the devil's work.

Puritan, c. 1630s

In the middle colonies, education involved more practical considerations, teaching boys work-related skills and reading, math, and religious subjects. In the South, schooling was more rudimentary, except for the children of aristocrats who could afford to hire tutors and governesses. However, education equipped most white males in the colonies with the tools needed to stay informed about outside events and develop a sense of identity transcending the family and the local community, thus facilitating communication with like-minded people elsewhere in the vast colonial empire.

The Puritans always tended to see themselves as a chosen people sent to the New World on a divine errand. However, social and political changes transformed Puritan thinking by the 18th century. Some conservatives, called Old Calvinists, continued to cling to old beliefs and practices. Several influential clergymen called the Old Lights, were eager to increase the church's appeal to the population, opening membership and preaching a more liberal doctrine.

The Great Awakening of the 1730s and 1740s brought new development, the evangelical New Lights, who built on old-fashioned Puritanism but set out to bring compelling, individual experiences of salvation to people throughout the colonies.

The Protestant clergy played a crucial role in preparing the colonial population for war against Britain, responding to British policies with severe denunciations, suggesting that Britain was doing the work of Satan, and referring to the king as the "Whore of Babylon." In retrospect, some Loyalists even claimed that the fervor and influence of Protestant preachers were the main reason behind the Patriots' success.

Enlightenment philosophers also influenced American political thought. Social contract theorists like John Locke and Jean-Jacques Rousseau (1712-1778) based their notion of political legitimacy on the idea that men were naturally free and equal, suggesting that differentials in power and status should be based on talent, character, and merit rather than traditional and hereditary privileges that had previously been ascribed to divine providence.

Political economist and philosopher Adam Smith (1723-1790) argued that economic privileges and monopolies should be abandoned in favor of free competition on open markets, allowing skilled individuals of any background to pursue their economic interests. He argued that market mechanisms would ensure that this pursuit of individual enrichment would also lead to better allocation of resources and a more prosperous economy.

Adam Smith, c. 1790

By the 18th century, science began to vastly increase human understanding of nature, which led Enlightenment thinkers to conceive that the social and political world could also be understood, explained, and improved with rational thought. Increasingly, intellectuals and activists questioned authority and doubted the legitimacy of existing social arrangements, including government structures.

Along with this new, more critical mode of thinking came suggestions for new models of government and society. Enlightenment thinkers favored systems based on freedom, toleration, equality, and consent. However, opponents often argued that reason alone could not build a better society than the wisdom of the ages and saw in some of the excesses of the French Revolution a confirmation of the dangers of a political system based on reason rather than tradition.

Thomas Paine (1737-1809) was a prominent intellectual figure during the American Revolution. His pamphlet *Common Sense* (1776) offered a blistering attack on the king and the concept of monarchy, suggesting that the people of the colonies had been forced to rise against the king to preserve their natural right to freedom.

In Paine's opinion, the government was a necessary evil at the best of times, always impinging on the rights of men. Only a republican government based on consent could avoid the kind of tyranny King George was trying to impose, so a complete break with history and tradition was necessary. Paine's writing style was so straightforward that it gained wide circulation in virtually every class of society, reaching anyone interested in political ideas and not just the educated elite.

Intellectual and cultural history – summary of the period

Native peoples and Africans in the Americas strove to maintain their political and cultural autonomy in the face of European challenges to their independence and core beliefs. European attempts to change American Indian beliefs and worldviews on underlying social issues such as religion, gender roles within the family, and the relationship of people with the natural environment led to American Indian resistance and conflict.

Clashes between European and American Indian social and economic values caused changes in both cultures. Spanish colonizing efforts in North America, particularly after the Pueblo Revolt, saw accommodation with some aspects of American Indian culture; by contrast, conflict with American Indians tended to reinforce English colonists' worldviews on land and gender roles. Despite slavery, Africans' cultural and linguistic adaptations to the Western Hemisphere resulted in varying degrees of cultural preservation and autonomy.

The New England colonies, founded primarily by Puritans seeking to establish a community of like-minded religious believers, developed a close-knit, homogenous society and—aided by favorable environmental conditions—a thriving mixed economy of agriculture and commerce.

Several factors promoted Anglicization in the British colonies: the growth of autonomous political communities based on English models, the development of commercial ties and legal structures, the emergence of transatlantic print culture, Protestant evangelism, religious toleration, and the spread of European Enlightenment ideas.

Resistance to imperial control in the British colonies drew on colonial experiences of self-government, evolving local ideas of liberty, the political thought of the Enlightenment, greater religious independence and diversity, and an ideology critical of perceived corruption in the imperial system.

During the 18th century, new ideas about politics and society led to debates about religion and governance and inspired experiments with new governmental structures. Enlightenment philosophers and ideas inspired many American political thinkers to emphasize individual talent over hereditary privilege.

Protestant evangelical religious fervor strengthened many British colonists' understandings of themselves as a chosen people blessed with liberty.

The colonists' belief in the superiority of republican self-government based on the people's natural rights found its most explicit American expression in Thomas Paine's Common Sense and the Declaration of Independence.

Relationship matrix

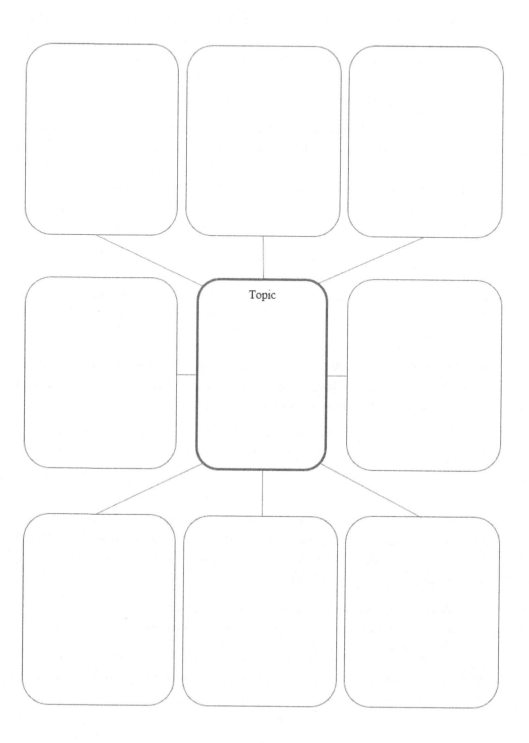

Notes for active learning

Notes for active learning

PERIOD 2

1790 to 1898

Political History: 1790 to 1898

Challenges to traditional imperial systems across the Atlantic World

The late 18th and early 19th centuries saw outbreaks of revolutions on both sides of the Atlantic Ocean, with profound and long-lasting consequences in the Americas and Europe. The American Revolution occurred and was secondary in importance only to the French Revolution, which had the most significant effects due to the status of France at that time and the fact that the influence of France spread with its military expansion during the Revolutionary and Napoleonic Wars. Haiti was affected early on in the Americas and later in Spanish America.

The timing of these events was not coincidental; the revolutionaries in different countries and colonies knew about each other and emulated each other. The ideals of republicanism, democracy, and human rights spread widely, threatening existing institutions such as monarchies, aristocracies, and influential state churches.

The revolutionaries professed Enlightenment beliefs, fighting for freedom and equality, and expanded opportunities for political participation and the rule of law. Their success demonstrated that starting from scratch with a brand-new system of government was possible and, in some cases, both valuable and accessible.

The Articles of Confederation and state constitutions

The Articles of Confederation served as the first constitution of the newly created United States of America. The Articles, like the Declaration of Independence, show the effects of Britain's rule. The founders created a confederation of states, which functioned almost as individual countries. A weak centralized government loosely joined this confederation of states. This was to avoid King George's dictatorial control over the colonies.

The Articles of Confederation, adopted by the Continental Congress in 1777 and ratified by all thirteen states by 1781, created a U.S. government composed simply of a legislature. The legislature only had one chamber and no executive or judiciary branch. Legislature members were appointed rather than elected, and each state had one delegate regardless of its population. This reflected the belief that the United States should be a decentralized confederation of states with limited powers and that all other powers should belong to state governments. The appointment of delegates by state legislatures rather than election by the populace similarly reflected that the founders had limited faith in democratic electoral politics.

Postage with an image of the Founding Fathers drafting the Articles of Confederation

At the same time, state constitutions moved power from the executive branch to the legislative branch, mainly due to the bad experiences dissident Americans had had with British-appointed governors. Pennsylvania went so far as to abolish the office of governor and the legislature's upper house, leaving only a unicameral legislature elected by all adult men who paid taxes.

The Pennsylvania constitution was far from typical, as most states placed significant restrictions on voting rights, even for adult white men, and even stricter restrictions on eligibility to hold elected office. In most cases, voter qualifications were similar to those from the British system, meaning that voters had to be free adult males who owned property and belonged to the established church in that state (in some states, there was no established church). The limitation of voting rights to property owners was justified by the claim that only those who owned property were independent men with a genuine stake in society.

The Articles of Confederation had a pronounced weakness: they allowed so many rights for each state that they also severely hindered the power of the federal government to enhance and protect liberty. For example, in his autobiography, Thomas Jefferson noted the issue of funding the U.S. Treasury under the Articles of Confederation. Most representatives' arguments acknowledged that the Treasury needed to be funded but lacked the intent to promise funds from constituents. It was challenging to achieve consensus when each representative wanted to promote their state's interests over the nation's.

The Articles of Confederation had limitations that, in the view of many critics, inhibited the development of effective governance and credible defense. The army was tiny and unpaid, and there was no navy. In the case of foreign threats, Congress neither had enough money voluntarily donated nor the authority to tax the citizenry, which meant that no authentic preparations for war could be made. Many states failed to honor the Articles, developing their foreign policies and sometimes violating the peace treaty terms with Britain.

Two factors exacerbated the money problem. The currency had become practically worthless, and the states failed to pay their taxes, meaning the national government could not pay foreign debts. By 1786, the United States was practically bankrupt.

The Articles of Confederation limited the U.S. government to powers over diplomacy and Indian affairs, issuing currency, handling the mail, and controlling a virtually nonexistent army. With no executive or judicial branch, there was no system to enforce the limits placed on the power of individual states. Thus, the problem of creating a unified and viable government was a serious one, mainly due to the lack of resources and the difficulty of making decisions, as all thirteen states had to agree on vital decisions.

Congress lacked the power to tax and received little from the states, who often preferred to issue their currencies and build their armies. They even imposed tariff regimes, placing tariffs on imports from other states. Economic and foreign policies suffered from inconsistency and a lack of coherence. When Spain restricted American navigation on the Mississippi River, the government lacked the means to do anything other than protest.

At last, the government even failed to defend itself. The event that best represents the country's inability to function uniformly is Shays' Rebellion in 1786 and 1787. Upset with the tax burden placed upon them to pay for the American Revolution, protesters began speaking out in Massachusetts.

When the legislature answered by passing laws to prevent mob actions and even suspended *habeas corpus* (a *writ* or written command for release by asserting unlawful detention), organizers in western Massachusetts mobilized to overthrow the government. They soon moved on to physical protests outside of local courthouses. While these protests did not turn violent, they stopped the county courts from meeting and disrupted business.

Anger grew as change seemed unlikely, and eventually, a group of men from Massachusetts—many of them veterans of the American Revolution—marched on a federal armory under the leadership of Daniel Shays (1747-1825), a Revolutionary War veteran.

When Shays' Rebellion broke out in Massachusetts (1786-1787), it was struck down by mercenaries rather than the United States Army. The federal government was unable to respond without funding for the military. Without an army, the state's merchant elite organized mercenaries to defeat the rebellion. Since thousands of people had taken up arms against the state government, Shays' Rebellion was an important factor in convincing political leaders that a new and more centralized and powerful federal government was necessary.

Portraits of Daniel Shays and Job Shattuck, leaders of the Massachusetts Regulators, c. 1786

The Constitution of the United States

In 1787, the Constitutional Convention assembled to solve the many outstanding problems of creating a viable federal government. Federal executive and judiciary branches were introduced, with many checks and balances to ensure that no branch of government could overpower the rest. At the same time, the Constitution was an attempt to strike a balance between the rights of the states and the need for centralization and leadership.

The new legislature was bicameral, with one popularly elected chamber representing the states according to the population. The members of the other chamber, the Senate, would be elected by state legislatures, and all the states would have the same number of senators. The Constitution was made the supreme law of the land, and the United States Supreme Court was given the authority to hear appeals in cases originating in state courts.

As some skeptics were critical of the new Constitution, especially the danger that a strengthened federal government might infringe on the rights of states and individuals, a series of amendments were later added. These first ten Amendments to the Constitution became the Bill of Rights, which secured for American citizens various freedoms and protections essential in everyday life, the development of civil society, and legal proceedings.

The new Constitution emerged from some compromises between the states. The first and most important was the Connecticut Compromise, which combined two original proposals, the Virginia Plan and the New Jersey Plan. The Virginia Plan suggested that the population in Congress should be proportional to each state's population. The New Jersey Plan called for equal representation in the system established by the Articles of Confederation. The Connecticut Compromise combined the two by proposing a bicameral solution where representation in one chamber was equal for all states and in the other – corresponding with the population.

The Connecticut Compromise solution then raised the question of the extent to which slave populations should be considered. The southern states insisted that enslaved people be considered when calculating state populations, while the northern states rejected this proposal. In the end, a compromise was made in the form of the three-fifths rule: one slave would count as three-fifths of a free person.

The southern and northern states clashed again over trade regulation. Southern elites were fearful that northerners might seek to abolish the slave trade and impose tariffs that would hurt the Southern export business. They wanted states, rather than the federal government, to regulate trade. The northern states thought that trade regulation should be a federal responsibility.

The Convention at Philadelphia, 1787

The Commerce Compromise meant that states would continue to regulate intrastate trade, but the federal government would regulate interstate trade. The case for import duties was accepted, but it was stipulated that there would be no export duties and no ban on the slave trade for the next twenty years.

Despite being short and concise, the Constitution is very well-balanced. Some of the fears of the anti-Federalists were well-founded, and the framers of the Constitution took steps to address them. The primary safeguard is the system of checks and balances between the three branches. This was implemented to keep any branch from gaining too much power.

Congress has the power to declare war, but the President does not. This would hopefully mean that all wars must be fully considered and debated before the U.S. military took action. However, in an emergency, the President can deploy troops for a limited time while seeking Congress's consent for further action. This way, the President cannot act alone on behalf of the nation but still has the power to respond to unforeseen events.

The President has the power to veto Congressional laws to protect against Congress, gaining too much political sway. Congress can override a veto to protect against a President trying to misuse his power. The Supreme Court is the final judge of whether any law is constitutional. In this way, the Constitution protects against abuses of power like those seen in many of the monarchies of Europe at the time.

The Bill of Rights

During the ratification process, some critics argued that the Constitution did not adequately enumerate the rights of people as a protection against government abuses. They felt that the federal Constitution should have a Bill of Rights attached to it, just like several of the state constitutions already in existence.

Founding Father James Madison (1751-1836; 1809-1817), who had been the formative influence on the original Constitution, initially felt that such an enumeration of rights might suggest that rights not enumerated were not protected.

President James Madison, c. 1817

Due to widespread skepticism, he finally proposed a series of amendments to the Constitution, of which ten were eventually ratified by the states (1791) and became the Bill of Rights. These amendments barred the federal government (but not necessarily the states) from interfering with the rights to free speech, free religion, and the right to bear arms.

The Bill of Rights outlines the fundamental rights given to all citizens during ratification. The Bill of Rights includes the right to free speech, assembly, and religion. It grants all citizens the right to own and use weapons to defend the country. It protects people against potential abuses of the military or police, like those that suffered under King George III. The Supreme Court analyzes the Constitution, its Amendments, and the constitutionality of laws and judicial rulings.

The Bill of Rights also offered protection from illegal seizures, cruel and unjust punishment, and unfair trials, among many other rights. In keeping with the concept of natural rights, the Ninth Amendment specified that the people retain rights not explicitly enumerated for the federal government in the Constitution.

The Bill of Rights 175th anniversary (left) and
James Madison Bill of Rights $5 commemorative gold coin (right)

Calls for abolishing slavery

During the revolution, critiques of British governance often referred to the situation of American colonists as a form of slavery. This way of speaking, along with the universalist language of freedom and equality for all, caused some Americans to reconsider the institution of slavery as it existed within farms, plantations, households, and shops around the country. Many began to doubt that differences in skin color alone could justify keeping an entire people in slavery. Soon, organizations working to abolish slavery were established, such as the Pennsylvania Abolition Society and the New York Manumission Society. In 1780, the Pennsylvania legislature passed a law that would allow "gradual emancipation" by declaring all children born of slaves free. The same act also banned the trade of enslaved people.

By 1788, eight states had abolished or suspended the slave trade. The northern states enacted gradual or immediate emancipation laws in the following decades. However, the southern states—where slavery was more prevalent—did not follow the northern states' lead. This led to mutual suspicion between the two sections, as when Abigail Adams questioned whether Virginians, with a propensity to enslave people, could love liberty as much as the people of New England.

Slavery was a problem for a country founded on ideals of freedom and equality. Founders like Washington, Jefferson, and Madison found slavery repugnant but held large numbers of enslaved people themselves. They did not see any practical way to end slavery. The Articles of Confederation did not mention slavery, and the Constitution failed to deal with slavery because of the divergent interests of the northern and southern elites. In exchange for concessions in other areas, the southern founders even forced the representatives of the northern states to accept a clause about fugitive slaves in the Constitution. Northern states were obliged to track down fugitive slaves and return them to their owners. Over the years, the question of slavery reappeared intermittently and created significant tensions between the North and South.

Westward expansion of late 18th century

Under the Articles of Confederation, the United States could not tax its citizens directly. The Land Ordinance was passed in 1785 to raise money. The Land Ordinance regulated the sale of western lands by the federal government and created a system for surveying public lands. The land was divided into townships that were six square miles, and these were, in turn, divided into thirty-six square sections. Once townships and sections had been surveyed, they could be sold to settlers and speculators (the two were not entirely distinct categories, as most settlers also speculated on the long-term increase in land values). One section in each township was to fund public schools in the area.

Surveying the Northwest Territory, c. 1788

Once the land had been sold, authority devolved from the federal government to local inhabitants, encouraging a strong sense of local autonomy in Western development. At the same time, local autonomy sometimes intensified conflicts between Indians and whites due to the lack of coherent and consistent policies toward the indigenous population.

The Northwest Ordinance of 1787 was of utmost importance because it defined the process of the westward expansion of the United States. It determined that the new nation would expand westward by creating new states, not by extending old states. It gave Congress the power to create new states out of federal lands and outlined the political development of these states-to-be. When they had 5,000 adult males, they would have a territorial legislature but a federally appointed governor. Once the free population surpassed 60,000, they could apply to become states. The Northwest Ordinance followed the Land Ordinance in emphasizing the importance of public education. It also secured religious freedom and private property. More controversially, it also prohibited slavery in the area. In some areas, notably southern Illinois and Indiana, settlers still brought in slaves and fought to legalize slavery.

Conflicts with American Indians and legal claims to seized lands

The French withdrawal from North America created a power vacuum in the borderlands between the British colonies and the territories previously claimed by the French. The backcountry was sparsely settled, and conflicts between settlers and Indians multiplied as more whites sought lands in these areas.

The Paxton Boys of Pennsylvania, who became famous for their atrocities against local Indians in the 1760s, turned to put pressure on the colonial assembly, demanding that more be done to protect the settlers against Indians. The Paxton Boys murdered and scalped peaceful women, children, and older men to achieve their goals. This was only one example of the increasingly violent and brutal confrontation between whites and Indians as the rise in the European population encouraged migration into the interior.

Paxton Boys' massacre of the Indians at Lancaster, December 14, 1763

These confrontations continued to take place throughout the revolutionary and national periods. From the mid-1780s to the mid-1790s, wars against the Indians played out in the areas west of the original thirteen colonies. The 1794 Battle of Fallen Timbers was the turning point, a decisive victory for a professionally trained American army that was followed by major Indian concessions in the Old Northwest.

The Constitution did not address directly how the relationship between the federal government and the Indians should be managed. An ordinance was passed in 1786, dividing U.S. lands into three districts with a superintendent for Indian affairs in each. In 1790, this was followed by the *Trade and Intercourse Act*, which described the process of licensing traders who ventured into Indian areas. It sought to define the terms of land acquisition by prohibiting white settlers from directly purchasing Indian lands.

All land purchases had to go through the federal government. Also, the Trade and Intercourse Act stipulated penalties for Americans who committed crimes in Indian country. This law was followed by several other trade and intercourse acts in the years that followed, meant to strengthen the protection of Indians against criminal whites attacking them and taking their lands.

World's first modern mass democracy

The search for a national identity characterizes the first half of 19th-century American history. The Americas were an empty slate for the Europeans who had colonized them. This, in turn, meant that the unstable government and lack of infrastructure impacted the changes in the newly-christened United States of America. Americans had to define a national identity based on their foundational democratic ideals while rapid changes occurred in the economy, territory, and population.

When the representatives from the colonies declared independence from Great Britain in 1776, they created a unique opportunity for themselves. The government that followed would be wholly new and original. There were no laws, treaties, or agreements to which they must adhere. While liberating, this lack of restrictions also meant frequent conflicts as the founders tried to create the most agreeable government for each very different colony. These colonies had been founded at different times with different charters. Each one had been shaped differently by Great Britain's tyranny. One of the most challenging problems facing the newly created United States was establishing how to work together to achieve a common goal.

Drafting the Declaration of Independence

The Declaration of Independence (July 4, 1776) is an excellent example of the early influences and struggles faced by the colonies. Written by a five-person committee, though usually attributed to Thomas Jefferson, the Declaration of Independence is heavily based on the significant political influences of the day, primarily the Enlightenment thinkers.

The declaration of "Life, Liberty, and the pursuit of Happiness" as fundamental human rights in the Declaration of Independence, for instance, is an echo of John Locke's *Second Treatise* (1689), where he explains that all men have a right to "their lives, liberties, and estates, which I call by the general name 'property.'"

Enlightenment concepts, such as fundamental human rights, spoke to the struggles that the colonies endured under King George III of England (1738-1820; 1760-1820) and that they hoped to eradicate from their government. Thus, the grievances listed against the King became the basis for the new government. However, even these were difficult to define.

Jefferson originally included an entire passage denouncing slavery and blaming the entire institution on George III, even though he enslaved people. This passage was struck from the final document to appease Southern representatives, who knew that an end to slavery would mean crippling the economic prosperity of the South. Eventually, the document was finalized and signed. War was upon the colonies, and while their soldiers fought for their independence on the battlefield, their next challenge would be framing the new government.

Political divisions

Even during the Revolutionary War, Americans had been divided between Patriots, Loyalists, and those who remained mostly aloof. After the war ended, divisions remained as some founders, highly skeptical of the new Constitution, became known as Anti-Federalists. In the 1790s, political conflict in the United States intensified and became partisan.

The Revolution in France and the continuing threat of war against either France or Britain put an enormous strain on citizens and members of the elite, who had different feelings about radical republicanism and different interests to preserve in terms of foreign policy. Disagreements over economic and financial policy were equally vehement, pitting proponents of a commercial, manufacturing civilization against those who relied on the civic virtue of the independent yeoman farmer in a predominantly rural republic.

To some extent, these conflicts reflected the need to come to terms with the legacy of the American Revolution. The radical and violent example of the French Revolution and the general instability of politics at home and abroad made this discussion increasingly necessary and challenging. It was apparent that the United States remained a tentative, experimental form of the republic that could not count on being left alone by the European powers. To some extent, this introduced an element of fear and apprehension into American political debate.

Although the father of the Constitution, James Madison, was an exception, most politicians, and Americans in general, did not believe that there was room for more than one legitimate political body in public life. As Patriots, they assumed that all reasonable people would be on the same side politically. Developing a party system was especially painful for the new republic, and opinions on both sides tended to be unyielding.

Newspapers added to this by being overtly political and highly critical of opponents. The great hero of the American Revolution, the President and father of his country, George Washington, was even attacked, vilified, and ridiculed by the opposition press, sometimes seen as an enemy out to destroy liberty and the republic. Even worse, abuse was heaped on the main protagonists of the party struggle, such as Hamilton and Adams on the Federalist side and Jefferson and Madison on the Republican side.

By the time of the 1796 election, the Federalists and Republicans both ran candidates at all levels, from local to state and national. They became more than mere factions, growing into influential political organizations based on firm principles. Even Madison, who had anticipated legitimate disagreement on political issues, had not expected anything other than temporary alliances built around, especially controversial issues.

However, voters were inclined to participate actively in politics and were not content with merely deferring to the elite. Thus, a competitive party system is sometimes marked by less civilized debate and confrontation. The strength of this system was exposed when Adams replaced Washington and later Adams with Jefferson. The peaceful exchange of power and position is a hallmark of political stability, despite Washington's insistence that parties were a grave threat to the republic.

The Federalists were supporters of centralization and a broad interpretation of the Constitution that would facilitate the use of government power to help the economy grow and develop. Those who supported Hamilton's policies promoting commerce, manufacturing, internal improvements, and national finance tended to support the Federalist Party. Merchants, creditors, and the urban middle class in the Northeast and New England were prominent among these supporters.

The opposition party that emerged during Washington's presidency was called the Democratic-Republicans, now sometimes called the Jeffersonian Republicans, to distinguish this party from the modern Republican Party, which emerged in the 1850s. Republican supporters were a diverse bunch, led by southern planters like Jefferson, Madison, and Monroe but also including farmers throughout the country. Unlike the Federalists, who were typical of English descent, the Republicans were a more heterogeneous party with many German and Scotch-Irish voters.

James Monroe's southern plantation, c. 1810

In the 1796 election, Federalists portrayed themselves as the more responsible party associated with the steady leadership of Washington. They suggested that Adams follow Washington, lest dangerous radicals take over the government and bring the chaos and anarchy of the French Revolution to American soil. The Republicans, meanwhile, often portrayed the Federalists as enemies of freedom and equality and as secretly scheming to introduce monarchy and aristocracy into the United States.

Adams thus came into power in a divided country and at a challenging time, given the explosive international situation and continued harassment of American shipping by both sides of the European conflict. His response to the vehemence of his critics led to the severe abridgment of civil liberties through the *Alien and Sedition Acts*. The response showed that the scope for legitimate opposition and debate was still being negotiated in the new republic.

Many voters disliked President Adams's heavy-handed tactics, and the election of 1800 showed that Americans' desire to participate in and influence politics was more durable than ever. The emotional appeals of the Federalists, arguing that a victory for the ungodly Jefferson would ruin the country, were unsuccessful.

The Republican insistence on curbing the centralization of political power was more effective. They criticized the Federalist military buildup, the encroachment on freedom during the Quasi-War, and the willingness of the government to borrow and spend. Republicans argued that the government should become closer to the people by leaving more decisions to state and local governments. This message was highly popular. Jefferson and the Republicans won a decisive victory, and the party remained in control of national politics for the next quarter of a century.

Influence of French Revolution on United States political debate

The French Revolution (1789-1799) threatened the old order in Europe, which the revolution in America had similarly challenged. Thus, Americans initially viewed the Revolution with delight, hoping it would usher in a new era of liberty and equality. The introduction of a constitution limiting the king's power was looked upon favorably.

However, the Revolution went much further than this. Soon, France was embroiled in war, a republic was declared, King Louis XVI was executed, and a reign of terror set in. The radicalism of the French Revolution even entailed the emancipation of enslaved people in the West Indian colonies. These new developments stirred debate and vigorous arguments between supporters and opponents of the Revolution across the Atlantic.

Illustration of an execution, Revolution Square, France

Federalists tended to support Britain, while Republicans preferred republican France in the ferocious war going on in Europe. Republicans like Jefferson saw what happened in France as part of a broader struggle against the old order. At the same time, Federalists believed that the radical tendencies of the French revolutionaries jeopardized the concept of social order altogether. These developments made many Americans believe that some of their fellow citizens held wrong and evil opinions and had to be suppressed, as they were by the *Alien and Sedition Acts*. Each side began to see the other as a threat to what they thought the United States should be.

The revolutionary wars in Europe created tensions between pro-French and pro-British factions in American politics. As such, international politics and foreign policy questions played an essential role in dividing the American political elite into two camps, constituting the first-party system in the United States.

By 1796, political contests were no longer personal but rooted in organized efforts to further certain principles and promote specific interests. The political climate became more unpleasant, and several politicians and newspaper journalists were arrested under new laws limiting the right to dissent. However, the election of 1800 showed the solidarity of the political system, as power passed peacefully from Federalist to Republican hands. Upon election, President Thomas Jefferson (1743 to July 4, 1826; 1801-1809) called for unity and reconciliation.

Emergence of political parties

The relationship between the federal and state governments continued to be the subject of contested and heated debates in the late 18th century. When the *Alien and Sedition Acts* were passed in 1798 during the undeclared war with France, legislatures in Kentucky and Virginia passed resolutions that held these laws to be unconstitutional, as they allowed the federal government to exercise powers not mentioned in the Constitution.

The Virginia version authored by Madison argued that the government's efforts to clamp down on free speech and a free press were perilous, as these were notably the necessary foundation for the defense of republican liberty and natural rights in general. According to Madison, Congress had not given the national government the power to infringe on these rights. Jefferson, who drafted the Kentucky Resolutions, argued that the states had the power to nullify (i.e., invalidate) laws passed by Congress, which the states found unconstitutional.

Before the outbreak of the Quasi-War with France, Madison, and Jefferson took issue with the Proclamation of Neutrality issued by President Washington when war broke out between France and Britain in 1793. Alexander Hamilton offered arguments for the proclamation by constitutionality, international law, and political expediency. Madison countered that a strict reading of the Constitution implied that Congress, not the President, should be responsible for foreign policy and suggested that supporters of the Proclamation represented anti-revolutionary and anti-republican sentiments.

These conflicts over foreign policy and constitutional matters contributed significantly to the development of two parties, with Republicans like Jefferson and Madison distancing themselves from leading Federalists like Adams and Hamilton. Another aspect of this conflict was disagreements over economic policy.

Hamilton presented ambitious centralizing financial plans that involved paying off debts incurred in the revolution by borrowing from the public to issue securities and suggested that only a central bank should be issuing currency. In this way, he sought to give the federal government financial credibility and make money available for investment in infrastructure projects.

Madison and Jefferson argued that this scheme was unconstitutional. Hamilton argued that the good of the nation depended on using any means necessary to further its interests if the Constitution did not expressly prohibit a policy. Madison, taking a much narrower view of constitutionality, suggested that the federal government not have the right to do anything that was not explicitly mentioned as one of its responsibilities in the Constitution.

Two distinct political parties fought to sway public opinion on rewriting the Constitution: the Federalists and the Anti-Federalists. The Federalists were led by John Jay (1745-1829), Alexander Hamilton (c. 1755-1804), and James Madison (1751-1836). They believed that a stronger centralized government would better protect the fundamental human rights of the citizens and the liberties gained during the American Revolution.

John Jay, c. 1829

The Federalists were well-funded and organized. They had the support of respected political figures like George Washington (1732-1799) and Benjamin Franklin (1706-1790). The anti-Federalists had legitimate fears about a strong central government. They pointed out that a stable centralized government would lend itself to the types of tyranny they fought a war to end. The ability of the President to veto decisions made by Congress had few legitimate restrictions. They also worried about the lack of protected rights for the citizens. Although the anti-Federalists were less organized and funded than their Federalist counterparts, they forced them to reevaluate their agendas and compromise to achieve a more balanced constitution.

In the 1790s, a new conflict between political parties arose immediately after the ratification of the Constitution. The Federalists and Democratic-Republicans had vastly different interpretations of the recently created legal system. The Federalists focused on economic prosperity by encouraging wealthy investors and favored an alliance with Great Britain. They believed Britain, a leading European government, would promote trade and encourage exports from the United States. They also felt that too much direct influence from voters would cause confusion in the government and that after being elected, all political figures should seek to distance themselves from their constituents.

Republicans viewed Federalist tactics as a holdover from colonialism and feared the political elite taking power on a national level. Therefore, they opposed connections with Britain, favoring the French as former American Revolution allies. They also sought to promote state and individual rights instead of the national rights that the Federalists focused on. This would keep the balance of power in favor of the individual states instead of allowing the federal government to have majority control.

These political parties were not stable. When Andrew Jackson entered the political arena (1796), a new set of political parties quickly replaced the Federalists and Democratic-Republicans. Democrats were in favor of reduced government spending and involvement. They found a ready constituency in those exposed to the market system, such as subsistence farmers. Whig politicians wanted the opposite: increased government spending and regulation. They were popular with the individuals who benefitted from a market system, particularly Northerners, who owned the means of production.

The second party system was the political party system operating in the United States from about 1828 to 1852 after the First Party System ended. The system was characterized by rapidly rising levels of voter interest, beginning in 1828, as demonstrated by Election Day turnouts, rallies, partisan newspapers, and high degrees of personal loyalty to parties. There were two main political parties during this period. One was the Democratic Party, led by Andrew Jackson. The other was the Whig Party, started by Henry Clay. The Whig Party was comprised of members of the National Republican Party and others who opposed Jackson.

There were also several minor parties. The Anti-Masonic Party (1827-34) was influential in developing political ideas and laws. The Liberty Party in the 1840s was an important abolitionist party (against slavery). The United States Free Soil Party in 1848 and 1852 was another anti-slavery party. The second party system reflected and shaped the political, social, economic, and cultural currents of the Jacksonian Era until the third party system succeeded.

The anti-immigrant support and slavery issues that could not be resolved adequately led to the disintegration of the second party system and the formation of sectional parties such as the Republican Party. While the issue of slavery was the focus, the country underwent economic and social changes during the 19th century, leading to the reordering of the political system based on separate lines.

During the compromise of 1850, the Democrats and Whigs were the only parties with voter loyalty. In the North, Democrats supported the compromise, and Whigs opposed it. Whigs supported the compromise in the upper South, and the Democrats opposed it. This competitiveness continued with the Fugitive Slave Law, but the two merged to solve the sectional conflict.

The changing economic structure made the traditional stand of the parties irrelevant, and the Whig ideals became less compelling in the wake of the gold rush (1848-1855) in California and the diversion of European investments to America. The Whigs' support of the high tariffs lost its appeal to the textile manufacturers of the North, as they wanted safety from foreign and local rivals.

The railroad issue caused competition between regions as opposed to political parties. The state constitutions that were introduced from 1848 to 1852 resulted in the weakening of party machinery, as they had fewer opportunities to strengthen party loyalty. The biennial legislative system reduced the capacity of the political system to pass laws and generated party allegiance.

Concerning nativism, the Democrats welcomed immigration, and the Whigs opposed it. The Whigs were forced to get help from Catholic immigrants in the 1852 presidential election to get votes. The election was the death knell for the Whigs, as they won only in four states. The Democrats won with a 2–1 majority in both Houses. This was mainly due to the controversy over slavery. The party's decline in the South after the Compromise of 1850, its loss of support in the North, and dissension within the party cadres over the support of the Catholic immigrants all led to the downfall of the Whig Party. This led to the fragmentation of the second party system and realignment efforts for the formation of new parties.

Influence of the judiciary

One of the Supreme Court's most important decisions happened due to the *Alien and Sedition Acts* endorsed by Federalist President John Adams. The *Alien Act* allowed the government to remove (i.e., deport) citizens who were suspected of plotting against the government. This was an effort to discredit French citizens and those who were vocal in their criticisms of President Adams. The *Sedition Act* that followed allowed the punishment of those who attempted to "stir up sedition" in the United States.

The passing of the *Alien* and *Sedition Acts* led to public outcry and widespread debate about the constitutionality of such laws. Several of Adams' political opponents and critics were tried under the *Sedition Act*, including Matthew Lyon, a Republican representative from Vermont, and Thomas Cooper (1759-1839), who wrote publicly about the President's *Alien Acts* and military actions and questioned the constitutionality. The *Sedition Act* and the political split with fellow Federalist Alexander Hamilton led to a defeat for Adams in 1800 to a political rival and Democratic-Republican Thomas Jefferson.

Recognizing that his power was fading after the election of his rival, Adams wanted to make sure that his party still had power in Washington. Thus, one of Adams' last actions as President was the *Judiciary Act* of 1801. It was a sweeping reform and expansion of the federal judiciary. The Act added sixteen federal judgeships for the six circuit judicial systems, giving them jurisdiction over all federal litigation where constitutionality was questioned. The Republicans worried that this might empower the federal system and weaken the state court systems. They also worried that Adams would appoint his Federalist supporters to the positions, precisely what he did with less than three weeks left in office. This earned Adams' appointments the title of "Midnight Judges" and meant that although Jefferson and the Republicans were taking hold of the government, they would have difficulty passing non-federalist legislation.

Thomas Cooper, 1759-1839

Jefferson stopped several of the commissions for the "Midnight Judges" before they were sent out and, in doing so, started proceedings on one of the most relevant judicial cases of the period. William Marbury petitioned the Supreme Court to force Secretary of State James Madison to send him his commission as Justice of the Peace in the District of Columbia. The Supreme Court's decision in *Marbury v. Madison* (1803) was not what Jefferson or others expected.

The court ruled in favor of Marbury and ruled that Madison's refusal to deliver the commission was illegal. However, they also stated that the *Judiciary Act* of 1789, which allowed an individual to petition the Supreme Court in this way, was unconstitutional because it extended the Supreme Court's jurisdiction beyond that laid out in the Constitution. This decision kept Marbury from his commission but also established the practice of judicial review. Judicial review allows the Supreme Court to review decisions made among the lower courts. If decisions are deemed unconstitutional, the Supreme Court has the jurisdiction to readdress the case. It also allows for the review of all legislation.

After the Panic of 1819 (a financial crisis that devastated the U.S. economy until 1821), the Supreme Court, led by Chief Justice John Marshall (1755-1835; 1801-1835), decided two pro-capitalist cases. In *Dartmouth College v. Woodward* (1819), the Supreme Court ruled that the state could not control private corporations, even if it created them.

Then, in *McCulloch v. Maryland* (1819), the Supreme Court ruled that the states could not legislate the Bank of the United States. These were important decisions because they established the limit of the government's power over private institutions and industry.

Conflict between democratic ideals and the reality of slavery

As the American economy began to bounce back, social issues like slavery moved to the forefront of politics. Like the economy, slavery was a complex issue that opposing sides attempted to simplify. Despite the outlawing of the international slave trade, the rise in the number of free African Americans in both the North and the South, and widespread discussion of various emancipation plans, the United States and many state governments continued to restrict African Americans' citizenship possibilities.

By 1808, it was illegal to import slaves into the United States from Africa or the Caribbean. This meant that most slaves bought and sold after these times were born in the United States (although an illicit trans-Atlantic slave trade persisted after 1808). However, slaves born in America were not considered American citizens and held very few rights.

Many Southerners embraced slavery as the "peculiar institution of the South" and saw slavery as part of their regional identity. They relied on enslaved people as a form of cheap labor and a ready workforce. Slavery allowed for higher profits because the workforce did not have to be paid. That is not to say that all slaves were laborers. Some enslaved people served inside houses as domestic servants and companions. These enslaved people might be taught skills inaccessible to other laborers. Domestic slaves, for instance, were the most likely to know how to read and write.

In the South, slave codes were published detailing the "rights" of enslaved people. These were manuals for enslavers and detailed how enslaved people could be legally treated. For instance, slave marriages were not considered legally binding, so those slave families could be broken up by their owners.

In the North, most states preferred to ignore the problem. Many states passed laws discouraging free slaves from settling in their state, like Ohio in 1804. In 1817, the American Colonization Society was founded to help formerly enslaved people return to Africa. While initially applauded for assisting the plight of African peoples, most people soon realized that the American Colonization Society was focused on removing freed African Americans from northern states than improving the situation of those still in slavery. Abolitionists fought against this negligence, trying to keep slavery an issue in the minds of the public.

The issue of regional identity versus national identity was constant during the 1800s. Movements helping one part of the country were inevitably met by resistance from another part of the country. Slavery was seen as a necessity in the South but was abhorrent to northerners. Tariffs on imports and exports inevitably helped the North and West while hindering the potential economic development of the South, and internal improvements in the North tended to distance the South.

Missouri Compromise

The federal and state governments had to negotiate to create an agreement as to the role that slavery should play in the West. The government kept a delicate balance between the number of slave and free states, splitting the twenty-two states evenly. This peace was maintained until Missouri requested to join the Union as a slave state in 1819. A fierce debate ensued as abolitionists fought the request. The government eventually decided upon the Missouri Compromise of 1820. Missouri would be a slave state, while Maine, formerly part of Massachusetts, would enter the Union as a free state.

Furthermore, the compromise drew an imaginary line across the nation to separate free and slave states. Few people were happy with the compromise. Southerners protested that the federal government was making rules related to slavery, a state issue, and northerners disagreed with the compromise on the premise that it allowed for the expansion of slavery, even if only below the compromise line. This uneasy peace existed for thirty years until it was repealed by the *Kansas–Nebraska Act* of 1854, which established the rule of popular sovereignty in both states. This meant Kansas and Nebraska could enter the Union as slave states despite being above the compromise line.

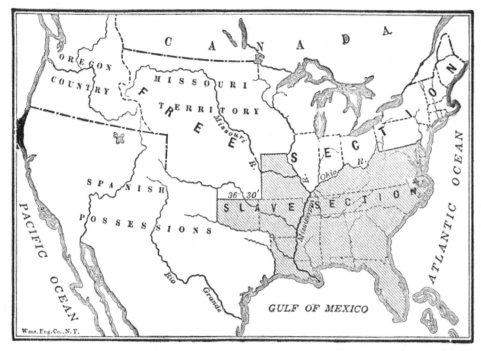

Missouri Compromise, 1820

Indian Removal Act

During the early 19th century, the United States increased in both power and geographical size. The Louisiana Purchase of 1803 more than doubled the nation's size, and the fertility and beauty of the new lands led to more westward expansion. Additionally, the Louisiana Purchase and the Treaty of Ghent—which ended the War of 1812—removed the foreign infringements in American territory. This proved detrimental to the Native Americans, as they had received protection from these foreign powers. While some Indian tribes ceded all their lands, many resisted the U.S. government.

While the Native Americans—especially the Cherokee—tried to resist the takeover of their ancestral lands by founding a nation of their own, the federal government used force and trickery to expel the Indians and exert its dominance over their lands.

With blatant disregard for the sentiments of the natives who had previously inhabited the lands, the government started using the land as if it rightfully owned it. The superior weapons and many armed troops made the settlers a dominant force, undefeatable to the Native Americans who did not have sufficient economic support or resources to fight.

Native American territories caused problems similar to those caused by the Missouri Compromise, as the tribes tried to establish their land and rules in the face of American migration. The incessant westward expansion by the United States forced several Native American tribes to resettle further west by force or by reluctant submission.

President Andrew Jackson (1767-1845; 1829-1837) tried to decide this issue with his *Indian Removal Act* of 1830, which required the relocation of eastern Indians to a territory west of the Mississippi River. The *Indian Removal Act*, passed by the United States Congress under President Andrew Jackson, authorized the exchange of lands east of the Mississippi River for the lands on the western side. From 1831 to 1839, the Five Civilized Tribes of the Southeast (Cherokee, Chickasaw, Choctaw, Creek, and Seminole) were relocated to the "Indian Territory" west of the Mississippi River.

Although heavily contested, the President ignored the opposition and pursued forced relocation of the American Indian tribes. While some activists protested the treatment of these people, many were willing to ignore their plight in favor of the opportunities opened by their relocation. The *Indian Removal Act* relocated over 100,000 Native Americans. Although, in theory, the Act was intended to be a voluntary submission of the Native Americans, immense pressure was applied to make them sign the removal treaties.

The Cherokee tribe contested the *Indian Removal Act* in court, and the Supreme Court decided in their favor in 1832. Chief Justice John Marshall ruled that the Indian tribes were "domestic dependent nations" and that the United States' function was that of a guardian. Later that year, *Worcester v. Georgia* (1832) held that the states do not have jurisdiction over Indian nations within their borders.

The heart of these rulings was that President Jackson's removal of native people from their lands was an abuse of power, though not technically unconstitutional. The President ignored the Supreme Court's sentiment and continued the forced relocation of tribes. This laid the foundation for the United States Native American policies. The idea of tribes as sovereign protected nations still legally holds.

The *Indian Removal Act* spurred massive destruction of the tribes, and the assimilations that followed their removal were even more devastating. The reservations to which these tribes were restricted separated them from their traditional life and forced them to embrace the European-American culture. Those who acknowledged U.S. supremacy accepted the teachings of missionaries, Christianity, and the inventions of white people. Some states even enacted laws forbidding the settlement of non-Indians on Indian lands to prevent white missionaries from helping the Indian resistance movement.

The conditions of their removal are often associated with the Holocaust from World War II. They were forced from their homes with few possessions and marched over land to their new territory. Disease was rampant among the natives, who had no immunity to many of the European plagues, such as smallpox.

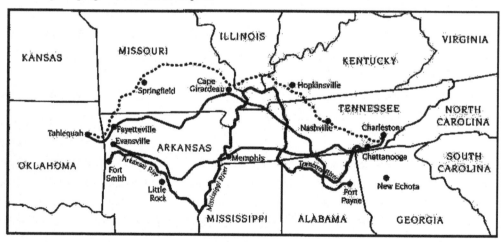

Map route of the Trail of Tears, the forced relocation of Native Americans in the 1830s

Many tribes did not leave their land peacefully, however. The Seminole tribe in Florida participated in three wars with the U.S. government to keep their land. The First Seminole War lasted from 1817 to 1818 and was a defense of tribal members. It was started when General Andrew Jackson, pre-presidency, attempted to recapture runaway slaves living with the Seminole tribe. The tribe was shaken by the encounter but defended its members.

The Second Seminole War (1835-1842) occurred after Jackson's Indian Removal Act. The tribe had many highly coveted lands that they refused to leave. This time, when soldiers approached, the tribe hid in the Florida Everglades and engaged in guerrilla warfare against the U.S. army. Their tactics were incredibly productive and might have continued that way if their leader had not been caught and ransomed back to them.

After the Second Seminole War, many members of the tribe moved west. The Third Seminole War (1855-1858) was focused on convincing the last remaining band to move west. Eventually, the federal government paid them to leave.

Seminole War: attack upon Fort King by the Indian forces under Osceola, c. 1840

Territorial expansion and slavery in 19th century

As northerners moved westward, the balance was maintained between the free and slave states. As slavery began to move westward, the nation had to decide what to do about slavery and the clear division in national attitudes. The federal government tried several compromises before tensions became too high for them to interfere directly.

While the Missouri Compromise preserved peace in the United States for thirty years, the slavery issues grew increasingly bitter over time. As slavery spread, so did the abolitionist movement and the firsthand accounts of cruelty under slavery. Formerly enslaved people, like Frederick Douglass, became famous orators and writers, spreading awareness of their cause and painting a picture of slavery that turned many Northerners against those in the South who practiced it. This, coupled with laws that allowed hunting parties to look for runaway slaves in the North, polarized the nation and caused a breakdown between the regions.

Over-cultivation depleted arable land in the Southeast. Slaveholders relocated their agricultural enterprises to the new Southwest. This increased sectional tensions over the institution of slavery and sparked a broad-scale debate about how to set national goals, priorities, and strategies. The *Kansas–Nebraska Act* of 1854 established the rule of popular sovereignty in all new states as a way for the federal government to keep from alienating any side or faction. While a worthwhile attempt, the result was a race to populate the state with supporters on both sides before the votes.

Texas, part of northern Mexico before 1836, had rebelled from Mexico to create the Republic of Texas, which was occupied in large numbers by white American settlers from the South. The Republic of Texas served as a haven for the African American slaves who settled there because of Mexican antislavery laws. Nearly 5,000 slaves lived in this republic, but when Texas decided to allow slavery, these people lost their rights.

While at first, the United States declined to annex Texas because of the reluctance of the political powers in the North against annexing another slave state, the annexation proceeded after James Polk (1795-1849; 1845-1849) was elected President. He wanted to re-annex Texas and reoccupy the Oregon Territory. Polk initiated talks on purchasing New Mexico and California. Mexico refused, leading to a declaration of war.

While the war was brewing, Representative David Wilmot (1814-1868) drew the Wilmot Proviso in 1846 to soothe the escalating tension between the North and South. According to the proviso, southerners could acquire new territories, but slavery would be banned in the newly annexed lands. The proviso was passed in the mostly-northern House, but the Senate did not acquiesce, so the proviso was not enacted.

David Wilmot, c. 1846

Mexicans led by General Antonio López de Santa Anna (1794-1876), who later became President of Mexico, could not defend their territory against the advanced artillery and superior rifles of the Americans. The treaty of Guadalupe Hidalgo, signed in 1848, established the Rio Grande River as the new border between the United States and Mexico, making California and the remaining territories north of Rio Grande a part of the United States. The territories were sold for $15 million, and Mexico lost New Mexico, Arizona, Nevada, Utah, and California – nearly one-third of its territories.

The Mexican-American War (1846–1848) was the first armed conflict fought by the United States entirely on foreign land. Although the U.S. invaded Canada during the War of 1812, this was part of a more massive war mainly fought in what is now the United States of America.

The Mexican-American War was controversial because it played a crucial role in expanding slavery. The North had been opposing the Mexican-American War, claiming that the South was trying to expand its slave power with the acquisition of new territories. The end of the war resulted in a compromise between the North and the South, but the status of slavery remained undetermined, spurring an intense debate that remained unresolved until 1863.

With a marked increase in the migrant population and the expansion of territories westward, many conflicts and encounters arose with Native Americans and Hispanics, leading to questions about their legal rights and social status. Mariano Guadalupe Vallejo, born in California in 1808, was affected by the marginalization of his tribe in their land during the territorial expansion of the Union. Born into a Californio family (i.e., a Mexican family living in Alto, California), he had been groomed to lead.

When Vallejo was fifteen years old, he joined the Mexican army. He participated in many Mexican and Indian expeditions and played a primary role in quelling the Indian revolts and establishing settlements to prevent Russian settlement in California. Vallejo identified himself with Mexican Liberals in supporting an efficient government independent of religious authority.

Vallejo favored the governing model of the United States and, in 1836, led a rebellion declaring California a free state. Although he supported the United States, American rebels poorly treated him in 1846. He was imprisoned by General John C. Frémont, leader of the Bear Flag Revolt. Vallejo's estate was damaged, and matters improved only when U.S. forces replaced the rebels under the leadership of Brigadier General Stephen Kearney.

Vallejo was made Indian agent for Northern California and was elected to the Senate in 1849. In the wake of the Treaty of Guadalupe Hidalgo, Vallejo lost most of his land. His life is an example of the fate suffered by many Californians under American rule. Despite their acceptance of the democratic U.S. government, they were treated as foreigners and could occupy only the lowest economic rung.

Although the United States was engaged in conflicts with the Indian tribes due to territorial expansion, the 1851 Treaty of Fort Laramie ceded extensive territory to the Indians. The terms of the treaty were renegotiated in 1861 by the United States after factors like the Pikes Peak Gold Rush (1858-1861). In 1861, Arapaho and Southern Cheyenne chiefs signed the Treaty of Fort Wise. This treaty reduced Native American land to one-third of the original amount. The Indian chiefs signed mainly to safeguard their people, but certain Lakota and Cheyenne tribes who called themselves Dog Soldiers opposed the treaty.

The Sand Creek Massacre was another effect of westward expansion on the country's Native Americans. In 1864, under orders from Colorado Governor John Evans, Colonel John Chivington attacked several Cheyenne camps in Colorado. More attacks followed in Kansas under the command of Lt. George S. Eyre. The Cheyenne attacked in retaliation, which increased tension between the U.S. forces and the Indians.

Eyewitness' depiction of the Sand Creek Massacre, 1864

On November 29, 1864, when most of the males were out hunting, the Colorado Territory militia, led by U.S. Army Colonel John Chivington, attacked the Indian villages of Arapaho and Cheyenne. Most of the people slaughtered were children and women. The massacre later came to be known as the Sand Creek Massacre.

Since the discovery of gold in Native American territory, tensions prevailed between the United States and the Indian tribes. When the tribes refused to move their reservations as ordered by the U.S. Army, they were attacked by Lieutenant Colonel George Armstrong Custer (1839-1876) in the Battle of Little Bighorn.

The Battle of Little Bighorn was fought in 1876 near Little Bighorn River; the federal troops under the leadership of Lieutenant Colonel Custer attacked Cheyenne warriors and the Lakota Sioux. The Indian tribes fighting under Sitting Bull outnumbered the armed forces and overwhelmed them in what was later termed Custer's Last Stand. Nearly 10,000 Native Americans joined the Indian camp at Little Bighorn River, which they dubbed Greasy Grass, in defiance of the war department's order to move their reservations.

In the Battle of Little Big Horn, 3,000 Native Americans defeated 600 of Custer's men within an hour. The battle was the highest victory by the Native Americans against the invading U.S. army and the worst defeat for the United States in their fight against the Indians. In the wake of the war, the government increased its efforts and confined the Cheyenne and Sioux tribes to reservations.

Tensions between the North and the South over slavery

The Southern states' concern over their rights and their nullification of the laws against their economic growth led to the Southern defense of portraying slavery as a sound system. One of the prominent southerners in this aspect was Democrat John C. Calhoun. A noticeable representative for the antebellum South, he helped the United States during its war with Great Britain and served as Secretary of War, Vice President, and Secretary of State.

Democratic Vice President Calhoun (1782-1850; 1825-1832) opposed the Mexican-American War and the annexation of California as a free state, and he was a renowned proslavery speaker. He initially supported the 1828 Tariff of Abominations, but after being criticized by the South, Calhoun protested it. Calhoun was elected as a senator for South Carolina and defended the slave system against the growing antislavery protests. He dominated the American political scene from 1815 to 1850 with his gift as a debater on political, economic, social, and philosophical issues.

Vice President John C. Calhoun, 1825-1832

The pro-slavery sections also had support from racist minstrel shows. The shows featured blackface, a theatrical makeup where white performers used stereotyping and makeup to represent a black person. The shows were popular during the 19th century and glorified the slave stereotypes such as "dandified coon" or "happy-go-lucky darky" on the plantation. The minstrel shows started in 1830 and continued for over one hundred years, becoming an essential tradition in American theater. The stereotypes embodied in the shows played a critical role in cementing as well as enhancing racist attitudes, images, and perceptions.

Repeated attempts at political compromise failed to calm tensions over slavery. They often worsened sectional tensions, breaking down the trust between sectional leaders and culminating in the bitter election of 1860, followed by the secession of southern states. Northerners attempted several measures to reduce the tensions that prevailed between the North and the South over slavery and other issues, including more power for the Southern states. The various attempts to solve the increasing sectional tendencies over slavery worsened the situation and led to the secession of the southern states.

The slavery conflict spurred by the annexation of territories in the wake of the Mexican-American War was resolved with the Compromise of 1850, which admitted California as a free state and allowed the territories of New Mexico and Utah to determine their slavery status by popular sovereignty. The compromise aimed at settling the border dispute between Mexico and Texas in favor of the latter and ending the slave trade in Washington, D.C., making it easier for the South to regain fugitive slaves. This compromise led to avoiding slavery and regional issues for many years.

The *Kansas-Nebraska Act*—passed in 1854—allowed territory settlers to decide on slavery based on a popular sovereignty mandate. The bill overturned the Missouri Compromise and thus invalidated the boundary for the free and enslaved person regions. Conflicts in the wake of the *Kansas-Nebraska Act* led to Bleeding Kansas, one of the causes of the Civil War in 1861.

This Act, which tried to organize the western territories, led to sectionalism and railroad development. It also split both major political parties, leading to the creation of a third party and a worsening of relations between the North and South.

Bleeding Kansas: slavery debate in Congress, c. 1854

While Kansas was given statehood in 1861, southern states started to secede from the Union. The antislavery Republican Party lost the support of the Northern Whigs and independent Democrats, causing further division within the political parties.

The *Dred Scott* (1857) Supreme Court case was instrumental in Abraham Lincoln being elected President in 1860. Dred Scott was an enslaved person who gained freedom via the American legal system. In 1857, the United States Supreme Court denied his plea for freedom, stating that a black man could not become a citizen. The abolitionists in the North were outraged by this turn of events.

Secession crisis

Prairie lawyer Abraham Lincoln (1809-1865; 1861 to April 14, 1865) enjoyed a short span in Congress from 1847 to 1849 and later embraced his law practice fully. He joined the Republican Party in 1856 when sectionalism was at its peak. The debates over the *Kansas-Nebraska Act*, slavery, and the role of the territories in these issues made him prominent nationally. However, he was unpopular in the South due to his antislavery ideals.

Lincoln was disliked by the South even before he took office as President in 1861. He was seen as an abolitionist and a fanatic of the caliber of John Brown. The South considered him a Republican who would not fear overriding the laws and constitution to arrive at a compromise of any nature. During his presidential campaign, Lincoln refrained from announcing any policies, fearing they may be misunderstood in the North and South.

President Abraham Lincoln

The secession crisis emerged because of a disagreement over the validity of the election outcome (Lincoln was elected with a thin minority of the vote and less than half of the Electoral College votes) and, more importantly, a disagreement between North and South about the appropriate boundaries between state and federal governmental powers.

Southerners advocated strong states' rights, while northerners favored a robust federalist system. Despite being elected by a majority of voters, Lincoln's authority was rejected by Southerners. Their threats of secession were a way to pressure Lincoln and the Republicans into accepting state autonomy.

The secession crisis was not new in 1860; it had existed for over a decade. While the Compromise of 1850 put down some of the ardor in the discord, the growing unrest among the Southerners made them repeatedly resort to the threat of secession.

The secession issue caused slaves and southern landowners to evaluate the changing political scene. The entire social system of slave and master had been challenged after Lincoln's election. The collapse of the prevailing political system made the slaves look for new opportunities. The slaveholders wanted the secession because they saw it as a positive step towards maintaining the stability of the master-slave balance. Northern intervention into their political and economic situation increased unrest among the slaves, and the deteriorating relationship between the masters and slaves led to their support of secession.

The Civil War

In 1860, Lincoln won the election without the support of the southern states. Lincoln decided to fight secession to preserve the Union rather than accept it. Lincoln believed in preserving the union of the North and South by prudent and, at times, forceful execution of power. His flexible tactics in an inflexible pursuit of reunification helped the North win the war. Lincoln's wise judgments on when to use or avoid military force (such as the intense military domination in Maryland and the moderate handling of the opposition in Kentucky) helped the North win and prevent secession.

Portrait of Lincoln surrounded by Civil War scenes, c. 1865

There are many reasons the Confederacy lost the Civil War (April 12, 1861, to April 9, 1865), but the main reason is that the North had more guns and men. The Union had overwhelming numbers of men, resources, and luck on its side, making it a very tough fight for the South. The enormous social divisions within Southern society are also cited as a reason for the Confederacy's defeat. Southern society was rife with racial, class, and even regional antagonisms, all of which contributed to the fall of the South. These factors, together with the lack of resources, arms, and men, enabled the Northern defeat of the South.

While it is broadly believed that the Union's resources were the main reason for their defeat of the Confederate army, some historians insist that it was the Confederate's approach that led to their defeat.

The Union had several advantages:

• Union had 22 million people against 9 million in the South (of whom only 5.5 million were white).

• North's firearm manufacturers had a higher capacity than those in the South.

• A robust naval blockade prevented the South from getting materials.

• Four slave states supported the Union: Kentucky, Maryland, Missouri, and Delaware.

• Some people in the Confederate states were not fully supportive of its cause.

Despite their many disadvantages, southerners were confident the Confederacy would win the war. The 750,000 square miles occupied by the South were considered a huge asset, making it difficult to occupy and conquer. The South had the advantage of defending their land instead of invading the North. Additionally, the rifles used at the time were best suited for defensive rather than offensive tactics.

Battle of Fort Sumter, Civil War, 1861

Geographically, the rivers flowing through North Virginia made it difficult for the Union armies to conquer Richmond, the capital of the Confederates. Finally, while the Northerners were engaged in the war in pursuit of a reunion, the Southerners had a more needy cause: defending their homes and lands, making their fight more psychologically immediate.

The Confederate victory in the initial major battle at Manassas (July 21, 1861) confirmed Confederate supremacy. Expert opinion contends that had the Confederate forces been more proactive and brought Britain on their side, they might have been more successful. Therefore, a combination of missed opportunities and lack of luck is also cited for the downfall of the Confederates.

When the war started, some northerners were against it, as they saw it as a crusade to end slavery. While most of the Democrats and conservative Republicans in the North opposed the expansion of slavery, they were against abolishing it entirely. In the wake of the First Battle of Bull Run (July 21, 1861) in Virginia, they reconsidered the role slavery played in the conflict. By 1862, Lincoln was convinced that without abolishing slavery, the war did not serve any purpose.

First Battle of Bull Run, stand of the Union troops at the Henry House, July 21, 1861

Therefore, after the big victory at the Battle of Antietam in Maryland, Lincoln issued the Emancipation Proclamation, declaring that enslaved people in all the rebelling territories would be declared free. The move was symbolic, as it freed only the slaves in the regions outside the control of the Union. However, it changed the main objective of the war from a reunification effort to the destruction of slavery.

Lincoln's Emancipation Proclamation was a critical document that changed the objective of the war. It is also one of the least understood documents in U.S. history. The Emancipation Proclamation was issued twice, in 1862 and again in 1863.

The Emancipation Proclamation applied only to the states that rebelled and intended to restrict the Confederacy. While the cabinet initially did not support the proclamation, it did so after witnessing the victory at Antietam and noting Lincoln's continued commitment to executing its ideals.

While the initial aim of the Civil War was to safeguard the Union from disintegration, freedom for the slaves became the primary objective after the Emancipation Proclamation was issued. Another advantage of the Emancipation Proclamation was that it prevented foreign nations from supporting the Confederates, as the European nations were against slavery.

The proclamation also helped African Americans to participate in their fight for liberation. Nearly 200,000 African Americans served in the Union Navy and Army by the end of the Civil War. The Emancipation Proclamation encouraged citizens to advocate and accept the abolition of slavery both in the North and South.

Events like Gettysburg and Sherman's March to the Sea reinforced that the Union won because of their plentiful resources, key victories, effective leadership, and efficient strategies. While the Civil War—like any other war—did not have one single moment that turned out to be the turning point, it did have many crucial moments that, in retrospect, clearly indicated the way it would end.

General Rober E. Lee's (1807-1870; 1862-1865) repulse of McClellan's army in Richmond in 1862, the victory of the Union in Antietam, the Emancipation Proclamation, and the successes that ensued at Gettysburg and Vicksburg in 1863 all transformed the fight significantly. General Lee's defeat at Gettysburg showed victory was imminent for the Union. The clear defeat and massive damage incurred by the Confederates, together with the final capture at Vicksburg, demoralized them and restored control of the Mississippi River to the hands of the Union.

The March to the Sea is another landmark event that strengthened Union supremacy. Led by General William T. Sherman, the Union army destroyed most of Georgia and captured Savannah from the Confederates in 1864. While Atlanta was a Confederate stronghold, Sherman had the needed supplies and troops to defeat the Confederates and destroy Georgia.

General Robert E. Lee

The Civil War ended with the surrender of the Confederate armies, which took place in several stages. The last major battle of the Civil War was the Battle of Palmito Ranch in Texas, fought on May 12-13, 1865. However, the last surrender on land did not come until June 23, when Cherokee Confederate General Stand Watie gave up his command.

On April 2, 1865, Union forces captured the Confederate capital of Richmond, Virginia, which was a major turning point in the war. On April 9, 1865, General Lee surrendered his army to Union General Ulysses S. Grant at Appomattox Court House in Virginia, effectively ending the war.

On April 14, 1865, President Lincoln was assassinated by stage actor John Wilkes Booth while attending the play *Our American Cousin* at Ford's Theatre in Washington, D.C. Lincoln was shot in the head and died the following day. After an initial escape, Booth was killed at the end of a 12-day pursuit. This was the first American president to be assassinated. Lincoln's assassination was part of a larger conspiracy intended by Booth to revive the Confederate cause. Wilkes believed that Lincoln was determined to overthrow the Constitution and destroy the South. After Lincoln's reelection in November 1864, Booth devised a plan to kidnap the president and take him to Richmond, where he could be ransomed for some of the Confederate prisoners languishing in northern jails.

However, that plan failed, and Booth decided to eliminate Lincoln and two other top federal government officials. His co-conspirators, Lewis Powell and David Herold were assigned to assassinate Secretary of State William H. Seward while George Atzerodt was going to kill Vice President Andrew Johnson. However, beyond Lincoln, the plot failed, and conspirators were later hanged for their roles in the conspiracy.

On May 10, 1865, Union forces captured Confederate President Jefferson Davis in Georgia. The president of the fallen Confederate government, his wife, and his cabinet had fled to Danville, Virginia after General Robert E. Lee informed him that he could no longer protect Richmond and advised the Confederate government to evacuate its capital.

Jefferson Davis (1808-1889),
first and only President of the Confederate States of America (1862-1865)

After Lee's surrender on April 9, 1865, Davis and his cabinet moved south, hoping to reach the trans-Mississippi area and continue the struggle until better terms could be secured from the North. However, Davis was captured before escaping to a sympathetic foreign nation such as Britain or France. Davis was imprisoned for two years at Fort Monroe, Virginia. Though he was indicted for treason, he was never tried and was released on bail in May 1867.

Reconstruction period

While the victory of the Union upheld the antislavery stand, helped resolve slavery issues, and put a stop to any idea of secession, unresolved issues remained regarding the extent of power wielded by the federal government and the rights given to the citizens. Some of these issues included the northern states' failure to return fugitive slaves, the northern support of abolitionists and insurrectionists such as John Brown, and the religious and political beliefs of the North, which the Southerners did not accept. The South was also against the idea of granting citizenship rights and voting rights to the slaves.

The Civil War (April 12, 1861, to April 9, 1865) and the period of Reconstruction (1865-1877) that ensued changed political relationships and power dynamics in all aspects, including the legislative, executive, judicial, and federal government policies. It also marked the end of slavery and the division of the Union. However, it did not resolve the questions related to the control of power and the change in economic and social patterns. Reconstruction entailed the first step taken by the United States to develop an interracial democratic system.

The war also resulted in the ratification of the Thirteenth, Fourteenth, and Fifteenth Amendments of the Constitution, which declared slavery a federal crime and brought in a new dimension to citizenship and universal male suffrage. This promised new powers and an active role by the government in enforcing the amendments.

The Thirteenth Amendment, passed in 1865 by the House of Representatives, abolished slavery in the United States and all places subject to its jurisdiction. During the war, the purpose of the struggle changed from the restoration of the Union to freeing the slaves, which caused Lincoln to issue the Emancipation Proclamation.

The Thirteenth Amendment was not accepted in 1864, as the Democrats were worried about the rights of the states. Lincoln's election, along with Republican majority votes in both Houses, helped pass the amendment successfully in 1865, leading to the eradication of slavery, which had left behind an indelible mark in the history of the United States. The Thirteenth Amendment was ratified eight months after the war ended. The Thirteenth Amendment represented the resolution of the long, drawn-out struggle for the freedom of the slaves.

Lincoln strongly believed in the need for a substantial constitutional amendment to end slavery ultimately. While Congress debated several proposals in 1864, which included incorporating provisions that would prevent discrimination against blacks, the Judiciary Committee of the Senate was the body that provided the final language of the amendment. The conditions were drawn from the 1787 Northwest Ordinance, which had banned slavery from the region north of the Ohio River.

The Senate passed the Thirteenth Amendment in 1864, and the victory of Republicans in the election guaranteed its successful implementation. The Radical Republicans wanted the complete abolition of slavery, while the Democrats wanted the restoration of the states' rights. Lincoln's victory in the election ensured the amendment's ratification was done smoothly. When the House passed the Thirteenth Amendment in 1865, it was sent to the states. After Georgia ratified the Thirteenth Amendment on December 6, 1865, slavery ceased to be an institution in the United States.

With the war's end, the fight for power emerged and was renewed as the moderate and Radical Republicans tried to change the power balance between the President and Congress. This led to leadership positions and political significance among the formerly enslaved people. Notable among the Republicans were Hiram Revels, Blanche K. Bruce, and Robert Smalls.

Republican Hiram Revels (1827-1901; 1863-1865) was the first African American to become a member of Congress when he was made a senator of Mississippi, filling in for Jefferson Davis, the former senator and Confederate President. He was part of the Labor and Education Committee in the District of Columbia.

While Revels was not predominantly for racial equality, he opposed the segregation of schools in Washington, D.C. He was also an advocate for the black people banned from working in the Navy Yard in Washington because of their racial identity.

Republican Robert Smalls (1839-1915; 1862-1868) represented South Carolina as an African American Congressman. He was enslaved until 1862, when he piloted a Confederate ship into Union waters. Smalls became actively involved in politics and, in 1870, was an influential leader in South Carolina. He was against segregation in railroads, eating establishments, and the military, and he opposed the western migration of African Americans in America as well as their emigration to Liberia.

Republican Blanche K. Bruce (1841-1898; 1875-1881) escaped slavery during the initial phase of the Civil War. He is the first African American to serve as Mississippi senator full-term and head a Senate session. Bruce wanted better treatment of the Native Americans and advocated army desegregation. He was part of the committee to improve navigation on the Mississippi River.

Despite several arduous efforts by the Republicans, especially the Radical Republicans, resolving slavery failed to bear fruit as the South steadily resisted all the moves towards altering their racial attitude. The sectional wounds wrought by the war failed to heal during Reconstruction.

The North tried to bring the South back into the Union and give it equal footing by reviving its economy and rebuilding the Southern landscape battered by war. However, deep divisions in the federal government prevented these goals from being realized. Furthermore, the assassination of Lincoln led to Andrew Johnson (1808-1875; 1865-1869)—a proslavery leader—becoming President. Democratic President Johnson started a Reconstruction plan that opposed rights for the formerly enslaved people. While the Confederates tried to enter power positions in government, Republicans had a dominant role in Congress and refused to give any leeway.

President Andrew Johnson

While the Radical Republicans opposed the Southerners, moderates and conservatives wanted the Southerners to be admitted. The Radical Republicans were committed to the total emancipation of slaves and the equal treatment and enfranchisement of freed slaves. During its formation in the 1850s, the Radical Republican Party—consisting of northern industrialists, altruists, practical politicians, and former Whigs—was not committed to abolitionism. However, it did attract some of the most fervent antislavery advocates.

While President Abraham Lincoln insisted that restoring the Union was the main aim of the Civil War, abolitionists in Congress also wanted emancipation included. The Radical Republicans formed the Joint Committee of the Conduct of the War due to agitation over the poor performance of the Union army and the lack of attention given to emancipation. The Radicals favored the inclusion of black troops and eventually broke with Lincoln over his Reconstruction policy and his reluctance to enforce the speedy abolition of slavery.

The areas in the South under military control were subjected to Reconstruction (1865-1877) under the command of Lincoln, who planned on including only 10 percent of the Southern electorate in forming the government. The Radical Republicans were not satisfied with Lincoln's Ten Percent Plan. They produced the Wade Davis Bill, which required fifty percent of the white male population of a state to take an oath of loyalty and excluded an increasing number of Confederates from taking part in the restored governments.

When Lincoln vetoed the bill, the Radical Republicans were enraged and launched an effort to deny Lincoln a second nomination. While they welcomed Andrew Johnson when it was clear that he pursued the same lenient policies in Reconstruction, they formed the Joint Committee on Reconstruction to ensure that Reconstruction was under congressional control rather than presidential control. They passed several measures to safeguard the political involvement of blacks in the South despite Johnson's vetoes.

Despite the Radical Republicans' efforts, white control of southern governments was gradually restored. The African Americans were frightened and prevented from participating in the polls by terrorist organizations such as the Knights of the White Camellia and the Ku Klux Klan.

Furthermore, the North lost its initial zeal over the continued military occupation of the southern states, and Reconstruction efforts failed by the end of 1877. One reason for this failure was the Northern politicians' lack of cohesiveness. Their commitment to emancipation and ending racial discrimination were the only threads that held them together. They were not united over critical issues such as labor reform, protectionism, and hard or soft money.

In the wake of the Civil War, the economic prosperity of the North—where the industrial inventions and output increased enormously—also led to a further divide between the North and the South. The subsequent depression and the northern boom made the Reconstruction efforts fail. Additionally, some of the white supremacy factions combined with Black Codes to dominate the freed slaves and deny them civil liberties. The Supreme Court rulings also limited the rights of the African-American population. The disparity in the sharecropping system pushed the African Americans into debt, which evoked their dependence during slavery. They remained oppressed and were afforded only second-class citizenship until the 20th century.

Continued westward expansion and treatment of American Indians

To bring about total westward expansion, the U.S. government supported the creation of a transcontinental railroad that would provide all the resources necessary to settle the West. The government was also forced to address the issue of Native American settlements, which had been promised in the earlier 19th century.

To address the issue of Native American lands, the U.S. government employed barbaric tactics, which included the extermination of the American buffalo, a life source of Native American populations. This coined the phrase, "*kill the buffalo and you kill the Indians.*"

Helen Hunt Jackson (1830-1885) worked to bring to light the government actions against Native Americans was told in detail in her book *A Century of Dishonor* (1881). This text perpetuated the concept of assimilation as a common good for the Native American populations, which were all but decimated by the end of the 19th century.

Helen Hunt Jackson, c. 1875

By 1890, all Native American tribes lost their legal entity status and over two-thirds of their former lands, and they were now living on reservations established by the U.S. government. The implications of such policy decisions were monumental, as the U.S. government effectively eliminated an entire way of life.

One so-called positive outcome of the reservation programs was the stabilization of the Native American populations following the devastation of life from ongoing military offensives, explosions of Anglican diseases brought by Western settlers, and relocation programs.

However, it is difficult to argue for any real benefits of the reservation programs employed by the United States during this period other than the opportunity for white settlers to continue their westward expansion.

As the Civil War ended, the West was sparsely populated. There were notable settlements in Texas, and lands promised to Native Americans, taking up most of Oklahoma and Kansas, but other sections of the West were considered wild and unsettled. This was quickly remedied with the conception of a transcontinental railroad, which would provide the people with goods and services necessary for the westward expansions called for by the government. During the 1870s and 1880s, the West grew alarmingly, causing many more to settle west of the Mississippi.

Using the railroad companies and governmental policies, the United States created large land grants that angered many settlers in the West. Examples were seen throughout the Gilded Age (1870s to 1900), where disgruntled settlers attacked land grant sites, cutting off railroads and temporarily stalling the progress made by these steam giants. Such opposition did not change the policies of the U.S. government, which sought to settle the wildlands of the West at any cost.

As the expansion continued, it seemed inevitable that it would be at the expense of Native American populations, who had been promised lands after being displaced from the East Coast following the initial American expansion of the Atlantic Seaboard. In hopes of bringing an end to Native American aggression, the United States sought to enact several treaties to eliminate coercive actions.

These included the Medicine Lodge Treaty signed in 1867, in which the federal government recognized the Great Plains as individual tribal lands allocated by the federal government. Other notable treaties of the period included the Fort Laramie Treaty, signed in 1868, which concluded warfare along the Bozeman Trail and promised vast areas of Wyoming, Montana, and the Dakota territories, including the Black Hills, to the Lakota people.

Many of these treaties would eventually be violated as the U.S. government failed to secure enough land in the western regions not already promised to the Native American populations. Land grants given to railroad companies in the West greatly influenced this process and would become commonplace along the frontier and in the settled West. The practice of land-grant colleges during this period strained the available territorial resources while establishing sixty-nine colleges. The Native American and Mexican populations, who believed the U.S. government would expand their territories until all other settlers were expelled and replaced with American frontier men and women, frowned upon the use of such policies but were powerless to stop them.

The long-term implications for such policies can be seen today, especially in the western portion of the United States, where Native American tribes maintain their traditions and culture on reservations surrounded by the unfamiliarity of the contemporary United States. Such policies brought criticism from many Americans during the period and later decades. As a result of the westward expansion, the American government was again forced to enact domestic policies to address growing concerns over its interactions with Native American populations. In the early 19th century, many Native American tribes had been allowed to remain on their native lands, with intermittent regulation attempts by the U.S. government.

By the mid-19th century, the government changed its policies to limit Native American access to land; they enacted the concentration policy, which removed Native American populations from areas white settlers wished to inhabit.

Following the Civil War, regiments of soldiers, most notably those led by Generals William Sherman, P. T. Sheridan, and George Custer, took up military offensives against Native American tribes. The policy of forcefully dispelling resistance was commonplace in the U.S. military during this period. It can be seen in the Sioux War (1876–1877) and Nez Perce conflicts, culminating in the battle at Wounded Knee in 1890.

In hopes of maintaining their livelihood and traditions, many Native Americans took up arms against the military forces and called upon their deities in hopes of evading assimilation. One notable example of the resistance movement by Native Americans comes from the Nez Perce tribe, initially located in the Northwest, mainly in Oregon. This tribe, led by Chief Joseph, fought to maintain their lands in Wallowa Valley; American military forces repeatedly engaged them and were eventually defeated in 1877.

The government initially promised relocation to ancestral lands but instead placed the remaining tribal members in malaria-infested camps in Kansas and Oklahoma, decimating the population. To avoid a similar outcome, many Native Americans began practicing ghost dancing to avoid forced relocation. On the eve of each new moon, many Native American tribes would practice this ritual, which eventually caused disturbance among white settlers. Authorities intervened, causing deaths and further soured relations.

In addition to military confrontation, the U.S. government sought to civilize the Native American populations through assimilation and education. This was first attempted under the *Dawes Act* of 1887, which granted the U.S. President the authority to allot tribal lands to the heads of households and others and the possibility of U.S. citizenship. While this legislation seemed beneficial to the Native American populations, it obliterated tribal customs and authority, eventually leading to the downfall of Native American culture in the United States.

Political history – summary of the period

In the late 18th century, new experiments with democratic ideas and republican forms of government, as well as other new religious, economic, and cultural ideas, challenged traditional imperial systems across the Atlantic World.

Many new state constitutions and the national Articles of Confederation, reflecting Republican fears of both centralized power and excessive widespread influence, placed power in the hands of the legislative branch and maintained property qualifications for voting and citizenship.

Difficulties over trade, finances, interstate and foreign relations, and internal unrest led to calls for significant revisions to the Articles of Confederation and a stronger central government. After experiencing the limitations of the Articles of Confederation, American political leaders wrote a new Constitution based on the principles of federalism and the separation of powers, crafted a Bill of Rights and continued their debates about the proper balance between liberty and order.

Delegates from the states worked through a series of compromises to form the Constitution for a new national government while providing limits on federal power. Calls for more significant guarantees of fundamental rights during the ratification process resulted in the addition of the Bill of Rights shortly after the Constitution was adopted.

During and after the American Revolution, increased awareness of societal inequalities motivated some individuals and groups to call for the abolition of slavery and greater political democracy in the new state and national governments. The constitutional framers postponed a solution to the problems of slavery and the slave trade, setting the stage for recurring conflicts over these issues in later years.

The United States policies that encouraged Western migration and the incorporation of new territories into the nation extended republican institutions and intensified conflicts between American Indians and Europeans in the trans-Appalachian West. As settlers moved westward during the 1780s, Congress enacted the Northwest Ordinance to admit new states and sought to promote public education, the protection of private property, and the restriction of slavery in the Northwest Territory.

The French withdrawal from North America and the subsequent attempt of native groups to reassert their power over the interior of the continent resulted in new white–Indian conflicts along the western borders of British—and later U.S.—colonial settlements and settlers were looking to assert more power in interior regions.

The Constitution's failure to precisely define the relationship between American Indian tribes and the national government led to problems regarding treaties and Indian legal claims relating to the seizure of Indian lands.

The United States developed the world's first modern mass democracy. It celebrated a new national culture, while Americans sought to define the nation's democratic ideals and reform its institutions to match them.Continued debates over federal power accompanied the nation's transformation to a more participatory democracy, the relationship between the federal government and the states, the authority of different branches of the federal government, and the rights and responsibilities of individual citizens.

As national political institutions developed in the new United States, varying regionally based positions on economic, political, social and foreign policy issues promoted the development of political parties. The spread of the French Revolution throughout Europe and beyond helped fuel America's debate about the nature of the United States' domestic order and its proper role in the world.

Although George Washington's Farewell Address warned about the dangers of divisive political parties and permanent foreign alliances, European conflict and tensions with Britain and France fueled increasingly bitter partisan debates throughout the 1790s. As the first national administrations began to govern under the Constitution, continued debates about the relationship between the national government and the states, economic policy, and the conduct of foreign affairs led to the creation of political parties.

As constituencies and interest groups coalesced and defined their agendas, political parties, most significantly the Federalists and Democratic-Republicans in the 1790s and the Democrats and Whigs in the 1830s were created or transformed to reflect or promote those agendas. The second party system ended when the issues of slavery and anti-immigrant nativism weakened loyalties to the two major parties and fostered the emergence of sectional parties, most notably the Republican Party in the North and the Midwest.

Supreme Court decisions sought to assert federal power over state laws and the primacy of the judiciary in determining the meaning of the Constitution. Concurrent with the increasing international exchange of goods and ideas, more Americans struggled to match democratic political ideals to political institutions and the social realities of slavery.

With the expanding borders came public debates about whether to expand and how to define and use the new territories. The desire for access to Western resources led to the environmental transformation of the region, new economic activities, and increased settlement in areas forcibly taken from American Indians.

The American acquisition of lands in the West gave rise to a contest over the extension of slavery into the Western territories as well as a series of attempts at national compromise. Enthusiasm for U.S. territorial expansion—fueled by economic and national security interests and supported by claims of U.S. racial and cultural superiority—resulted in war, the opening of new markets, the acquisition of new territory, and increased ideological conflicts.

The acquisition of new territory in the West and the U.S. victory in the Mexican-American War was accompanied by a heated controversy over allowing or forbidding slavery in the newly acquired territories.

As the territorial boundaries of the United States expanded and the migrant population increased, U.S. government interaction and conflict with Hispanics and American Indians increased, altering these groups' cultures and ways of life and raising questions about their status and legal rights.

States' rights, nullification, and racist stereotyping provided the foundation for the Southern defense of slavery as a positive good. National leaders made various proposals to resolve the issue of slavery in the territories, including the Compromise of 1850, the *Kansas-Nebraska Act*, and the *Dred Scott* decision. However, these ultimately failed to reduce sectional conflict.

Lincoln's election on a free-soil platform in 1860 led some southern leaders to conclude that their states must secede from the Union, precipitating civil war. The Union and the Confederacy mobilized their economies and societies to wage war even while facing considerable home-front opposition.

Lincoln's decision to issue the Emancipation Proclamation changed the purpose of the war, enabling many African Americans to fight in the Union army and helping prevent the Confederacy from gaining support from European powers.

The North's more considerable manpower and industrial resources, leadership, and the decision for emancipation eventually led to the Union military victory over the Confederacy in the devastating Civil War. Although Confederate leadership showed initiative and daring early in the war, the Union ultimately succeeded due to improved military leadership, more effective strategies, key victories, significant resources, and wartime destruction of the South's environment and infrastructure.

The Civil War and Reconstruction altered power relationships between the states and the federal government and among the executive, legislative, and judicial branches. The issues of slavery and secession were settled, but unresolved questions about the federal government's power and citizenship rights remained. Social and economic patterns were largely unchanged.

The Thirteenth Amendment abolished slavery, bringing about the war's most dramatic social and economic change, but the exploitative and soil-intensive sharecropping system endured for several generations.

Efforts by radical and moderate Republicans to reconstruct the defeated South changed the balance of power between Congress and the presidency. The result was some short-term successes, reuniting the union, opening political opportunities and other leadership roles to former slaves, and temporarily rearranging the relationships between white and black people in the South. Radical Republicans' efforts to change Southern racial attitudes and culture and establish a base for their party in the South ultimately failed due both to determined Southern resistance and to the North's waning resolve.

As transcontinental railroads were completed, bringing more settlers west, U.S. military actions, the destruction of the buffalo, the confinement of American Indians to reservations, and assimilationist policies reduced the number of American Indians and threatened native culture and identity.

Post-Civil War migration to the American West, encouraged by economic opportunities and government policies, caused the federal government to violate treaties with American Indian nations to expand the land available to settlers. The U.S. government generally responded to American Indian resistance with military force, eventually dispersing tribes onto minor reservations and hoping to end American Indian tribal identities through assimilation.

Notes for active learning

Notes for active learning

Economic History: 1790 to 1898

States' resistance to federal economic authority

While President Jackson sought to repeal parts of the American System, such as the National Bank, Congress was considering another tariff, like President Adams' Tariff of 1828, which was called the Tariff of Abominations. The new tariff was very similar. A protectionist tariff attempted to protect local producers from foreign competition. It did this by taxing imported goods, raising prices, and making buying American products more appealing.

The issue was that any tariff that taxed imports would benefit the North over the South. The North's products, like textiles, would be cheaper than foreign products, causing northern markets to flourish. Southern markets, mainly cotton, would suffer because foreign traders could buy fewer products.

Southerners protested the tariff vehemently, but on July 14, 1832, Andrew Jackson signed it into law. The southern states, which were to be the hardest hit, were outraged. South Carolina particularly resisted the new tariff, and in the winter of 1832, the state government declared it null and void because they considered it unconstitutional.

In response, President Jackson issued a proclamation disputing South Carolina's ability to ignore federal law. Congress soon passed the *Force Act*, which allowed a military force to be used against any state that refused to comply with the tariff acts. As tensions grew, a deal was brokered by Henry Clay (1777-1852) and Vice President Calhoun.

The Compromise Tariff of 1833 gradually reduced taxes to their set levels from 1816. This conflict quickly demonstrated the tensions between the federal and state governments. It also illustrated why regionalism was inherent in American culture.

Regional attitudes towards slavery

During the early 19th century, territorial expansion became a full-fledged activity in the U.S. effort to protect its states and further its economic status. A critical factor that influenced expansion policies, opened new markets, and caused ideological conflicts was Eli Whitney's (1765-1825) invention of the cotton gin in 1793. This machine reduced the time required to separate seeds from cotton fiber, previously a laborious process that required manual labor and primitive tools.

The cotton gin increased the profitability of the cotton industry in the South, and the increase in profits led to a rise in slavery, which many historians cite as the main reason for the Civil War (April 12, 1861, to April 9, 1865). Due to the flourishing cotton industry, the American economy improved dramatically, and cotton was exported in plenty. While the South benefited from the exports, the North—particularly New England—benefited from the ample raw material supply for its textile industry.

Eli Whitney watching the cotton gin, c. 1793

The first Industrial Revolution (1790 to 1830) was also influenced by Whitney's large-scale musket production, one of the earliest examples of the American mass-production system. The muskets were made of standardized and identical interchangeable parts, enabling faster assembly and repair. This led to the massive production of arms, which was highly profitable for the country.

Unlike the southern elite of the antebellum era, who tended to glorify slave society, most early American leaders from both the North and South saw slavery as distasteful and outdated. They envisioned that slavery would eventually die out on its own. The Virginian founders who later became Presidents (including Washington, Jefferson, Madison, and Monroe) were all slaveholders interested in the gradual abolition of slavery.

The Northwest Ordinance also banned slavery in the vast northwestern territories of the United States without much protest from Southern politicians. Southerners were content that it would be challenging to grow competing tobacco in the new territories without slave labor. The introduction of new breeds of cotton and the invention of the cotton gin allowed for explosive growth in cotton agriculture in the South. At the same time, the mechanization of textile manufacturing, the first stage of the Industrial Revolution, led to a vastly increased demand for cotton, especially in Britain. As new cotton lands opened in the West, slaveholders in the East saw the value of their slave property increasing as the prices of enslaved people rapidly increased.

Gathering cotton in the field of a plantation, c. 1793

Meanwhile, slavery was disappearing in the North. During the Revolutionary War, blacks in New England were agitating for emancipation. During the 1780s, several states passed laws of gradual or immediate emancipation, and by 1804, all the northern states had taken such steps.

Vermont joined as a free state, and the new states carved out of the Northwestern Territory would also become free states. Kentucky and Tennessee entered the Union as slave states, and the lands to the southwest were prime candidates for cotton plantations worked by large numbers of enslaved people.

Boston-born Benjamin Franklin (1706-1790), a former slaveholder, became one of the most vocal opponents of slavery. In 1790, the octogenarian petitioned Congress, proposing that slavery should be abolished throughout the United States. Quakers from Pennsylvania were also agitating for the same policy. Their petitions provoked great anger and controversy in the House of Representatives.

Southern representatives argued that slavery was justified by the Bible and economically necessary in the South. They also feared that any debate on this topic might inspire slave rebellions. Some northern representatives claimed that the Constitution did not protect slavery and was directly contradictory to the message of the Declaration of Independence.

Benjamin Franklin, c. 1780

As a response, South Carolina and Georgia threatened to secede from the union. To avoid disintegration, hostilities, or possibly even civil war, Madison brokered a solution that suggested Congress had no right to abolish slavery, as it was a state matter.Slavery continued and expanded into the new lands west of the original southern states. By the time of the Civil War, twice as many enslaved people had been taken from the Eastern Seaboard into the new states as had arrived from Africa in the whole of colonial and national history. This expansion of slavery and slave-owner power and wealth would become the most divisive political issue of the 19th-century United States.

The expansionist policies and worsening divisions regionally led to contested debates over slavery and its abolition. In addition to the raging slavery issue, the cultural, economic, and political changes that occurred during the period led to civil war. These issues included the abolition of slavery, the control of governments, nullification, and sectionalism. The institution of slavery and its attendant ideological debates, along with regional economic and demographic changes, territorial expansion in the 1840s and 1850s, and cultural differences between the North and South, intensified sectionalism. The central conflict that separated the North and South and increased sectionalism between them was slavery.

The United States was not able to bring about a balance between the northern free states and the southern slave states, although there were numerous legal documents signed in attempts to resolve the issue. The South also felt dominated by the North due to the increase in the northern population. This limited the chance of getting a President who supported the pro-slavery policies of the South. The South faced increased tariffs as it primarily relied on agriculture and plantations. The North was mainly industry-based and thrived on manufacturing. The South needed more land to create a better economic balance with the North. The economic disparity between the two sections increased tensions and led to the Civil War.

Impact of international conflicts on American industries

As the government and the country grew, the United States had to assess its place as an economic market. By 1805, constant conflict between Britain and France started putting military, financial, and social pressure on America. When British ships began targeting American vessels on the high seas and abducting American soldiers using the practice of impressment, Jefferson implemented the *Embargo Act* of 1807, which prohibited American goods from being exported overseas.

The intention was to withhold several raw materials that the British and French relied on economically, like cotton. Jefferson hoped that this would pressure both countries into leaving American vessels unmolested. The *Embargo Act* did more to hinder American growth than French or British aggression due to European stockpiles. James Madison repaired the relationship with France but not Britain, setting the stage for the War of 1812.

Transporting cotton, c. 1810

While the *Embargo Act* made sense nationally, most states were against it because it would hurt them individually. Many northern states were unsuited for the agricultural specialization that flourished in the South. They were less arable, and the lack of enslaved people in the North meant that labor was more expensive. Eventually, the northern states began to industrialize, building factories that supplied the country with materials Europe had previously supplied. During the War of 1812, Europe supplied most of its farming tools and weapons to the United States. The North also protested vehemently because the northern states were heavily involved in the shipping industry. They stood to lose a significant amount of money because of Jefferson's embargo.

In the South, agriculture was the primary profession. Products like tobacco and cotton made southern plantations very lucrative. This was due in part to the cheap labor provided by slavery. Southerners primarily sold goods to Europeans, although, as the North industrialized, clothing factories began competing for southern cotton. Both regions opposed the idea of the embargo because it gave them less opportunity to market and sell their goods. Disputes like this between the state and federal governments persisted as regional interests differed from overarching national plans.

Technological shifts in agriculture, manufacturing and labor force

The early 1800s saw some significant shifts in technology and business. Suddenly, machines that could do the work of multiple men with less strain and effort were available. This rocked the market foundation of the country and opened the door for some possibilities. These rapid and far-reaching changes affected everything from where new communities settled to gender roles and family relationships.

Two central problems faced the new U.S. agricultural market: communication and transportation. With long-distance communication existing only in letters, it was challenging to determine product markets and establish fair buying and selling practices. For example, a tobacco farmer in North Carolina may not have wanted to sell his tobacco in North Carolina because most other farmers in the state also grew tobacco, saturating the local market. Farmer had to find a different market for his goods to profit. The farmer's market options were limited due to the difficulty of transportation. If the farmer could not get his items to a new market, they were virtually worthless. This changed as infrastructure created safer and more accessible transportation and with the creation of the telegraph by Samuel Morse in 1844.

Samuel Morse making the telegraph, 1844

America's economic development was very dependent on technological innovation. Samuel Slater (1768-1835) is often called the father of the American factory system. After covertly memorizing the setup of a British textile mill, Slater came to the United States and put his mill into practice. While he used previously conventional methods in Britain, they were new to Americans and revolutionized how northerners looked at their labor force.

Slater changed the factory system by constructing a small town for his factory. Slater believed he could improve production by employing families and housing them at the factory. This system gave families an option outside of semi-subsistence farming—the typical lifestyle at the time—although most factory families obtained some of their food through farming.

Samuel Slater, c. 1835

Other innovators focused on agriculture. Cyrus McCormick (1809-1884) is not well known in the modern era, but his company became part of International Harvester in 1902, which still supplies farming equipment today. McCormick's invention, the mechanical reaper, meant that harvesting was no longer limited to the amount that could be cut by hand. Beyond inventing the mechanical reaper (1831), McCormick created an entire industry, including creditors and a service department utilizing the new concept of interchangeable parts. His business model is relevant in the modern market, and many enterprises follow a similar plan.

Likewise, John Deere (1804-1886) started his company with the manufacture of plows that could tackle the prairie lands where grassroots made the sod thick and difficult to penetrate. His innovative design began what is still a successful agricultural business. The Slater method of employment, in which entire families were housed and taken care of by the factory, was later adapted by Frances Cabot Lowell (1775-1817), who employed farm girls and young women instead of whole families. The girls were housed in supervised dormitories and provided educational and cultural opportunities. While this situation often raises suspicion about working conditions and pay, the Lowell system benefited its workers.

Lowell drew in a ready and willing labor force by hiring young women, typically from rural communities, who would not have had many opportunities to improve themselves. Lowell's system impacted the Women's Rights Movement, helping to encourage more women to join political movements and empowering them to demand rights and education equal to their male counterparts.

Lowell women at the loom, c. 1815

With the progression of the market and the development of new factories, the discovery of anthracite coal deposits in Pennsylvania was a blessing to the nation. As industrialization continued, it became evident that there were not enough trees to power the growing factories. Coal was a good solution, especially anthracite, with its high carbon content, allowing it to burn longer than most other types of coal.

Finding ways to mine and transport coal proved difficult. It took an entire generation to prepare the mountainous areas of Pennsylvania for coal mining. Canals were built to connect the coal mines with cities that needed their product. Eventually, railways replaced water transportation, which meant more coal could reach the market faster. It also meant that coal tycoons, having control of the product and the means of transportation, could sway the future of entire regions.

Cotton industry domination in the South

One of the country's most important agricultural products was cotton. While important before the Revolutionary War, cotton became one of the most influential American products in the world after Eli Whitney developed the cotton gin in 1793. Whitney's machine increased cotton production at unheard-of rates: nearly 800 percent in the first decade. King Cotton, as it was called, was an excellent money-maker that created high competition and provided good returns on investment. It did not spoil the way produce did and could be sold in distant domestic markets and overseas.

Typically, cotton was grown in the South and sold to factories in the northern states or to England, whose thriving textile factories could not be adequately fed by European wool. If sold to England—and, on average, 80 percent was—cotton was transported on northern shipping vessels. This meant that the North also prospered from the sale of cotton. The increase in production also meant an increase in labor; slavery became even more deeply ingrained into the Southern economy as new labor forces were always needed to keep up with growing demand. Slave ships illegally transported cargo from Africa and the Caribbean to southern markets.

Picking cotton, c. 1831

Many slave women were encouraged or forced to produce children. Poor farmers, those who did not enslave people and could not afford to buy them, often stopped planting other crops to focus on cotton. Southerners were eventually forced to seek new farmland as their one-crop system quickly drained the land of its resources. This eventually raised the question of whether slavery should be allowed to spread into new territories, and this is why the cotton gin is often cited as a cause of the Civil War.

The American System of economy

Cotton was not the only thing tying the North and South together. John Quincy Adams, son of former President John Adams, focused on America's internal integrity using the American System. Secretary of State Henry Clay (1777-1852; 1825-1829) created the American System, which consisted of three main pieces. A tariff designed to promote American industry, a national bank to help establish productive business and enterprise, and federal monetary support for infrastructure to help agriculture reach new, more profitable markets inside the United States.

While the American System was unpopular, especially with Adams' political opponents, it achieved significant infrastructure strides. For example, the Cumberland Road, also known as the National Road, connected the Potomac and Ohio Rivers and allowed for westward expansion at an exponential rate.

Adams also commissioned a series of canals that opened America's waterways to encourage economic growth. This was partially due to the *Gibbons v. Ogden* (1824) Supreme Court decision, which allowed the federal government the right to regulate interstate trade. The county's prosperity grew as railroads and canals made interstate commerce easier. As Adams left office, the national debt had been reduced to one-third of its size. Adams hoped its continued economic growth could unite America, but many people, particularly Southerners, disliked his American System because it limited the number of markets for products like cotton. This meant a limit on competition and price.

The North was less impacted because it could adapt its shipping industries inward. The North and Western territories grew closer as more commerce and movement opened. The South, in comparison, stayed relatively isolated by its beliefs and economic and infrastructural differences.

Efforts to exploit the nation's natural resources led to government efforts to promote free and forced migration of American peoples across the continent and to compete for ideas about defining and managing labor systems, geographical boundaries, and natural resources. Natural resources were abundant in the Americas.

Virtually untouched, America had immense forests that could be turned into boats or tools. They could be shipped to Europe, where lumber was more expensive and less plentiful. Abundant supplies of fresh, clean water supported the creation of new towns and communities while allowing for faster travel of people, resources, and news. America had vast, untapped mineral wealth, including coal, iron, copper, silver, and gold. As each resource was discovered, an industry grew to harvest it for consumption elsewhere. These jobs were dangerous but profitable, so a steady labor supply was available. Disease and bodily harm created concerns about job safety, and regulation became a topic of national interest.

Regional patterns

Many scholars believe several variables affected where and when settlement occurred in the United States in the 1800s. Before 1815, settlements were relatively slow to expand and branch out, particularly beyond the Appalachian Mountains, because there was very little immigration due to the wars in Europe and the War of 1812 in America. Following the war, immigration to the United States increased rapidly, with the promise of new land in the Louisiana Territory.

Businesses tended to differ from region to region, depending on the type of environment. For instance, in the agricultural areas, cities were very far apart, as settlers claimed the land for farming. In areas where the growing season or land was not conducive to agriculture, people tended to band together to form larger cities for economic growth and prosperity. This meant that the societal makeup for these different areas differed significantly.

The market revolution helped to widen the gap between rich and poor, shaping the emerging middle and working classes. It caused an increasing separation between home and workplace, which led to dramatic transformations in gender and family roles and expectations. With the rapid changes in industry, workers started to band together to form protective agencies called unions. Unions focused on improving workers' conditions by creating safer working conditions and offering fair wages.

In 1834, the National Trades Union made a short appearance, yet most labor unions functioned better locally than at the national level. Previously, the American economy was based mainly on small-scale agriculture and local commerce. By the middle of the 19th century, America turned into a capitalist marketplace. The Industrial Revolution changed America's economy and boosted urbanization, while agricultural development spread to the West. As settlers moved towards the West, their conditions improved, and they flourished as hunters and farmers.

Cheap land and plentiful resources attracted new settlers, and merchants and artisans followed farmers toward the Western occupation. Chicago, Illinois, which in 1830 had been a trading village, became the richest and largest city by the time its original settlers breathed their last. The *Preemption Act* of 1836 allowed people to stake claims on land, and after 1862, people could acquire their land just by occupying it and making improvements.

The steel plow, invented by John Deere in 1837, made it easier for farmers to plow their land, while the mechanical mower and reaper, invented by Cyrus McCormick in 1834, replaced manual scythes and sickles for large-scale agricultural practices. Soon, mechanical seeders and threshers were introduced. The technological innovations and persistent westward movement resulted in large-scale commercial activity in the West.

The transportation revolution also helped the country economically. The Pony Express, steamboats, and clipper ships were some inventions that helped bind the nation together and connect it with other parts of the world. The clipper ships first launched in 1845 had tall masts and several sails and could sail faster than a steamer in a good breeze. They carried highly-demanded tea from China to America and transported goods to prospective merchants in California. The transportation revolution integrated the continent into a single economic and cultural entity and instilled a more profound nationalist spirit.

Economies divided by slavery and free labor

The main economic difference between the North and South was the labor systems they employed. While industry played a vital role in the North, with commerce taking priority, the South was mainly agricultural. The Southern economy was based on plantations that relied on enslaved people as cheap labor to produce cotton and tobacco. The expanding economy in the North and its dependence on the free-labor manufacturing economy led to a sharp divide between the North and South.

Sectionalism, a term used to describe the needs of one section of a nation being given precedence over the needs of the entire nation, was rife before the Civil War. The antislavery stand of the North remained a significant cause of sectionalism. Additionally, each section wanted to pass laws that benefited their land. This resulted in the free states supporting the North and the slave states supporting the South. The westward expansion widened this divide.

Tariffs imposed on imports affected the South more heavily, as Southerners relied on importing goods from Britain and exporting their cotton overseas. While the North wanted the tariffs to safeguard their industries, the South opposed them, and tensions rose. The South argued their right to the nullification of the tariffs and antislavery laws that the North was intent on passing. Even before the Civil War, the relationship between the North and South worsened due to taxes. While the taxes imposed on the imported goods by Congress helped industrial development in the North, it weakened the economy of the South because, with its agriculture-targeted economy, the South needed to import machinery from foreign countries.

During the 1850s, when the recession peaked, Congress raised the import tax from 15 percent to 37 percent. In response, the South threatened to secede from the Union. The North was livid, as Southern secession would significantly reduce foreign trade and strike a heavy blow to the American economy. Secession would mean that the coastwise trade, which the South dominated, would also leave the Union.

Therefore, shipping would remain idle without the involvement of the South. Given these economic implications, the Union decided that war was the only alternative to a situation that would land them in financial ruin.

Southern industry. C. 1840

The Gilded Age

The emergence of entrepreneurs, corporate conglomerations, innovators, and economic and social reformers embodied the spirit of the Gilded Age and set the United States on a trajectory for today's political, economic, and social system.

Following the damage and desolation of the Civil War, it was difficult to define the American spirit and national identity. This changed as Americans moved into the 20th century. Twentieth-century Americans were confident, resourceful, and urbanized, and they began to call into question social oppression involving gender and racial discrimination.

In response to these transitions, the U.S. government set out to expand into its western lands, address workplace misgivings and lack of regulations, and embrace the newly expanding consumer and production cultures. Americans began to question the government's land-use practices and, for the first time, were concerned with massive conservation attempts, highlighting the change in American planning from reactive policy agendas to those crafted with the future in mind.

The rise of big business in America determined the national identity associated with the United States heading into the 20th century. Without this boost in industrialization and manufacturing capacities, it is difficult to say whether the United States would have acquired and maintained its position as a global power in the 20th and 21st centuries. This exceptional growth rate was crucial for the economic reforms under the Progressive movement in the early 20th century.

The major political players of the late 19th century envisioned an economic market with no restrictions, and it was because of their laissez-faire economic policies many Americans began to question the level of control and influence these magnates held over the American political system.

As the entrepreneurial spirit swept across America, the government and the public struggled to adjust to the fundamental changes in urban development and technological innovations. Improved workplace technology, such as conveyor systems, expedited the time required to produce goods, causing an influx of goods and later services. To meet these demands, the American perception regarding consumerism had to change. As more Americans required more goods, the market became less saturated and more stable, propelling the economic machine of the late 19th century.

In addition to consumer trends and exponential growth in production capabilities, the American public witnessed monopolies begin with the emergence of company trusts and interlocking directorates. Such business consolidation by buyout processes caused the wealthy elites in America to increase their fortunes while limiting access to such ambitions. While the entrepreneurial spirit was never more evident than in this period, the former wealthy class did not welcome newcomers. It was resistant to embracing the nouveau riche of the Gilded Age.

Mr. and Mrs. Goodhue Livingston and Mrs. Vanderbilt, American Gilded Age, c. 1895

In addition to technological achievements, the Gilded Age was also responsible for explosive expansion in various areas, the evolving economy, urban dwellings, city living, and unparalleled growth in the West. These transitions and their initial successes caused the U.S. government to promote growth, which would have catastrophic results for the Native American populations of the United States.

The developments in communication technologies were unprecedented during this period; Alexander Graham Bell's introduction of the telephone (1847-1922) was an impressive jump from the telegram a few decades earlier. Additional transformations in information sharing were also seen using mass-circulation newspapers such as the *New York World,* the *New York Journal,* and the *St. Louis Post-Dispatch.* National magazines and bestselling novels of the Gilded Age also transformed communication and information or idea sharing in the last years of the 19th century.

Many viewed the displacement and resettling of Native Americans as a necessary sacrifice for the American dream. This was perceived as an opportunity to give an uncivilized population the proper training and resources to live in the 19th century. The lasting influences of this period are all-pervasive and have directly impacted the economic and social systems we see today. The Gilded Age of business expansion and the American spirit of Nationalism were vital in developing today's perception of the American dream.

Alexander Graham Bell

In hopes of reunifying the United States following the disastrous Civil War, many believed growth and expansion—connecting the Atlantic and Pacific coasts—were necessary. To accomplish this monumental task, the U.S. government began investing in the transcontinental railroad, a source of communication, travel, and much-needed work for minorities and whites.

To promote the success of the railroads, the government and railroad companies used land grants and other incentives to lure workers out west. Leaflets and brochures widely distributed in the United States and parts of continental Europe proved successful advertising tactics. The draw of land and better wages following the economic and political uncertainties of the earlier 19th century caused many working-class citizens, both native-born and immigrant, to support westward expansion, thus promoting the railroad's success and—by default—the federal government.

As the magnates of this period realized the opportunity for financial return from the new railroads, many jumped on the expansion projects, attempting to corner market sectors such as ownership of the only railway leading into New York City. This type of economic strategy saw the emergence of the first monopolies, which were able to dictate the labor policies of the railroads while also greatly influencing the political landscape of the period.

The lasting influence of such political agendas and strategies can be seen in the monopolies created during the Gilded Age, as they were the first of their kind and incredibly influential. However, the backlash these same monopolies experienced just a few years later reflected the social upheaval average Americans experienced during this period and served as a precursor to the social revolutions of the 20th century.

The domestic politics of the United States during the Gilded Age focused primarily on economic and social transitions produced due to the unregulated markets and the tremendous expansion of the industrial capacities of the factories where most Americans now worked. After years of struggling to subsist in their new urban surroundings, many in the working and immigrant classes began seeing the role of the government as too limited and accommodating the members of big business.

Regarding corporate expansion, the American public had seen the rise of empire and monopoly in the United States using the railroad and steel companies dominated by the Vanderbilt and Rockefeller families. The banking industry of this period had been wholly influenced by J. P. Morgan, who stabilized the financial markets many times before finally being defeated by the chaos of the Great Depression (August 1929 to March 1933). These hands-off policies in the manufacturing, production, and economic sectors would end, for the most part, in the early years of the 20th century.

Tariffs were also a concern for many factory workers, consumers, and factory and manufacturing owners during this period. While the use of tariffs benefited the owners, it had the opposite effect on consumers, who typically were working class. The two types of tariffs included *revenue tariffs*, which fund agencies, and *protective tariffs*, which allowed American companies to compete with the prices and services of foreign companies at the expense of the consumer. Such policies were heavily influenced by the business elite and caused division between the management and working classes.

Currency was another topic of interest and contention during this period, causing further division among Americans, this time into soft currency supporters and opponents. In 1873, The *Fourth Coinage Act* was enacted to create the gold standard, which was opposed by those who argued that silver was a more logical choice given that the mines were already producing vast silver reserves. This began a new rivalry among those who called for silver backing of currency instead of a gold standard.

By 1890, six new states had been acquired in the West, and President Benjamin Harrison (1833-1901; 1889-1893) was facing ever-mounting pressure to adopt some form of silver backing. In 1890, the *Sherman Silver Purchase Act* was enacted, requiring the government to purchase silver every month to be converted into coins and certificates.

The influence of the currency and tariff debates allowed many Americans to have a more direct say in the economic policies of the United States than ever before. With this being said, many Americans, especially the working and farming classes, were adamantly opposed to silver- and gold-backed currency instead of calling for the expansion and circulation of greenbacks, which would supply the currency markets with more money without the backing of gold or silver. Such currency would have also allowed Americans to pay their debts.

Labor practices and labor movements

As the magnates of the Gilded Age experienced periods of criticism, many were quick to use the ideas of social Darwinism, which transformed the social sciences also beginning in this period, to secure their new status within the political and economic systems. The most notable entrepreneurs of the Gilded Age included John D. Rockefeller (1839-1937) and J. P. Morgan (1837-1913). These men initiated the economic production and markets of the late 19th century and forever transformed the notion of the American dream and the accumulation of wealth during the Gilded Age.

Some Gilded Age business practices would be illegal today. The use of interlocking directorates and the buying up of corporations under parent umbrellas to create monopolies were new ideas in this period. Such tactics were wildly successful for those managing the companies. This was typically at the expense of shareholders and, sometimes, the American public. Business dealings, such as the Union Pacific interlocking directorate scandal, caused great dissatisfaction and mistrust between the working class and the ruling or business class. These sour relationships continued until the late 20th century, when, for the first time, progressive activists and presidents sided with labor and not its big business partners.

John D. Rockefeller, born into a modest family in New York, became one of the leading magnates of this period and spent much of his time acknowledging and defending the fortune he had amassed. In 1870, Rockefeller struck liquid gold with petroleum and quickly established the Standard Oil Company, valued at one million dollars. Rockefeller perfected the use of trusts to eliminate his competition in the oil markets. By 1877, Rockefeller controlled nearly 95 percent of the oil refineries operating in the U.S. After eliminating his competition, such as the Vanderbilt family, he monopolized the global petroleum market.

Like Rockefeller, J. P. Morgan was also a revolutionary figure for this period. He gained his foothold in finance, drastically influencing the economic laissez-faire policies of the period. Morgan was born into a wealthy family, and through his scrupulous economic dealings, he expanded his family's empire to include banking and steel.

195

John D. Rockefeller, c. 1935

Morgan was able to perfect the use of the interlocking directorate, placing a puppet board of directors in charge of multiple companies he oversaw. Morgan was able to buy out his competition when they were reeling from the 1890s depression. After buying out Andrew Carnegie (1835-1919) from the steel business, Morgan formed the first billion-dollar corporation in 1901 with the creation of the United States Steel Corporation.

Andrew Carnegie was less than persuaded by the arguments of superiority put forth by the social Darwinists but capitalized on the unregulated financial markets of the Gilded Age. Unlike his counterparts, who bought out the competition and created monopolies, Carnegie employed a tactic known as vertical integration, where he systematically integrated all the steps in his steel production. Carnegie owned the coal production plants, the steamships that transported iron ore found in the Great Lakes, and the railroads that transported his materials to his flagship city, Pittsburgh. By controlling all variables in the production process, Carnegie improved efficiency and quality while decreasing cost.

Andrew Carnegie, c. 1915

In 1900, Carnegie sold his stock in steel to J. P. Morgan, effectively eliminating himself from economic policies and instead focusing on philanthropic works, which he believed to be the responsibility of the wealthy elites. These men were instrumental in crafting the perception of the American dream to include anyone and everyone from any background. Some of these men broke through social classes and stereotypes to create some of America's largest and most influential companies.

As industrial and manufacturing giants dominated the period's political landscape, they were often met with strong opposition from the immigrant classes and the emergence of labor unions and planned strikes. These had a drastic impact on the future of labor movements in America. As immigration labor fueled the railroad expansion, which would unify the country through transcontinental means, it was also the first to experience labor strikes due to the newly formed unions.

One drawback of exponential labor reserves—as seen in the immigration explosions of the late 19th century—was that it made workers expendable and decreased their wages. Keeping vocational practices in this light caused increased social tensions and issues within the railroad companies, which soured the relationship between workers and management.

These first influential labor movements allowed many Americans the right to go on strike or demand better workplace conditions regarding health and safety. These concepts became the common workplace expectations of all Americans leading into the 20th century, forever altering the conception of union and labor movements in America. The drastic increase in labor movements and strikes highlights an American landscape amid a tumultuous and challenging transition.

Strikers at the Burlington Railroad shop yards, 1888

The years between 1881 and 1900 saw close to 23,000 strikes, which involved more than six million workers. Confrontations within the railroad, steel, and mining sectors led to bloody strikes typically dispersed using force by the federal government on behalf of businesses. The policies enacted by corporations and the federal government would serve to sour and detach the relationships between the working class and the government.

Some labor activists who faced legal action for their role in union strikes were convicted and hung, leading to martyr unions working against management regardless of the cost. For example, Molly Maguires, a secret Irish society member, became best known for their activism among Irish immigrant coal miners in Pennsylvania. While the facts are much debated among historians, the group was involved in violent conflicts with industrialists and other groups, and their actions led to the conviction of twenty suspected members for murder and other crimes. These members were executed by hanging in 1877 and 1878.

Such events would continue to drastically impact the labor movement of this period, as most labor activists saw little to no result of the actions taken against the railroad, coal, and steel corporations.

As the workforce continued to expand, it became increasingly clear that children and minority groups were now encompassing more and more of the workforce. Many social and labor activists detested the use of child labor. Child labor was commonplace in big business in the 20th century. By 1890, nearly 18 percent of the workforce comprised children aged ten to fifteen. A vast expansion of women in the workforce also defined this period; between 1880 and 1890, the number of working women jumped from 2.6 million to 8.6 million, causing some men to question their quick ascension into urban work. Men in this period viewed women working for wages as a threat to the overall wage levels. This sentiment was typically shared by most labor unions as well.

As the labor movement took hold, corporations fought back against these institutions. If workers began to contest hours or working conditions, many companies would blacklist the worker and replace him or her with another worker who would be willing to work for even fewer wages and typically without the promise of any benefits. The abundance of unskilled laborers due to immigration and migration following the Civil War was considered harmful. Workers were no longer commodities and were being treated accordingly. This influx in unskilled and skilled labor changed the economic conditions for many working class during this period.

However, this same workforce, which would propel the industrial and manufacturing giants to a new level of economic prosperity and influence, would also bring about the rise of the labor movement and unions, causing the business giants' eventual decline. The use of cheap labor and deplorable working conditions caused many to support the labor movement as their means of equal representation in the industrial and manufacturing systems.

The use of child labor would go mostly unchallenged until the progressive reforms. This was due in part to the financial needs of struggling families but also because the social norm of the day was not to actively speak out against child labor.

Child labor in the textile mills, c. 1890

As the industrial and manufacturing giants of the period amassed wealth and influence, the working classes struggled to be protected or fairly represented. To combat this social and economic issue, many social activists emerged to fight for the rights of the working class. Workplace conditions in 1866 led to the first labor union, the National Labor Union, which supported implementing an eight-hour workday, using greenback-labor members, enforcing health and safety regulations, and repealing laws that made importing labor easier. This latter concern embodies the sentiment of nativism, which spread during this period.

In 1869, the Knights of Labor was formed, which encompassed both skilled and unskilled laborers and worked toward equal pay between genders—a revolutionary concept at the time—as well as an eight-hour workday, codes for health and safety in the workplace, and the use of greenback or soft currency to expand the supply of currency being circulated while also elevating pressure on debtors.

Knights of Labor pentagram, c. 1870

Other notable unions of this period include the American Federation of Labor (AFL), which was founded in 1886 and was an example of the emergence of craft unions. The establishment of such unions would become common in the early 20th century, as many more Americans began to embrace the idea of organized workers bargaining with management and going on strikes when an agreement could not be reached.

Mary Harris Jones (1837-1930), often referred to as "Mother Jones," was an influential character in the labor movements of the late 19th century. She was an Irish American immigrant who worked tirelessly for the advancement and protection of industrial workers. Aside from planning and implementing vast strikes, Jones was also the co-founder of the World's Industrial Workers in the early 20th century, which fought against child labor and the exploitation of the industrial workforce.

Some significant strikes of this period included the Great Strike of 1877, where the workers of the Baltimore and Ohio railroads went on strike following a drastic pay cut of almost 10 percent. The strike ended with the intervention of federal troops sent by President Hayes (1822-1893; 1877-1881). The Homestead Strike occurred in 1892 at the Carnegie Steel Company's offices in Homestead. It was an industrial lockout and strike which lasted for four months and resulted in the deaths of three Pinkerton detectives and nine factory workers.

The Pullman Strike, which began in 1894, was also a result of decreased wages and the increased cost of living and resulted in violence between railway strikebreakers, sometimes called "scabs," and the rail workers. Little action was taken to address the grievances of the working class. The rail company fired all those who went on strike and blacklisted many more from working in the railroad industry. This was the typical response to strikes in the late 19th century and undoubtedly led to the culmination of full labor reforms during the 20th century.

Pullman strikers outside Arcade Building. Chicago in 1894

As a result of the Confederate defeat in the Civil War, many Southerners began to question the economic practices of the past, specifically the economy's sole reliance on cotton. With the emergence of the "New South," many hoped to see a diversification of the goods and services offered there.

As the southern markets and goods expanded, the South found a new market to invest in northern exports. Many northerners imported the tobacco grown in the South and industrial exports such as lumber, iron, and coal. Though some called for the industrialization of the South, this seemed rather unlikely. The southern society was agriculturally based and continued to be so after the Civil War. The introduction of secondary crops such as tobacco, rice, and sugar cane all reestablished the agrarian traditions of the past.

Supported by people such as Seaman Knapp, who perfected the cultivation of crops in the South, the newly formed local and state governments established and expanded agriculture education and production programs to assist those farming in the New South. This was particularly important, as much of the New South's tradition and the effects of Reconstruction still centered around implementing an agrarian society rather than one dominated by the industrial and manufacturing movements seen elsewhere.

In addition to agricultural transitions, which were moving away from cotton and into tenant farming, the New South explored industry in cities such as Birmingham, Alabama. Here, southerners found natural resources of iron, limestone, and eventually coal, which were extremely important to the economic development needed in the South following the disastrous Civil War and the railroad and manufacturing booms experienced in the North, Midwest, and Western territories.

Industries expanding during this period included lumber exports of prized southern pine trees—which were found to be in high demand around the country—and new markets for paper, clay, and glass production. While the New South struggled to shed its image of outdated agrarian life, it became clear that the impact of industrialization in the Midwest and Northeast influenced Southern politicians, but not enough to transform the economic landscape of the Southern states. The re-emergence of the South as a sustainable, operating entity was a vast accomplishment of the Reconstruction period (1865 to 1877) and the capitalist system and greatly influenced the future of political and social reforms, or lack thereof, in the region.

Government–industry relations in the Gilded Age

Leading up to and during the Gilded Age, many Americans perceived the government's role as one that enforced law and order but stopped short of ensuring the social welfare of the American population. However, this idea began to change in the late 19th century and caused many to embrace new ideas surrounding regulating business and corruption by local, state, and federal officials.

One notable incident that caused many to support regulation was the American transcontinental railroad scandal (1872-1873), where the Union Pacific and Crédit Mobilier companies had engaged in an interlocking directorate. After investigation, it was discovered that Union Pacific had paid Crédit Mobilier at highly inflated rates, making the supply company rich at the expense of the American public and Union Pacific shareholders.

East and West shaking hands at the laying of the last rail of the Union Pacific Railroad

The Gilded Age (1870s to 1900) introduced business conglomerates and trusts into a governmental system that was easily manipulated by the leading businesspeople of their day, and this was evident in the political agendas of the late 19th century.

While the management and elites became wealthier, the working and immigrant classes struggled to maintain their day-to-day lives, eventually culminating in the desire for social and political changes. In seeking these changes, many Americans who lacked support from the government turned to the neighborhood and fraternal organizations that could provide services to those typically neglected by state and federal institutions.

As these organizations grew, they became substantially more powerful and could influence and infiltrate the political entities of the cities for which they provided services. Such influence and lack of federal or state regulations quickly led to corruption, "under the table" dealings, and establishing the "*good ol' boy*" network.

As Americans saw this corruption, now fully integrated within the government system, they began to embrace ideas of socialism, which had been entirely out of the question before. Reformers working against machine politics, most notably those embraced by William "Boss" Tweed at Tammany Hall in New York, convinced the American population of the need for reforms. These efforts culminated in the passage of the *Interstate Commerce Act* in 1887, which created the Interstate Commerce Commission, responsible for the federal monitoring of the economic systems.

In addition to the Interstate Commerce Commission, which was the first of its kind, in 1890, Republican President Benjamin Harrison took the first step with the passage of the *Sherman Anti-Trust Act.* The Act was the first of three antitrust laws outlawed monopolies and trade limitations. Some politicians believed the law was for show and difficult to enforce.

President Harrison, c. 1893

Subsequent presidents greatly added to these progressive policies, such as the *Hepburn Act* (1906, Roosevelt) and the *Clayton Anti-Trust Act* (1914, Wilson). Most significant was a campaign against cronyism and monopolies, which earned Republican Theodore Roosevelt (1858-1919; 1901-1909) the name *"Teddy the Trust Buster."*

Republican President Teddy Roosevelt used the *Sherman Anti-Trust Act* and the Federal courts to break up forty-five trusts (e.g., J. P. Morgan's Northern Securities Company, Standard Oil, and U.S. Steel). Republican President William Howard Taft (1857-1930; 1909-1913) confronted over seventy-five significant monopolies.

The impacts of the calls for reform were monumental for the future of American economic policies, as seen in the Progressive movement and Presidents such as Democrat Franklin Roosevelt (1882-1945; 1933-1945). The ideas, policies, and laws enacted regarding this period's economic system foreshadowed the American people's sentiment until the substantial reforms of the New Deal.

The boom years of the Gilded Age (1870s to 1900) brought about great prosperity, research, and invention; these same trends created monopolies and caused a transition in economic policies and schools of thought. As Americans experienced these economic changes and the volatility in the economy in that period, some perceived the attitudes of the bankers and industrialists to be reckless and demanded expanded government involvement and oversight.

These changes, coupled with the rapid urbanization that followed the booming industrial periods, caused many transitions in the social norms of America. As urban dwellers began earning higher wages and a middle class emerged, the new expectations of city life included department stores, banks, insurance companies, and corporate headquarters. This widespread rapid urbanization culminated in domestic economic growth and pitted traditionalists, like farmers and agrarians, against industrialists, who saw the future of America in cities and factories.

Such polarization would come to embody this transition period, as many Americans sought new job opportunities, a change in the accepted economic class structures, and a different form of government than had previously been seen. However, not all Americans embraced this sentiment of change. Many traditionalists argued for a return to the roaring prosperity and cultural expectations that accompanied the early years of the 20th century.

Industrial transitions and economic shifts

In addition to the scientific innovations of the period, America also saw the emergence of industrialized monopolies in the form of railroads and new modern factories. These transformative business practices allowed Americans to propel their economy and production capacities past those of their European rivals. The unchecked power and influence of monopolies within the American government also created great dissatisfaction among the working population.

The Gilded Age substantially impacted the formation of America following the devastating Civil War and leading into the two world wars. Without the industrial advances of the period, America would have lacked the resources necessary to become a world power. The manufacturing and industrial capabilities that emerged during this period laid the infrastructure of the American economy, creating railroads and the surge in factory and manufacturing production that would lead to a more efficient workforce in America.

By 1894, the United States ranked first in manufacturing nations worldwide, proving that a significant transformation from an agrarian-based society to industrialization had undoubtedly occurred. The key players in the later years of the Gilded Age, such as Rockefeller and J. P. Morgan, continued to influence economic and industrial affairs, though on a more restricted level, as seen in the progressive presidencies of Roosevelt, Taft, and Wilson.

This influence saw continued decline, leading to the World Wars following the Great Depression (August 1929 to March 1933). Many Americans wanted a stronger policy against monopolies and trusts that dominated the landscape of this period.

The manufacturing sector was enhanced with new technology, implementing mass production techniques that allowed companies to produce high-quality goods much faster. Given this new technology, factories could lower costs while maximizing profits.

As a result of such efficient operations and artificially high money supply, many companies produced more goods than could be sold, resulting in a saturation of the market and economic chaos. This oversupply also explains why industrialists wanted to expand into foreign markets in the Western Hemisphere.

This industrial transition shed light on the widening class gap seen since the beginning of the Industrial Revolution of the 19th century. This contrast in wealth caused some to be concerned with class war, while those who had traditionally been the elites of society were displeased with the rise in the "nouveau riche," or new rich. This created a new social rivalry characteristic of the social tensions that developed in the late 19th and early 20th centuries.

Small business owners and farmers saw monopolies of corporations as unfavorable. They worked with local and federal legislators to limit the size and influence of such entities. These corporations also held significant political influence regarding foreign policy. Evidence of this is seen in the tactics used by President Taft and others who tried to infiltrate the foreign markets of the Western Hemisphere, creating an intense U.S. hegemony. Following the World Wars, this unipolarity would continue giving the United States an advantage in many international affairs regarding the global system's economic and political futures.

President Taft, c. 1913

Following the industrial boom of the Gilded Age, which spanned from 1870 to 1900, the federal government decided to reevaluate its former laissez-faire business policies. Instead of continuing this hands-off approach, state and national institutions began implementing more regulatory measures, falling in line with the public opinion surrounding monopolies and the desire for the government to intervene on behalf of the populace. These economic transitions and a mass explosion of urbanization compelled many Americans to transform their day-to-day activities, which incited rivalries within the social and political classes.

In the late 19th century, the United States also saw an agricultural transition to farmers producing crops more efficiently with a smaller labor force. This smaller labor force was due to 1) new technology (such as the steam-powered tractor) that increased efficiency; 2) increased difficulty hiring workers due to mass urbanization and the increase of opportunities and wages created by capitalism for the average person; and 3) industrial projects that were beginning to dominate the American landscape.

Economic history – summary of the period

The federal government's attempts to assert authority over the states brought resistance from state governments in the North and the South at different times.

The expansion of slavery in the lower South and adjacent western lands and its gradual disappearance elsewhere began to create distinctive regional attitudes toward the institution. Intensified by expansion and deepening regional divisions, debates over slavery and other economic, cultural, and political issues led the nation into civil war.

With the acceleration of a national and international market economy, Americans debated the government's role in the economy. At the same time, diverging economic systems meant that regional political and economic loyalties often continued to overshadow national concerns. A global market and communications revolution, influenced by technological innovations, led to dramatic shifts in agriculture and manufacturing. Innovations, including textile machinery, steam engines, interchangeable parts, canals, railroads, the telegraph, and agricultural inventions, extended markets and brought market efficiency to production.

Increasing numbers of Americans, especially women in factories and low-skilled male workers, no longer relied on semi-subsistence agriculture but made their livelihoods producing goods for distant markets, even as some urban entrepreneurs went into finance rather than manufacturing. Southern cotton furnished the raw material for manufacturing in the Northeast. In contrast, cotton production and trade growth promoted the development of national economic ties, shaped the international economy, and fueled the internal slave trade.

Despite some governmental and private efforts to create a unified national economy, most notably the American System, the shift to market production linked the North and the Midwest more closely than either was linked to the South.

Regional economic specialization, especially the demands of cultivating southern cotton, shaped settlement patterns and the national and international economy. The economic changes caused by the market revolution significantly affected migration patterns, gender and family relations, and the distribution of political power.

The North's expanding economy and its increasing reliance on a free-labor manufacturing economy contrasted with the South's dependence on an economic system characterized by slave-based agriculture and slow population growth.

The rise of big business in the United States encouraged massive migrations and urbanization, sparked government and widespread efforts to reshape the U.S. economy and environment, and renewed debates over U.S. national identity.

Following the Civil War, governmental subsidies for transportation and communication systems opened new markets in North America. At the same time, technological innovations and redesigned financial and management structures such as monopolies sought to maximize the exploitation of natural resources and a growing labor force. Despite the industrialization of some segments of the southern economy, a change promoted by southern leaders who called for a "New South," agrarian sharecropping, and tenant farming systems continued to dominate the region.

Large-scale production—accompanied by massive technological change, expanding international communication networks, and pro-growth government policies—fueled the development of a "Gilded Age" marked by an emphasis on consumption, marketing, and business consolidation. Business leaders consolidated corporations into trusts and holding companies and defended their resulting status and privilege through theories such as social Darwinism. Gilded Age politics were intimately tied to big business and focused nationally on economic issues—tariffs, currency, corporate expansion, and laissez-faire economic policy—that engendered numerous calls for reform.

The industrial workforce expanded through migration across national borders and internal migration, leading to a more diverse workforce, lower wages, and increased child labor. Labor and management battled for control over wages and working conditions, with workers organizing local and national unions and directly confronting corporate power.

Corruption in government—especially related to big business—energized the public to demand increased popular control and reform of local, state, and national governments, ranging from minor changes to major overhauls of the capitalist system.

Large corporations' continued growth and consolidation transformed American society and the nation's economy, promoting urbanization and economic growth, even as business cycle fluctuations became increasingly severe. Large corporations dominated the U.S. economy as they increasingly focused on producing consumer goods, driven by new technologies and manufacturing techniques. Governmental, political, and social organizations struggled to address the effects of large-scale industrialization, economic uncertainty, and related social changes such as urbanization and mass migration.

Notes for active learning

Notes for active learning

Foreign Relations: 1790 to 1898

International spread of American revolutionary ideas

Although the United States was a sparsely populated country very far away, Europeans were impressed and heavily influenced by developments in North America during and after the American Revolution. The Declaration of Independence codified a new way of discussing human rights, and many in Europe adopted the language and ideas of American revolutionaries. The French Revolution, for example, was, in part, inspired by the American precedent.

The United States was the "first new nation," created, as it seemed, by applying philosophy and principle rather than justified by tradition and heredity. The notions that government should be based on the consent of the governed and the preservation of liberty and that monarchs who failed to do so could be disposed of were powerful ideas that inspired enthusiasm in some and animosity in others. Meanwhile, the language of freedom and equality did not grant freedom and equality for all in the United States. Women did not have the same rights as men, and slavery and the removal of Indians from their territories remained key elements of the new American reality.

The American Revolution inspired liberals, republicans, and nationalists in Europe and the Americas. They saw the United States as an example of putting Enlightenment ideas into practice in the name of liberty and equality. The Revolution encouraged the Irish to seek more freedom from the British and the Belgians to seek independence from Austria. The French Revolution became another example of a fight against privilege and tyranny in support of universal human rights.

However, when slaves in Haiti rebelled against their owners, the United States was not especially supportive. The American government cooperated with the Haitian revolutionaries when vocal slavery opponent John Adams was President, but the tide turned when Jefferson became President in 1800. Southern enslavers found the spectacle of a slave rebellion and a republic led by blacks terrifying, and the United States did not recognize the independence of Haiti until 1862, long after France had done so.

When the Spanish colonies in South America sought independence in the early 19th century, they were keenly aware of the examples of the United States and Haiti. They rallied around ideals of freedom and national independence while fearing that the government of Spain could not protect them against slave rebellions. The disorganized state of the Spanish government during the lengthy revolutionary wars and Napoleonic Wars in Europe (1803-1815) made Latin American separation and independence possible.

Diplomatic challenges of the new republic

Independence brought several foreign policy problems to bear on the American experiment. American ships were no longer sailing under British flags. Until the Jay Treaty of 1795, they were restricted from selling their goods in the British West Indies, an essential market for foodstuffs and other agricultural products for southern planters and farmers. American sailors even risked being enslaved by North African pirates.

On the mainland, Britain and Spain retained vast territories in North America and often acted hostilely. The British refused to vacate the forts in the Old Northwest for more than ten years after the Revolutionary War's end, citing the new republic's failure to compensate Loyalists for losses due to confiscation during the revolution.

The Jay Treaty also resolved this problem. Similarly, Spanish authorities refused to accept American sovereignty south of the Ohio River and closed the Mississippi River to American traders. They even got involved in secret conspiracies with prominent Americans to secure the Old Southwest for Spain.

However, Florida and Louisiana were peripheral parts of the sprawling Spanish Empire in the Americas, and the differences over borders and trade were eventually settled in Pinckney's Treaty, signed in 1795.

The Jay Treaty, signed by the United States and Britain in 1794, resolved some of the issues of contention that lingered since the end of the Revolutionary War. The architect behind the treaty was Federalist Alexander Hamilton, who sought rapprochement with the British and expansion of American trade. The moment seemed opportune to Hamilton, as Britain became involved in a new war with France.

The treaty was a victory for the United States because it finally ended the British occupation of the forts in the Old Northwest. The departure of the British was especially significant because it demoralized Indians who had hoped to stop American expansion into their lands. At the same time, the treaty resulted from the defeat of the Western Confederacy of tribes at the Battle of Fallen Timbers in 1794.

As the Indians seemed unable to resist the American military, the British no longer had any fundamental role in the area. The British justification for holding on to the forts had been unpaid wartime debts related to confiscating Loyalist property; both parties now agreed to send this matter to arbitration. The Jay Treaty made the Spanish fear a future alliance between the United States and Britain. Spain closed navigation on the Mississippi to Americans but now agreed to reopen commercial channels and negotiate boundaries.

The Battle of Fallen Timbers, 1794

By 1795, this resulted in Pinckney's Treaty, where Spain ceded most of what is now Mississippi and Alabama to the United States. Navigation rights were restored, and the Spanish pledged not to incite and arm the Indians against the United States.

Thus, by playing the European powers against each other, the Washington administration tightened the country's grip on frontier territories and reduced the risk of outside powers intervening in its dealings with the Indians. This facilitated the ongoing westward expansion of the United States.

The War of 1812

The War of 1812, sometimes called the Second War for Independence, resulted from Anglo-American tension brewing since the American Revolution. The tension increased with the British impressment of American sailors during the Napoleonic Wars, one of the leading causes of the embargo in 1807.

When Jefferson implemented the *Embargo Act* of 1807 in response to British ships bullying American vessels on the high seas, he intended this Act to punish the British and French by withholding resources and thus convince them to leave American ships alone. This Act strained the relationship between America and the French and British, hurting American traders more than European traders.

James Madison, who succeeded Jefferson, mended the relationship with the French, but America's relationship with Britain remained tense, leading to the War of 1812. The British were also encouraging the resistance of Native Americans as settlers began to move west into the newly purchased Louisiana Territory.

In 1812, encouraged by the War Hawks in Congress, James Madison and Congress declared war on Britain. American troops were immediately dispatched to Canada (then a British colony) and were pushed back due to their under-preparedness.

War of 1812, Battle of New Orleans

The British had several successes in the war, including the capture of Washington, D.C., and the burning of the White House in 1814. The Americans held control of the Northwest Territory and had several naval victories.

When Fort McHenry in Baltimore withstood more than twenty-four hours of sustained bombardment, the British Navy moved south towards New Orleans. The Treaty of Ghent was signed, and the war was supposed to be over. However, communication was slow, and the British did not know that the war had ended when they attacked New Orleans, where American troops led by Andrew Jackson defeated them. The war and its consequences highlighted the need for America to be active in the international community.

Foreign relations to preserve and expand American territories

In the 1820s, America began to look abroad at its influence in the international theatre. Democratic-Republican President James Monroe (1758-1831; 1817-1825), in the spirit of former President Jefferson, wanted to encourage other countries to leave the Americas alone regarding colonization. To this extent, and with the support of the British, he issued the Monroe Doctrine in 1823 during his State of the Union Address.

In 1823, nearly all Latin American colonies were moving towards independence. Monroe wanted to ensure that no one would step in and fill the void as the colonies established themselves as governments. Monroe clarified that any action to gain control of these colonies would be met with American intervention.

In turn, Monroe promised that America would not interfere with existing colonies. This has been referred to as the Monroe Doctrine; numerous Presidents have upheld it and still play an integral part in American foreign affairs.

President James Monroe, c. 1810

In 1836, Texas successfully rebelled against Mexico and formed its state. The United States offered the new territory diplomatic recognition and left it alone until 1844, when Whig President John Tyler (1720-1862; 1841-1845) started negotiations for annexation. As a result, Mexico severed all economic and diplomatic ties with the U.S. Failing on the first vote, Texas was eventually added to the Union in 1845. Relations with Mexico tensed as a result, especially as the Mexico–Texas border had not been resolved before annexation.

When buying the disputed territory did not work, President Polk gained congressional support for declaring war against Mexico. American troops captured Mexico City in 1847, and the treaty to buy the disputed territory was reexamined. Mexico agreed to give the United States over half of its pre-war territory, provided that it pay Mexico $15 million and forgive $3.3 million in debts owed by Mexican citizens.

Mexican-American War, the battle of Palo Alto, May 8, 1846

Several of the international diplomatic initiatives during this period involved Great Britain. In 1842, Secretary of State Daniel Webster met with British Ambassador Lord Atherton to negotiate some key points. The issue of the Canadian border was quickly resolved by establishing a fixed latitudinal border and discussing actions to be taken in the event of an accidental violation. The issue of the international slave trade was similarly finalized. The British agreed to stop searching American ships if the Americans agreed to police the coast of Africa to look for slave ships flying the American flag. With Anglo-American tensions relaxed, the two countries could focus on other areas, such as China.

However, tensions flared again in 1846 as the Oregon Territory became a pressing matter. In the end, England conceded its claim to some territory in exchange for uncontested control of the northern territories. With the border established from sea to sea in the North, America had almost established its present-day continental size.

From 1844 to 1877, a series of events and issues, including the expansion policy of the United States and the growing unrest among antislavery organizations, led to the Civil War. In 1844, when Democrat James K. Polk (1795-1849; 1845-1849) was elected President, the country attracted migrants due to its lucrative economic development policies. President Polk supported expansion, as the Democrats believed in republican virtue being upheld if more lands were opened for the yeoman farmers.

Texas annexation (1845) and the acquisition of Oregon County (1846) increased the country's influence on the continent. While organizations against slavery existed before this period, they gained political mileage only after 1840, when the Liberal Party grew discontented with abolitionist organizations and began to fight slavery via political methods.

In addition to its westward expansion within North America, the United States wanted to extend its base overseas, especially in Japan, for three reasons. First, the United States needed a coaling base (i.e., a fueling port) for its steamships. Since Japan is in the same latitude as San Francisco, it served as an ideal location for a coaling base. Although Hawaii was already used as a coaling base, the U.S. Navy wanted another port in the East.

Secondly, an American presence in Japan would ensure that shipwrecked sailors reaching Japan received proper treatment. Lastly, the United States sought to increase its revenue by trading with other countries.

Before Commodore Oliver Hazard Perry's mission to Japan in 1854, only the Dutch could land ships on Japanese soil, and all other countries were prohibited. After a few visits to Japan, Perry (1785-1819) convinced the Japanese to sign the Treaty of Kanagawa in 1854, enforcing the Japanese provision of food, water, coal, and other needed supplies to the American ships that docked in Nagasaki. Ultimately, Japan consented to trade with the United States, ending two hundred years of isolation.

Commodore Perry, c. 1854

The treaty brought vast foreign money and significantly damaged the Japanese economy. It paved the way for Russia, France, the Netherlands, and Great Britain to sign unequal treaties with Japan, granting Japan fewer rights than the foreign nations. Furthermore, the treaty helped overthrow Japan's Shogun government, previously considered an undefeatable force.

Foreign trade

As the United States began its inward expansion, many influential businessmen and politicians also looked into the global system in hopes of finding influence, resources, and alliances. The industrial machine had to influence foreign markets in Asia and Latin America to establish the United States as a real-world power. Following this expansion-style foreign policy agenda, the United States was highly interested in securing the natural resources required to sustain the industrial and manufacturing boom of the Gilded Age.

With the expansion of manufacturing and production, the United States and its business magnates sought fresh markets. Some of the most notable examples were the investments in Asian and Latin American countries to gain regional influence. The United States established its 20th-century foreign policies by undertaking these investment and export opportunities while simultaneously creating a more pronounced rivalry between its European counterparts. Such foreign policies foreshadowed the decisions in the latter decades of the 20th century.

As the U.S. government faced pushback from conservationists, some industrialists sought the natural resources of other less regulated countries. To maintain the massive expectations of manufacturing and production, the United States needed to secure vast amounts of natural resources, including but not limited to iron ore, coal, lumber, and oil. The long-term implications of resource security can be seen in the World Wars and every period that followed, highlighting the incalculable value of such resources during the Gilded Age and the contemporary period.

Iron and steel company in Johnstown, Pennsylvania, c. 1890

For the first time during this period, Americans realized the economic potential of steel and oil refining. The United States went to great lengths to cultivate relationships and economic partnerships with countries where these commodities were not readily available, ushering in the century of American hegemony. One might also argue that such policies were successful, as, under President Taft, a similar strategy was employed using dollar diplomacy.

Following the "closure" of the western border by the Bureau of the Census in 1890, many Americans began to look abroad in hopes of influencing and maintaining America's interests in the form of newly acquired territories, such as the Philippines, Guam, and Puerto Rico following the Spanish-American War. Others invested in foreign markets to dispel a European hegemony in the Western Hemisphere. President Taft endorsed foreign policy by continuously supporting his policies of dollar diplomacy.

By 1898, the United States replaced many European countries as the dominant influence in international affairs, allowing for the gradual transition into a global power that surpassed European countries in consumer products and led the rebuilding effort in Europe in hopes of maintaining a stable and continuous peace.

In addition to economic interests, social Darwinism persuaded many in America to view other ethnicities and nationalities as needing guidance from more developed people. This ideology, termed "*survival of the fittest*," caused many Americans to view themselves in a genetically dominating role. This sentiment was quickly adopted by imperialists and interventionists who were able to garner support for colonial aspirations. This mindset of a "closed" frontier was important in understanding the desire for colonialism during this period.

Foreign relations – summary of the period

While the new governments continued to limit rights to some groups, ideas promoting self-government and personal liberty reverberated worldwide. The American Revolution and the ideals outlined in the Declaration of Independence reverberated in France, Haiti, and Latin America, inspiring future rebellions.

The continued presence of European powers in North America challenged the United States to find ways to safeguard its borders, maintain neutral trading rights, and promote its economic interests.

As Western settlers sought free navigation of the Mississippi River, the United States forged diplomatic initiatives to manage the conflict with Spain and to deal with the continued British presence on the American continent. Regional interests continued to trump national concerns as the basis for many political leaders' positions on economic issues, including slavery, the national bank, tariffs, and internal improvements.

U.S. interest in increasing foreign trade, expanding its national borders, and isolating itself from European conflicts shaped its foreign policy and spurred government and private initiatives. Struggling to create an independent global presence, U.S. policymakers sought to dominate the North American continent through military actions, judicial decisions, diplomatic efforts, and to promote its foreign trade.

Following the Louisiana Purchase, the drive to acquire, survey, and open new lands and markets led Americans into numerous economic, diplomatic, and military initiatives in the Western Hemisphere and Asia.

The United States became more connected with the world as it pursued an expansionist foreign policy in the Western Hemisphere and emerged as the destination for many migrants from other countries. The U.S. interest in expanding trade led to economic, diplomatic, and cultural initiatives westward to Asia. Businesses and foreign policymakers increasingly looked outside U.S. borders to gain more considerable influence and control over markets and natural resources in the Pacific, Asia, and Latin America.

The perception in the 1890s was that the western frontier was "closed." Economic motives, competition with other European imperialist ventures, and racial theories all furthered arguments that Americans were destined to expand their culture and norms to others, especially the nonwhite nations of the globe.

Notes for active learning

Notes for active learning

Social History: 1790 to 1898

Unity and divide

After the revolution, Americans tried to create a unified national identity founded on equality, civic virtue, and commercial success. At the same time, the country was deeply divided along cultural, geographic, economic, and racial lines. Migration within North America, cooperative interaction, and competition for resources raised questions about boundaries and policies and intensified conflicts among peoples and nations. It led to contests over creating a multiethnic, multiracial national identity.

Even though the Constitution established the political future of the United States, there were still conflicts between factions and parties. The authority of the Supreme Court did not stop people from disagreeing with the decisions it reached. With conflict occurring in the political arena, creating a stable social reality that reflected stated political goals was hard. Many groups tried to arrange these conflicting ideas into some form of truth that supported the ideals of the country's founding documents.

Proponents of slavery ignored the pathos-driven arguments of the abolitionists and focused instead on what they considered practical reasons for slavery. They claimed that slavery was a historical constant. Enslaved people have existed in all major societies since ancient times as a form of fast and cheap labor. Proslavery advocates asserted that slavery made economic sense. The Egyptians used enslaved people to build the pyramids, and the Americans used enslaved people to pick plants, which would surely whither on the vine if slavery was ended.

They also argued that not only were enslaved people necessary to the nation's continued economic growth but that if all enslaved people were freed, there would be a substantial social impact. Because enslaved people were not citizens and had no rights, these pro-slavery advocates argued that emancipation would disrupt the running of society and create widespread unemployment as slaves entered the workforce and competed for jobs.

Supporters of slavery also turned to the Bible for justification of their views. They argued that several Christians had slaves, and God still supported them. King Solomon, the blessed king of the Israelites, had owned slaves. Similarly, the Ten Commandments chastised those who coveted their neighbor's possessions, and supporters of slavery interpreted "possessions" to include slaves. Therefore, they argued that God both condoned slavery and condemned attempts to enslave people away from their owners.

Furthermore, by bringing enslaved people to America and educating them in the Christian faith, many enslavers thought that they were saving their slaves from hell. Senator John C. Calhoun claimed in a proslavery speech to the Senate, "Never before has the black race of Central Africa, from the dawn of history to the present day, attained a condition so civilized and so improved, not only physically, but morally and intellectually."

Calhoun described slavery as an institution "indispensable to the peace and happiness of both" races. Slavery, according to him, was a better condition to live in than the ignorance of their native Africa. Calhoun insisted that Southerners stop apologizing for the institution of slavery, and his comments defined the proslavery arguments for several decades.

While First Lady Martha Washington (1731-1802; 1789-1797) relied on enslaved people in the presidential household, First Lady Adams (1744-1818; 1797-1801) helped a young black man learn how to read and write.

While groups like the abolitionists looked at the founding documents and concluded that all humans—not just whites—had rights, many people had the opposite sentiment. Many citizens were concerned about what the inclusion-based policies of the federal government would mean if extended to all people, especially the rights afforded to citizens.

Thus, a rise occurred in anti-black and anti-Indian sentiments. If these groups were made citizens, they would be able to vote, and that would change the political field. Similarly, as land opened in the West, xenophobia spread. Americans began demanding the federal government deal with the waves of immigrants traveling to America.

Abolitionism movement

While the population in the North continued to grow and change, the population in the South stayed reasonably similar. This created a unique class system separating the North and South. While the North had industrial empires like those of the railway barons, the South developed a landed gentry or aristocracy amongst those that could afford large plantations and the enslaved people to work them.

Below this class were those who could afford some slaves, but not as many as were needed to turn the massive profits of the genteel Southerners. Below them were those who were too poor to afford any outside labor. Called "white trash" by their neighbors, these citizens were almost at the level of formerly enslaved people. This social system baffled and deterred northerners and immigrants, allowing the South to strengthen its ties with Europe.

The sectional conflicts and reform movements that happened during the early part of the 19th century focused on slavery and led to the abolitionist movement in the North. This movement aimed at abolishing slavery and represented the best efforts by the North to defeat the pro-slavery Southerners. Southerners resisted this movement, and sectional conflicts grew.

The abolitionist movement fought for the immediate emancipation of enslaved people and the ending of segregation and racial discrimination. Immediate emancipation differentiated abolitionists from the antislavery advocates whose moderate stand encouraged gradual emancipation. The abolitionists also differed from the free-soil advocates who wanted to restrict slavery to the existing areas and prevent it from spreading west. Radical abolitionism was also encouraged partly due to the Second Great Awakening fervor, which motivated people to support emancipation based on religious conviction. Abolitionist ideas became more prominent in the churches and politics in the North during the 1830s, creating more animosity between the North and South and eventually leading to the Civil War.

Of the abolitionists, some notable personalities include:

- William Lloyd Garrison. Garrison was the publisher of the newspaper *The Liberator* and the most vocal of the abolitionists, writing in a blunt and coarse language that struck at the core of the matter.

- Fredrick Douglass. Born enslaved, Frederick Douglass became an author, orator, and reformer. He devoted his life to the abolition of slavery and the pursuit of rights for black people.

- Harriet Tubman. This African American helped free hundreds of slaves and was the leader of the Underground Railroad that helped slaves flee to the free states or Canada.

- Sojourner Truth (1797-1883). Like Tubman, Truth was born into slavery without any formal education. She ran away from her master and became a preacher, attacking the organized religious beliefs that favored the whites and the privileges they were given.

- Nat Turner (1800-1831). This preacher and black slave led one of the most famous slave revolts in the history of the United States. In 1831, he and seventy other slaves killed sixty whites in Virginia, including his master, Joseph Travis. Turner was captured by the Virginia militia and hanged, and this led to southern states passing stricter laws for controlling slaves, especially the slave preachers.

Nat Turner and his confederates in conference, c. 1831

Another influential abolitionist, Scottish-born Frances Wright (also known as Franny Wright), was a proponent of utopian communities and believed that they could be used to resolve the American issue of slavery (the term "utopian" comes from Sir Thomas More's *Utopia* (1516), in which she theorized about the perfect society). These settlements tended to experiment with different models of government, marriage, labor, and wealth to find the perfect society.

In 1825, Wright (1795-1852) published *A Plan for the Gradual Abolition of Slavery in the United States without Danger of Loss to the Citizens of the South*. She urgently suggests that land be put aside to create a colony for freed blacks based on the utopian communities of the time. Wright was so sure that her plan would work that she invested her money in a 640-acre tract in present-day Tennessee. She called the land *Nashoba* and populated her colony with enslaved people that she bought and freed in exchange for being a part of her colony. Soon after the colony was founded, however, she was forced to leave. When she returned, she found it destroyed.

Frances Wright, c. 1850

Still insistent that her plan could work, she published a well-received newspaper article defending her idea, and in 1830, she planned for the Nashoba enslaved people to be emancipated to Haiti.

Many enslaved people, unwilling to live in the horrible conditions they were subject to, attempted to escape. If caught, they would be killed or returned to their owners. If successful, they would flee to Canada, where slave catchers were banned after 1819.

In 1804, the Underground Railroad was established in Pennsylvania by abolitionists hoping to help runaway slaves. The "railroad" was a connected line of safe houses where slaves could hide. They would be given food and shelter and transported from one house to the next until they were free. The different station houses did not necessarily know each other.

Conductors led runaway slaves, often runaway slaves themselves. Perhaps the most famous of these conductors was Harriet Tubman, credited with assisting over 300 enslaved people to freedom. She made at least nineteen trips to the South, never lost a passenger, and was never caught.

Other African Americans served as an example of what freed enslaved people could be. Most notable are James Forten (1766-1842) and David Walker (1796-1830). Forten apprenticed with a sailmaker in Philadelphia and took over the business when the owner passed, refusing to make rigging for any slave trading vessels. He was an inspiration to the African American community and actively fought for an end to slavery.

Harriet Tubman, the Moses to her people, c. 1850

Forten opposed the American Colonization Society because he was an American and belonged to the United States. Forten also financially supported William Lloyd Garrison's (1805-1879) abolitionist paper, *The Liberator* (1831-1865). Similar publications spread across the northern states and allowed abolitionists to band together.

Some of the more extreme abolitionists took after John Brown. Brown attacked the federal arsenal at Harpers Ferry, Virginia, with the intent to lead slaves in an armed insurrection. Although Brown's actions shocked and were criticized by many, they earned him great respect from others.

The North was against slavery, and the South thrived on it. The northern culture depicted the Southerners as un-Christian sponges and decadent people. When the Free Labor Movement–supporting the Republican Party, won the elections, and Abraham Lincoln was made President of the Union in 1860, southerners interpreted the move as a coup d'état by the northerners.

John Brown at Harpers Ferry Raid, October 16-18, 1859

The cultural and economic fear of the people instigated the Civil War. Contrary to popular belief, slavery was not the only issue. Although the Republican Party was against slavery, it was not abolitionist. Abraham Lincoln's Emancipation Proclamation of 1862 supported the freeing of slaves only in the regions occupied by Confederate forces. All the other slave-holding states, which had supported the Union by fighting for it, were exempted.

Lincoln addressed the issue directly, saying that he did not have the right or inclination to interfere with slavery. He said that if he could have saved the Union from division without freeing the enslaved people, he would undoubtedly do it, but that it was not an option. According to Secretary of State William H. Steward (1801-1872; 1861-1869), the Emancipation Proclamation was meant to emancipate slaves in regions where the Union could not help and keep slaves in bondage in regions where they could easily be set free.

Emergence of women's rights movement

Women saw a surge in culture as they realized their place in the new nation. While less volatile than slavery, gender equality was another polarizing issue of the time. Women in the early 1800s did not have a place in the public sphere and were considered an accessory to their husband's image. This trope, often known as "the cult of domesticity," strictly defined gender roles for women and men.

As abolitionism spread, women began their fight for rights. They questioned their subservience to men and felt that the abolitionist movement should be extended to include all human rights. This split the abolitionist movement, particularly over whether women could serve as officers and speakers.

The women's suffrage movement in America was founded by women actively involved in abolition and temperance movements. Founded in the mid-19th century, the women's rights movement met in Seneca Falls, New York, in 1848 to discuss women's rights. They passed a resolution to secure the elective franchise and discussed equal rights to employment and education. Although the Seneca Falls Convention was ridiculed by the public and several supporters of the women's rights movement refrained from supporting them, their resolution marked the beginning of the women's suffrage movement in the country. When Elizabeth Cady Stanton (1815-1902) was snubbed at the World Anti-Slavery Convention in London in 1840, she joined Lucretia Mott and Susan B. Anthony (1820-1906) to create a separate women's movement.

Susan B. Anthony, c. 1905

The resulting Seneca Falls Convention of 1848 in New York earnestly established the women's movement. The convention encouraged speakers to share their perspectives on women's rights in the United States, and delegates drafted a Declaration of Sentiments based on the Declaration of Independence.

The Declaration of Sentiments demanded specific rights and improvements for women, including protection in divorce (especially with custody laws that tended to grant the father custody), equal property rights to men, fair wages, and access to higher-level professions. The primary demand and the vehicle through which women sought to achieve these changes was suffrage.

The first national convention on women's rights was held in 1850. It continued annually, improving the focus on the women's suffrage movement. The right to vote would allow women to pursue the changes they wanted on a national level and would grant them an equal say in other political issues, like slavery. While the women's movement was separate from the abolitionist movement, there was still significant support for abolition amongst the delegates. Sojourner Truth demonstrated this relationship at a women's rights convention of 1851 when she gave her famous speech, *Ain't I a Woman?* In the speech, she reminds her fellow women that the fight for women's rights does not end at suffrage for white women but is for all women. Later, this issue would divide the organization.

Territorial expansion and Manifest Destiny

After the acquisition of the Louisiana Territory, expansion became a certainty. In 1803, Thomas Jefferson commissioned the Corps of Discovery, better known as the Lewis and Clark Expedition (May 14, 1804, to September 23, 1806). Meriwether Lewis (1774-1809) and William Clark (1770-1838) led the Corps over 8,000 miles from 1804 to 1806 to chronicle the new territory's land, plants, animals, and people.

Meriwether Lewis (left) and William Clark (right), c. 1803

During the journey, Lewis recorded observations in a detailed journal, so the expedition was well preserved for posterity. They were aided by several native tribes who provided supplies and assistance and their guide and interpreter, Sacajawea, a native. Their discoveries helped to expand the knowledge of the new territory, plants, and animals that had never been seen before. The expedition was heralded as a success, and Meriwether Lewis was given a governorship upon their triumphant return. Lewis and Clark made it to the Pacific Ocean, and their example spurred others to turn west.

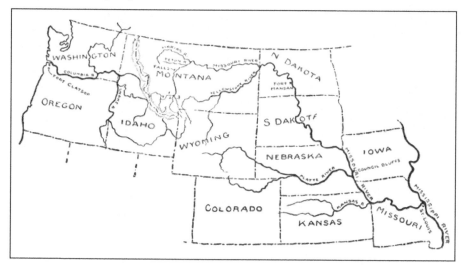

Map of the general route followed by Lewis and Clark, c. 1804

Manifest Destiny, a phrase coined around 1845, was the belief that Americans were meant to conquer the entire continent from east to west and became a prevalent force in society. Two issues held up the expansion of these western territories: the nation had to decide how to deal with Native Americans and the question of slavery.

Manifest Destiny fueled the Western territorial expansion. Manifest Destiny was first coined in 1845 by John O'Sullivan, editor for *The United States Magazine and Democratic Review*. It was proclaimed as an effort to expand the continent, which Providence gifted to help the multiplying millions of Americans flourish.

John O'Sullivan, c. 1895

Manifest Destiny encouraged the belief that the American settlers were destined to expand and move across the New World to spread their culture, traditions, and institutions and to enlighten the primitive nations of the world. Some American settlers considered the Hispanics and Indians as inferior beings who needed to be cultivated.

The settlers considered Manifest Destiny the best way to bring order to the country and remake the world in a way that mirrored their image. This belief that the American people had the mission of imposing their virtuous life on others led to westward expansion, the acquisition of new territories, and war with Mexico in the 1840s. O'Sullivan's (1813-1895) article focused on the recent Texas annexation. It hinted at the annexation of the territories acquired during the Mexican-American War through negotiations with the British for Oregon and the proposed annexation of Cuba from Spain.

Western expansion had some resistance from the people of the East, who worried that their dominant role in national affairs would be restricted by expansion. Regardless, in his address in 1844, President James K. Polk reiterated the nation's commitment to expanding existing territories and acquiring new ones to strengthen the bonds of the Union, provide security and economic development opportunities, and grant its people more agricultural land.

Intra- and intercontinental migration patterns

As with the utopian communities, new areas in the western territories created connections outside the familial to encourage migrations. Small towns and communities were typically close-knit, as the individuals living there relied on each other for continued survival. This meant that fellowship through uniting ideas, such as religion, tended to replace familial relationships, and town life would revolve around these uniting opinions and goals.

Most of the immigrants moving into the western territories were Europeans because trade with China was tentative at best, and Africa was still off-limits due to the legislation regarding the slave trade. These European settlers typically started in the northern states, where the shipping business made it easier to travel from Europe. Then, they set out west, typically among easily traveled paths like rivers or established trails. Similar groups tended to stay together, and scholars believe they may have sought locations that reminded them of their original land.

Emigrants to the West, c. 1840

The westward expansion and migration within the country, the influx of immigrants, and the end of slavery changed the social boundaries in North America. This created several conflicts due to the cultural identities, issues of citizenship, and protecting the rights of all the different groups of inhabitants—Asians, African Americans, Hispanics, and Native Americans. The unresolved slavery issue and voting and citizenship rights for immigrants and formerly enslaved people were major issues that had significant economic, religious, and political impacts on the nation.

During the pre–Civil War period, many international migrants entered the United States, including over one million Germans, over three million British, and four million Irish. While before 1845, only Irish Protestants migrated to the United States, after 1845, Irish Catholics started migrating in huge numbers mainly due to the Great Famine. Additionally, Greeks, Italians, Hungarians, Poles, and other Slavic nationals migrated to America after 1880. These immigrants served to make up the bulk of the American labor pool and were instrumental in making the country a leading economic giant worldwide.

Religious discrimination

The nativist, or Know-Nothing, movement of the 1850s had opposed the German and Irish Catholic immigration. The movement was powered by fear within the nation of the domination by Catholic immigrants who were considered opposed to American values. While the movement did not meet with much success, it was joined by many of the Protestant groups and middle-class people who were unresolved over the slavery issue.

The Know-Nothing movement (1855-1860) aimed to purify American politics by ending the influence of Irish Catholics. The movement wanted to uphold Republican values and curb naturalization and immigration.

Political poster, Know-Nothing Party, c. 1855

The anti-Catholic sentiment that began with the influx of Irish Catholics in the 1840s resulted in the conviction that Catholic children needed to be educated in public schools to learn American values. Despite opposition from the Protestants, the Irish Catholics built their parochial schools nationally and formed the Catholic Educational Association, later called the National Catholic Educational Association. Piety, strict discipline, and orthodoxy were prominently taught.

The Catholic schools were founded in reaction to the increasing number of schools publicly funded by Protestants. The American Bible Society in 1840 declared that the Bible would be read in each classroom. In 1875, a constitutional amendment was called for by President Grant, who favored the Know-Nothing Party for prohibiting the use of public funds for sectarian schools and making free public schools mandatory. The amendment was motivated by anti-Catholic views and the fear that ambition, superstition, and greed, which were believed to be fueled by the Catholic Church, would go against the values of intelligence and patriotism. Grant supported public schools free of pagan, sectarian, or atheistic teachings.

Although the amendment was defeated, it laid the groundwork for the Blaine Amendments, which were incorporated into the thirty-four state Constitutions over the next few decades. The Blaine Amendment passed in 1875 forbade using tax money to fund the parochial schools or parish schools operated by the Irish to protect their Catholic religion, culture, and language.

The white, African American, and Asian populations had migrated to the West to capitalize on the plentiful economic opportunities there as well as to seek religious refuge. The Mormons' history is one stark example of a religious exodus across the continent and the successful establishment of a strongly religious society.

The Mormon Church originated in western New York. Joseph Smith Jr. (1805-1844), a fourteen-year-old migrant farmer's son, claimed to have experienced supernatural revelations and spiritual visitations that led to the establishment of the Mormon Church. This Church was later named the Church of Jesus Christ of Latter-day Saints.

Mormonism attracted antebellum crowds in New York, who began to be inexplicably drawn by the promises of buried treasure, mystical visions, and magical talismans that Mormonism portrayed. Smith offered hope and promise to a weak, weary, and persecuted group searching for divine manifestation.

The antebellum people were economically backward when compared to the industrially wealthy northerners. They were easily enticed by the promise of emancipation offered by the Mormons. The movement was threatened by local authorities and moved to Kirtland, Ohio, where the first temple was built, and later to Missouri and Illinois, when the government ordered their extermination.

Smith was shot in 1844 by a mob while he was in prison. The anti-Mormon protests were primarily due to the struggle for political and economic power, as people believed that the Mormons, with their large number of followers, could upset the balance. The Mormon practice of polygamy also fueled the protests.

Smith's first vision, 1820

Early 19th-century American society supported monogamy, individualism, and private property. Since these principles contrasted with Mormon values, they did not accept Mormonism. The Mormons' main objective was to establish God's kingdom on Earth.

Religious rivalries and oppression were seen during this period, which is to be expected given the transition from traditional Victorian values into modern interpretations of religion and science. Many people immigrated during this period to experience greater freedoms of religion and escape persecution in their native lands, examples being Russian Mennonites and migrant Mormons, who made a home for themselves in Utah.

While many embraced the transitions of the period, others worked tirelessly against such changes, arguing that the tradition and cultural norms of the early 19th century were not broken and certainly did not need fixing. However, it seems these traditionalists quickly lost the public's ear, and many Americans were excited and eagerly awaiting the emergence of progress in the 20th century.

Resettlement patterns and the Homestead Act

The rise in wheat, corn, and cotton prices helped the southern plantations dominate the small-scale farmers. The displaced farmers moved westward to unoccupied forested land with more affordable conditions. Those settling in the West during this period demanded preemption, which allowed them to settle land initially and pay later. Eastern economic forces opposed this, fearing the cheap labor available for their industries would be lost.

The economic growth of the United States was impacted by the gold rush of 1848. Before the peace treaty with Mexico, gold had been discovered in California in 1842 by Francisco Lopez, a Californian. The announcement of the discovery of gold by James Marshall in 1848 in the San Francisco newspaper *The Californian,* spurred a gold rush in which people from all over the country landed in California with shovels and picks.

The gold rush attracted speculators from China, Latin America, France, Germany, Australia, and Britain. The population of San Francisco spiked from 459 to 20,000 in just a few months and transformed it into an ethnically diverse, violent, and unruly society. This sparked many murders of Native Indians, Mexicans, immigrants, and white people.

Gold washing in California, c. 1848

The unprecedentedly high number of immigrants to America settled in the West, drawn by its economic prosperity. The advanced transportation in the form of roadways and new canals reduced the dependence of the West on the New Orleans harbor. Furthermore, England's repeal of the Corn Laws opened new markets for American agricultural exports. Thus, the West faced many locals and immigrants searching for fertile land.

Despite these improvements, the homesteading laws were opposed on different fronts. The North bemoaned the loss of cheap labor, and the Southern states were worried that the settlers would form new antislavery states. Homestead laws were proposed and defeated thrice in 1852, 1854, and 1859. In 1860, the Homestead Bill passed by Congress was vetoed by Democratic President Buchanan (1791-1868; 1857-1861).

The *Homestead Act* of 1862 was passed due to land distribution issues occurring prevalently during westward migration. The land policies before the Act made it financially impossible for prospective homesteaders to acquire land. All this changed due to the Mexican-American War in 1846. Popular pressure occurred to alter policy according to the evolving demographics, improving the economy, and shifting the social climate of that period.

While the new allocation methods were chaotic and arbitrary, resulting in frequent disputes over borders, the *Homestead Act* had a tremendous political and regional impact. When Republican President Abraham Lincoln signed the *Homestead Act* in 1862, eleven states defected from the Union. The southern states' removal from the Union led to the Act being passed and signed as law. The new law established filing for application, improving the land, and filing for title deeds as its threefold process.

Certificate of the first homestead according to the Homestead Act, 1868

While the physical frontier conditions initially prevented people from making a claim, the *Pacific Railroad Act* (1862) led to new railroads and easy access to goods, tools, weapons, and other necessities for the homesteaders. Such resources allowed homesteaders to improve their facilities by building towns, schools, and eventually new states.

As Americans began their massive westward expansion, it quickly became evident that these exploits would be undertaken at the cost of great violence and instability. The *Homestead Act* had given many white settlers an advantage over Mexican or Native American settlements, which dotted the western landscape.

The expansion of westward migration opened several new transformations in farming, mining, and ranching markets. Such expansion became possible only with the transcontinental railroad's introduction of mass transportation. With the implementation of the *Homestead Act*, the government stopped selling land as a means of revenue. Instead, it was used to encourage the settling of the West, mainly by farming families and those moving west to find their Gilded Age niche, such as ranching, mining, or working as a cowboy.

The main detriment of farming on the Great Plains during this period was the unpredictability of the climate, which could have disastrous effects on the crops and economic sustainability of the farm. In addition to difficulties with the weather, the political landscape of the West was barren, and a lack of law and order pervaded the West, leading many to enact forms of vigilante justice. This was especially the case in disputes between ranchers and homesteaders, who, during this period, still shared prairie lands on the open range.

Western Expansion: street in Abilene, Kansas, c. 1865

Women experienced more significant roles of independence and equality in the westward expansions than those living in the urbanized Northeast. The ratio of men to women in some frontier settlements in the West was more than 100–1. This gender differential afforded women many more privileges and the respect of their peers as they worked side by side with men in the farms and western communities.

Establishing trading hubs on the Pacific Seaboard, such as San Francisco, embodied the West's diverse population, which comprised nearly half of immigrant populations, including but not limited to Hispanic, Asian, and European backgrounds. Such diversity culminated in sources of conflict, including anti-immigration sentiment against Chinese populations in California, most notably in San Francisco, as well as Hispanic-Anglo aggression along the southern border of the United States.

At the height of westward expansion's farming and mining booms, the Great Plains also experienced a period of open-range policies. During this period, farmers, cowboys, homesteaders, and native populations struggled to maintain boundaries, which culminated in frontier justice such as vigilante courts and killings.

Between the 1870s and 1880s, cowboys, ranchers, and farmers embraced the cattle industry with no feeding pattern, which was unsuccessful and caused the end of open-range farming and ranching. By the later 1880s, the Great Plains and unsettled West had been fenced up, which was made possible by Joseph Glidden's (1813-1906) invention of barbed wire. This caused conflict as homesteaders settled in new areas allotted to Mexican and Native American settlements.

Geronimo, c. 1905

Notable acts of violence include those undertaken by Geronimo (1829-1909), an Apache leader who waged guerrilla warfare against American and Mexican settlements in the West. Geronimo surrendered in 1886 at Skeleton Canyon, Arizona. There were also vigilante acts of terror and aggression by Mexican settlers against the railroads and the American working-class settlers. These acts continued until the end of the 19th century. They perpetuated uneasy feelings toward westward American expansion and the Mexican settlers, who dominated the southwestern portion of the United States for decades.

Such ongoing tensions resulted in a chaotic and unlawful frontier dominated by vigilante justice and countless descriptions of terrible atrocities at the hands of whites, Mexicans, and Native Americans alike. These attributes made the Southwest and the Pacific Coast seem like continuous sources of domestic conflict, both welcomed and scorned by the American people following the Civil War.

Reconstruction efforts failed to advance civil rights

The failure of Reconstruction (1865-1877) was due to the South interpreting its efforts as a northern concept. Furthermore, the North had no clear plan for properly implementing Reconstruction. This led to the failure to reintegrate the South with the Union and to conflicts related to the rights of African Americans, minorities, and women. While at the end of the war, it seemed that the formerly enslaved people were given equal rights to whites, racism prevailed. Thus, Reconstruction (1865-1877) failed to integrate freed slaves into society.

The Fourteenth and Fifteenth Amendments were adopted as part of the Reconstruction efforts. These were aimed at eliminating discrimination over the right to vote based on racial identity or previous servitude conditions. Before the amendments, the states were in control of determining the qualifications of voters.

While support for the amendments was an effort to help the formerly enslaved people, there was a deeper reason behind it. The black votes from the South would gain the majority for the amendments' supporters. The main reason for the Fifteenth Amendment was that the Republicans wanted the support of black votes to gain power in both the North and South. While the Fifteenth Amendment was temporarily and moderately successful in providing voting rights to the blacks living in northern and southern states, opposition to the amendments started in the Confederate states.

Voter intimidation, poll taxes, and grandfather clauses were used to limit the voting rights of freed slaves. In the latter part of the 1870s, the Southern governments nullified the Fourteenth and Fifteenth Amendments, stripped the privileges given to African Americans, and Southern states engaged in strong discriminatory practices (e.g., literacy tests, violence, intimidation) to prevent African Americans from exercising their right to vote.

While the Fifteenth Amendment banned any explicit disenfranchisement based on racial factors or prior enslavement (i.e., incidents of slavery), the southern states used three overlapping methods to disenfranchise blacks between 1868 and 1888. These included violence, illegal tactics, and massive fraud (e.g., cumulative poll tax by Georgia).

The Supreme Court supported this disenfranchisement by gutting federal laws passed to protect blacks. The Supreme Court undermined the federal executive powers that protected the voting rights of blacks and refused to acknowledge racial discrimination, even if it was proven to allow constitutional violations by citing specious reasoning.

While the Thirteenth Amendment abolished slavery, the complete elimination of racial discrimination was not possible due to the conflicting interests, motivations, and goals that prevailed during the Reconstruction period. The status of the freed slaves was unclear, and they did not receive proper legal protection to counter Southern coercion.

Ratification of the Thirteenth Amendment, December 6, 1865

The Fourteenth Amendment was passed in the wake of the *Dred Scott* (1857) decision, which occurred before the war and declared enslaved Black people as nonpersons. The Fourteenth Amendment sought to restore their status as citizens with natural rights, recognize their allegiance to the country, and give full representation in the legislation so that Southern efforts to keep them permanently oppressed could be thwarted.

For women's rights advocates, the Fourteenth Amendment was a disappointment. Based on Section One of the Fourteenth Amendment, women were given the right to vote, but the Republicans, while supporting the protection of freed slaves, did not support women's suffrage. This was solved by the introduction of Section Two, which specified the counting criteria of the inhabitants of a state for legislative representation.

The three-fifths clause of the Constitution was amended, and the specification of voting rights and citizenship to black males denied women their right to vote. This enraged women's rights activists. Most of the Congressmen who had supported the rights of black men now opposed women's right to vote, and the women's rights activists turned their attention to gaining women's suffrage rather than broader reforms.

When gender was not specified in the Fifteenth Amendment during Reconstruction, the National Women's Suffrage Association was formed. Founded by Elizabeth Cady Stanton and Susan B. Anthony, the association tried to push for women's suffrage via the U.S. Constitution. Lucy Stone (1818-1893), the first woman in Massachusetts to earn a college degree, formed the American Woman Suffrage Association and worked towards the same goal. Both these groups joined to form the National American Woman's Suffrage Association in 1890. In 1869, the Wyoming Territorial Legislature became the first jurisdiction in the United States to grant women the right to vote.

Lucy Stone, c. 1893

While the Reconstruction Amendments—namely the Thirteenth, Fourteenth, and Fifteenth Amendments—adopted in the wake of the Civil War helped to implement the Reconstruction of the South, they were also a historic step towards developing a single national identity for all Americans.

The Fifth Amendment (Bill of Rights, December 15, 1791) provided a due process clause to protect citizens' natural rights and limit the federal government's powers. The clause did not restrict the powers of the states, enabling the states to violate the Bill of Rights Amendments, and fundamental (natural) rights were only partially protected.

The Fourteenth Amendment (1868) prohibits violations of fundamental rights by the states. It extends the fundamental rights to persons born or naturalized in the United States.

Based on the *equal protection* clause of the Fourteenth Amendment, the government has two tasks in securing fundamental rights for the people: 1) the federal government should not infringe upon or threaten the rights of citizens, and 2) the federal government should take decisive measures to protect the persons within its governing territory.

While the *due process* clause addresses the former function, the *equal protection* clause ensures the latter. The states, however, were not duty-bound to protect rights, as the original Constitution did not make it mandatory. States were thus legally free to deny rights by their actions or by failing to prevent others from violating rights.

The amendments were required because the earlier protection clause did not have a reliable standard for protecting all persons. While Congress seriously considered language akin to the full protection of laws, these were not clear-cut standards, as they left room for violation. Equal protection provided a manageable standard, offering protection like that given to the most favored members of the community. The courts and Congress arrived at a behavioral standard by enforcing these amendments.

The *immunities and privileges* clause does not guarantee natural rights, as it applies only to citizens, thereby lacking the universal *natural rights* provision. Similarly, the Fifteenth Amendment is not favorable for protecting natural rights and involves the right of a citizen to vote. The Fifteenth Amendment denies states the right to abridge laws on a racial basis about the right to vote. However, states may abridge the right-to-vote clause on any basis other than racial discrimination.

Historians have identified four different categories of rights, which were debated in the nineteenth century: civil, social, political, and natural. Each has different claims and statuses to protect. While natural rights are for all human beings, political rights are not universal, and eligibility is subject to the community's decision.

The Fifteenth Amendment states that race is not a valid reason for determining the right to vote, but it leaves other ways of denying the right to vote (such as literacy) open. Thus, the actual intention of the amendment was circumvented for several years by crafty exploitation of such loopholes states used to deny minorities the right to vote. While these amendments aimed at giving freedom, rights of citizenship, and voting to the slaves, they were slowly but effectively eroded by the federal court rulings and state laws – called "Jim Crow laws" after a mythical southern white racist – during the latter part of the 19th century.

Women were prohibited from voting, which led to Susan B. Anthony trying to vote in the presidential election of 1872 as an act of agitation against the rules. The Jim Crow laws passed by some states limited the rights of formerly enslaved people.

Furthermore, the *Slaughterhouse* (1873) and *Plessy v. Ferguson* (1896) Supreme Court cases undermined the rights given by the 13th, 14th, and 15th Amendments. The freed slaves enjoyed the full effects of their rights only after laws such as the 1964 *Civil Rights Act* and the 1965 *Voting Rights Act* were passed.

Environmental and agricultural movements

The transitions experienced by farmers during the late 19th century varied and sometimes met with considerable pushback; one notable example of this was the farmers' dependence on rail transportation of goods to East Coast markets. Most farmers operating in the Great Plains did not welcome this new relationship, eventually leading to opposition movements, including the Grange and Populist movements. The Grange movement, also called the Patrons of Husbandry, was founded in 1867 and was meant to facilitate the advancement of agricultural technologies while also voicing the social and economic concerns of farmers operating in the Midwest.

As the government faltered in addressing farmers' economic, political, and social concerns, the Grange movement saw a drastic increase in membership during the 1870s. Farmers were distraught with the rising costs of transporting goods by train and the fact that the government opted for gold-backed currency instead of silver.

Grangers adopted the slogan "I pay for all," which embodied their stance as the breadwinners of American society, where farming was the cornerstone of American industry and progress during this period. Such policies, along with failing crops, decimated the farming populations of the 1870s, leading farmers to support Populist and later Progressive movements concerned with the well-being of the American farmer.

U.S. postage stamp honoring the Grange movement

As the American industry exploited the natural resources of the Midwest and West, some believed that action by the federal government was necessary to preserve national resources, including land and water. The difficult westward expansion taught settlers the importance of protecting resources like water for future generations of farmers.

In 1871, one of the first steps toward such conservation was the formation of the Office of Commission of Fish and Fisheries, also known as the Fish Commission, which was signed into law by Republican President Ulysses S. Grant (1822-1885; 1869-1877). Fisheries were one of the first renewable resources to receive the federal government's attention because Americans saw a drastic decline in the fisheries' production, calling into question the sustainability of fishing practices.

In addition to concerns regarding fishery practices following the industrial boom of the Gilded Age, the federal government began looking closer at its policies regarding forestry. As a result, in 1891, the *Forest Reserve Act* was passed, allocating lands for national forests, which later came under the control of the National Forest Service. Such policies would be expanded in the first years of the 20th century under President Theodore Roosevelt.

Another notable organization seeking to limit federal and state control was the Las Gorras Blancas, which took a more coercive approach to removing government regulations. From February 1889 until the summer of 1891, members of Las Gorras Blancas went on night rides, terrorizing the ranchers enclosing the Land Grant Common of Las Vegas and railroad companies in the region. These vigilantes were acting against what they perceived to be the perpetrator of land grants in the West.

Others engaged in the battle to protect natural resources against the machine of industrialization. One notable example is John Muir, who, in 1892, founded the Sierra Club, which was concerned with the protection and conservation of what was considered wildlands. Even today, the Sierra Club advocates on behalf of wildlife and for resource conservation.

The actions of conservationists during this period would have profound implications leading into the 21st century. Without these initial programs, resources, and lands might have been lost to the consumerism and manufacturing of the period.

Future Presidents, such as Republican Theodore Roosevelt (1858-1919; 1901-1909) and Democrat Franklin D. Roosevelt (1882-1945; 1933-1945), expanded these programs, bringing more water and land security to the Great Plains and the western settlements. Such advancements were crucial to maintaining the progress of the Gilded Age and migration to the West without decimating natural resources highly valued by many Americans today.

The Colored Farmers' Alliance (C.F.A.) was also influential during this period. It worked against the influence of the federal and state governments, as well as racial stigma and persecution following the Civil War. The C.F.A. was formed in 1886 as a separate entity because the Southern Famers' Alliance declined to admit African Americans. Though the Colored Farmers Alliance was short-lived, it sought to advance African American farmers and citizens advocating for independence and private property ownership, such as homes, while eliminating debt.

The formation of such groups shows the impact each demographic had on the political system during the late 19th century; every walk of life in America was greatly influenced by the ideals and economic strategies of the Gilded Age (1870s to 1900). This was certainly the case for those living on the western frontier, experiencing firsthand the resistance of private entities to being regulated by the federal government or corporate powers. However, this would prove to be the norm in the early decades of the 20th century, as the magnates and big businesses of the Gilded Age influenced the federal government.

While the farmers' call for more regulation and reforms of the influence exercised by the railroads went unnoticed, Populism, another social movement, emerged. Like its predecessors, the Populist movement was an attempt by disenfranchised farmers to have their grievances aired and addressed. The Populist movement was influential in the New South. It asked white and black farmers to work toward a common cause rather than being separated based on race.

By the late 1880s, farmers had experienced years of failed crops, the lack of credit institutions, insufficient marketing, a lack of regulations by the federal government to protect farmers' rights, and declining prices. These conditions, coupled with the tense relationships shared between railroad management and farmers, caused the explosion of the Populist movement in the later years of the 19th century.

However, the Populist movement dissipated by the late 1890s with the defeat of the candidates of the Populist and Democratic Parties, such as William Jennings Bryan, as the Populist Party lacked popularity among the American public. In the years following, many who supported the Populist and Grange movements would find some common ground with the Progressive movement.

Though the Populist movement was unable to maintain its popularity, it was influential because it laid the groundwork for later movements, such as the Progressivism movement of the 20th century. This movement highlights another example of division within the American population, culminating in social upheaval in later decades. This is an early example of a biracial organization after the Civil War. For many in the South, this was an accomplishment. The concept of government accountability and fair representation of all Americans originated in such social and political movements.

As industry and manufacturing giants dotted the American landscape following the Civil War, it seemed a new war on natural resources and conservation had been declared. The industrial magnates of the period exploited and sought the natural resources of continental America in hopes of continuing their dominant role within the new economy. However, many conservationists, who sought policies more in line with preserving and maintaining the natural resources and unspoiled wilderness of the United States, quickly opposed this.

The exploitation of natural resources by business interests centered mainly on iron ore, coal, oil, and lumber. Iron ore created steel and pig iron by the railroad companies and in building bridges and buildings. Coal was needed to propel the steam engines in the railcars after replacing using wood as fuel. Other industrial machines also used coal as a fuel source, making it necessary for the Gilded Age. Oil was used as kerosene in lighthouses and cities during this period. It also created a new industry, petroleum refining, which would later evolve into multi-billion-dollar corporations. Lumber was in high demand during this period.

Hauling coal locomotive, c. 1915-1925

The creation of national parks was a great victory for conservationists and would allow for advancements in conservation by later progressive Presidents. This transition away from policies supporting big business towards those that gave a voice to workers can be seen as the transition from the Gilded Age into the Progressive Age of the early 20th century.

New economic opportunities

As modern culture emerged out of the Civil War, many African Americans, immigrant workers, and women saw their futures as having more opportunities than before. This manufacturing explosion saw the increased need for skilled labor, which had been supplied by immigration influx in the past. It appears that the industrial and manufacturing advancements of the Gilded Age would allow for all minority groups to expand their vocational opportunities. However, many quickly realized such ambitions would exist within the same class structure as in the past and would be drastically limited by the opportunities afforded to white males.

As America entered the end of the 19th century, it was quickly becoming evident that social reform and revolution were on the horizon, and many seemed to embrace this unprecedented period of growth and transition. The impact of the Gilded Age, western expansion, urbanization, and industrialization changed America's political and social landscape for decades, resulting in the global power it became by the mid-20th century.

The expansion of the western territories following the Civil War shows the most exceptional example of gender and racial equality of the period. In the western territories, women and minority groups such as African Americans, Chinese immigrants, and other European immigrants experienced more freedom and vocational opportunities than were afforded to them in the urban settings of the Atlantic Seaboard. This was due to the need for skilled and unskilled laborers and life circumstances in the western territories.

As economic opportunities grew in the West, women who settled there were given more freedoms and responsibilities associated with running a homestead. Immigrant groups were able to settle in the West with fewer experiences of prejudice than on the East Coast while also being afforded more significant financial opportunities.

One notable example is laundress and seamstress shops opened by Chinese immigrants who saw a gap in the market and capitalized on the demand for laundry services in mining communities. African Americans found greater work opportunities (e.g., ranchers, farmers, cowboys, railroad laborers) in the West than in the New South and northern states.

As America began its transition westward or into urban centers, many immigrants worldwide looked to the United States to accomplish dreams unattainable in their native lands. Many immigrants moving from Europe and Asia sought better economic and vocational conditions. In contrast, others looked for expanded religious freedoms, as seen with the period's Eastern Orthodox and Jewish immigrants. African Americans, who had survived slavery and the Civil War, looked for the freedoms and equality promised by the Emancipation Proclamation.

As America experienced the boom of initial urbanization, many immigrants and minority groups looked at these cities and vast economic opportunities for better wages and the amenities of city life. While many groups that had previously experienced discrimination were able to find work, social and class expectations still stifled the ambitions of many people living in the city.

The westward expansion proved less rigid in class and social structure, allowing many African Americans and immigrant classes to hold various jobs, including those that would have previously been designated strictly for white males. Such examples included mining, ranching, and homesteading. These initial opportunities would become the foundation of further calls for equal job opportunities, rights, and protection within the political system.

The implications of such expansion were critical to propelling the United States into a more developed, unified country following the ravaging it had experienced during the Civil War. It also allowed many Americans to find opportunities previously unavailable, perpetuating the American dream of a new wave of citizens.

As the manufacturing and industrialization boom continued, thousands of native-born Americans and immigrants flocked to the newly developed cities to find work. Transportation was unavailable to most working-class people during this period, so many lived within walking distance of their factories. These new cities also provided work in construction and infrastructure, as housing projects and more prominent buildings were necessary to accommodate the massive influx in urban populations.

Within the urban city, one could easily find mini-cities divided by nationalities, such as "Little Hungary" or "Little China," where new and seasoned immigrants could enjoy some of their native traditions. These communities typically embraced their own, making the transition into American society and culture easier for each new wave of immigrants. However, the programs offered within the community were provided with the understanding that once someone had become successful, he or she would extend his or her services to those in need, thus perpetuating the cycle.

As the American population began its transition from rural to urban, many new sectors of employment opened to new demographic groups, including immigrants, minorities, and women. These new opportunities and global instability caused many to see immigration to the United States as a way to become prosperous and financially secure. The development of cities created new job markets. By the end of the 1890s, close to one million women transitioned into the workforce, holding positions as bookkeepers, telephone operators, secretaries, and seamstresses.

Most working women were unmarried and came from lower-class backgrounds, while socially acceptable vocations for upper- and middle-class women included teaching and nursing. This initial explosion in women entering the workforce set the groundwork for vocational advances during the World Wars and the following years. Once women began to earn better wages and hold stable jobs, they were determined to maintain these advancements and continue to fight for recognition and equality.

This urban boom, which created leisure time and a middle class, was driven by theological ideals, including expansion and a new American dream. Highlighted by Massachusetts-born Horatio Alger (1832-1899), the concept that hard work, rather than divine intervention or status, led to success garnered support among many working classes. This vision also embodied the ideals of many Americans entering the early 20th century who wished to work for themselves and create their versions of an urban paradise.

Horatio Alger, c. 1898

As immigrants came to America, they, like native-born citizens, sought to attain their version of the American dream, which typically meant more freedoms, better wages, and a better day-to-day existence for the working class. During the Gilded Age, the American manufacturing sector needed skilled and unskilled laborers to sustain the booming economy. Because of this demand, many industrial elites welcomed the exploding immigration patterns of the period.

These immigrants could maintain a sense of their homelands, as many assimilated into American culture with the help of other immigrants who lived in relative proximity and came from the same country, such as Poland, Russia, or China. In the West, entire settlements consisted of Chinese immigrants who minted the gold and silver caches of the West and supplemented agriculture during times of conflict, such as the Civil War.

Following the Civil War in 1865, women and African Americans found new opportunities in the West and North, igniting the desire for equality and vocational opportunities. One example was the emerging cowboy hired to round up and drive longhorn cattle across the Great Plains.

Men from every background worked as cowboys, including Mexican settlers, former slaves, and various European immigrants. Women and other minority groups could also make opportunities for themselves as homesteaders; like other Western ambitions, this was difficult, and many were forced to pursue other work, such as lending themselves to other farms as hands or servants.

The efficiency of the city system would prove to have drastic implications for later waves of American urbanization in the 20th century and establish the expectation of urban living and production for future generations. Following the Gilded Age, Americans never looked to agrarian means to support the economy or population. Instead, it supported industrialization and manufacturing advancements, allowing the United States to remain a global power in the 20th century.

Discrimination and socioeconomic inequalities

At the end of Reconstruction in 1877, many Americans wondered what freedoms had been gained since the end of the Civil War in 1865. While many African Americans found new opportunities in the northern cities, African Americans in the South faced an exponentially long road to real equality. This was the case for all minority groups, including but not limited to the Chinese and southern and eastern European immigrants.

As a result of Reconstruction, many Southerners wondered what emancipation would look like. It was quickly realized that the South looked very similar, especially regarding racism, as it had before the Civil War. One such example, which would have explosive implications, was *Plessy v. Ferguson* (1896), where the Supreme Court ruled in favor of segregation, coining the idea of "separate but equal." Such examples highlighted the rampant racism still evident in the 20th century.

Religious differences were another source of discrimination. Protestants and Catholics took aggressive actions against one another. These events culminated in the American Protective Association (APA) creation in 1887. The founder, Henry Bowers, was a Mason and used his connections to forge significant political influence.

The American Protective Association quickly grew into a widespread organization while also highlighting what some would later call Protestant Paranoia. As a result of the 1893 economic crisis, the APA attracted thousands of new members, and eventually, the group claimed over one million members. During this period, many Americans embodied a sense of nativism, which was increasingly evident as immigrants migrated in waves throughout the late 19th century.

As these new immigrants settled into American society, many connected themselves with other nationalities who were also recent or first-generation immigrants and created transplant communities called "Little Italy" or "Little Hungary." These communities fed the tensions and violence between nativists and immigrants. Such interactions would continue into the 20th century and highlight the beginnings of the anti-immigration sentiment maintained by the American public for many years.

In response to the massive influx of immigrants, the U.S. government passed the *Chinese Exclusion Act* in 1882, which stopped the immigration of all skilled and unskilled Chinese immigrants for ten years. This Act was expanded in 1888 with the *Scott Act*, which banned re-entry into the United States after visiting China, regardless of legal status.

Such actions significantly soured the relationship between the United States and China until 1943, when the immigration ban was lifted in hopes of garnering support for the war against Japan from Chinese nationals. Discrimination and oppression limited many Chinese from immigrating after the anti-immigration legislation of the 19th century.

The immigration restrictions imposed during this period highlight a change in thinking from the marginal acceptance of immigrants in the early and mid-19th century to the complete denial of immigration during the late 19th century, coinciding with the rise in nativism and Nationalism. These movements continued to influence both domestic and foreign affairs for America leading into the 20th century, and they caused many Americans to claim racial superiority over other ethnicities. Such an attitude can be seen in the legislation passed during the Red Scare as well as the World War II internment camps used to hold thousands of Japanese Americans.

Immigrants and international migrants were also able to seek work in industrial and urban settings; many suffered workplace abuses and continued discrimination. This xenophobia caused increased tensions between native-born Americans and the massive influx of immigrants seen between 1890 and 1920. This negative perception of immigration did not lessen the number of immigrants hoping and willing to settle in America to make a more prosperous future for themselves and their families. These new vocational opportunities were the precursors for the advancement of women and minority groups seen during the war years. These transitions were instrumental in beginning the conversation of the women's and civil rights movements of the latter part of the 20th century.

The explosion of city living illuminated the drastic and deplorable contrast between the wealthy elites and the working classes. This disparity had never been more evident than during this period. As thousands of workers flooded the city, it quickly became apparent that many did not have the resources or services necessary to live in these urban metropolises. Due to a lack of space, the tenement houses were crowded and typically had communal bathrooms.

The sewer and water facilities provided by the city were typically overloaded and unable to provide service to all those living in the cities, greatly straining the sanitation system. The trash piled up on the streets of New York and Chicago, and health concerns mounted, partially due to the spread of communicable diseases such as tuberculosis.

The child mortality rate was extremely high in Chicago in 1900. Poverty and low standards of living caused many to despise the wealthy classes who, during this period, lived in a new sense of luxury. As a result of continued income inequality, many living below the poverty line joined neighborhood gangs, such as the Hell's Kitchen Gang or the Rock Gang, who subsided by shoplifting and other petty thefts.

In addition to boundaries derived from nationalities, the city grotesquely displayed the class and income inequalities of the period, with a small percentage of elites living in luxury and the working class managing through the slime of the newly minted city. This class inequality would be the foundation for many social movements in the later 19th and early 20th centuries.

The Gilded Age—from 1876, at the end of Reconstruction, to about 1900—was a period of exponential growth and innovation in America. However, accompanying these developments was a great deal of corruption, mainly stemming from government policies and business practices. The tremendous highs of the Gilded Age experienced by the wealthy elites and the economic lows felt by the working classes and new immigrant populations highlighted the stark economic and social differences of the late 19th century.

The social and political rivalries prevalent between the working classes, the elites, and the management in government during the Gilded Age were the precursors to the social upheavals seen during the late 19th and early 20th centuries. Such social movements and changes in perception among the American population also set the groundwork for economic reforms and the political changes of Progressivism in the 20th century.

Social movements of the period

As Americans entered an unprecedented period of economic and social development, it became clear that reform was on the horizon, and many social groups, including women, the working class, and immigrants, would benefit from these eventual reforms. Late 19th-century America had unregulated work environments, overzealous and sometimes corrupt politicians, and a population unhappy with the influx of recent immigrants. These divisions highlighted the difficulties faced by average Americans but also showed the abundant and varying solutions and perceptions of the American public.

In hopes of addressing various forms of racial discrimination, many abolitionists and formerly enslaved people worked to end the racial norms of the Civil War era using organizations and support groups whose goal was to help assimilate formerly enslaved people into post–Civil War America. Socioeconomic inequalities were addressed by attempts to reform the workplace, guaranteeing shorter workdays, wage protection, and forming unions.

As the federal government was unable to provide abundant services to the immigration and working classes seen during the explosion of urbanization, fraternal, neighborhood, and social groups were able to fill the gap, garnering substantial political influence during the Gilded Age. These relationships were hugely influential in establishing the stability sought by those living in urban America during the late 19th century. Such influence caused the government to enact many social programs in the early 20th century, which placed the social dependence of the population back on the expanding federal government rather than privately organized ethnic or fraternal entities.

In 1874, the Woman's Christian Temperance Union (WCTU) was founded in Cleveland, Ohio. This evolved into an influential women's groups in the 19th-century political landscape. By 1879, the leadership of the WCTU was under Frances Willard (1839-1898), who propelled the group to voice its opinions regarding labor laws, prison reforms, and women's suffrage. However, upon Willard's death in 1898, the group became staunch supporters of prohibition and fell away from the main thrust of the women's movement.

Mary Greenleaf Clement, founding member of WCTU, c. 1910

Another notable organization that championed social change was the National American Woman Suffrage Association, formed in 1890 by combining two former rival groups. The first president of the WCTU, Elizabeth Cady Stanton, sought to show the American public that women deserved the right to vote not because they were equal to men but because they were different. She focused on other positive traits, such as maternal instincts and ideals equating to political morality.

Eventually, Stanton withdrew from mainstream feminism, but she is still attributed, along with Susan B. Anthony, with creating the foundation of the women's suffrage movement. The implications of such organizations are paramount to understanding the social and civil movements of the 20th century. These divisions amongst the population regarding the women's suffrage movement also bring into focus, yet again, the social instability and rivalries seen during this period. Such conditions would inevitably lead to sweeping reforms and laws during the 20th century.

As many struggled with the social transitions of the Gilded Age, minority groups such as women and African Americans attempted to achieve the equality and opportunities promised to all Americans. Booker T. Washington (1856-1915), who was born into slavery, worked tirelessly throughout his life to garner better funding for African American education, as well as overall equality for African Americans following the Civil War.

Booker T. Washington, c. 1910

In 1881, Washington founded the Tuskegee Institute in Alabama, which was dedicated to the education of teachers and advancing this vocation in an industrial economy. Washington would go on to advise the federal government on matters of education and create the National Negro Business League in 1901. During a time of high racial tension and uncertainty, Booker T. Washington advanced the rights of African Americans using accommodation to a place of conversation within the political system, leading to the civil rights movements of the 20th century.

Ida Wells-Barnett, also born into slavery, was a critical member of the early civil rights struggles experienced during this period. Wells-Barnett worked in various capacities, such as social activism and writing, in hopes of shedding light on the white violence still experienced in this period by African Americans, specifically the practice of lynching. In 1896, with the help of her husband, Wells-Barnett organized the National Association of Colored Women, which opposed the accommodating tactics proposed by Booker T. Washington while fighting for equality in race and gender.

Another notable activist concerned with the advancement of women's suffrage and civil rights in this period was Elizabeth Cady Stanton, who formed the National Woman Suffrage Association in 1870. Stanton was the front-runner of the women's suffrage movement, advocating more liberal divorce laws and women's reproductive rights. Though Stanton was influential early in the women's movement, she became more detached by the 1890s and was less in tune with mainstream perceptions and opinions. Stanton's work would eventually culminate in the passage of the Nineteenth Amendment (August 18, 1920), giving women the universal right to vote.

These activists greatly influenced the civil rights movements of their period and future periods of history, inevitably setting the foundation for future civil rights advancements. Such work was undeniable in achieving the advancements experienced by minorities and women in this period and led to women's suffrage and equal pay ambitions.

On a different front of social change, there was Dorothea Dix (1802-1887), who tried to bring social reform to the treatment of the mentally ill. In 1841, while teaching Sunday school at a women's prison in the East Cambridge Massachusetts Jail, Dix discovered that the living quarters for the prisoners were not hospitable, especially those holding the mentally ill. Many of the rooms had no heat. Outraged by the way these women were being treated, she petitioned the courts for an order to improve the standard of living in the prisons.

Concerned about the plight of others, Dix traveled around the state to research the living conditions in prisons and poorhouses. This led to her writing a proposal for the Massachusetts legislature to expand and improve the State Mental Hospital at Worcester. Satisfied with her work at home, Dix began a national tour to improve patient conditions. Her continued success at the state level encouraged her to move into the federal arena.

In 1848, she requested an endowment be put aside to treat the mentally ill, deaf, and blind. The House and the Senate passed the bill, but Democratic President Franklin Pierce (1804-1869; 1853-1857) vetoed it. Discouraged but not defeated, Dix began to travel internationally, recommending reforms worldwide.

Utopian communities

Several utopian communities existed during the period. Few had any lasting impact on society, but each experimented with different social structures, an indicator that the young country was still trying to define itself. In 1841, Brook Farm was founded by Unitarian Minister George Ripley.

Known as the Transcendentalist Romance, the community was the first purely secular utopian community. The foundational idea was that by living together, farming together, and sharing their labors, members would have more time to spend on academic pursuits. The community disbanded relatively quickly when finances became an issue. Nathaniel Hawthorne (1804-1864), an influential Romantic writer, was a community founder.

Nathaniel Hawthorne, c. 1864

Author Louisa May Alcott spent seven months of her childhood at Fruitland, Harvard, MA, a utopian community founded by her father and Charles Lane. Though it claimed to be based on principles of gender equality, Alcott's scathing reflection detailed a very different story.

New Harmony, in Indiana, was a more fruitful endeavor. Founded by social reformer Robert Owens, the community was populated by scientists and succeeded in establishing a center for scientific discovery outside of the Northeast. It disbanded after four years.

The Shaker is a utopian group that exists today. Shakers practice celibacy and communal ownership of goods. Both aspects were typical of religious utopias. However, they also believe in strict gender roles and keep the sexes separate. Their prosperity is based mainly on a source of income, namely furniture design and manufacture.

As intellectuals of the Gilded Age period struggled to conceptualize the transitions of the Gilded Age, many turned to utopian viewpoints, wildly popular amongst Nationalists, Populists, and Socialists. One such advocate of utopian America was Edward Bellamy (1850-1898), most famous for his work *Looking Backward, 2000–1887* (1888), which inspired many utopian settlements in the 1890s. Bellamy's work spurred the new concept of Nationalism, which, according to the book, can create a state with a correctly functioning nationalized industrial sector, similar class structures, and equal distribution of wealth.

In 1888, Bellamy also founded the Bellamy Nationalists Clubs, which spread his message of evolutionary-led transitions into utopian Nationalism. The works of Bellamy highlight the superbly utopian models of government and politics following the radical transition from Victorian-era policies into the more progressive ideas of the Gilded Age. While many initially supported the movement, membership waned and, by the mid-1890s, had all but expired. Other critics of capitalism emerged but were typically silenced, leaving many to embrace other movements, such as Populism.

The Social Gospel and other utopian movements can be seen as a direct result of the abundant social transitions during this period. As Americans struggled to find their place in an ever-evolving market and social structure, it became clear that some Americans longed for the traditional Victorian values of the early 19th century. Others looked to the future, full of social and economic transformation, overflowing with new opportunities and innovation.

Social history – summary of the period

Many white Americans in the South asserted their regional identity through pride in the institution of slavery, insisting that the federal government should defend that institution. Resistance to initiatives for democracy included proslavery arguments, rising xenophobia, anti-black sentiments in political and popular culture, and restrictive anti-Indian policies.

The South remained politically, culturally, and ideologically distinct from the other sections while relying on its exports to Europe for economic growth. Abolitionists, although a minority in the North, mounted a highly visible campaign against slavery, adopting strategies of resistance ranging from fierce arguments against the institution and assistance in helping enslaved people escape to a willingness to use violence to achieve their goals.

American groups and individuals initiated, championed, or resisted the expansion of territory and government powers. The idea of Manifest Destiny, which asserted U.S. power in the Western Hemisphere and supported U.S. expansion westward, was built on a belief in the particular virtues of the American people, their destiny to expand throughout the continent, and a sense of American cultural superiority; it helped to shape the era's political debates.

With the opening of canals and new roads into the western territories, native-born white citizens relocated westward, relying on new community systems to replace their old family and local relationships. Migrants from Europe increased the population in the East and the Midwest, forging strong bonds of interdependence between the Northeast and the Old Northwest.

Westward expansion, migration to and within the United States, and the end of slavery reshaped North American boundaries. It caused conflicts over American cultural identities, citizenship, and the question of extending and protecting rights for groups of U.S. inhabitants.

Substantial numbers of new international migrants—who often lived in ethnic communities and retained their religion, language, and customs—entered the country before the Civil War, giving rise to a significant, often violent nativist movement that was strongly anti-Catholic and aimed at limiting immigrants' cultural influence and political and economic power. Asian, African American, and white peoples sought new economic opportunities or religious refuge in the West, efforts that were boosted during and after the Civil War with the passage of new legislation promoting national economic development.

Westward migration, new systems of farming and transportation, and economic instability led to political and popular conflicts. The competition for land in the West among white settlers, Indians, and Mexican Americans led to an increase in violent conflict. The constitutional changes of the Reconstruction period embodied a northern idea of American identity and national purpose. They led to conflicts over new definitions of citizenship, particularly regarding the rights of African Americans, women, and other minorities.

Although citizenship, equal protection of the laws, and voting rights were granted to African Americans in the Fourteenth and Fifteenth Amendments, these rights were progressively stripped through segregation, violence, Supreme Court decisions, and local political tactics. The women's rights movement was emboldened and divided over the Fourteenth and Fifteenth Amendments to the Constitution.

The Civil War Amendments (13th, 14th, and 15th) established judicial principles stalled for many decades. The Supreme Court's decisions undermined civil rights.

Farmers adapted to the new realities of mechanized agriculture and dependence on the evolving railroad system by creating local and regional organizations that sought to resist corporate control of agricultural markets. Government agencies and conservationist organizations contended with corporate interests about extending public control over natural resources, including land and water. The growth of corporate power in agriculture and economic instability in the farming sector inspired activists to create the People's (Populist) Party, which called for political reform and a more substantial regulatory role in the American economic system.

Business interests battled conservationists as the latter sought to protect sections of unspoiled wilderness by establishing national parks and other conservationist and preservationist measures. The industrial culture in the United States led to more opportunities for and restrictions on immigrants, minorities, and women.

Increased migrations from Asia and southern and eastern Europe, as well as African American migrations within and out of the South, accompanied the mass movement of people into the nation's cities and the rural and boomtown areas of the West.

Cities dramatically reflected divided social conditions among classes, races, ethnicities, and cultures but presented economic opportunities where new businesses proliferated. The United States continued its transition from a rural, agricultural society to an urban, industrial one, offering new economic opportunities for women, internal immigrants, and international migrants who continued to flock to the United States.

Immigrants sought both to "Americanize" and to maintain their unique identities; along with others, such as African Americans and women, they could take advantage of new career opportunities even in the face of widespread social prejudices. Increasingly prominent racist and nativist theories, along with Supreme Court decisions such as *Plessy v. Ferguson*, were used to justify violence as well as local and national policies of discrimination and segregation.

As cities grew in size and number, some segments of American society enjoyed extravagant "conspicuous consumption," while many others lived in relative poverty. International and internal migrations increased urban and rural populations, but gender, racial, ethnic, religious, and socioeconomic inequalities abounded, inspiring some reformers to attempt to address these inequities.

In an urban atmosphere, where access to power was unequally distributed, political machines provided social services in exchange for political support; settlement houses helped immigrants adapt to the new language and customs. Women's clubs and self-help groups targeted intellectual development and social and political reform.

Challenging their prescribed "place," women and African American activists articulated alternative visions of political, social, and economic equality. Some critics challenged the dominant corporate ethics in the United States and sometimes capitalism itself, offering alternative visions of a good society through utopianism and the Social Gospel.

Notes for active learning

Intellectual and Cultural History: 1790 to 1898

Traditional cultures

Although America tried to cultivate a cultural identity separate from the rest of the world, creating purely American art forms took time. Americans had not been around long enough to break away from traditional art forms, and it was trendy to mimic the highly sophisticated styles of Europe. This changed during the first half of the 1800s, primarily as a reaction to the opening of the western territory and the development of many regional identities, which were then expressed and preserved.

The early 1800s saw distinct cultures emerge within numerous communities. For the Native Americans, this was a resurgence of traditional values. Through trade with the Europeans and Americans, many tribes changed and adapted their cultural practices. They used new agricultural methods, learned to read and write in English, and adopted new technology at the expense of some of their traditional practices.

Many natives encouraged a shift back to older ways. For instance, in 1811, three Cherokee in Georgia reported seeing a vision denouncing European goods. The Cherokee deities were unhappy with the way Cherokees allowed settlers to treat animals and the land, demanding that they return to the old ways.

Expression of abolitionism through art

Enslaved people and free African Americans were creating their own culture during this period. In 1794, Richard Allen created the first black denomination: the African Methodist Episcopal Church. Spirituals were sung in the fields as enslaved people worked to create a sense of community and family. They also had the dual role of acting as coded messages for runaway slaves. *Follow the Drinking Gourd*, for instance, explains how to travel north to freedom by following the Big Dipper (Ursa Major), which includes the North Star.

Runaway and formerly enslaved people began sharing stories that detailed their lives under former masters. Frederick Douglass wrote arguably the best known of these works: *Narrative of the Life of Frederick Douglass, An American Slave* (1845). Douglass' text and others like it were published in the North and opened the eyes of many northerners to the evils of slavery by making slavery about a person instead of an institution.

David Walker published his thoughts on slavery in *An Appeal to the Colored Citizens in the World* (1829), which he smuggled into the South using sympathetic sailors as contacts. Slaves who read his works—writing that defended them against slavery in the South and discrimination in the North—were uplifted and inspired. Slaveholders soon had a bounty on his head, but he refused to flee to Canada and insisted on staying in the public eye. Another publisher, Elijah Lovejoy, was killed for publishing anti-slavery messages.

Frederick Douglass, 1895

Many white abolitionists encouraged the spread of African American art forms to polarize the issue and encourage more people to join the abolitionist movement. However, even amongst abolitionists, there was discord.

For example, with *The Liberator*, Garrison intended to bring abolitionists together and spread their ideas. Garrison scorned the idea that solely political action would have any impact on ending slavery. This put him in direct opposition to the Liberty Party, which tried to influence abolitionist change using the existing political system.

Others thought that by emulating and popularizing slave narratives, they could gain attention. Harriet Beecher Stowe (1811-1896) wrote one of the most famous pieces of literature from this period, *Uncle Tom's Cabin* (1852). Her take on the slave narrative style was widely popular and earned her and the abolitionist movement a wealth of support.

Harriet Beecher Stowe, c. 1895

The Second Great Awakening

While less politically charged than many other conflicts, religion rapidly changed during the early 19th century. Before the American Revolution, most people belonged to one of three major Protestant denominations: Congregationalists, Anglicans, and Quakers. Congregationalist churches were the descendants of Puritan churches, and Puritan influence on America can still be seen in many American ideals, such as hard work and community.

The Anglican Church was the American branch of the Church of England. After the Revolution, they were the Episcopalians. The Quakers were a "peace church" like the Amish. After the American Revolution, the major denominations changed, and the three foundation denominations gave way to evangelical Methodists and Baptists as revivals swept the nation. This period is the Second Great Awakening.

Charles Finney, c. 1875

At the heart of the Second Great Awakening were revivals. These were large meetings, typically held in fields where a preacher, or several preachers, would stand and speak. Charles Finney (1792-1875), called the Father of Modern Revivalism, was one such preacher. He shared his faith at revivals, and his style impacted the movement. Finney allowed women to pray out loud in public meetings of mixed gender, which was not done during the period due to the cult of domesticity and national understanding of gender roles.

Charles Finney created the "anxious seat," a place for non-Christians considering converting. They could sit in the anxious seat to receive prayers. He habitually censored individuals by name during his services and preaching extemporaneously for an audience. Using methods like these, these speakers masterfully controlled the crowd's energy. An account of a 20,000-person revival in Kentucky reads:

The noise was like the roar of Niagara. The vast sea of human beings seemed to be agitated as if by a storm. I counted seven ministers, all preaching at one time, some on stumps, others on wagons...Some of the people were singing, others praying, some crying for mercy. A peculiarly strange sensation came over me. My heart beat tumultuously, my knees trembled, my lips quivered, and I felt as though I must fall to the ground.

—James Finley

The ministers at these revivals reached out to their audience at the emotional level and upheld ideals that the average person could agree with. Evangelical churches generally favored ordinary people over elites. They felt that a truly pious individual was more capable of leading others to salvation than a formally trained minister, like those required by many traditional churches. These open policies meant that many flocked to the Evangelical faith.

While these religious revivals did not directly threaten any established order, they did encourage activism on a full scale. The movement stressed the concept of free will and a person's choice to accept their lot in life or work to better their position. It was a very optimistic outlook, allowing the choice of religious salvation instead of the fatalistic views held by other denominations. However, it was also one that encouraged conflict with social norms. White women, who were invited to take leadership roles for the first time, found themselves in a position to enact social change for women's rights. African Americans were allowed to participate actively in the new religion. The stressing of individual salvation caused many to question the religion-based proslavery arguments.

Art, literature, and architecture

Artists adapted original American styles as the country struggled to establish a national identity amidst the chaos of conflict. It became fashionable to document scenes of everyday life for different classes and in different regions. As territory opened in the West, landscapes became the dominant art form. Styles like the panoramic landscapes of the Hudson River School showed the country's beauty and vitality.

Tonalism and Luminism movements invoked a spiritual serenity in landscapes, reflecting the ideas of westward expansion and Americans as chosen people. Artists expressed the serenity of America, which was embroiled in conflicts and searching for its place in the world. In a sense, they were capturing the fundamental ideals that founded the nation.

Painter John James Audubon (1785-1851) established a very different style and body of work that still managed to capture the myth of America. His goal as a painter was to accurately capture the majesty of the numerous American birds. While this may sound simplistic, he became famous in the United States and abroad. His birds managed to capture the majesty and youth of America. In addition to painting, Audubon practiced science. Audubon made the first American bird bands and used them to track and identify a group of Eastern Phoebes that returned annually to his neighbor's yard.

John James Audubon, c. 1850 (left), Passenger Pigeon by Audubon (right)

Romanticism, a famous literary style characterized by philosophical idealism, gave way to transcendentalism, one of the first American literary styles. Though it is sometimes mistaken for religion, transcendentalism is about interpreting relationships. Transcendentalist authors were trying to encapsulate the same mythology as visual artists of the period; they wanted to define what it meant to be an American and write about the spirit of America.

Famous transcendentalists are Ralph Waldo Emerson (1803-1882) and Henry David Thoreau (1817-1862). Emerson's essay *Self-Reliance* (1841) is still widely read and speaks to the inability of humans to obtain meaning from others. Emerson wrote that the truth had to come from within. Thoreau's best-known work is his essay, *Civil Disobedience* (1849).

In *Civil Disobedience*, Thoreau encompasses many of the same ideas that Emerson illuminated. His most well-known excerpt is his description of the night he spent in prison following his refusal to pay taxes to fund a war that he did not support. In the excerpt, Thoreau mocks the idea that a man whose conscience is clear could ever be "imprisoned." Like other transcendentalists, he valued the mental over the physical and felt that his actual "body" could never be touched.

Perhaps the premier artistic style to impact the early history of America was neoclassicism, characterized by a renewed interest in classical forms and ideas. It can be seen in stunning variety in America during the early 19th century.

Many of the political ideas from the Enlightenment had their roots in Greco-Roman culture. Epics, a literary form used by Greek and Roman poets, became popular and compared well with the slave narratives and westward expansionism of the day. Even the buildings that housed the government showed an obvious homage to the Greek and Roman ruins. One of the most noteworthy members of this movement was Thomas Jefferson, an accomplished architect, and a leading statesman.

Ralph Waldo Emerson (left) and Henry David Thoreau (right)

Jefferson wanted his admiration of the Roman Republic to be manifested, not only in the political institutions of the new nation but also visually in the nation's public buildings, to remind the citizens that they lived in a Republic. The White House uses the same column style as the Pantheon in Rome. Neoclassicism serves as an excellent metaphor for the early American people. They were attached to the past to remain connected to their ideas, yet they were prepared to change.

Technology and innovation

The Gilded Age produced many modern amenities that are appreciated today, including but not limited to the telephone, deliverable electricity, and photographic and motion picture technology.

Some of the most notable inventors of the period include:

- Nikola Tesla (1856-1943) invented the first motor that transformed alternating current (AC) electrical power into a usable mechanical force.

- Alexander Graham Bell invented the telephone in 1876, which revolutionized communication in America.

- Thomas Edison (1847-1931) produced the first record player or phonograph in 1877 and the light bulb in 1879, culminating his lifelong achievements with the establishment of the first direct current (D.C.) electric power station in Manhattan in September of 1882, which propelled electricity throughout businesses and homes in America.

Thomas Edison, c. 1930

Cultural and intellectual arguments of the Gilded Age

As the success of the Gilded Age continued, some argued that considering the wealthy class's success and status within the political and social systems, they should be required to support those less fortunate. Others argued that the current condition was as it was meant to be designed with a class structure in mind and predetermined social statuses, which would inevitably lead to the right people exercising power. Such division regarding social issues highlighted the tensions and polarization of the American public leading into the 20th century.

Leading intellectuals of the day debated the social formula necessary for creating a productive and sustainable America. One such person was Henry George (1839-1897), who held vocations in many areas, including but not limited to writing, politics, and economics.

Through his studies, George proposed a "single tax," which would be placed on land at the undeveloped price. This tax would fund the projects required of the U.S. government without the limiting effect of other taxes levied, such as income or agricultural taxes. George embodied economic and socialistic motives, arguing that by creating land as common property, the taxes levied against it would create the funding necessary to maintain the economic models.

Andrew Carnegie also shared this idea of required actions by those in economic and political positions of power regarding the protection of the lower social classes. In his famous essay, the *Gospel of Wealth* (1889), Carnegie argues that successful Gilded Age entrepreneurs can and are obligated to eliminate poverty in a capitalistic society. Through philanthropy, American society could be transformed to highlight the common and public good rather than the opportunistic landscape seen in cities. Others argued against the concept of social welfare, stating that the natural order of this period was determined by the social classes, with some destined to rule and manage. In contrast, others were meant to work and supply the factories.

Henry George, c. 1895

Social Darwinism, introduced in the 1870s, influenced many to believe evolution selected the fittest to rule. This theory regarding the right to influence the political landscape was expanded upon by some American elites of the period.

Theories of racial superiority were also hugely influential in the early years of the 20th century and were used by Nazi Germany as support for their campaign of racial cleansing. While the theory was not employed on this level in the United States, it was applied to the Native American populations, which were viewed by many as a lesser species of human compared to the Anglo-Americans. During this period, it was common to seek the affirmation of political or social ambitions through new forms of social science, such as Darwinism and racist theories.

While this period is characterized by conflicts over slavery, women's rights, and Native American rights, great strides were made in other forms of activism. In 1837, Horace Mann (1796-1859), often called the Father of the Common School, used his position as the secretary of the newly-created Massachusetts Board of Education to enact significant education reform. He started the Common School Movement to ensure that all children would have a primary education at the state's expense.

Mann believed that society could only flourish when all citizens were literate and had a general understanding of civics. He argued that it was only with an educated public that a democracy, dependent upon the will of that public, could reach its fullest potential. Mann created teacher training schools, called normal schools, so that professionals would educate children. He also recruited and trained women for what was, at the time, an all-male vocation.

Horace Mann, c. 1858

New culture of the Gilded Age

Urbanization, which began during the Gilded Age, caused many to make social and economic transitions and inspired concern in those who worked to maintain the traditional customs with which they were comfortable. Some of the challenges faced during this period included the decline in popular religion, most notably in Protestantism, which caused many to fear that the American public was becoming immoral.

In addition to intellectual debates, many spiritual leaders of this period were concerned with the transition in popular religion seen in America. As factory workers adapted to their urban lives, many became less interested in religion or membership in church organizations. While many were concerned with such a trend's spiritual and social ramifications, others saw the financial concerns associated with a declining membership base. However, the working class, particularly the factory workers, saw no need to attend church, considering their unprecedented work hours.

In response to such changes, the Social Gospel grew and tried to adapt the teachings of the Bible to contemporary issues. Many church leaders took up social causes as well. One of the most notable examples was Washington Gladden's (1836-1918) support of the right to strike and his fight against child labor.

In hopes of addressing urban issues, churches created organizations such as the Young Men's Christian Association and the Young Women's Christian Association, which aimed to revitalize religion among the younger populations. Some have labeled such transitions as the Third Great Awakening of religion in America, which was a direct result of the urbanization of the period.

The intellectual movements of the period highlighted a new way of thinking developed during the Gilded Age (1870s to about 1900) but also demonstrated the shortcomings of the period, such as racial and ethnic discrimination and gender and social inequality. The period's literature speaks to these concerns and gives insight into the common perceptions of racism and industry following the end of the Civil War.

Some see the Gilded Age as an American Renaissance, as the public experienced new art forms, literature, and living standards. In a wealthy American home of the period, one could expect to find the latest tapestries and stained-glass lighting from Louis Comfort Tiffany, a famous company of the period. Americans sought new types of literature, most notably from Mark Twain (1835-1910), including *Tom Sawyer* (1876) and *Adventures of Huckleberry Finn* (1885).

Mark Twain, c. 1900

Famous poets of the period included Walt Whitman and Emily Dickinson. Painting blossomed during the Gilded Age too, and many were engrossed in the paintings of Winslow Homer, who gained fame after his publications in *Harper's Weekly*. The arts of the period following the Civil War gave people hope, which was generally in short supply. The culture of this period was a bonus to the industrial and manufacturing initiatives of big business.

Intellectual and cultural history – summary of the period

While Americans celebrated their nation's progress toward a unified new national culture that blended Old World forms with New World ideas, groups of the nation's inhabitants developed distinctive cultures.

Groups of American Indians, women, and religious followers developed cultures reflecting their interests and experiences, as did regional groups and an emerging urban middle class. Enslaved and free African Americans, isolated at the bottom of the social hierarchy, created communities and strategies to protect their dignity and family structures, even as some launched abolitionist and reform movements aimed at changing their status.

The Second Great Awakening, liberal social ideas from abroad, and romantic beliefs in human perfectibility fostered the rise of voluntary organizations to promote religious and secular reforms, including abolition and women's rights. A new national culture emerged, with Americans creating art, architecture, and literature that combined European forms with local and regional cultural sensibilities.

"The Gilded Age" witnessed new cultural and intellectual movements in tandem with political debates over economic and social policies. New cultural and intellectual movements buttressed and challenged the social order of the Gilded Age. Cultural and intellectual arguments justified the success of those at the top of the socioeconomic structure as both appropriate and inevitable, even as some leaders argued that the wealthy had some obligation to help the less fortunate.

Relationship matrix

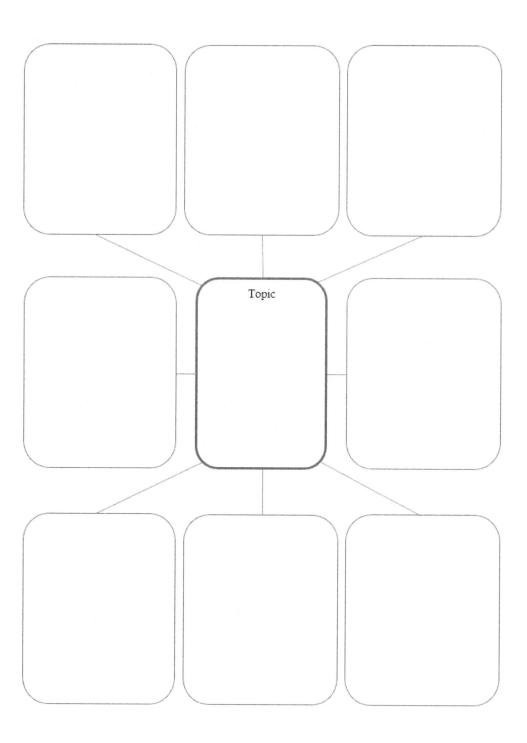

Notes for active learning

Notes for active learning

PERIOD 3

1899 to Present

Political History: 1899 to Present

Immigration policies

Beginning in the late 1890s and continuing into the 1920s, America experienced a great influx of immigrants, met with opposition by many native-born Americans. Many Americans believed that this massive influx would change or tarnish the image of America, both internally and abroad. The government administrations of the period respected the sentiment by using immigration quotas; one notable example is the *Emergency Quota Act* of 1921.

The *Emergency Quota Act* limited the entrance of migrants of certain nationalities to only 3 percent of that nationality's current representation per the 1910 census. This significantly limited the number of new immigrants accepted at Ellis Island, New York. Given the census material provided, it became evident that the immigration of people from Asia and eastern and southern Europe would be drastically limited in the following years.

Supplementing this bill was the *Johnson-Reed Immigration Act* of 1924, which extended and expanded immigration quotas leading into and following World War II. While many in government supported the anti-immigration sentiment sweeping across the United States, one notable Congressman spoke out against the bill. Robert H. Clancy, who represented various nationalities in Detroit, labeled it "un-American" and argued that Jewish, Polish, and Italian immigrants were just as American as anyone. These policies were in place until World War II, setting the tone for immigration reforms in the 1960s.

Another situation that intensified the xenophobia seen in America came from the Zimmerman Telegram in 1917, which caused many Americans to fear an assault by German and Mexican forces. Such concerns convinced many Americans that the country should look inward to solve problems rather than welcome outside influences through immigration, focused on the message of isolationism following the atrocities of World War I.

The exception to these anti-immigration policies was seen in Mexico, where the U.S. government encouraged thousands of Mexicans to migrate seasonally to maintain agricultural production during periods when the United States lacked an adequate workforce. This was most typical during World War I (July 28, 1914, to November 11, 1918) and World War II (September 1, 1939, to September 2, 1945).

While the United States was against immigration from Europe and East Asia to meet its labor needs, it found no issue with the continued influx of unskilled laborers from Latin America, specifically Mexico. This highlighted contradictions within U.S. foreign policy, causing many to wonder why the border remained virtually open to Mexico and other countries in the Western Hemisphere.

This need for unskilled laborers in agricultural production was satisfied as the Mexican Revolution intensified between 1910 and 1920, resulting in a mass exodus of refugees north into the United States from all parts of war-torn Mexico. Close to 900,000 Mexican Americans, many of whom were sick and in poverty, immigrated to the United States between 1910 and 1920, quickly filling the void in the American workforce.

These policies also highlight the rivalry between European countries and the United States leading into and following World War I. The United States exercised hegemony within the Western Hemisphere and believed it could do so by influencing political and economic policies in Latin America and North America. By allowing the influx of Mexican American immigrants, the U.S. government believed it could hold some influence in later situations of the region. Such agreements created instability and uncertainty along the U.S.-Mexico border, as well as soured relationships between the United States and Native Americans as westward expansion continued.

Restrictions on civil liberties

As with other periods of conflict, the civil liberties of Americans were sacrificed during World War I (July 28, 1914, to November 11, 1918) and during World War II (September 1, 1939, to September 2, 1945) to maintain the national security of the country. These restrictions most notably influenced freedom of speech, causing many Americans— both native-born and immigrants—to fear the legal and judicial actions of the American government. One example comes from the Espionage and Sedition Acts of 1917 and 1918.

The *Espionage Act* prohibited any negative conversation regarding the outcome of U.S. foreign policy in the war, as well as about military forces or the American flag. Those guilty of speaking against the government during a war could be fined up to $10,000 or sentenced to twenty years. The *Sedition Act* greatly impacted immigrants, as anyone who opposed engagement in World War I, the military draft, or the newly imposed limitations on the freedom of speech were susceptible to legal action taken against them, including but not limited to fines and deportation.

American Socialist Party Logo

Another implication of the Espionage and Sedition Acts was limiting newspaper mailing privileges of publications considered a concern by the U.S. government. These groups included German-language newspapers, German American newspapers, pacifist publications, and publications owned by the Industrial Workers of the World or the American Socialist Party. Almost seventy-five newspapers lost their operating privileges due to the Espionage and Sedition Acts.

Though the *Espionage Act* initially came under fire as unconstitutional, the Supreme Court inevitably supported the law as necessary during times of conflict, ruling that the government has the authority to punish anyone who would create a clear and present danger. Close to 1,000 immigrants were tried and convicted of sedition. Many immigrants were deported, but none were convicted of spying or sabotage.

The lasting implications of the Espionage and Sedition Acts are varied; the *Sedition Act* was removed shortly after the war's end but was adamantly contested while in practice. The *Espionage Act* remained in action through the end of World War I, the Red Scare in 1919, World War II, and the Cold War.

Following the end of World War I (November 11, 1918), America entered a period of racial and political oppression. A common practice during this period included vigilante justice by the citizenry and infringement of civil liberties. One example comes from the summer of 1919, referred to as "the Red Summer" due to the vicious racial attacks on and murders of African Americans. Though the National Association for the Advancement of Colored People (NAACP) requested an investigation by Democratic President Wilson (1856-1924; 1913-1921), little was accomplished at the local and federal levels.

The Red Scare from 1919 to 1920 resulted from fear regarding the spread of Bolshevism in the United States following World War I. The goal of the Red Scare policies was to expose and remove radicals and socialists from the U.S. government. The Palmer Raids occurred between 1918 and 1921, spearheaded by Democratic Attorney General A. Mitchell Palmer (1872-1936). The Red Scare raids produced little evidence of wrongdoing or malevolent intent against the United States but resulted in extensive deportations.

Eventually, the public lost support for Palmer and his raids, questioning their constitutionality. Other notable events during the Red Scare include the trial and execution of Nicola Sacco and Bartolomeo Vanzetti. Italian immigrants and anarchists were accused of murdering a guard and paymaster of a shoe factory; the trial and appeal continued for seven years. The proceedings were met with considerable protest by many in the United States. In August of 1927, both men were executed, arguably because of their immigrant background.

Protest to save Sacco and Vanzetti, c. 1927

Global influence

Under President William Taft, the United States pursued a foreign policy agenda influenced by the interventionist mindset, which garnered both short-term alliances and long-term resentments. By pursuing dollar diplomacy, Taft, a staunch interventionist, propelled the United States to the forefront of influence in the economic, political, and military sectors.

However, President Wilson, an anti-imperialist, worked from a position of humanitarian diplomacy and sought to expand human rights and create a stable and lasting peace. The intent of both men to influence the international system by different means highlights the desire for American influence within the newly emerging international system.

The role of the United States in the global system drastically changed in the years following World War I and leading into World War II. Unlike most world powers, the United States experienced minimal destruction in the Great War. The United States could profit from the arms and resources sold during the war. This profit, coupled with a drastic increase in economic production and manufacturing, allowed the United States to influence international affairs directly and indirectly in both the Western and Eastern Hemispheres.

The Allies conquered the Axis powers (Germany, Italy, and Japan) through political posturing, military cooperation, and technological advancements. Such examples include the Manhattan Project, investment and research into ballistic missiles and space technology, and the introduction of sonar technology.

The Atlantic Conference & Charter in 1941 was a culmination of British and American war aims, reinforcing the political alliances necessary to combat and defeat Nazi Germany and its Axis powers. Also discussed were the goals of the Allies in postwar Europe, which determined the political landscape and U.S. hegemony leading into the Cold War era.

Advancements in sonar and radar technology allowed military leaders to plan and carry out surprise attacks against their enemies, strategies that would have severe implications for the United States and Japan; evidence of this was seen in the December 7, 1941, Pearl Harbor attacks. This type of long-range radar navigation (also called LORAN), predated today's GPS, clearly shows the advancement of warfare technology.

The introduction of plastics had a significant impact on the American war effort, allowing for the manufacturing of incendiary bombs, including napalm, flamethrowers, and smoke screens. The factories that produced these materials had formerly been used for domestic consumer production. Following the domestic mobilization program pursued in the United States, these factories produced materials for the war effort. Such materials were transformative in the conflict and set the stage for future conflicts, as seen in the Korean (1950-1953) and Vietnam (1954-1975) Wars.

Medical advancements allowed the U.S. many advantages. Service people could fly at higher elevations safely, using superior technology. Penicillin (discovered by Alexander

Fleming in 1928) and pesticides like DDT, which killed the mosquitos transmitting malaria and fought venereal and tropical diseases, were crucial for a victorious U.S. campaign in the tropical South Pacific. Scientific feats, such as blood transfusions and supplemental oxygen, caused innovations in the medical sector following the end of World War II.

Several types of military cooperation were seen throughout World War II. One notable example is the North African offensive undertaken by U.S. and British forces. This offensive eventually led to the capture of the *Desert Fox*, General Erwin Rommel (1891-1944), and the surrender at El Alamein. This was a decisive blow for the German forces and was seen by some as a turning point in the war.

General Leslie Groves (left), military head of the Manhattan Project,
with Professor Robert Oppenheimer (right)

The most notable technological advancement of World War II was the atomic bomb, which was the culmination of the Manhattan Project. At the project's inception, two cities were chosen—Oak Ridge, Tennessee, and Hanford, Washington—to cultivate different processes for bomb-making: one based on uranium and the other on plutonium. The program was designed to guarantee that the United States would be the first country able to create an atomic bomb successfully. This type of efficiency and speed was necessary as Nazi Germany, Japan, and the Soviet Union were competing in the nuclear armament race.

With the help of European scientists, America was able to use both a plutonium bomb in Nagasaki and a uranium bomb in Hiroshima, effectively ending World War II in the Pacific. This technology had unimaginable implications in the years following World War II, most notably in the Cold War and the arms race undertaken by the United States and the Soviet Union (which ended on December 25, 1991).

Anti-communism policies

During this period, the most significant concern of many Americans was the rapid spread of the Soviet Union and its communist ideology. To prevent the infiltration of communism in America, many argued that staunch regulations, legislation, and policies should be in place to prevent such a political and social crisis, as communism stood against everything valued by Americans.

A second Red Scare dominated the American public during the late 1940s and early 1950s. In response, Democratic President Harry S. Truman (1884-1972; 1945-1953) enacted some of the first anti-communist policies in the United States. Executive Order 9835, issued in 1947, allowed the attorney general to list membership in fascist, communist, and subversive organizations as grounds for dismissal from work. Many academic institutions, such as Harvard and Columbia, were targeted by the government for supporting communist sympathizers or discussing the political and social attributes of communist society. Between 1947 and 1953, close to 5 million workers were questioned and investigated by the federal government using the Federal Loyalty Program, resulting in the termination of approximately 3,000 workers and the resignation of nearly 12,000 more.

Such policies would eventually bring about the installation of the House Un-American Activities Committee (HUAC) and the *Internal Security Act* (1950), all of which actively sought to label and expel those working against America on American soil. By 1954, the American public—as well as those in the Senate and the Republican Eisenhower administration (1953-1961)—had grown tired of right-wing Senator Joseph McCarthy (1947-1957) and his exaggerated claims of communist infiltration within the U.S. government. Though McCarthy himself lost the support of the American public, the sentiment of anti-communism and anti-subversive policies continued for many years and is arguably perceived as his legacy following his death in 1957.

President Dwight D. Eisenhower, 1953 – 1961

The implications for such domestic policies were far-reaching, leaving the American public weary of federal investigations. Many Americans were wrongfully accused of supporting subversive movements or communism itself, which brought into question the use of the federal government's power against its population.

As American Presidents exerted unprecedented executive power, the American people began to question specific policies and legislation, causing an influx of both criticism and support for the executive branch and its newly acquired authority.

One of the earliest examples of executive authority during this period comes from President Truman, who was able to craft the rebuilding of Western Europe and financing states threatened by communism through unprecedented legislation. Such actions would mold the international system in postwar Europe, and the actions of one man allowed the United States to ascend into its position of hegemony.

Growing executive power

Another example of new executive authority came from infrastructure development using the *Federal Highway Act* of 1956, which granted President Eisenhower (1890-1969; 1953-1961) the ability to build and develop a sizeable federal highway system, a crucial component for commerce in continental America.

To finance the project, Congress approved a rise in gas taxes and instituted highway and toll taxes for some roads; the federal government financed nearly 90 percent of the project. Some argue that this legislation is the most extensive domestic success of the Eisenhower administration. Critics insist that the excessive force used to produce these highways decimated arming lands and isolated parts of the country.

The most notable and far-reaching example of executive authority during this period comes from the Gulf of Tonkin Resolution (1964), which effectively gave the executive branch the authority and means to pursue a total war against the Northern Vietnamese. Many argued that the escalation of the Vietnam War was due to the reactive policies of the Johnson administration. These policies allowed the conflict to be perpetuated into a chaotic state of total war. Later, Presidents such as Nixon (1913-1994; 1969 to August 8, 1974) would cite the resolution when defending military offensives (e.g., Cambodia in 1970).

The American sentiment surrounding expanded executive powers was hot and cold; at certain times, the public called upon the federal government to protect their interests and promote social programs. During times of conflict or dissatisfaction, the public turned away from these expansive powers. Long-term implications for such political events and contexts would be seen in contemporary times as the United States entered the 2003 Iraq War, where the American public again called into question the absolute authority of the executive branch.

Military-industrial complex and nuclear arsenal

As Americans attempted to assimilate into the Cold War period, it became clear that the use of nuclear weapons was a concern for almost all Americans and caused many to question the use and maintenance of a vast nuclear arsenal. Some Americans saw this arsenal as protection against the threat of the Soviet Union and its nuclear arsenal; others believed that nuclear war was imminent and built bomb shelters in their backyards.

The "military-industrial complex" was a term used before the Cold War era by those in World War I and II to describe war profiteering. The term gained prominence during the farewell speech given by President Dwight D. Eisenhower in 1961. This sentiment was a culmination of the arms races and struggles seen during the Cold War by those living in the United States and the Soviet Union.

While Republican President Eisenhower believed a degree of the military-industrial complex was necessary to deter the use of nuclear weapons by the Soviet Union, the increased military spending during his presidency also concerned him because it limited his ability to reduce the tax levels below those of Democratic Presidents Roosevelt and Truman.

President Eisenhower saw the expansion of ideas such as the military-industrial complex as an expansion of federal power, which he did not necessarily support. Like other conservatives, President Eisenhower sought to limit the federal government's authority in most matters and believed that state and local representation (i.e., state and county governments) could address most American issues. While many supported this concept of the expansion of federal power, others sought to illustrate the negatives of the military-industrial complex, arguing that it would significantly alter the source of power within the United States by placing it in the hands of a few elites. Others argued it was a liberal policy that allowed the overspending of the national security budget while hampering the arms-reduction efforts that were fiercely pursued considering the period and nuclear threats.

As Americans tried to adjust to the Cold War's nuclear scares and their nuclear past in Hiroshima and Nagasaki, many began to look to the federal government to limit the threat to national security. Some demanded a more aggressive foreign policy against the Soviet Union, and others sought to question the role of the President in foreign and military affairs. Such concerns were highlighted in the 1960s.

Democratic President Lyndon B. Johnson (1908-1973; 1963-1969) was given rights by Congress via the Gulf of Tonkin Resolution (1964) to take whatever actions he deemed appropriate against the North Vietnamese attacks to maintain the peace and security of Southeast Asia. These types of decisions by the federal government would perpetuate the conversation regarding the President's role in contemporary conflicts and politics. This legislation had a far-reaching influence, as it was the legal foundation from which Democratic Presidents John F Kennedy, Lyndon B. Johnson, and Republican Richard Milhous Nixon would launch their campaigns in the Vietnam War (1954-1975).

Civil rights movement

Americans moved into the 1960s with a new sense of stability and prestige, and the successes of the previous decade seemed to spur on new social movements, most notably the civil rights movement and the counterculture movement, which dominated domestic politics during the 1960s. During this period, the United States continued to expand its influence within the international system as a constant adversary to communism, which was in line with how many Americans believed foreign policy should be handled.

To address the failed system of segregation, the United States finally began to adopt legislation and policies that would eventually bring equality to African Americans. To address the social concerns of the counterculture, the federal government attempted to expand rights in the workplace, ending segregated hiring practices and limiting gender discrimination practices. However, many struggles were yet to come, and many would march, protest, and sit-in before any real action was taken.

Americans looked to the federal government for financial assurances and protection of their freedoms. In 1965, President Lyndon B. Johnson issued an executive order requiring all federal contractors to use affirmative action in hiring, eliminating workplace discrimination for minorities and women. Many large companies that held government contracts were now required to hire more minorities and women.

President Johnson, who supported the civil rights movement, attempted to recognize the concerns of the African American population by appointing Thurgood Marshall (1908-1993; 1967-1991) as an Associate Justice to the Supreme Court; Marshall was the first African American to hold this position.

U.S. Supreme Court Justice, Thurgood Marshall, c. 1991

The actions of the 1960s set in motion the future social expectations of the 20th and 21st centuries. After this decade, many Americans concluded that everyone should have an equal voice in the democratic principles of the United States, minorities and women included. Social demonstrations became an avenue many Americans accessed to have their grievances heard and addressed, perpetuating the idea that the United States is a land of freedom and opportunity for all.

Social programs to address poverty and inequality

Under President Lyndon B. Johnson, the United States experienced the most massive expansion of domestic social programs since President Franklin D. Roosevelt. He advanced the "Great Society" – a set of policy initiatives to combat poverty and political and social inequalities determined by race and gender. President Johnson's firm stance against communism caused many Americans to view the presidency as a continuation of the ideas put forth by President John F. Kennedy (1917 - November 22, 1963).

In March 1964, President Johnson wrote to Congress, calling for the end of poverty in America, which he hoped to accomplish through social programs comparable to the reforms of the New Deal. To address poverty in rural America, President Johnson initially proposed a $962 million aid package; however, by 1966, this package mushroomed to close to $3 billion. President Johnson also sought to create jobs using social programs to bolster aid and federal support to educational services, the civil rights movement, and people experiencing poverty. This followed in the footsteps of President Kennedy, who founded the Volunteer in Service to America (VISTA) program, which provided volunteer services to rural and underprivileged areas across the United States.

President Lyndon B. Johnson

President Johnson also embraced the civil rights movement and continued to show presidential support for the equality of African Americans across the country. By asking Congress to continue President Kennedy's legacy using civil rights legislation, President Johnson formed and enacted the most substantial civil rights reforms since the Reconstruction era. In 1965, he heralded the *Voting Rights Act* as monumental legislation.

Continued expansion of social programs and oversight by President Johnson resulted in forming the Department of Housing and Urban Development, initiating Medicare and Medicaid. Implementing a Head Start program also allowed preschool students to be better prepared in the educational system. Other notable policies of the Great Society included conservation efforts emerging throughout the country, the creation of the food stamps system, and the protection of the American public as consumers.

President Johnson differed from his predecessor, Kennedy, on foreign affairs such as involvement in the Vietnam War and the expulsion of communism at any price. During this period, Johnson cautiously expanded the United States' role in the conflict by signing secret negotiations and policies that allowed American military forces to take covert actions against the North Vietnamese. These policies expanded to limited bombing raids on Northern Vietnam, and following the passage of the Gulf of Tonkin Resolution; President Johnson led the United States into a full-scale war against the North Vietnamese and communism.

Rise of conservatism

During the postwar years, many liberal Presidents, most notably Presidents Kennedy and Johnson, were able to bolster domestic affairs while struggling to maintain foreign affairs. Due to this shortfall in global politics, many in the government, most notably conservatives, questioned the soft policies toward communism and domestic spending on social programs. This revitalized the conservative movements in the American public and government.

Though the conservatives had been out of favor in Washington for several years, the failures of the liberal government in the 1970s meant that people were more open to the conservative messages of smaller government and social conservatism. When Republican Ronald Reagan (1911-2004; 1981-1989) beat Democrat Jimmy Carter (1977-1981) in 1980, he was well-liked for his optimism and his effectiveness as a spokesman for the government, which earned him the moniker "The Great Communicator." People supported President Reagan as they rallied around their beliefs. This set the stage for a period of conservative successes, a trend continued by his successor, George H. W. Bush (1924-2018; 1989-1993).

Still, the conservative movement's success was mitigated by several government programs implemented in reaction to social issues. Programs like Social Security and governmental healthcare were too deeply entrenched in the government to allow for genuine change. Similarly, any attempts to change aspects of these programs were often met with contention from the public.

Economic and political debates

As the economic and political atmosphere changed, the policies for their regulation changed. Public debates characterized the end of the 20th century as Americans attempted to determine the direction American foreign and domestic policies should take. Globalization legislation, like the North American Free Trade Agreement (NAFTA), characterized international relations, while domestic policy debates focused on welfare policies.

NAFTA was designed as a contract between the United States, Mexico, and Canada. The idea was to phase out the tariffs and trade regulations between these three powers to achieve economic growth in all three nations. Since one-third of all imports and exports were headed from or to these two countries, the agreement had great promise for the American economy, though experts disagree on the outcome.

All three countries did experience economic growth. That growth could have been coincidental and would have occurred without the new agreement. A similar argument can be made for many of the harms of NAFTA. While NAFTA made it easier for businesses to move to Mexico, it did not impact movement to Asia as businesses were still located there.

President Bill Clinton signing NAFTA (1993)

Domestically, the debate focused instead on social welfare programs like health care. The primary concern with programs like Medicare, Medicaid, and the new Obamacare (April 23, 2010) is that these programs are hard to implement and sustain. Some have gone so far as to deem them unconstitutional. Many people fear that nationalized healthcare is a step towards socialism. Problems with socialized medicine are seen in some countries, and people were concerned with what was happening in America as these programs continued to expand.

A common problem in socialist countries is the wait time to see a doctor, as the number of physicians decreases due to a lack of financial incentives; however, many view this as an opportunity to perfect methods and encourage innovation in medicine. Others argue that any program that allows citizens to opt out of the national plan in favor of a private plan cannot be deemed socialist.

Constitutionality was a concern raised by Obamacare taxes. The *Affordable Care Act* (2010) requires all citizens to have health insurance and taxes them with a fine if they do not comply. Proponents of the Act claim that Congress can impose taxes and carry out programs for the wellness and betterment of the American people. Opponents of the Act remind Congress that they are not allowed to force individuals to buy products they do not want from private companies.

Similarly, the questions regarding Social Security reform do not question if changes need to be made, but what changes need to be made and when. Social Security is on the precipice of failure. Some believe this is because of the population increase, while others see mismanagement as the problem. The baby boomer generation is approaching the Social Security retirement age. It is projected that the Social Security system will be unable to fund all claims by 2033, as the government will not collect enough taxes to fund the payouts, and the trust funds held in reserve for crisis years will be depleted.

Thus, the government has four options: increase income through taxes, reduce spending in other areas, divert the funds to Social Security, borrow the money from another source, or eliminate the Social Security program. The impending deadline for changes worries many economists and only 50 percent of the American public has indicated that they have faith they will receive payouts when they retire. Others say small changes over some years will fix the problem and create continued solvency.

Natural resources and environmental concerns

The world governments consume an amazing amount of oil and gasoline every year. Fossil fuels allow for transportation and provide electricity and the means to produce materials like rubber and plastic. The amounts of oil deposits on Earth are finite; they cannot be replaced once used. This, among other impacts, has caused many to question the United States' consumption of fossil fuels.

Availability is a primary concern. While energy demands increase, the amount of oil does not. Additionally, the ability to refine and produce usable oil is also limited. Infrastructure limits the capacity and amount of a product that can be produced at any given time. Many nations have started to express concerns over their energy stores and are stockpiling reserves in the event of natural disasters or political events like the 1970s embargo.

The United States has several refineries and plans for the Keystone Pipeline, an oil pipeline from Alberta, Canada, to refineries in Texas and Illinois. Many people supported these measures because they would return the means of production to the Americans and drastically decrease the dependence on Middle Eastern oil. This is a concern, especially when one considers that the sale of oil to the United States and other Western powers may be funding anti-American terrorist organizations. Opponents of this self-sufficiency plan claim that the environmental impact would be too severe.

Environmentalism is another question when analyzing fossil fuel usage, particularly climate change. Every year, the climate changes minutely, but over the last century, the climate's total change has been 1.4 degrees Fahrenheit. Many environmental groups are concerned that global temperatures may continue to rise and that most of this change comes from greenhouse gases, like carbon dioxide, released into the air when fossil fuels (e.g., gasoline) are burned.

These gasses function like a greenhouse around the Earth, thus giving them their name. They trap warmth by absorbing the sun's rays and allowing less radiation to leave the atmosphere. This makes the Earth slowly warm. Because of these adverse effects, many forms of alternative energy are attempting to achieve saturation in the same way fossil fuels have.

The issue with alternative energies is that they are dependent on uncontrollable factors. Wind energy only works in places with enough wind to be harnessed. Solar power only works during the day, and while it can be stored in battery packs, these batteries are often more harmful than the original fossil fuels would have been. Until a sustainable form of energy is created that allows the ease of use and low cost of gasoline and oil, it is unlikely that any real change will occur.

Wind farm in Power County, Idaho

While the United States could not answer the energy crisis alone, the United Nations worked to solve many of the world's energy concerns through collaboration. The United Nations created its United Nations Framework Convention on Climate Change (UNFCCC) in 1992 to affect real change. The UNFCCC worked for several years, developing what they felt were achievable goals and standards for countries and their environmental impacts.

The piece of legislation that they put forward was the Kyoto Protocol because it was ratified in Kyoto, Japan, in December 1997. Fifty-five countries agreed to the Protocol, which was considered enough for ratification. Further meetings among the UN delegates better defined the goals and standards of the Kyoto Protocol. In 2001, the United States refused to participate, claiming no interest in the Protocol. Since then, many other countries have ratified it, and in 2007, 191 countries signed the Protocol.

The goal of the Kyoto Protocol was to stabilize the amount of greenhouse gas in the atmosphere to mitigate the gas and stop global warming. There are some legally binding practices. All member nations were asked to submit emissions status reports periodically and attempt real change within their nation by promoting climate-conscious technology and educating the public about emissions and prevention. The goal was to reduce emissions, but only industrialized nations were asked to meet any commitment.

Developed nations like the United States and most European nations were asked to reduce their emissions to pre-1990 levels. These nations were also asked to share any technology they might develop to aid these efforts with developing nations. Developing nations are nations that are still industrializing. Industrializing is an essential process in the economic growth of a country, and it was considered impractical for industrializing nations to conform to the same policies as industrialized nations.

Therefore, their agreement to reduce emission levels was voluntary. The Kyoto Protocol implemented three innovative programs to help industrialized countries meet their goals: the clean development mechanism, joint implementation, and emissions trading.

While many nations believe the United Nations is progressing in the right direction with climate change, others have expressed concerns. In 2011, Canada left the group, claiming that while they valued the efforts and goals of the Protocols, there was no point in remaining a member, considering that the world's largest emissions producers (China and America) had not signed the agreement.

As of 2023, China led the world in greenhouse gas emissions, producing 27% of global carbon dioxide (CO_2) and 33% of worldwide emissions. The United States generates emissions of 12%, followed by India and the EU at 7% each. This meant that even if every nation were to reduce emissions, there would be almost 45 percent of emissions that could not be changed. The Kyoto Protocol was extended into 2020, but the United States has not become a signatory to the Treaty.

Political history – summary of the period

The global ramifications of World War I and wartime patriotism and xenophobia, combined with social tensions created by increased international migration, resulted in legislation restricting immigration from Asia and southern and eastern Europe. Several acts of Congress established highly restrictive immigration quotas. At the same time, national policies continued to permit unrestricted immigration from nations in the Western Hemisphere, especially Mexico, to guarantee an inexpensive labor supply.

World War I created a repressive atmosphere for civil liberties, resulting in official restrictions on freedom of speech. As labor strikes and racial strife disrupted society, the immediate postwar period witnessed the first "Red Scare," which legitimized attacks on radicals and immigrants. Global conflicts over resources, territories, and ideologies renewed debates over the nation's values and role while propelling the United States into a dominant international military, political, cultural, and economic position.

The United States and its allies achieved victory over the Axis powers in World War II through a combination of factors, including allied political and military cooperation, industrial production, technological and scientific advances, and widespread commitment to advancing democratic ideals. Americans debated policies and methods designed to root out communists within the United States, even as both parties tended to support the broader Cold War strategy of containing communism.

Cold War policies led to continued public debates over the power of the federal government, acceptable means for pursuing international and domestic goals, and the proper balance between liberty and order. Americans debated the merits of a massive nuclear arsenal, the "military-industrial complex," and the appropriate power of the executive branch in conducting foreign and military policy.

Liberalism, based on anti-communism abroad and a firm belief in the efficacy of governmental and primarily federal power to achieve social goals at home, reached its apex in the mid-1960s. These generated a variety of political and cultural responses. Liberalism reached its zenith with Lyndon Johnson's Great Society efforts to use federal power to end racial discrimination, eliminate poverty, and address other social issues while attacking communism abroad.

Conservatives achieved some political and policy goals. The enduring popularity and institutional strength of some government programs and public support for the cultural trends of recent decades limited their success. Policy debates intensified over free trade agreements, the size and scope of the government's social safety net, and calls to reform the U.S. financial system. Conflict in the Middle East and concerns about climate change led to debates over U.S. dependence on fossil fuels and the impact of economic consumption on the environment.

Notes for active learning

The Great Depression

The economic uncertainties of the late 19th century and early 20th centuries were a precursor to the economic collapse of the Great Depression (August 1929 to March 1933). Many who engaged in the markets and economic sector experienced periods of depression and crisis leading up to the 1930s. One such example came in 1893 when the United States experienced a considerable economic depression and was only stabilized following drastic intervention by financial giant J. P. Morgan.

In 1907, J. P. Morgan was again called upon to stabilize a failed attempt at Wall Street speculation. At this point, the conservative school of thought and powerful "money trusts" dominated big eastern cities and adamantly opposed the progressive movement. Some Americans began supporting progressive ideas and questioning the lack of government supervision in the stock market and banking sectors, with some calling for a central banking system.

These bouts of instability would continue, eventually leading to the Great Depression. By the 1930s, banking and industrial magnates such as J. P. Morgan could not buy out the American economy as they had previously done. This inability left many people to place their support, criticism, and expectations with the federal government rather than the private businesses that previously dominated the markets.

This was a pivotal moment for Americans' financial and economic mindset and would be transformative in the years following the Depression. Some economic reforms drastically influenced banking following the Great Depression and moving into the later years of the 20th century. They arguably molded the financial mindset of many Americans today concerning regulations and oversight. Notable among these policies was the *Regulatory Bank Act* (1933), signed by Democratic President Franklin Roosevelt (1882-1945; 1933-1945).

The economic instability of the early 20th century also highlighted the political polarization between progressives and conservatives, a battle that would continue into the late 1930s and beyond. This series of events also highlights how often the United States toed the line of economic collapse before finally faltering in the Great Depression.

The New Deal

Democratic President Franklin Delano Roosevelt pursued a domestic agenda that placed social programs ahead of a balanced or limited federal budget, especially during the Great Depression. To bring stability to the economy, Roosevelt's first act as President was to place the banks on a four-day holiday. After the banking sector stabilized, his next task was to put people back to work. His first request of Congress in 1933 was the passage of the *Unemployment Relief Act*, which created the *Civilian Conservation Corps* (CCC).

Civilian Conservation Corps was responsible for employing, housing, and feeding young men who could support their families from their earnings in the program. Congress passed the *Federal Emergency Relief Act* (FERA) in 1933 to support families and the unemployed, funding state works and welfare programs with an additional $3 billion. Farmers and homeowners received aid through the *Agricultural Adjustment Act* (1933) and *Home Owners' Loan Corporation* (HOLC), which delayed foreclosures and repossession of farms.

President Franklin Delano Roosevelt

Whether or not New Deal policies mitigated the Great Depression is a subject of continuing debate. The prevailing assumption among historians has always been that these interventionist policies were a success. Recently, some historians have argued that these policies forestalled a natural return to full employment by artificially inflating wages and prices. World War II ended the depression with the immense production of war goods.

Franklin Roosevelt promoted the Tennessee Valley Authority (TVA) to supplement these programs, which became a model for future mandated projects. He also promoted the Federal Housing Administration (FHA) and the National Recovery Administration (NRA), which addressed both short- and long-term concerns stemming from the economic crisis. At the same time, these policies supported the average American citizen by creating a minimum wage and maximum work hours, enhancing Roosevelt's appeal to more voters.

Roosevelt's most notable New Deal policy was the creation of the Works Progress Administration (WPA), which employed nearly 8.5 million people and created jobs through various projects, including building bridges, public buildings, parks, roads, and airports. Additionally, subgroups of the WPA, such as the Professional Projects Division, employed women and men in federal art, theater, music, and writers' projects.

The implications of the New Deal policies are vast and transformative; some argue that without these social reforms, the U.S. economy may not have emerged as strongly following World War II. This, in turn, would have questioned the dominant role it played in international affairs during the postwar and Cold War eras. New Deal programs, such as the *Federal Deposit Insurance Corporation* (FDIC), *Securities Exchange Commission* (SEC), and the *Social Securities Act*, set expectations of government-sponsored assistance programs.

These policies also transitioned the voting demographics of the Civil War Era. Minority groups who had previously voted Republican due to President Abraham Lincoln now saw themselves more appropriately represented by the Democratic Party. This sentiment evolved and transitioned in the years following the New Deal.

Populist movement

The farmers and agrarian populations faced difficult times leading into and during the Great Depression; many could not pay the rents or mortgages maintained by East Coast financiers, leaving them hopelessly indebted to the banking sector following the stock market's collapse. In hopes of having their concerns managed, many farmers joined the Populist movement, which originated in the 1890s due to a revolt led by farmers against Democrats and Republicans who had previously ignored these growing concerns.

The rural Populist movement had its roots in the Grange movement, which published a list of demands and grievances called the "Farmers' Platform" in 1857, which was directly influenced by the work of Karl Marx (1818-1883). Some of their grievances centered on the lending practices of East Coast banks, resentment towards the emergence of railroad monopolies, and the technological transition taking place because of industrial and urbanization booms.

In addition to the Populists, union movements propelled workers' rights and representation to the forefront of domestic politics. The American Federation of Labor (AFL), a notable labor union organization of the period, was concerned with its members' economic prosperity and advancement. Immigrant cigar maker Samuel Gompers spearheaded the union from 1886 until he died in 1924.

Huey Long, cover of Time, 1935 magazine

President Roosevelt and liberal politicians sought to limit the economic catastrophe of the Great Depression using New Deal policies. However, the conservatives met the Roosevelt administration with considerable pushback. Such resistance was seen in judicial rulings of the Supreme Court during this period.

In 1934, Congress passed the *Frazier-Lemke Farm Bankruptcy Act*, ordering the postponement of mortgage foreclosures for five years. The Supreme Court struck down the law as unconstitutional shortly after that.

In *Butler v. the United States* (1935), the Supreme Court ruled that the government had unconstitutionally collected taxes to manage the agricultural markets. Roosevelt faced pushback from the Supreme Court in the *Schechter* case, ruling that the government exceeded its authority regarding regulating local businesses with no interstate connections.

The 1935 assassination of Huey Long (1893-1935), a radical populist and opponent of big business and Wall Street, illustrated the polarized political climate Franklin D. Roosevelt and the American population faced following the Great Depression. Many felt the government should enact policies that protected small farmers against the devastating instability of the Depression and, later, the disparity of the agricultural disaster of the Dust Bowl.

Economic reforms

In addition to supporting the public through social programs, Franklin D. Roosevelt and his administration also sought to reform the economic sector, especially the stock market and banking industry, following the chaotic periods of growth and decline in the early 20th century. Examples of this are the previously mentioned four-day bank holiday and the Emergency Banking Bill of 1933.

In hopes of limiting the continued outpouring of capital, Roosevelt gave the banks a reprieve while at the same time using his "fireside chats" on the radio to bolster the perception of bank security and encourage Americans to keep their money in the bank instead of under the mattress. This stabilized the banking sector and eventually led to the creation of the *Glass-Steagall Act* (1932) and the *Federal Deposit Insurance Corporation* (FDIC). Financial policies such as the FDIC have been instrumental in ensuring the integrity of the bank sector for millions of Americans following the Depression and in the future.

To create reforms, Roosevelt created the Securities and Exchange Commission (SEC) in 1934, which oversaw and regulated all stock market trading, creating an equal footing for all investors. Leading into the Depression, many traders and anxious investors began pulling stocks to maintain their high prices. This mass exodus from the stock market manifested in a domino effect, causing panic and market collapse in October 1929.

As shareholders continued to sell their stock, the market plummeted, and between October and December 1929, the market lost $40 billion in value. Many hoped this type of trading would be limited by creating federal supervision through the SEC.

One of the more notable reforms of Roosevelt's New Deal was the *Social Security Act* of 1935. This law created government-sponsored insurance for the disabled, dependent children, retirees, and the unemployed. Again, this is an example of a policy with both short- and long-term benefits. Many conservatives opposed the passage of the *Social Security Act*, labeling it as an unsustainable form of socialism.

Economic recovery driven by the World War II

To be victorious in war-ravaged Europe and the Pacific, the United States and its civilian population had to fill many jobs held by men now fighting in the global conflict. This allowed women and minority groups to work in previously unavailable positions. Close to 6.5 million women entered the workforce during the war years.

Using the Office of War Information, the U.S. government undertook a domestic advertising campaign encouraging women to enter the workforce and support the military effort. One notable example of this ad campaign is Rosie the Riveter. First Lady Eleanor Roosevelt convinced her husband to create women's auxiliary forces for the Army (WACS), Navy (WAVES), Air Force (WASPS), and Coast Guard (SPARS).

Rosie the Riveter poster

In addition to the actions taken by women during the war effort, African Americans also found significant roles within the American war machine. Millions of African American men and women served the United States during World War II, over a million in the military, and 8% of the civilian workers in the war industries. Though many served in construction or service capacities, this was a great sacrifice and opportunity for blacks in America, still reeling from racial bias and oppression.

Native Americans also engaged in the war, most notably the Navajo Code Talkers, who assisted Allied forces by creating a code system based on the Navajo language. By the war's end, more than 500 Navajo Nation members were working for the United States Marine Corps in this capacity. Comanche fighters and over 300,000 Mexican American servicemen also engaged the Axis powers (Germany, Italy, and Japan) in the European theater. On the home front, Mexicans were encouraged to cross the border to assist with the harvest season in the Bracero Guest Worker Program.

The national war effort allowed American and Allied troops to continue their attack on Nazi Germany and was instrumental in winning the war. It also had enormous economic implications, as it pulled the American markets and economy out of the Great Depression and into a period of great prosperity. Wartime programs gave new opportunities to women and minority groups, which would set the tone for future civil rights conversations in the 1960s and 1970s. However, even in this time of great sacrifice, the biases of racism and sexism were still present and would be seen throughout the modern history of the United States.

As many Americans experienced unprecedented growth and leisure, many others still struggled to maintain a reasonable standard of living, falling below the poverty line and making less than $3,000 annually during this period. To combat these issues, President Kennedy and President Johnson enacted significant legislative measures using social programs to address poverty in America.

President John F. Kennedy

Under Democratic President John Fitzgerald Kennedy, Congress appropriated nearly $5 million in urban renewal efforts to ease poverty in cities across America. The passage of the *Area Redevelopment Act* in 1961 also worked to provide economic aid to impoverished rural and urban populations while attempting to address unemployment in these demographics. President Johnson continued these efforts through his version of the New Deal, which provided additional aid and support to the lower-income demographics.

Shifts in manufacturing and means of production

The American economy, one of the most powerful in the world, had to change in reaction to outside forces and the globalization of the world economy. This led to fear and instability as investors and businesses took advantage of new policies and practices. At the same time, the workforce often felt the negative impact of these newer and cheaper alternatives to American labor. The government attempted to aid both sides while still considering the fate of America over any group.

As the business composition of the United States changed in reaction to the government and policy changes, the workforce was also forced to change. As the United States moved from domestic manufacturing to a more service-oriented economy, with production outsourced to foreign nations, it also had to consider how to maintain a thriving economy without the means of production in the United States.

The American economy saw rapid growth in the wake of World War II. Most of this growth was due to new production methods and businesses manufacturing goods and materials for sale worldwide. Not only were Americans enjoying new manufactured goods like Maytag appliances and Levi Strauss jeans, but the rest of the world was also looking to America to fill the gap left by the destruction of their means of production. The war had decimated Germany and Japan. They needed to rebuild a nation and an economy from the ground up.

American products suddenly became the gold standard worldwide. The new industry also meant new jobs and job growth, spurring the rise of a middle class composed of well-educated citizens who filled highly profitable production or management roles. By 1965, just over 50 percent of the economy was tied to manufacturing jobs. As the global economy rebounded from the war and foreign nations began to develop their means of production, the demand for American goods decreased. Manufacturing went from 53 percent of the economy in less than twenty-five years to 39 percent. By 2004, manufacturing accounted for less than 10 percent.

The loss of manufacturing jobs had several immediate and long-term impacts. During the 1970s, it was estimated that one-fourth of the nation was working for manufacturers. By 2005, it was less than 10 percent. Perhaps the best example of this decline can be seen in the automotive industry.

In 2005, General Motors cut over 30,000 jobs and closed nine American plants to make the business competitive internationally. The same year, Ford cut 30,000 jobs and closed ten plants nationwide. In one year, these automotive giants alone accounted for the loss of 60,000 jobs and nearly twenty factories. Citizens began to ask why these jobs were disappearing. It should be noted that these losses did not result in a permanently lower level of employment in the U.S.A., as the creation of new jobs in other areas offset them.

General Motors headquarters in Detroit

Two factors impacted the loss of manufacturing jobs in the United States: globalization and outsourcing. Globalization speaks to an international economy where goods and services can be traded quickly and inexpensively over national borders. Outsourcing is when a domestic industry moves the means of production overseas, typically to take advantage of lower regulation and labor costs.

The *North American Free Trade Agreement* (NAFTA) in 1994 allowed many countries to set up factories in Mexico. CAFTA, a similar agreement with Central American countries, continued the trend. India and China are also home to many American businesses because of their cheaper labor costs.

Outsourcing has meant a significant decrease in people joining labor unions because competition increases as manufacturing jobs decrease. Businesses are less willing to meet the unions' demands when other workers are willing to come in as strikebreakers and keep their jobs after the strike is broken. Union members began to fear their place in the business if they spoke out too much, and union membership deflated rapidly. Some labor unions stayed strong because jobs in their industries cannot be outsourced (e.g., teachers' unions and first responders) and because, in most instances, all new employees are required to join the union and pay membership dues.

Outsourcing allows for substantial profits for American businesses, but much of that money is spent in foreign countries to create the means of production. For instance, when factories were built in America, they were built by Americans and staffed by Americans. Most of the investment money was eventually returned to the American economy. With the advent of outsourcing, American companies pay foreigners to build and staff their factories.

This means that the only money returning to the economy is from advertising, corporate taxes, and state sales taxes. As more money is leaving the country via imports than entering the country through the sale of exports, America is experiencing a trade deficit. Some commentators argue that products are cheaper, but Americans are more impoverished, as most service industry jobs pay lower wages than manufacturing jobs.

Economic conservatism

The 1980s ushered in a period of fiscal conservatism. Conservatives believe that the government should remove itself as much as possible from economics and that business runs best when it is not regulated. To this end, Ronald Reagan began a tax cuts and deregulation trend that would continue for several decades. Reagan's economic policy, often called the *trickle-down theory*, was based on supply-side economics. This means that Reagan supported tax cuts for businesses.

The idea behind this economic policy is that if production is less expensive, it encourages businesses to increase employment and business size, eventually benefiting the consumer base by increasing living standards through less expensive and higher-quality products. This is trickle-down economics because an increase in consumption by the wealthy and businesses benefits the lowest-income earners through increased employment and wage levels over time.

To this end, in 1981, Ronald Reagan signed the *Economic Recovery Tax Act* (ERTA) into law. ERTA reduced individual tax rates by 25 percent across and was implemented over three years. It also allowed additional tax breaks for education and investment. This meant that someone investing in a business would pay fewer taxes to reward their investment in the economic market. Individuals who pursued higher education would also receive a tax write-off. In 1986, Reagan signed another tax act, which cut taxes for high-income taxpayers from around 70 percent to 30 percent in another effort to boost his trickle-down policies.

While President Reagan's economic policy was later criticized, it was a good fit for his presidency. His policies favored investment in businesses, which led to the advent of venture capitalism and entrepreneurship. Reagan also had tax incentives for education; the new opportunities were reflected in the number of students enrolling in higher education. Reagan's first term saw a revolution in the information industry by creating some of the most influential tech companies (e.g., Intel, Dell, Microsoft, and Cisco). With promised tax benefits, Americans were more willing to risk some of their hard-earned money, and the stock market began rallying.

In 1994, as Democrat Bill Clinton was President, more than 300 Republican Congressional candidates signed a promissory document called the Contract with America to support several critical conservative values. Newt Gingrich, Speaker of the House of Representatives, led the contract presentation at a press conference in September 1994. The contract was based on three core principles: accountability, responsibility, and opportunity.

Accountability meant being accountable to the American people to counteract the disconnect between the people and their politicians. Responsibility spoke to the personal responsibility of the American people; the conservative Republicans felt it was important for the government to let its citizens be responsible for themselves.

President Bill Clinton (left) and Newt Gingrich,
Speaker of the House of Representatives (1989-1995) (right)

The opportunity section augments this. People need to have personal responsibility, but they also need to be able to achieve it. The opportunity section was, therefore, focused on restoring the opportunities for Americans and immigrants to achieve the American dream.

The Contract with America had ten bills submitted to Congress that would be used to achieve eight primary goals. The first goal was to bring Congress back to the people by mandating that all laws applied to others apply to Congress.

The second goal was to use government resources best by hiring an independent company to audit the federal government for waste or misuse. Reducing the number of committees by one-third was planned to help decrease waste, a term limit for committee chairs was meant to increase productivity and encourage new ideas, and a ban on proxy votes in committees would now be open to the public for observation. The seventh goal was to limit taxes by requiring a three-fifths majority for any new tax increase.

Finally, the Contract with America called for a zero-baseline budget to keep the country accountable and monetarily sustained. In the end, the success of the contract was mixed. Several of the proposed bills could not come to fruition because of either a lack of support or vetoes issued by President Bill Clinton. However, several did pass, and their success helped bolster conservative values under liberal leadership.

When Republican George W. Bush (2001-2009) became President in 2001, the recession came in with him. Bush quickly reacted to help bolster the economy. Like Reaganomics, Bush's tax cuts were multi-pronged and included incentives. Bush reduced income tax rates across the board to be implemented over several years.

Despite popular rhetoric, these tax breaks did not focus on the wealthiest members of society. Instead, Bush tax cuts focused on the middle class and had several tax breaks and incentives directed toward them. For instance, Bush doubled the child tax break for working families.

Bush's tax breaks did not change the country's momentum fast enough. In 2003, Congress stepped in and added several other tax code changes. They phased out the "Death Tax," or the estate tax on inheritance. They also encouraged people to invest their money by cutting the cost of investments. Their interference worked, and the economy started to stabilize and grow. Bush's tax cuts were unique because they had a ten-year timeline before they became defunct unless reissued. Some policies were renewed while others could expire, meaning the subsequent tax rate is higher than under President Bush.

President George W. Bush

Debates over social programs

While conservatives celebrated many economic victories during the eighties and nineties, there were some programs that they could not limit or eliminate, such as Medicare and Medicaid. The debate for national health insurance started during the Great Depression when most people could not get the necessary care. The initiative failed but continued to spark debate.

In the 1960s, bills were passed to encourage states to provide health care for the elderly. Not all states did so, and those that did often provided inferior care. Eventually, Medicare was signed into law in 1965. Its basic premise was to provide health care for all Americans over sixty-five, regardless of their financial situation. In 1972, this was expanded to include younger adults who had disabilities. Medicaid, also founded in 1965, is an assistance program. This program is open to people of all ages, provided they can demonstrate financial need. Both programs work to offset medical costs for those who cannot afford private medical insurance.

Several steps have been taken to limit Medicare and Medicaid spending. However, the programs are so popular with voters that it is difficult to achieve real change while remaining responsible to a constituency.

For instance, the 1988 *Catastrophic Coverage Act* was celebrated as a great way to protect seniors from the stress of nursing home bills until it became apparent that Reagan's administration was expecting the elderly to pay for the new coverage without a tax on those not receiving coverage.

Seniors were furious, and the Act was repeled a year later. Many people worry about the spending on Medicare and Medicaid, but funding has been projected to exceed demands for the baby boomers, meaning the program is likely to survive. The newest addition to the healthcare debate is the highly contested *Affordable Care Act* (ACA), or Obamacare (March 24, 2010). The ACA attempts to expand coverage to all Americans while limiting spending through restrictions on insurance companies.

Social Security is another social welfare program that conservatives have tried and failed to restructure. Social Security provides funds for individuals who cannot work or are retired. The program is called a "pay-as-you-go" program, which means monthly money is collected from workers and employers through Social Security deductions from paychecks. This taxpayer-contributed money is then paid to those who have retired or are disabled. It is estimated that one out of every four families receives Social Security payments.

The concern with the Social Security system is, of course, monetary solvency. As life expectancy in the United States continues to rise, the federal government is paying more and more Social Security dollars to more and more citizens. With the baby boomer generation soon reaching full retirement age, many economists are concerned that the program will run out of funds. Some options have been considered, including raising the full retirement age; however, change is slow and laborious.

President George W. Bush discusses strengthening Social Security at the
Lake Nona YMCA Family Center in Orlando, FL, 2005

By current estimates, Social Security could run out of solvency within two decades. The concern is that if these programs are not solvent, they will require increased taxes and money borrowing that the country cannot afford. Conservatives tend toward fiscal restraint and worry about what happens in the event of defaulting on a debt of this size. These issues are compounded by the national debt, which hit $34.2 trillion in December 2023.

Economic history – summary of the period

Even as economic growth continued, episodes of credit and market instability, most critically the Great Depression, led to calls for the creation of a more robust financial regulatory system. The liberalism of President Franklin Roosevelt's New Deal drew on earlier progressive ideas. It represented a multifaceted approach to the causes and effects of the Great Depression, using government power to relieve people with low incomes, stimulate recovery, and reform the American economy.

Radicals, labor unions, and Populist movements pushed Roosevelt toward more extensive reforms, even as conservatives in Congress and the Supreme Court sought to limit the New Deal's scope. Although the New Deal did not overcome the Depression, it left a legacy of reforms and agencies that endeavored to make society and individuals more secure, and it helped foster a long-term political realignment in which many ethnic groups, African Americans, and working-class communities identified with the Democratic Party.

The mass mobilization of American society to supply troops for the WWII victory effort and a workforce on the home front ended the Great Depression. It provided opportunities for women and minorities to improve their socioeconomic positions.

Despite the perception of overall affluence in postwar America, advocates raised awareness of the prevalence and persistence of poverty as a national problem, sparking efforts to address this issue. The increasing integration of the United States into the world economy was accompanied by economic instability and significant policy, social, and environmental challenges.

Conservatives enjoyed significant victories related to taxation and deregulation of many industries, but many conservative efforts to advance moral ideals through politics met inertia and opposition. Although Republicans continued to denounce "big government," the size and scope of the federal government continued to grow after 1980, as many programs remained popular with voters and were challenging to reform or eliminate.

Notes for active learning

Foreign Relations: 1899 to Present

Expansionism of late 19th century

During the final years of the 19th century, Americans made a significant push for expansion abroad. Several groups were interested in foreign policy dealings, including industrialists who hoped to bring goods to new markets and extract cheaper resources. Nationalism, a popular sentiment at the time, also embraced this concept of overseas expansion to establish a perception of authority and influence within the growing international system.

This mindset was a response to the formerly dominant European colonial models, which some Americans, such as interventionists and imperialists, now envisioned as appropriate for the U.S. Others called for expanding American values, democratic traditions, and religions through missionary activities. Social Darwinists argued that Americans had some obligation to the less developed peoples abroad, and authors like Josiah Strong perpetuated such theories.

In 1898, the last remnants of the Spanish Empire in the Americas were obliterated when America and Spain fought a short war, which America won. The Spanish-American War was a conflict between the United States and Spain that lasted from April to August 1898. The war was fought mainly over the issue of Cuban independence, which had been ongoing for several years. The United States intervened in the conflict and emerged victorious after several naval and land battles.

The Treaty of Paris of 1898 officially ended the war. It resulted in Spain relinquishing sovereignty over Cuba (where future President Theodore Roosevelt led the famous cavalry unit called the "Rough Riders"), ceding Puerto Rico, Guam, and the Philippines to the United States while receiving $20 million from the United States for Spain-owned infrastructure. Puerto Rico, the Philippines, and Guam became American territories and would each follow a different path in the twentieth century. The war marked the end of the Spanish Empire in America and Asia.

One year after Spain granted Puerto Rico self-rule in 1897, Puerto Rico became a protectorate of the American government on October 18, 1898. American troops raised the U.S. flag over the island nation of one million people, claiming U.S. authority over it. In December 1898, the Treaty of Paris was signed to end the Spanish-American War and officially formalize the cession of Puerto Rico to the United States.

While military means were used to subjugate these places and Hawaii just before the Spanish-American War (April 21, 1898, to August 13, 1898), American missionaries established schools, orphanages, leper colonies, and other philanthropic institutions. These institutions were benevolent but played the dual role of cultural diffusion, which the more cynically nationalistic Americans actively promoted. Once these territories had been acquired, American natural resource industries developed in them.

From a military and political standpoint, territorial expansions and intervention abroad allowed the United States to become a global power during World War II. Many, including influential writer Alfred Thayer Mahan, believed the key to international influence was control of the seas, which could be accomplished in the 20th century by expanding and maintaining geopolitically strategic military bases. Evidence of this school of thought can be seen in the United States acquisition of naval base rights in Newfoundland and the Caribbean in return for wartime aid to the British.

Alfred Thayer Mahan, c. 1914

American involvement in the Spanish-American War (1898), the Panama Canal project (c. 1904-1914), and Republican President Theodore Roosevelt's corollary policies highlight the extensive partnership the United States built in Latin America in the early 20th century. During this period, military intervention and dollar diplomacy were commonplace for U.S. foreign policy in the Caribbean and Latin America. As Latin America and the Caribbean countries faced revolution and internal strife, the United States intervened, causing further U.S. hegemony within their territories and their neighbors.

The Panama Canal in 1915

As a result of the American victory in the Spanish-American War, the United States obtained the Philippines and the islands of Guam and Puerto Rico, furthering its influence abroad and creating rivalries with other European states for status and power. By the time the United States entered World War I, it was a global power, maintaining territories abroad while propelling its interests ahead of its European counterparts. These types of policies predicated the rise of U.S. influence during the two world wars, the reshaping of Europe following the collapse of Nazi Germany, and the rise of the Soviet Union.

American foreign interests in early 20th century

As America entered the 20th century, many questioned its role in the international system. Some supported the expansion of imperialism and argued that the United States should continue to maintain its overseas colonies. Many officials aimed to maintain U.S. international commercial interests while dispelling European aggression. Republican President Taft (1909-1913) implemented dollar diplomacy, using the economic power of the United States as a foreign policy tool to influence markets and maximize its influence abroad.

By limiting the influence of European countries, Taft believed he would bolster the U.S. economy while also growing its international influence. This influence was intensified when the United States obtained territories following the Spanish-American War and left many anti-imperialists calling for their release. However, interventionists believed the United States would maintain its interests by influencing international affairs.

As America looked toward Latin America to build relationships, it struggled with its neighbor Mexico and its various revolutions in the early 20th century. Many fled from Mexico into the United States following the instability, causing tense border relations and ongoing conflict. Approach and response to situations like this varied greatly depending on leadership, as the United States under Democratic President Wilson (1913-1921), a staunch anti-imperialist, played a limited military role in the revolutions, undoing much of the foreign policy agendas of President Taft, an enthusiastic interventionist.

The implications of dollar diplomacy can be seen in the influence the United States garnered in the international system. President Taft created short-term relationships that he hoped would blossom into more fruitful interactions. The use of dollar diplomacy could only be so effective against the coercive policies of World Wars I and II. The lack of Mexican intervention under President Wilson is evidence of his anti-interventionist and anti-imperialist mindset; however, it contradicts his interventions in World War I.

American involvement in the World War I

The spread of democracy, freedoms, and morality marked the Presidency of Woodrow Wilson. Democratic President Wilson saw the role of the United States as one that would facilitate the spread of peace and stability throughout the international system. Following its entrance into the war in April 1917, the United States, led by President Wilson, sought a stable peace to create a new period of international prosperity.

Rather than working against a German state that was already in shambles after the devastating loss, Wilson sought to move forward to create a more stable international system void of aggressive conflict and coercive policies following World War I. Notwithstanding this, devastating war reparations payments, demanded by the European allies, would be imposed on Germany in the Treaty of Versailles, signed by Wilson.

In January 1918, President Wilson outlined his famous Fourteen Points speech to a joint session of Congress. These policies would become the center of the peace accords agreed to at Versailles and were respected by many leaders across the globe, notably Lenin and those in the Allied forces. Though the United States participated in the conflict on a smaller scale than its European counterparts, President Wilson was able to influence post– World War I Europe using his political theories and models.

President Wilson believed that the government's responsibilities included remedying the wrongdoing of the state and putting the needs of the people before the state. This type of foreign policy agenda is necessary because it influenced contemporary U.S. foreign policy regarding the expansion and maintenance of human rights and democratic institutions. As seen in the formation of the League of Nations, this type of foreign policy would dominate the international system for the next several decades. Some would argue that Wilson's policies crafted and molded the expectations for global powers regarding international perception and influence in the late 20th and early 21st centuries.

President Wilson (left) and French President Minister Poincaré (right), c. 1918

The League of Nations

The leadership of President Wilson is apparent in the Paris Peace Conference and the Treaty of Versailles, as well as the formation of the League of Nations, though America abstained from membership. A foreign policy based on morality and idealism was a vital attribute of the Wilson Presidency, and this is evident when examining Wilson's reasons for entering World War I.

The Treaty of Versailles (January 10, 1920) culminated in the Paris Peace Conference that convened in January 1919. In response to the end of World War I, the victorious Allied forces sought to punish the military aggression of Germany and its allies. Excerpts of the treaty include the limiting of German naval and armed forces, the trial of Kaiser Wilhelm II and other high-ranking German officials as war criminals, the surrender of 10 percent of Germany's prewar territories, and a $5 billion immediate payment.

Long-term war reparations were set at an amount estimated today to be the equivalent of 96,000 tons of gold (three trillion U.S. dollars). The Treaty of Versailles created great animosity in Germany and contributed to the rising hostilities leading to World War II.

The League of Nations was the culmination of President Wilson's foreign policy aspirations and a response to the atrocities seen during World War I. The League of Nations' goal was to establish an international organization to maintain peace, foster international cooperation, and provide security for its member states. The ideals proposed by the League of Nations were popular worldwide, as many countries were exhausted by the war effort and sought a return to normalcy.

Senator Henry Cabot Lodge, c. 1924

The United States' membership in the League of Nations was hotly debated. The opposition was led by Senate majority leader Henry Cabot Lodge (1850-1924) from Massachusetts, who believed membership in the League of Nations would limit the United States' ability to protect its interests in an expensive obligatory relationship with other members. Lodge was successful in his campaign; the United States never became a member of the League of Nations. The global implications of the Treaty of Versailles and the formation of the League of Nations were countless. President Woodrow Wilson established an international model free of conflict and aggression.

Additionally, the agreements reached by President Wilson in the Treaty of Versailles (January 10, 1920) left many issues unresolved in Germany. They caused many Germans to hold a great sense of resentment toward the rest of Europe. This resentment eventually culminated in the German aggression seen at the onset of World War II.

Post World War I diplomacy

Following World War I, the United States pursued a foreign policy agenda that used diplomacy using treaties and financial partnerships, rather than force or military commitment, to reestablish and maintain stability and normalcy in the international system. One of the first examples of this diplomacy was the Washington Naval Conferences in 1921 and 1922, where all the great naval powers converged to discuss disarmament and the de-escalation of the conflict in East Asia.

The Stimson Doctrine, which began in late 1931 following the Japanese invasion of northeast China, stated that the United States would not acknowledge any territory acquired through aggression as it violated the international system. Without committing military action, the United States, led by Republican President Hoover (1874-1964; 1929-1933) and his Secretary of State, Henry Stimson, could clearly outline its stance against aggression or coercive policies in the international system.

Continuing to abstain from European conflicts, the U.S. government passed a series of Neutrality Acts. The *Neutrality Act* of 1935 prohibited trading all implements of war, ammunition, and arms; it also stated that arms manufacturers operating within the United States must apply for an export license. It also warned American citizens traveling in conflict zones that they did so at their own risk. Americans could no longer extend lines of credit or loans to countries considered belligerent.

The *Neutrality Act* of 1937 experienced tremendous support from the public, considering aggressive fascism in Europe and the outbreak of the Spanish Civil War (1936-1939). The revised *Neutrality Act* forbade arms transports by U.S. merchant ships to belligerent countries, regardless of the country of origin. The Act produced the "cash and carry" policy, which allowed the transport of materials except arms by U.S. merchant ships to belligerent countries, at the discretion of the President, in return for immediate payment.

The final *Neutrality Act* was passed after much debate in November 1939 and lifted the arms embargo previously described instead of viewing all trade under the provisions of the "cash and carry" policy. Eventually, these policies would be scaled back as the Lend-Lease program began.

These policies would significantly impact the outcome of World War II. Without the U.S. aid to the Allied forces, Germany would have certainly overtaken British forces before the United States entered the war. They also greatly influenced the map of postwar Europe, which was now dominated by U.S. hegemony.

Following the horrible destruction and tumultuous years of World War I, the United States questioned its role within the international system. Despite European influence, the United States began a direct and steady path toward isolationism while focusing most of its energy on securing its interests within the Western Hemisphere.

Outside of economic investments, the United States shied away from involvement on a large scale with other developed countries; many believed that after the dealings of the Great War, the only sensible foreign policy agenda was extreme isolationism. This mindset, coupled with the economic collapse of the Great Depression, which impacted American and global markets, caused many nations to look inward, ignoring their neighbors while trying to rebuild their state system.

To pursue these interests, the United States continued to invest in rebuilding Europe and economic engagement with Latin America, building on the previous dollar diplomacy enacted by President Taft. Such policies were designed to give American interests an advantage in the rebuilding of the developed world while at the same time sowing seeds of influence in the developing world.

By investing in foreign markets, President Taft and those who supported dollar diplomacy hoped to buy influence within international affairs and eliminate any possible European influence within the Western Hemisphere. The United States also sought to limit arms production and negotiate peace treaties to avoid a second global conflict.

The implications of World War I can be seen in the U.S. foreign policy agenda of isolationism, which was the center of its diplomatic efforts until the mid-1930s. While America wanted to experience its role as a global power through influence, it typically did so through economic and diplomatic means, avoiding any commitment to the conflict.

However, soon after the end of the Second World War, it became clear that tensions and unresolved issues remained, causing many to fear the outbreak of the next conflict. In the U.S. government, some sought to bolster aid and support of the British and French allies, while others continued to call for complete and extensive isolation from European affairs.

America in the World War II

Following World War I and the instability of the Great Depression, most Americans had lost any appetite for conflict, and for many years leading up to World War II, they were content to maintain an isolationist mindset towards Europe. By 1940, the foreign policy of the United States began to transition in preparation for the inevitable conflict with Nazi Germany. Rather than entering the war, the public opinion of Americans now focused on supplying and supporting the Allies against the Axis powers (Germany, Italy, and Japan).

By September 1940, the United States agreed to give the British over fifty obsolete destroyers in return for ninety-nine-year lease agreements to territories in Newfoundland and the Caribbean. These territories would operate as joint air force bases, expanding U.S. influence throughout the Western Hemisphere. In December 1940, the British could no longer pay for their supplies; President Roosevelt introduced the Lend-Lease Program, which required no immediate payment for the supplies sent abroad. The Lend-Lease Program was expanded to over thirty countries and rendered nearly fifty billion dollars in aid to those fighting the Axis powers (Germany, Italy, and Japan).

USS California sinking at Pearl Harbor on December 7, 1941

Any resistance to entering the war was quickly dispelled when Japan attacked the United States at Pearl Harbor on December 7, 1941. The following day, Democratic President Franklin D. Roosevelt declared war on Japan. Germany quickly followed suit, declaring war on the United States and propelling America onto the global stage of the conflict. The United States now faced a war on two fronts: in the Pacific against the Japanese and continental Europe against the Axis powers.

The public perception of the war effort, molded by U.S. officials, was a fight of good against evil, protecting democracy and the human rights of those worldwide. The prominence won by the United States following its military and political victories in World War II could not have been achieved without the public support of the American people.

The implications of the attack on Pearl Harbor and the U.S. entrance into World War II are almost incalculable. Some WWI historians speculate that without this attack, the United States might have waited to enter the war, allowing Germany to strengthen its grip on continental Europe and the British Isles. This delay could have had drastic implications for the outcome of World War II. In any event, the declaration of war against Japan by the United States caused Nazi Germany to open a new war front, as well as involving a new player on the original fronts, which led to the decline of the Third Reich.

Given the military victories and political successes of the United States following World War II, including but not limited to the acquisition of new territories, the disarmament of Germany, and a prestigious role in international affairs, it is no surprise that the United States maintained a dominant role within international politics in the postwar world.

Even during the war, the United States secured its interests in postwar Europe by acquiring new allies and resources, accompanying its rising global influence. The U.S. was able to exercise its influence at various wartime conferences. As a member of the "big three," with Great Britain and the Soviet Union, the United States enjoyed a substantial presence and position in world politics and affairs.

At the Casablanca Conference in 1943, the U.S. and British forces agreed to fight Germany until its unconditional surrender. This was crucial, as it stopped Germany from being able to eliminate the dual threat it faced on the eastern and western fronts. The Tehran Conference in 1943 promised Soviet aid to the United States against Japan, critical to ensuring amicable relations between the United States and the Soviet Union.

The most critical wartime conference came in February 1945 at Yalta, where President Roosevelt and Prime Minister Churchill (1874-1965; 1940-1945 and 1951-1955) agreed to the eventual hegemony of the Soviet Union in Eastern Europe following the war. The big three also agreed to general occupation and war reparations for Germany, something for which Stalin desperately argued.

The Potsdam Conference in 1945 was also influential in postwar Europe, as tensions leading into the Cold War were undeniable. No agreements were reached at this conference; the United States and the Soviet Union used these exchanges to build their arsenals against one another. The United States, under the leadership of General Douglas MacArthur (1880-1964), also spearheaded the occupation and reconstruction of Japan, allowing the United States to influence East Asian affairs significantly post–World War II. Such influence would be crucial in maintaining U.S. interests in the Cold War era.

Towards the end of the Second World War, it was clear that the U.S.A. would displace Great Britain as the unchallenged global power. The war economically drained Great Britain, which could no longer suppress nationalistic movements in its remaining colonies, like India and significant parts of Africa and China. This was not lost on the numerous Americans who believed in America's anti-colonial origin and self-identity.

Militarily, America grew the most massive army and navy in the world. It was the sole occupying power of a defeated Japan, previously the only modern power in Asia. This meant that America replaced Japan as the sole military and economic power in the Pacific. America was, until 1949, the only nation with the atomic bomb.

A new threat was emerging even before the war ended: the rise of the Soviet Union. Fearing communism, the U.S.A. used its military hegemony and its new image as a great liberator to gain the trust of the devastated world as the only nation that could stop the threat of Soviet expansion.

President Truman was prudent in using economic policy to garner popularity away from communists. The Marshall Plan gave thirteen billion dollars in direct aid and trade concessions to Western European nations to enable them to rebuild their nations as capitalist democracies. Thus, eliminating dire poverty, the U.S. government thought, would diminish support for communism there. The U.S.A. also established two other international entities immediately after the war, focusing on stopping the spread of communism: the United Nations and the anti-Soviet North Atlantic Treaty Organization (NATO).

American leadership in the post-war world

As the United States emerged from World War II, it was clear that the politics and global powers of the prewar period had been forever changed, and this transition would propel the United States into a state of unipolarity within the international system. Though the United States now holds more power than before, the postwar period was filled with chaos and tension that would culminate in the Cold War that spanned much of the late 20th century.

Such conditions included rebuilding Western Europe and establishing governments that supported the Western goals and ambitions pursued by the United States, embodied by the Truman Doctrine. Such policies provided countries facing authoritarian or outside aggression with economic, military, and political resources. One notable example was Greece's $400 million emergency funding on behalf of the United States.

By 1947, relations between the United States and the Soviet Union deteriorated, causing many in the government and the American public to see the Soviet Union as a new adversary. As an immediate response, President Truman and his Secretaries of State George C. Marshall (1947–1949) and Dean G. Acheson (1949–1953) crafted the containment policies, which would shape the United States' foreign policy during the Cold War.

President Truman with Secretary of Defense George C. Marshall,
Secretary of State Dean Acheson and Secretary of the Treasury John Snyder,
upon the President's Return from the Wake Island Conference.

Another notable event during this period that had a transformative influence on the 20th century's politics was the Chinese Revolution, which occurred in October 1949 and culminated in the accession of Mao Zedong and the Communist Party in China. Such an event highlights the "sphere of influence" policies used by the United States and the Soviet Union during this period and throughout the Cold War.

In addition to the ongoing Cold War, the United States also engaged in the Korean War (1950–1953) and the Vietnam War (1954–1975), which had significant implications for the United States internationally and domestically, seen mainly through the antiwar movements in the United States during this period. Aside from antiwar protests, the United States faced several other domestic concerns, the most notable being the civil rights movement, which dominated the 1960s.

As the Truman administration and following presidencies struggled to deal with the growing power and influence of the Soviet Union, they would enact foreign policy agendas with one common goal: to diminish the spread and influence of communism. Such attempts can be seen in a wide variety of policies, including but not limited to containment, massive retaliation, and the formation of global monetary institutions such as the International Monetary Fund (IMF) in 1944.

Marshall Plan aid to France:
bulldozer to help rebuild the French electric power system

The United States expanded its role again in postwar Europe after it promised to rebuild and support the war-torn nations of Western Europe while at the same time actively denouncing the rebuilding efforts of the Soviet Union. Using the Marshall Plan, the United States was able to create a relatively stable Europe by the end of the 1950s, which depended heavily on American financial backing and its military resources.

The United States quickly needed a more collective security policy to create a more abundant international security system. By creating the North Atlantic Treaty Organization (NATO) in April 1949, the United States and its allies formed an entity that could support and maintain peace by force and coercive policies. This enraged the Soviet Union and allowed Western Europe to feel a sense of security over the growing threat of communism.

In addition to NATO, the United States pursued individual peace and security agreements that set the foundation of the spheres-of-influence conflicts that would come to dominate the Cold War. In October 1949, President Harry Truman signed the Mutual Defense Assistance Program. By January 1950, bilateral agreements had been reached with eight of the NATO countries that requested military assistance from the United States. The agreements resulted in vast military supplies and financial aid rendered to many of the war-torn countries of Western Europe.

The long-term implications for such foreign policies are vast; some argue that without NATO and the aid of the United States, Western Europe would have staggered into the late 20th and early 21st centuries. Others argue that the presence and eventual expansion of NATO intensified and perpetuated the Cold War, leading to the ongoing rivalry between the two late 20th-century global powers, creating a true bipolarity in the international system for the first time. The alliance forged between the United States and Western Europe due to these foreign policies has undoubtedly influenced the 20th and 21st centuries international system and arguably allowed the United States to maintain a global hegemony.

Collective security and anti-communist coalitions

As a result of the Soviet Union's explosive rise in Eastern Europe—and, in turn, a global rise in communism—the United States and others who opposed communism sought to cooperate and expel such ideology from their regions and spheres of influence. Immediately following World War II, the United States pursued this expulsion via the Truman Doctrine and later the Marshall Plan.

Established in 1947, the Truman Doctrine stated that the United States would come to the economic, military, or political aid of any country that faced an outside threat, most notably in the form of communism. As former world powers like Britain were preoccupied with domestic issues (including rebuilding efforts), the United States and the Soviet Union saw a power vacuum and acted accordingly.

The United States, led by President Truman, argued that if aid were not given to countries where Britain had recently ceased its aid and involvement, such as Greece and Turkey, the Soviet Union would intervene and gain additional communist satellite states. As a result, over $400 million was approved by Congress in aid to both Greece and Turkey, effectively engaging the Soviet Union in a sphere-of-influence conflict.

Following the success of the *Truman Doctrine* in March 1947, Congress passed the *Economic Cooperation Act*, commonly known as the Marshall Plan, which funded the European Recovery Program and rendered close to $13 billion for the rebuilding projects of Western Europe. Such economic aid would allow most of Western Europe to be rebuilt by the mid-1950s and caused many European countries to become reliant upon the United States for economic cooperation and military resources.

Successful economic cooperation came from the Berlin Airlift Crisis (1948–1949), in which Soviet forces exercised their power and influence within postwar Europe with frightening results. The crisis began in June 1948, when Soviet forces in East Berlin enacted a blockade of rail, road, and water passages leading into West Berlin. To combat this threat, American, Canadian, and British forces airlifted supplies into West Berlin. The blockade ended in May 1949, as Soviet forces lifted any land restrictions from West Berlin.

The United States tried to combat the Soviet Union and contain the threat of communism. The policies developed by President Truman and diplomat of the Department of the State George Kennan set forth the containment policies, which would be influential in the Cold War and later periods of the 21st century. To combat the Soviet threat of expansion into satellite states and the spread of global communism, the United States engaged in two major wars during this period: the Korean War (1950–1953) and the Vietnam War (1954–1975). Both conflicts were unpopular with the American public and seemed only to inflame the struggle between the East and West.

In addition to the conflict of the Cold War, the U.S. used technological advancements to promote its status within the international system. Under orders from President Truman, the U.S. produced the first hydrogen bomb. Edward Teller (1908-2003), a former Manhattan Project scientist, advocated during and following the end of World War II, pressing for advancement in nuclear arms. However, not all scientists and politicians supported the project.

Others in the scientific community, such as Italian Enrico Fermi (1901-1954) and J. Robert Oppenheimer (1904-1967), adamantly opposed the concept of the hydrogen bomb. Like the scientists who produced the arms race of the 19th century and the atomic bomb of World War II, many believed the creation of such a weapon was immoral and could catapult the global system into one dominated by destruction and war.

Edward Teller, c. 1985

However, the production of the bomb continued, and in November 1952, the United States conducted the MIKE Test, which detonated a 10.4-megaton hydrogen device in the Marshall Islands in the Pacific. Subsequent testing included the BRAVO Test, which took place in March 1954, also on the Marshall Islands of the Pacific; this test produced the first deliverable hydrogen bomb.

Massive retaliation or response policies made famous by Secretary of State John F. Dulles (1888-1959; 1953-1959) under the Eisenhower Presidency in the mid-1950s were used as deterrents to the expansion of the Soviet Union. Dulles and later presidents, such as President Eisenhower, argued it was impractical to assert a national defense budget at the level being presented by the Soviet Union; it would bankrupt the United States. Instead, it would deter Soviet aggression using nuclear weapons and the threat of full-scale American aggression.

One final military sector where the United States and the Soviet Union collided was the Space Race, made famous by Project Mercury, Warner Von Braun, and the Soviet satellite Sputnik. On October 4, 1957, the Soviet Union launched the first human-made satellite, Sputnik, causing jubilation in the Soviet Union and dread and fear in the United States. The following month, the same Soviet scientists successfully launched another satellite, this time carrying live dogs into space (along with some other species, all of which returned alive)—a monumental accomplishment for humanity. Such advancements spurred the Americans to begin their space program, and in early 1958, the United States successfully launched Explorer I, its first satellite. During this same year, President Eisenhower announced his support for creating the National Aeronautical and Space Administration (NASA), which also mandated that Project Mercury, newly formed, would send a man into orbit before 1959.

Robert R. Gilruth, responsible for Project Mercury

The Space Race was influenced by the lack of qualified scientists and researchers produced by the U.S. educational system during this period. In 1958, the *National Defense Education Act* was established to promote better teaching resources, math, science, modern language applications, higher education, and college scholarships, all intended to produce the academic minds needed to compete with the USSR in the Space Race.

The implications for the technological and military advancements during this period are far-reaching, even in today's political and international systems. Without the initial advancements of the ballistic missile, the technology could not have been transformed to create the intercontinental ballistic missiles of today. Additionally, the development of the hydrogen bomb set a new precedent, even above that of the nuclear annihilation seen in Japan following World War II, which troubled many scientists and American families alike.

The investment in academics and research due to the creation of NASA has been monumental in maintaining the perception of the United States as a global power, and the results have transcended the physical boundaries previously in place for humankind. Additionally, the space technology that had once been such a source of rivalry between the United States and the Soviet Union eventually became a bridge to cooperative interactions between the two countries.

Cycles of US–Soviet confrontation

As the bipolarity of the Cold War system emerged, it became clear that neither side would be able to wage war on its rival actively or sustainably. Thus, periods of great conflict followed by nonaggression and coexistence were seen during much of the Cold War. The most notable examples of direct conflict between the United States and the Soviet Union are the Vietnam and Korean Wars.

Both wars created intense polarization among the American public and the international community regarding the spread of communism and the anti-communist campaigns of the West. These wars were also instrumental in the spreading or expulsion of communism during this period. Other examples of indirect conflict in the sphere-of-influence battles between the Soviet Union and the United States were illustrated by communist satellite states and the establishment of NATO.

While both global powers maneuvered to secure their position within the international system, they found themselves in periods of détente—a French word meaning a release of tensions—which eased the nuclear ambitions of both sides.

One such example came from President Nixon, who in 1972 made historic trips to China and the Soviet Union to meet with foreign leaders. These trips allowed him to highlight his foreign policy successes rather than his domestic blunders.

President Richard Nixon and Premier Alexei Kosygin sign the Cooperation in the Fields of Science and Technology Agreement between the United States and the Soviet Union

The détente period ended with the signing the Strategic Arms Limitation Talks (SALT) and was revisited with subsequent trips in June 1973 and 1974. These later talks produced little to no agreement, as was seen in the initial talks, but they did perpetuate a sense of universal peace between the two powers. Such foreign policy ambitions aimed to increase trade between the countries and nuclear de-escalation, which both parties hoped for.

These periods of fluctuating tensions would be essential to set the groundwork for future Russian and American relations following the end of the Cold War and the collapse of the Soviet Union. These periods of relaxed relations also allowed the American public to see the Soviet Union as less of a threat, which was crucial to lowering the anti-communist rhetoric seen in the United States following World Wars I and II.

Global decolonization period

After World War II, the period of global decolonization began, which fundamentally reshaped the world. Dozens of countries gained their independence, ending an age of colonialism in which mostly European empires ruled nearly a third of the world's population. From 1945 to 1960, over three dozen new states were formed in Asia and Africa, bringing the global transition away from colonization into context.

Breaking away from colonial rule entailed years of violence or protest. Furthermore, even after independence, leaders faced the challenge of building governments to provide their citizens with physical and economic security and political rights. The era of decolonization brought attention to historically neglected global issues such as economic inequality and foreign military intervention. Millions of formerly disenfranchised people voted for the first time, and new, postcolonial leaders emerged. During this colonization period, the United States struggled to find an even tone of authority and security while maintaining its stance as a champion of democracy and self-representation in the international system.

Not all governments were pleased with this new policy agenda; many in America feared that the relinquished colonies would quickly be influenced or intimidated by the Soviet Union, which would cause the expansion of communism. It seemed that decolonization could cause security concerns for the United States and its allies. Examples include the Indonesian War of Independence (1945–1950) against its colonial rulers in the Netherlands and the conflict between the Vietnamese and French (1945–1954).

Spheres of influence during the Cold War

Political revolts and rebellions in Eastern Europe also plagued the Cold War period. Notable examples include the Hungarian Revolution, which ended in November 1956, and the revolt of the Czech population, ending in August 1968 at the hands of Soviet forces. Such transition and instability caused the United States to pursue a foreign policy agenda that included financial aid and support, military intervention when necessary, expansion of alliances to include the new influx of states created following World War II and an end to widespread colonialism.

As the Cold War heated up and the United States and the Soviet Union continued to pursue aggressive policy agendas, it was clear to the newly emerging countries of the 20th century that each must support or oppose communism. However, many states wanted to be excluded from the sphere-of-influence conflict. They decided to form the Non-Aligned Movement, which focused on internal development rather than foreign policy agendas. The Non-Aligned Movement was cultivated in 1955 at the Bandung Conference; it quickly gained momentum among newly nationalized or formed states.

These newly created independent states became even more interested in the 1950s and 1960s when the international community saw the influence such states could have on the United Nations Council. Due to their colonial past, these states were typically wary of European-style government and management. They tried to distance themselves from the former ruling models they had seen used in Europe and North America.

In hopes of limiting the influence of the Soviet Union and communism within the Western Hemisphere, the United States took drastic and sometimes concerning actions to welcome non-communist-based governments into its fold. The first formal attempt at welcoming these alliances following World War II came from the Inter-American Treaty of Reciprocal Assistance, also known as the Rio Treaty, enacted in 1948, which stated that aggression against one country in the Americas would be seen as an attack on all the countries.

Such foreign policy decisions would significantly impact the relationships between American states and Soviet relations with these same states, causing some to turn towards communism and others to turn towards other forms of government, in most cases, not real democracies. Before the two world wars, the United States had consistently pursued a path of isolation from global affairs; however, following the wars—and certainly during the Cold War era—this was neither practical nor possible.

As the United States worked to install and support governments opposed to communism, it also found itself orchestrating the demise of the governments it perceived as pro-communist. Such examples can be found throughout the Cold War era and include the US-sponsored coup in Iran in August 1953, Guatemala in June 1954, and Chile in September 1973, all of which resulted in the overthrow of acting governments.

The United States attempted to stay the tide of negative perception in Latin America due to its extensive involvement in the early 20th century. Notable examples include the Organization of American States (OAS), which was formed in 1948 shortly after the Rio Treaty and called for the cooperation of American states against the spread or infiltration of communism into the Western Hemisphere.

The global ramifications for such policies can be seen in the immediate Latin American response and future relationships between the American countries. Mistrust and concerns grew from the relationship between Latin America and the United States during this period. The United States failed to see substantial results from OAS, which never experienced the surge of anti-communism they hoped to see in the Latin American countries.

Additionally, the continued unilateral use of force by the United States in Latin America caused many to question whether the United States had genuinely embraced a new path of foreign policy towards its American continental neighbors or just insisted upon being perceived in this way.

The Middle East

During World War II, the Soviet Union deployed and maintained military resources to Iran, an oil-rich nation, to protect its resources from Axis aggression. However, its continued military presence in the country following the war caused many Americans to be concerned about the future of the Middle East following the end of the two world wars.

After the Soviet Union backed an armed rebellion in 1946, it became clear that Soviet "satellite states" in the Middle East were a real concern, and U.S. involvement in the region escalated as a result of the Tehran Conference violations. In hopes of eliminating threats to the global oil markets, the United States and other global and regional powers established institutions that could better control the markets.

One such institution is the Organization of the Petroleum Exporting Countries (OPEC), created in September 1960 at the Baghdad Conference. Original members included Iraq, Saudi Arabia, Iran, Kuwait, and Venezuela. Its main goal was to regulate and unify member state policies regarding oil production to produce fair and stable petroleum markets for producers. Following several oil crises, the formation of OPEC was a safeguard against future mishandling.

However, this was not necessarily the case, and OPEC acted against what it perceived to be its threats and adversaries. In 1973, oil diplomacy was enacted by OPEC; it called for an embargo on oil against states that supported Israel's Yom Kippur War against Egypt, Syria, and Jordan. This included the United States and other Western allies who relied upon the oil of the Middle East to feed their energy needs.

The Suez Crisis also highlighted the energy concerns of the postwar period. On October 29, 1956, Israeli military forces invaded Egypt and progressed toward the Suez Canal. This military offensive came after Egyptian President Gamal Abdel Nasser (1918-1970) nationalized the canal in July 1956. The conflict escalated when British and French forces joined with Israel, almost enticing the Soviet Union, which supplied Nasser with arms, into the conflict. Forces were eventually withdrawn in late 1956 and early 1957.

OPEC ministers

The Eisenhower Presidency worked to deter its allies from inciting a Soviet conflict. It had to be careful of policies that seemed soft or too accommodating of Soviet expansion. The long-term implications of the formation of OPEC would cause the United States to pursue national policies toward the oil markets and its producers, namely, OPEC states.

Later administrations attempted to influence Middle Eastern states, most notably Saudi Arabia, Iran, and Iraq, to stabilize the global oil markets while exercising American influence for regional hegemony. This is ascribed to the sphere of influence during the Cold War, which positioned states against other states in the Soviet-American game.

Reagan's foreign policy toward the Soviet Union

When Reagan entered office, it was with a definite focus on anti-communist policies, especially as they related to Latin America. El Salvador, Nicaragua, and Cuba were of interest, but the President was determined to stop any new communist regime in the Western Hemisphere. Reagan proved this when, after a successful Marxist coup in the Caribbean nation of Grenada, he authorized troops to invade and reinstall an anti-communist government. The invasion included the death or capture of some 700 Soviet-supported Cuban soldiers. It drew a hard line in the sand for any government factions considering a communist regime in the Western Hemisphere.

This hardline on communism gave rise to the *Reagan Doctrine*, which provided American support for any anti-communist revolution. Reagan supported the anti-Soviet freedom fighters in Afghanistan with weapons and training, for example. In 1979, after Nicaragua fell to the Sandinista Marxist group, a decade of civil war followed, which was the most critical test of the Reagan Doctrine.

Reagan approved the covert training of Nicaraguan rebels, colloquially called Contras, and the CIA assisted until commanded by Congress to end all aid. Reagan quietly looked for ways to side-step Congress' decree and permitted the CIA to sell weapons to the Iranians, provided that all proceeds go to the Contras. In 1986, the plot was revealed, and the Iran–Contra scandal had severe political backlash from all involved, including the President. Four years later, the Marxist government of Daniel Ortega was routed in a national election.

Reagan's administration also wanted to strengthen ties with China to contain the Soviets, but the President would not allow any policies that did not support Taiwan. The Taiwanese have had conflict with China since the 1940s when they first sought independence. During the height of the Cold War, the United States made a declaration that any attacks on Taiwan would be met with American retaliation.

This meant the United States could not strengthen relations with China unless an agreement were reached. However, this also meant that military support for Taiwan mainly threatened the Chinese government. While the formal relationship with China improved under the Reagan administration, the central conflict was not solved during his presidency.

President Reagan did structure policy for foreign influence. His tendency toward hard lines in the sand and sticking to a set of ideals was supported, for the most part, by Americans. This inspired other leaders to try similar approaches after Reagan's term in office ended. Both Bush Presidents fought foreign wars using the same sort of techniques that Reagan utilized.

Ronald Reagan's presidency was instrumental in ending the United States' Cold War with the USSR. He, like most Americans at the time, saw communism as a threat to American interests. In 1983, the *Strategic Defense Initiative* (SDI) was founded under Reagan's administration. This program was called "*Star Wars*" because it was a missile defense system positioned in the Earth's orbit. The program aimed to find a way to protect the United States from nuclear attacks. The program relied on technology that was not available at the time but could be developed, particularly a super-computer system that could identify nuclear warheads as threats and use lasers to destroy them while they were still in the atmosphere.

The program garnered much criticism. Many thought the SDI violated the Strategic Arms Limitation Talks (SALT). Some analysts felt that the SDI was an excellent idea but were concerned about costs; others felt that successfully implementing it would give the United States too much of an advantage over the USSR and might cause them to strike preemptively. Due to constant setbacks and struggle to find funding, the SDI was eventually put aside.

Gorbachev (left) and Reagan, c. 1985

In the end, it was probably for the best that the SDI was never completed, as an unlikely relationship began to develop between Mikhail Gorbachev, then the leader of the USSR, and the Reagan presidency. In 1981, President Reagan attempted to implement better communication between the White House and the Kremlin.

The USSR was controlled by General Secretary Leonid Brezhnev (1906-1984), who was unresponsive to Reagan's attempts. Brezhnev died in November 1982. His successor, Yuri Andropov (1914-1984), died less than two years later, and he was succeeded by Constantine Chernenko (1911-1985), who died a little over a year later.

Chernenko's successor, Mikhail Gorbachev (1931-2022), finally responded receptively to Reagan's overtures. The two met in Geneva, Switzerland, in November 1985 to improve relations. They spoke about the differences and similarities between their two countries and tried to find common ground on which to build a relationship. The first meeting was a success, and a year later, they met again in Reykjavik, Iceland.

This summit did not go as well as the first due to a disagreement about America's missile defense systems. Gorbachev wanted a promise that America would end its plans for a space-based missile defense system. Reagan refused to hinder American security that way but offered to share the technology with the USSR to protect both countries. When Gorbachev refused, the summit was called to an end.

Many people thought that the failure in Iceland would keep Reagan and Gorbachev from being able to achieve anything. Eight months later, Reagan demonstrated his faith in the relationship when he successfully called on Gorbachev to tear down the Berlin Wall that separated East and West Berlin in Germany.

Reagans arriving in Moscow, May 29, 1988

In December 1987, Gorbachev and his wife were welcomed to Washington for their third summit. The third summit in Washington was an unprecedented success, with both leaders signing the Intermediate-Range Nuclear Forces (INF) Treaty, which eliminated ground launching ballistic and cruise missiles. The Reagans returned the favor the next year and traveled to Moscow for the next summit. President Reagan signed the INF Treaty, which both governments had ratified.

The fifth and final summit meeting happened in December 1988 as President Reagan and George H. W. Bush, both the Vice President and President-elect, traveled to New York, where Gorbachev came to meet them. Reagan considered this a way for him to hand off the relationship between the two countries to President-Elect Bush.

Reagan's call for Gorbachev to tear down the Berlin Wall was crucial in their relationship. In 1945, after the defeat of the German army and an end to the Western Front of World War II, the Allies met to determine what to do with the German territory and people. They split the country into four occupation zones: the United States, the USSR, Britain, and France. The German capital of Berlin was in the Soviet territory, but the Allies agreed to split it up, which annoyed the communists. The USSR was rankled to have a Western capitalist city in the middle of their territory, so they attempted to slowly force the Allies out through starvation, cutting off all supplies to the western side of Berlin.

Woman waving over the Berlin Wall, 1961

Instead of leaving, the United States, Britain, and Canada began airlifting food and supplies to their sections of Berlin. Realizing starvation would not work, the Soviets turned to other pursuits but soon had to refocus on Berlin as thousands began defecting from East to West Germany. In August 1961, nearly 2,400 Germans defected in a single day at the height of the defections. Embarrassed by the flow of people from East to West, the Soviets decided to end the privilege of free movement across occupational zones.

Within two weeks, the Berlin Wall was constructed and in place. Once separated, the two halves of the city grew independently. East Berlin suffered under-inflation and lack of resources, while the capitalist Western half was rapidly rebuilt and flourished.

On June 12, 1987, President Ronald Reagan stood before the Brandenburg Gate in Berlin and called for Gorbachev to tear down the wall because it was an outdated symbol. Two years later, on November 9, 1989, that dream became a reality as the gates were opened, and citizens began removing the wall from their city. This, perhaps more than any other action, symbolized the ending of the Cold War and strengthened the relationship between the East and West.

Dismantling of the Soviet Union

While good relations between the East and West were primarily accredited to Reagan, his counterpart, Mikhail Gorbachev, also affected real change, leading to the end of the USSR and improved economic prosperity in the Soviet nations.

When Mikhail Gorbachev (March 15, 1990) assumed the leadership of the USSR, he understood that things needed to change. His country was stagnant and weakened by oppression. To combat this, he introduced two new sets of policies. The first was "*glasnost*," or political openness. Glasnost encouraged Gorbachev to connect with Reagan, which had tremendous effects on his nation. It allowed people to relax with new liberties, like freedom of the press and open and honest elections.

The second policy was "*perestroika*," which means economic restructuring. Gorbachev realized that the Soviet policies of a communist command-based economy were not working, and he shifted the control of the means of production from the state to private citizens and businesses.

While these policies would eventually mean economic prosperity, that prosperity did not manifest before the old system collapsed, causing frustration and outrage throughout the USSR. With the command economy in tatters and rationing a reality, it was no surprise when the Soviet Union began to crumble as individual states pulled away and fought for their independence. The Velvet Revolution in Czechoslovakia quickly followed the Polish revolutions in 1989. Quickly, the other states began pulling away, and soon, the USSR was officially disassembled.

The end of the USSR looked like a failure to many people living there; the world viewed it as progress. In 1988, Time magazine named Gorbachev their "Man of the Year" to support his continued efforts to work with the United States for peace and a diplomatic end to the Cold War. In 1989, they upgraded him to the "Man of the Decade." While only a single magazine, it became apparent that they spoke for the world when Gorbachev was given the highly coveted Nobel Peace Prize in 1990 for his work to end the Cold War and the Nuclear Arms Race.

President Reagan Giving a Speech at the Berlin Wall, Brandenburg Gate, June 1987

Bush's term as President saw good relations with Gorbachev, as both men continued the work that had been started in their own countries and abroad. It also completed the first Strategic Arms Reduction Treaty (START I). The treaty was a huge success and limited the United States and Russia (after the USSR was divided in the early 1990s) to 6,000 nuclear warheads each. Each country was also limited to 1,600 nuclear delivery vehicles. This limitation was a fantastic success and dramatically reduced stockpiles. It also served as an example of the New START Treaty in 2010, which reduced the limits.

America's role in the world after the Cold War

As the Cold War ended, the United States was forced to redefine its place in the global theater. This was affected by some factors. The collapse of the Soviet Union meant a restructuring of former Soviet republics and Soviet-bloc countries and a shift in global political power that had to be filled by other nations. It quickly became apparent that the United Nations also needed to be strengthened and reformed during the period immediately after the Cold War.

While the United States pulled back and attempted to act mainly through the United Nations during the 1990s, they were called upon to function as "police" during several significant conflicts. The 2000s saw America return to the forefront of international politics after the September 11, 2001 attacks. The resulting War on Terror redefined both domestic and foreign policy.

As the United States and Russia ended the Cold War hostilities that had long polarized international relations, the question of American power and intervention arose. Most people favored a new international approach and placed their faith in the United Nations, whose military and member countries donate peacekeeping forces. In response, the United Nations changed how it approached missions, focusing on agreements that led to sustainable peace. Peacekeeping was no longer just a military role. Instead, the United Nations realized that peacekeeping had to include an effort to change all a country's ills, including infrastructure and government.

Several peacekeeping efforts were successful, but it soon became apparent that there were problems with the new systems. Yugoslavia, Rwanda, and Somalia were three places where the peacekeeping efforts failed, and the United Nations was criticized for its ineffectual practices and structure. Many Americans questioned their place in an organization that would allow genocide to occur without attempting to stop it. The United Nations looked to reform and change to address their weaknesses and failings. They have since moved on to more complex missions and have maintained a helpful role.

The United States could not remain behind the United Nations, however. In 1990, Iraq, under the leadership of Saddam Hussein (1937 to December 30, 2006), invaded their neighbor Kuwait. Hussein's validation for the invasion was that Kuwait was a part of Iraq and not a separate territory. He claimed that the Western powers had carved out Kuwait and used the country, as well as other nations like Saudi Arabia, to keep oil prices artificially low.

Saddam Hussein, c. 2000

The other countries of the Middle East were concerned by Hussein's actions and condemned them. President of Egypt Hosni Mubarak (1928-2020; 1981-2011) attempted to host a negotiation between the two countries. However, Hussein was not receptive, and on August 2, 1990, Iraqi forces invaded the country, causing King Fahd of Kuwait to flee into exile.

The other Middle Eastern Nations immediately called upon the West to intervene. The United Nations responded the next day, issuing instructions for the Iraqi forces to leave Kuwait and return to Iraq. Hussein summarily ignored them. After several days, King Fahd of Kuwait (c. 1921-2005) came to the United States directly and requested military and political aid. Within several days, a coalition of American and NATO troops joined Middle Eastern troops in Saudi Arabia. The plan for Operation Desert Shield was to serve as a barrier between the Iraqi forces and Saudi Arabia, containing the problem until a solution could be met. Knowing his weak position, Hussein tried some measures to garner support for his invasion. He tried to claim that he was fighting a jihad, or Muslim holy war, against the coalition.

Hussein attempted to garner the support of the world by turning the occupation into a political move to represent the struggle of the Palestinians. He offered to leave Kuwait if the Israelis would leave Palestine, the land that had become Israel after World War II. When it became apparent that these measures were not working to sway public opinion and that violence was imminent, Hussein made a deal with Iran to swell his military's ranks and prepare for war.

At the end of November, the United Nations gave Iraq a deadline. They were to withdraw all troops from Kuwait before January 15, 1991. Operation Desert Storm began two days after the deadline (August 2, 1990, to February 28, 1991). The hope was to end the war quickly and decisively with the least damage to Kuwait and its citizens. To this end, the United States and allied nations used the newest technologies. They thought an air offensive would create the most minor damage in total. Therefore, utilizing planes and "smart" bombs, which had a built-in laser guidance system, the Allies attacked Iraqi planes, runways, communications systems, and weapons plants.

These air attacks were helpful but did not lead to the end of the war as quickly as hoped. The air attacks were soon carried out on ground troops and high-profile targets. With the air operations working as effectively as they could, ground troops were soon necessary to finish the job, and Operation Desert Sabre managed to last less than a week before the Iraqi soldiers retreated. The United States pursued them deep into Iraqi territory.

Members of the coalition forces drive a tank during Operation Desert Storm

The United States declared a ceasefire on February 28, 1991. In return for their withdrawal, the allies negotiated for Iraq's recognition of Kuwait's sovereignty. Iraq also agreed to destroy all weapons of mass destruction (WMD) like nuclear missiles. While the war was considered a definite success for the Allies, the effects of the war were felt for several years. Non-compliance with the UN regulations and mandates meant that people continued to question the validity of the United Nations as an international peacekeeping body. Resentment also grew in the area, and eventually, several unresolved issues sparked another war with Iraq in 2003.

Global War on Terror

America changed drastically at the turn of the century when terrorists carried out the first international attack on American soil since the bombing of Pearl Harbor. Much of America's political and economic future changed seemingly overnight. The terrorist attacks of September 11, 2001, drastically impacted the U.S. economy, as the World Trade Center disappeared, and American airlines were crippled. Recession, already building from Clinton's time in office, was imminent.

Politically, the United States had soon pledged itself to two costly and unpopular wars, which set them at odds with several other political leaders and earned them an international bias. At home, the political sphere became polarized, and people began to question the federal government, as liberty and privacy were quickly put aside by the need for security. The place of the United States in world politics was once again in question. Additionally, the country and citizens had to revisit the founding documents, as security and privacy issues were at odds.

The United States was fundamentally changed in September of 2001. The Middle Eastern terrorist organization known as al-Qaeda, headed by Osama bin Laden, had planted sleeper agents inside the United States. These agents prepared to perpetrate an attack on American citizens by learning how to fly commercial airliners. On the morning of September 11, 2001, these al-Qaeda terrorist operatives hijacked four American airline flights and crashed them into political targets.

The first plane to crash was directed into the North Tower of the World Trade Center in New York City. Each plane was filled with enough jet fuel for a cross-continental flight, and the damage was extreme. It was followed eighteen minutes later by the second plane, which crashed into the South Tower.

Another of the hijacked planes was directed to Washington, D.C., where it crashed into the E Ring of the Pentagon, the central hub of the United States military. As the Pentagon burned, the situation in New York became even more critical. The towers of the World Trade Center, unable to handle the burning jet fuel and structural damage, collapsed. Only six people left in the towers at their collapse survived.

A fourth plane was hijacked but was late in taking off. The passengers learned of the situation in New York and grew suspicious when they were not immediately returned to the airport. The current belief is that this plane was supposed to crash into the White House, Camp David, or a nuclear power plant. Wherever it was intended to crash, the plane did not reach its destination. The passengers on the plane revolted against the four hijackers. The plane crashed in an empty field, killing all forty-five of the people on board.

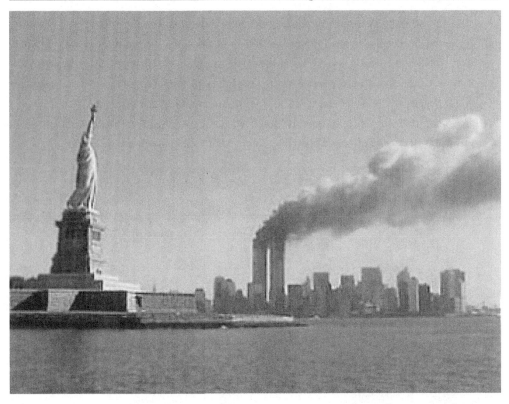

World Trade Center on September 11, 2001

More than 3,000 people lost their lives in New York. Over 10,000 others were treated for injuries, many quite severe. In Washington, 125 people died in the Pentagon, and 64 people died on the plane. These events shook the nation. Citizens had a difficult time comprehending what they were seeing. President George W. Bush was in a Florida classroom, making a public appearance at the time of the attacks. Bush quickly returned to Washington to aid the country in rallying behind the rescue efforts and to offer direction and leadership as the country mourned. In an address to the American people that night, Bush promised that there would be no distinction made between the terrorists who had perpetrated these attacks and those who protected them.

Al-Qaeda claimed responsibility and, within one month of the attacks, Operation Enduring Freedom, an international effort to end the Taliban regime in Afghanistan and bin Laden's associated terrorist network, had boots on the ground in Afghanistan. Within two months, the Taliban was officially removed from power, but they continued to utilize guerrilla tactics as they fought the U.S. troops from a base in Pakistan.

In 2003, the War on Terror was extended. Seeing America's vulnerability, President Bush moved decisively against anyone he felt threatened the United States. Iraq, under the control of Saddam Hussein, was funding the terrorist organizations that Bush was attempting to destroy. Coupled with erroneous reports that Iraq still had Weapons of Mass Destruction (WMDs) despite a UN Mandate, it led to a joint American-British invasion. Like the war in Afghanistan, the war in Iraq quickly achieved its first objective: the overthrow of the government. The occupation and guerrilla violence led by an insurgency followed.

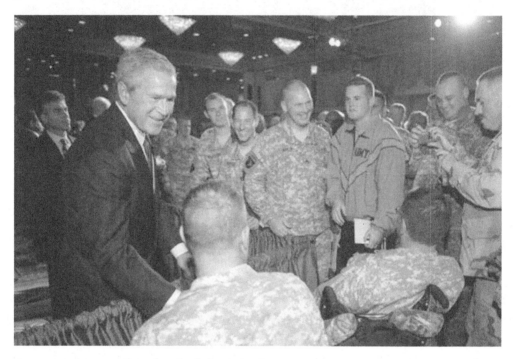

President Bush discusses the war on terror, c. 2007

In 2007, violence in Iraq began to decrease. In response, the United States started to pull out troops until the withdrawal was completed in December of 2011. The United States still has troops in Iraq but as advisors and teachers only. In May 2011, Osama bin Laden was finally tracked down and killed by the Naval Special Warfare Development Group (Navy SEAL) Team Six.

One month later, President Obama called for a reduction of troops in Afghanistan, with a full withdrawal by the end of 2014. As with Iraq, some troops remain to maintain peacekeeping efforts in the area.

America has continued to question its role in the international arena. Due to the unpopular wars in Iraq and Iran and several illegal forays into the sovereign territory—like the 2011 killing of Osama bin Laden in Pakistan—the United States has been criticized internationally for acting as the world's police. A sufficient balance between action and inaction has yet to be determined.

Foreign relations – summary of the period

In the late 19th century, many Americans began to advocate overseas expansionism, leading to new territorial ambitions and acquisitions in the Western Hemisphere and the Pacific. The American victory in the Spanish-American War led to the U.S. acquisition of island territories, an expanded economic and military presence in the Caribbean and Latin America, engagement in a protracted insurrection in the Philippines, and increased involvement in Asia. Questions about America's role in the world generated considerable debate, prompting the development of various views and arguments between imperialists and anti-imperialists and, later, interventionists and isolationists.

After initial neutrality in World War I, the nation entered the conflict, departing from the U.S. foreign policy tradition of noninvolvement in European affairs in response to Woodrow Wilson's call to defend humanitarian and democratic principles. Although the American Expeditionary Force played a relatively limited role in World War I, Wilson was heavily involved in postwar negotiations, resulting in the Treaty of Versailles and the League of Nations, which generated substantial debate within the United States.

Following World War I, the United States pursued a unilateral foreign policy that used international investment, peace treaties, and select military intervention to promote a vision of international order while maintaining U.S. isolationism, which continued to the late 1930s. World War I and its aftermath intensified debates about the nation's role in the world and how best to achieve national security and pursue American interests.

The involvement of the United States in World War II, while opposed by most Americans before the attack on Pearl Harbor, vaulted the United States into global political and military prominence and transformed American society and the relationship between the United States and the rest of the world.

The dominant American role in the Allied victory and postwar peace settlements, combined with the war-ravaged condition of Asia and Europe, allowed the United States to emerge from the war as the most powerful nation on Earth. The United States responded to an uncertain and unstable postwar world by asserting and attempting to defend a global leadership position, resulting in far-reaching domestic and international consequences.

After World War II, the United States sought to contain the growth of communist military power and ideological influence, create a stable global economy, and build an international security system. The United States developed a foreign policy based on collective security and a multilateral economic framework that bolstered non-communist nations.

The U.S. government sought to "contain" Soviet-dominated communism through a variety of measures, including military engagements in Korea and Vietnam. The Cold War fluctuated between direct and indirect military confrontation periods and mutual coexistence (or détente).

As the United States focused on containing communism, it faced increasingly complex foreign policy issues, including decolonization, shifting international alignments and regional conflicts, and global economic and environmental changes.

Postwar decolonization and the emergence of powerful nationalist movements in Asia, Africa, and the Middle East led both sides in the Cold War to seek allies among new nations, many of which remained nonaligned.

Cold War competition extended to Latin America, where the United States supported non-communist regimes with varying levels of commitment to democracy. Ideological, military, and economic concerns shaped U.S. involvement in the Middle East. Several oil crises in the region prompted attempts at creating a national energy policy. The Reagan administration pursued a reinvigorated anti-communist and interventionist foreign policy that set the tone for later administrations. Reagan initially rejected détente with increased defense spending, military action, and bellicose rhetoric, but later developed a friendly relationship with Soviet leader Mikhail Gorbachev, leading to significant arms reductions by both countries.

The end of the Cold War and new challenges to U.S. world leadership forced the nation to redefine its foreign policy and global role. The end of the confrontation led not only to new diplomatic relationships but also to new U.S. military and peacekeeping interventions, as well as debates over the nature and extent of American power in the world.

Following the attacks of September 11, 2001, on the World Trade Center and the Pentagon, U.S. foreign policy and military involvement focused on a war on terrorism, which generated debates about domestic security and civil rights. In the wake of 9/11, U.S. decision-makers launched foreign policy and military efforts against terrorism and lengthy, controversial conflicts in Afghanistan and Iraq.

Notes for active learning

Notes for active learning

Social History: 1899 to Present

Urbanization and social stratification

The social structure of this period, highlighted by the great income gap, influenced the social reforms, but it is difficult to say how great of an impact it had. While many continued to work towards better workplace treatment and more efficient city services, others lived below the poverty line. It is also interesting to note that regardless of this period's manufacturing and technical accomplishments, the European elites still looked down on Americans as wealthy barbarians who had undoubtedly achieved innovative technologies but lacked social sophistication and grace.

Social classes in the U.S. experienced the impacts of large-scale industrialization and urbanization. The elites became wealthier, maintaining a firm grip on domestic policies, while the working class could experience more varied vocational opportunities and improved quality of life. This was one of the first periods when working-class Americans could transition into the middle class, allowing for consumerism. Leisure activities such as shopping and listening to the radio preoccupied many upper- to middle-class Americans. The introduction of vast department stores, theme parks, theaters, and operas inspired many city dwellers to enjoy the benefits of urbanization, contrasting the poor living conditions of the lower social strata.

In contrast to the slums many Americans inhabited in the city, the wealthy class had experienced an incredible increase in their standard of living. The term "millionaire" was coined earlier during the 19th century but was not actively used until this period, which should give some insight into the levels of excess and decadence experienced by the American elites. One such example of over-the-top opulence came from a formal dinner party thrown by the wife of a railroad tycoon in honor of her dog, who entered the party wearing a $15,000 (today approximately $400,000) diamond collar. The economic instability leading to and culminating with the Great Depression altered the spirit of the American public, causing many to question the safety and supervision provided by the government.

Women's rights movement

As women and minority groups began expanding their roles in the economy and politics, it quickly became evident that social and political abuses were ongoing, causing many to take up their causes with local and federal organizations. The National American Woman Suffrage Association (NAWSA) was formed in 1890, culminating in previously formed groups working towards women's suffrage.

Elizabeth Cady Stanton and Susan B. Anthony (1820-1906) shared the presidency and worked tirelessly for women's rights. A few years later, Alice Paul (1885-1977)—also working towards suffrage by different and sometimes more aggressive means, such as White House pickets and hunger strikes—founded the National Woman's Party.

Alice Paul, c. 1930

By 1910, most western states granted partial suffrage rights to women, though the South and Northeast opposed such a political transition. By August 1920, President Wilson finally signed the Nineteenth Amendment into law, giving women the right to vote.

Minority groups, specifically African Americans, worked together to be treated equally in 20th-century America. The *Niagara Movement* (1905) was the first attempt at national equality for African Americans. Though many whites labeled the movement as extremist, many African Americans saw a commonality in its theology.

In 1909, four years after the Niagara Movement began, *the National Association for the Advancement of Colored People* (NAACP) was founded. The NAACP's goal was to improve the public perception and self-image of African Americans while providing them equal opportunities in American society. These organizations and institutions became fundamental components of America following this period and began conversations about civil rights, which peaked in the 1960s and 1970s. Without these grassroots efforts, many minority groups, including African Americans and women, would not have been adequately represented.

Progressive movement

Those who supported the progressive movement held the government responsible for overseeing many sectors, most notably the economy, the environment, and the workplace abuse of the early 20th century. To achieve the transition from a formerly conservative ruling structure to one based on progressive principles, politicians and American citizens alike championed efforts towards improved working conditions, better pay, more responsible and stable economic policies, and maintenance of our national wonders and resources. This movement, supported by progressive Presidents Roosevelt, Taft, and Wilson, was a transition from the conservative voices of the Gilded Age into a more progressive period.

In addition to economic and political supervision, the progressive reformers sought to maintain, protect, and enhance our natural resources and environment. This was a newer concept and a useful employment tool in the New Deal policies using mandated projects such as the completion of the Hoover Dam in the 1930s and other jobs pertaining to the National Park Service. These environmental policies were instrumental in creating and expanding the current National Parks system.

Hoover Dam site, c. 1930

The progressive movement was in full swing by the early 20th century and climaxed with the passage of the *Federal Reserve Act* in December 1913. The hotly debated law called for a compromise between the interests of the private banking sector and popular sentiment, which was achieved by creating a decentralized bank. President Woodrow Wilson saw this law as a compromise between the progressive and conservative schools of thought.

The creation of the *Federal Reserve Bank*, as directed by the *Federal Reserve Act*, was instrumental in bringing stability to the economic crises of the period; however, it also had lasting implications for the financial well-being of the United States.

In 1914, President Wilson signed the *Clayton Antitrust Act*, which limited unlawful restraints and monopolies, exclusive sales contracts, local price cutting, and interlocking directorates in corporations valued at $1 million or more in the same field. The progressive movement was making strides away from the former economic policies of the Gilded Age.

During this period, many were also concerned about the environment and social exploitation in the workplace. In 1916, President Wilson created the National Park Service, which oversaw thirty-five national parks and monuments and maintained the beauty of America for future generations.

Philadelphia-born Florence Kelley (1859-1932) was a renowned social and political reformer who substantially influenced the regulation of workplace abuses. Kelley advocated for the improved treatment of women, children, and factory workers, the implementation of an eight-hour workday, and the protection of wages.

Florence Kelley, c. 1920

The instability of markets in the late 19th and early 20th centuries, coupled with the disparity of the Great Depression, caused many American citizens to question the banking system. The lack of federal supervision embodied the former laissez-faire business policies of the 1920s, leading to the economic crisis.

In response to the economic instability, many progressive Presidents, such as Theodore Roosevelt, began to transition the U.S. model away from capitalism towards more of a welfare state that supported people in need and maintained economic norms during periods of crisis. The New Deal highlights examples of such policies, passed under later President Franklin Roosevelt. Presidents Roosevelt, Taft, and Wilson championed the spirit of Progressivism.

The progressive school of thought argues that former laissez-faire economic policies and social Darwinist theories are intellectually incorrect; President Wilson went so far as to label these ideals as morally and intellectually unjust. Progressives also claimed that the government and the populace could right what they perceived as "wrongs" of the free market. Such ideas were perpetuated by their predecessor movements, including the populist movement, which laid the groundwork for social change.

The long-lasting implications of the progressive movement are evident in today's social programs. It also highlights a transition in the thinking surrounding the federal government's role in times of crisis and prosperity. Such ideals are seen today; notable examples were in the recent economic crisis of 2008, where the federal government bailed out banks and assisted average Americans with maintaining financial health.

Political and social conflicts

The early 20th century saw high polarization in American politics, economic policies, and immigration reforms. Evidence of this is seen in rural or agrarian prominence being replaced by urban expansion, which caused hostility, on behalf of farmers, towards the banking sector and the new wealth derived from the industrial boom. Evidence of the tense relationships during this period came from the workers and management of industrial projects, most notably the railroad system.

Several strikes and walkouts occurred during the railroad boom between 1890 and 1945. The most notable strikes included the Pullman Strike in 1894 and the United Mine Workers Strike in 1902. Management in all sectors tried to combat the rising tensions among its workers by limiting or expelling unions through yellow-dog contracts (contracts that contain a clause in which a hired worker agrees not to join a union) and lockouts.

The massive immigration influx experienced by the United States during these years also irritated the native-born Americans and new groups of immigrants from Southern and Eastern Europe and East Asia. Americans viewed these immigrants as unskilled laborers lacking education or English-speaking skills. These unskilled laborers were considered undesirable in the political climate of the period. This tension was met with immigration quotas placed on Chinese and later Jewish populations in hopes of quelling the anti-immigration sentiment expressed by Americans in this period.

Fundamentalist Christianity also found an adversary in early twentieth-century America, as many sought to explain the world through scientific modernism. Such transitions were difficult for many Americans to embrace and received much pushback from traditional religious groups. Again, Americans were divided on the subject. An example of this can be seen in the opposition and support for prohibition.

Ratified in 1919, the Eighteenth Amendment banned the sale, manufacturing, and transportation of alcoholic beverages. Protestants and progressives argued that prohibition would increase production, reduce crime, and limit organized crime. Many others disagreed with this position and embraced speakeasies as a means of skirting the law.

After World War I, many men returned from the front, and some civilians, dissatisfied with the current political structure, began feeling disillusioned. However, others felt a sense of high idealism at the close of the war, creating a source of tension between those who had experienced the atrocities of the First World War and those who had not. This is another example of social tensions in America because of the conflicts America entered into abroad and the domestic issues addressed by the American government.

The division of the American public in this period made it difficult to create a unified front, regardless of the topic. However, this would change following the December 7, 1941, attack on Pearl Harbor, which incited a deep and dominant sense of Nationalism.

Post-war migration waves

In addition to economic turmoil, the American public also struggled with its perception of massive migrations in the late 19th and early 20th centuries. While some welcomed the unskilled labor forces, mainly from Latin American countries, many others supported anti-immigration policies, again leading to escalated tensions among various social groups.

An explosion in industrial production and the need for unskilled workers caused a massive influx of immigrants. From 1890 to 1920, the United States admitted approximately fifteen million people. During this period, the immigration patterns were predicated on the flow of the economy; in times of prosperity, immigration rose, and in times of crisis, it stalled.

These years of growing immigration also spurred social unrest, as many Americans embodied a strong sense of Nationalism and opposed the acceptance of "new immigrants." Unlike their predecessors, these new immigrants came mainly from China or southern and eastern Europe, were typically poor, and lacked schooling. Many continued to practice their old-world traditions and were less interested in assimilation, causing social tensions with some native-born Americans.

Hungarian immigrants celebrating the sunflower harvest in Cleveland, c. 1915

Following the terrible years of World War I, many worldwide attempted to return their lives to some normalcy, but for many in Europe, this was almost impossible. The United States, though involved in the global conflict, did not suffer extensive damages like Europe and emerged from the Great War with an improved economy. This improvement and America's rapid industrialization made it an appealing immigration center from the Eastern and Western Hemispheres.

Immigration patterns were a response to economic instability caused by the two world wars. In contrast, the social pressures of immigration and rising Nationalism influenced the U.S. immigration policies in the 20th century. In hopes of quieting criticism at home, the United States instituted exclusion policies regarding immigration from countries outside the Western Hemisphere. One such example came from California, where Japanese immigrants experienced harsh discrimination and oppression, finally resulting in segregated schooling and cultural separation. In hopes of stopping the influx of Japanese immigrants, the United States penned the informal Gentleman's Agreement of 1907, which promised separate schooling in return for limited immigration. However, the agreement did allow Japanese women to enter the country to form families with men who had already immigrated.

During the Great Depression, countless Americans traveled for work, consistent food, and adequate housing. Workers were displaced by more efficient methods of operation and technological advances, such as the implementation of the assembly line, and by changes in demand from industries that previously provided steady work, such as railroads, factories, and the automobile industry. Farmers also struggled during the Depression, causing many to abandon their farms and homes to seek an income to sustain a family.

As America prepared for World Wars I and II, the need for wartime production labor was overwhelming. As the men who previously occupied these positions left for war, women and minority groups were expected to fill the labor gap. World War II bolstered the American economy following the Great Depression, which could not have happened so successfully if not for the domestic support of the wartime populations.

Women and minority groups flocked to armament factories and industrial plants in hopes of securing higher-paying jobs while also supporting the national war effort, which was glorified continuously by wartime propaganda. As these groups worked in new positions, they gained a sense of importance and growth; this was an unprecedented time for women and minority groups in the workplace.

Following the labor shortages of the Great Depression and World Wars I and II, America solved its labor problems by encouraging the influx of Mexican immigrants and seasonal workers, who maintained the agricultural production of the United States and provided an abundant source of unskilled labor. One such program was the Bracero Program, which began in 1942 and ended in 1964. This program resulted from multiple bilateral agreements between the United States and Mexico regarding American labor shortages.

Some social activists fighting for Mexican labor and social causes appeared during this period. One notable example was Luisa Moreno, who organized union workers, led labor strikes and organized the first National Congress of Spanish-Speaking People in 1938. Moreno was a symbol of the struggle Mexican Americans felt during the social abuses of the Great Depression and world wars.

During times of inflammatory anti-immigration sentiment, most notably during the Great Depression and other periods of economic instability, thousands of Mexican American laborers and their children were deported back to Mexico. Native-born Americans harbored heightened immigration concerns during periods of economic crisis, and such deportation policies caused many in America and abroad to wonder if the United States addressed the humanitarian concerns of Mexican immigration.

To deal with the chaotic deportations on the Mexican border, the U.S. Farm Security Administration (FSA) provided some families with housing, medical resources, and the promise of protection from the petty crimes typically associated with migrant work camps and Mexican labor conditions. The policies enacted by the U.S. government against Mexican immigration mirrored those of other anti-immigrant sentiments. However, these were particularly volatile, with considerable fluctuations depending on economic and social circumstances. This unpredictability in policy caused many immigrants to yearn for stability and citizenship.

The first Braceros arriving in Los Angeles by train in 1942

Discrimination and segregation

Some U.S. wartime policies, such as the creation of Japanese and Italian internment camps, caused debate and, at times, concern in the United States and abroad. Governments may limit civil liberties to maintain security during conflict or crisis. One example is the Supreme Court ruling in *Korematsu v. United States* (1944), where the Court sided with the government in preventing national security threats through detention and internment camps. Italian immigrants faced interrogation policies like the Japanese. Close to 700,000 Italian Americans were required to register as enemy aliens during World War II. Almost 10,000 Italian Americans were forcibly relocated from coastal areas.

Segregation in the armed forces caused some to question the morality of the leadership. While African Americans were eventually allowed to enter the war, using two combat units and a few auxiliary forces like the Tuskegee Airmen, the racial bias remained. Other minorities serving in the military included the Navajo Code Talkers, the Comanche, and several thousand Mexican Americans, who fought on the European front but were not formally segregated. Again, racial bias remained.

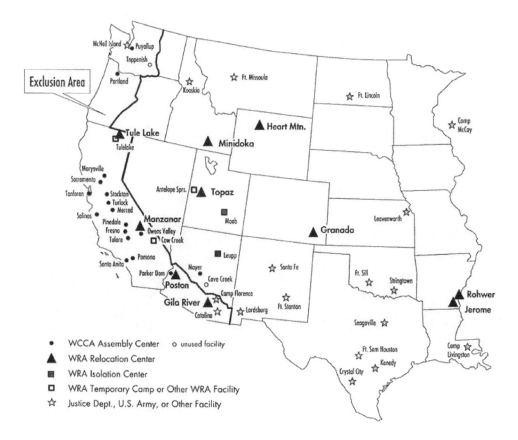

Map showing Japanese American Internment Camps in World War II

The American public and leadership questioned the brutality of the atomic bombs dropped on Hiroshima and Nagasaki, ending the war in the Pacific. As a country that claimed to spread freedoms, liberties, and democracy, it is seen by many as odd that the U.S. government ordered the use of two atomic bombs on civilian populations. This extent of U.S. military power and superiority was unprecedented, resulting in a drastic transition in the global system, felt most keenly during the Cold War era. Some military strategists argued that the use of the atomic bomb was necessary and saved thousands of American lives, as it stalled the planned invasion of Japan (i.e., code name Operation Downfall), scheduled for November 1, 1945.

Under Democratic President Roosevelt, there was disregard for civil liberties in America by Executive Order 9066, Japanese American incarceration. Incarceration also applied to German Americans as well as Italian Americans. EO 9066 resulted in the relocation of more than 10,000 Italian Americans and restricted the movement of 600,000 Italian Americans. These actions caused many Americans to question the morality of their government. In the years following the internment camps, the U.S. government failed to acknowledge its mistake, and it was not until 1988 that Congress awarded surviving detainees $20,000 each in restitution.

As African Americans entered the 20th century, the conditions in the post–Civil War South were still deplorable and unjust; legalized segregation and outbursts of violence-plagued many still living there. While many stayed in the South following the Civil War, others undertook the Great Migration north and west, hoping to obtain new opportunities. Newspapers spread information regarding job recruitment; advertisements were taken out in black newspapers such as the *Chicago Defender*, and stories of successful African Americans in the northern and Midwestern workforces were printed.

As African Americans converged in northern cities, it became clear that many had similar circumstances and ambitions. All faced segregation, oppression, and a lack of economic opportunity. As thousands journeyed north, it became clear that work opportunities would be found in the industrialized cities. By 1919, nearly one million African Americans fled the South, vying for jobs and housing in the crowded major cities of New York, Chicago, Philadelphia, and Detroit.

During this same period, there was a resurgence in Ku Klux Klan membership; by 1923, it peaked at five million members. In the summer of 1919, the large cities experienced a series of race riots, most notably in Chicago, which lasted thirteen days and left 537 injured and 38 dead. Such situations highlight the tense relationship between northern whites and African Americans following the initial flood of the Great Migration.

The Ku Klux Klan on parade down Pennsylvania Avenue in Washington, D.C.

Fight for civil rights

During the late 1940s and 1950s, civil rights activists continued to fight the social and racial inequalities experienced by many African Americans in the United States. While progress was sometimes slow or even stagnant, the movement persevered and eventually culminated at the end of racial segregation.

Rosa Parks and Dr. Martin Luther King Jr

Initial social and legal victories were seen in *Brown v. Board of Education* (1954) and the Montgomery Bus Boycott after the arrest of Rosa Parks in December 1955. The Bus Boycott also sparked progress within the civil rights movement, this time across the country, as news reports regarding the boycott garnered civil rights supporters from the American public. Eventually, lower courts determined that the segregation of the public bus system was unconstitutional.

The emergence and leadership of Dr. Martin Luther King Jr. (1929 to April 4, 1968) also sparked renewed interest and support for the civil rights movement, continuing the momentum that culminated in the *Civil Rights Act* of 1965. To stem the tide of segregation and racism in America, many social activists worked tirelessly with the help of the federal government to create equality for all in the late 20th century. Many notable social activists came from this period, including Fannie Lou Hamer, Thurgood Marshall, and John Lewis; all worked by different means to bring social equality to the United States.

Fannie Lou Hamer (1917-1977) was a civil rights activist who worked for the Student Nonviolent Coordinating Committee and co-founded the Mississippi Freedom Democratic Party in 1964. Hamer worked endlessly against racial discrimination in politics, promoting democratic voting rights to inadequately represented African Americans.

In 1962, Hamer, along with seventeen other African American activists, registered to vote despite local and state obstruction by police forces and white Americans in the South, who met such actions during this period with fierce resistance and interference. Hamer was fired from her job at a plantation where she lived and worked for two decades. However, she saw this action as a blessing and began pursuing civil rights on a more intensified scale.

John Lewis (1940-2020) was a U.S. Congressman and avid civil rights activist who championed Americans' rights and freedoms. Lewis maintained leadership roles in various organizations, and he was the Chairman of the Student Nonviolent Coordination Committee and the director of the Voter Education Project (VEP). Lewis was also instrumental in the 1963 March on Washington, where he was the keynote speaker, and the Selma march on March 7, 1965. Lewis was arrested more than forty times during the civil rights era and was able to put in place a monumental framework for racial and social equality.

Thurgood Marshall was another influential civil rights activist who maintained membership with the NAACP and championed the court cases of *Brown v. Board of Education* (1954). Marshall was appointed an associate justice of the United States Supreme Court by President Johnson in October 1967 and served through October 1991. Marshall was the 96th justice and the first African American on the Supreme Court.

Such events had an immense impact on the civil rights movement. The use of sit-ins, boycotts, freedom rides, peaceful marches, and the protection offered by the Supreme Court facilitated slow but constant progress in the fight for racial equality. In attempts to create real racial equality, the U.S. government—using the judicial, legislative, and executive branches—facilitated significant progress in the civil rights movement of the 1950s, 1960s, and 1970s. Notable examples included the entire desegregation of the armed services following the historic Supreme Court ruling in May 1954 in *Brown v. Board of Education*. The Supreme Court ruled that the "*separate but equal*" segregation laws in public schools were unconstitutional, transforming the civil rights movement. This ruling would be used repeatedly to delegalize federal and state segregation.

The *Civil Rights Act* of 1957 established the Civil Rights Division of the Department of Justice, which empowered the federal government and prosecutors to obtain court injunctions (court orders) against interference with the right to vote. This was monumental in accomplishing a fair democratic representation of the African American population.

Adding to this success was the Twenty-Fourth Amendment, which eliminated the poll tax that required payment to participate in federal elections and limited voting. *The Civil Rights Act* of 1964 outlawed discrimination based on race, religion, sex, or national origin, enforced equal employment and ended segregation in public places. These acts of legislation and rulings by the Supreme Court forever altered the political and judicial landscape of the United States, finally affirming to the nation and others that true equality is obtainable through the cooperative efforts and hard work of social activists and the American public.

As civil rights activists made progress in their pursuits, some Americans—most notably in the South—adamantly rejected desegregation and equal rights for African Americans. This sentiment was embodied in several period crises, including the Montgomery Bus Boycott, the Little Rock desegregation, and the Watts riots.

Following the call for public desegregation, many local and state governments in the South attempted to pursue their policies by raising funds to create white-only private schools or defunding public school programs, as exemplified in 1956 by Virginia legislatures.

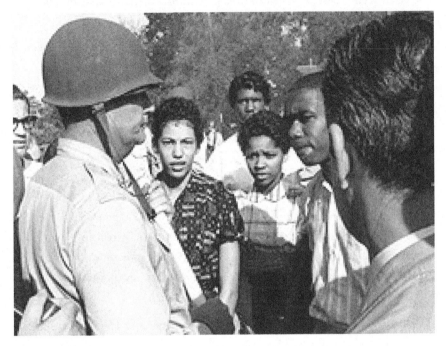

Black students turned away in Little Rock, Arkansas 1957

During this period, southern state legislatures passed nearly 500 laws attempting to block the Supreme Court decision of *Brown v. Board of Education.* Unfortunately, the measures taken by some state governments opposed to desegregation were quite efficient, and the federal government typically lacked the ability or desire to intervene.

By 1957, the federal government was forced to intervene in Little Rock, Arkansas, as the school system, under Democratic Governor Orval Faubus, refused to integrate African American students. With the help of the National Guard, nine students were escorted to school and protected by federal troops. The Virginia legislature, led by Democratic Senator Byrd, ordered that public high schools close rather than be fully desegregated, which was enforced until April 1959 following the Supreme Court ruling that the school system reopens.

The racial tensions of this period created severe sources of conflict and aggression; most times, these actions were taken against African Americans. In August 1965, African Americans protested in Watts, California, leading to massive riots that lasted upwards of a week and left thirty-four dead and countless injured. These initial riots would foreshadow unrest in the summer of 1966 and embodied the sentiment of frustration among young African Americans. These racial riots spread across the country and impacted cities such as Cleveland, Chicago, and Detroit, which had to request federal troops and National Guardsmen to quell the riots. Such racial tensions between young African Americans and the police forces in urban areas would continue into the 21st century.

As the civil rights movement lagged, some activists began to seek a different way to achieve racial equality. Prominent black separatist Malcolm X (1925 to February 21, 1965) advocated a drastic departure from King's methods for some years but did not garner the public support necessary to propel his social revolution. Malcolm X embodied a different perception of the civil rights movement, as he was willing to resort to violence to right the wrongs of American society.

The Black Panther Party for Self-Defense—also known as the Black Panther movement—founded in Oakland in 1966 by Huey Newton (1942-1989) and Bobby Seale (1936-), employed similar tactics. The movement, which attempted to police minority communities against the federal government's threats, also wished to enact revolutionary socialism for the minority and working classes. The Black Panther movement highlighted the frustration of many African Americans who argued that the federal government had done too little to grant equality.

Groups like the Black Panthers argued that no real action had come from the accommodating policies of Dr. Martin Luther King Jr., and acts of violence would more effectively force the hands of the federal government into action. The Student Nonviolent Coordination Committee (SNCC) also followed the path of Malcolm X and the Black Panthers. The SNCC had previously been part of the MLK camp of nonaggression towards racial injustice. Stokely Carmichael from Brooklyn led the organization and called for active participation in Freedom Rides to desegregate the bus systems.

Recognition of minority groups

As African Americans and women began seeing the progress of the civil rights and women's movements, other minorities who faced similar oppression and prejudice worked to promote their equality and bring to light injustices.

Cesar Chavez (1927-1993) led the United Farm Workers (UFW), a nonviolent labor movement, from 1963 until 1970. This movement led to the unionization of Mexican American farm workers. For the first time, it gave appropriate credence to the difficulties immigrant and nonimmigrant workers faced in the American Southwest.

Another organization that pursued equality for Mexican Americans was La Raza Unida, or the National United Peoples Party, which successfully elected many Mexican Americans to local and state government positions. La Raza Unida's goal was to procure better-paying jobs, better educational opportunities, and adequate housing.

Cesar Chavez, c. 1993

The Native Americans were also pursuing better recognition and rights on behalf of the U.S. government during this period. The American Indian Movement (AIM) was an Indian activist organization created to monitor police activities, promote cultural renewal, and coordinate vocational opportunities among urban and rural Native American populations. The AIM was a concern for the federal government in the early 1970s, as it occupied the Bureau of Indian Affairs headquarters in 1972 and the Pine Ridge Indian Reservation at Wounded Knee, South Dakota, in 1973.

While the federal government faced criticism at home regarding its stalled interaction with the civil rights movement, other organizations criticized the United States for its foreign policies. Students for a Democratic Society, who initially voiced concern over income inequality, racial justice, and participatory democracy, quickly gained traction in the antiwar protests of the period. This group was a more radical entity of the counterculture and worked against the U.S. military actions domestically and abroad.

Such social movements were influential in creating the perception of free speech among university campuses nationwide while giving a voice to impoverished urban minorities who had been ignored for decades. These organizations were critical of the federal government and allowed many students to march against inequalities and injustices, a freedom that is much prized by many Americans today.

Feminism

Following the booming 1950s, most Americans viewed the family structure in a traditional sense, with a domesticated stay-at-home mother and a father who worked outside of the home. Such perceptions were amplified following the baby boom, which projected women as subservient maintainers of the traditional values of the family.

However, other women, mainly those who occupied vocational posts during the war years, wanted to experience a new American dream of working outside the home while maintaining their families and personal lives. This change in public opinion resulted in the popularity of feminist movements during the period but also highlighted a countermovement that viewed women's rightful place in the home and worked to promote the social norms maintained during the 1950s.

As the American population adjusted to the postwar political climate, it became clear that women would continue to maintain many roles acquired during the war years, especially in the workforce. Following the domestic war boom, former munitions factories and manufacturing plants, which had been used for arms production and military rearmament, were transformed to meet the demands of the newly emerged consumer culture, providing new avenues of work for women.

Women struggled for equality during the 1950s, 1960s, and 1970s. During this period, all demographic groups experienced publication and social activist recognition; this was also the case regarding the emergence of sexuality following the counterculture. Many women activists, such as Gloria Steinem, sought to shed light on the gender inequalities and discrimination of the period. One example of such activism came in 1963 when Steinem went undercover at the notorious New York City Playboy Club, where she detailed the degrading experience women faced in the workplace. Such publications were read everywhere and received by many women as a gratifying criticism of the sexism faced in America.

During this period, the feminist movement took a strong position within the American public and caused the equality conversation to not only encompass women but gays and lesbians as well. This conversation would begin during the 1960s but continued to evolve in the 21st century. Notable figures of the feminist movement during this period included Betty Friedan (1921-2006) and Gloria Steinem (1934-).

Betty Friedan's *The Feminine Mystique* (1963) criticized domestication and challenged the perception of women as housewives, which was widely circulated in the 1950s. This book sought to educate women on vocational opportunities outside the home and encouraged women to be more than homemakers. Gloria Steinem was also a social activist and writer of the period who worked to promote women's rights and equality using political and vocational opportunities.

Steinem worked to create *New York* magazine in the 1960s and, during the 1970s, founded the National Women's Political Caucus and *Ms. Magazine*, a feminist publication. The feminist movement of this period would eventually catapult into a full-gender movement encompassing the rights and freedoms of gays and lesbians within the American community.

Phyllis Schlafly (1924-2016) was an opponent of women's equality laws and an opponent of Gloria Steinem. Phyllis Schlafly argued that women would suffer if further equality measures were taken because such changes would enter women into the draft, revoke protection from the law in sexual assault and custody cases, and—most importantly—destroy the traditional American family. Schlafly promoted the Stop ERA campaign, which worked against the efforts of feminists and proponents of women's rights and eventually caused a resurgence of concern amongst the public about the sanctity of the traditional American family.

During World War II, many women joined the workforce in factories and cities, filling the void left behind by the predominantly male workforce that had gone to war. During this period, close to 25 percent of the workforce was made up of women. During the later years of the 20th century, women continued to expand their roles within the workforce, and between 1945 and 1960, they made up nearly 50 percent of the total American working population. This transition in social perceptions would be monumental for continued women's movements of the late 20th and early 21st centuries. It also highlights the social divisions of the period and shows the United States as a country striving to provide equal rights and opportunities for all. Women and other minorities would continue to experience setbacks—such as the failure to ratify the Equal Rights Amendment in 1972—but would continue to work towards equality.

Role of the Supreme Court in civil liberties

The United States Supreme Court ruling in *Miranda v. Arizona* (1966) resulted in the decision that police officers must make detainees aware of their constitutional rights to an attorney and against self-incrimination upon arrest. The case highlighted the judicial struggles of Americans against a system they did not always understand.

Ernesto Miranda, a Phoenix resident, was arrested on charges of rape, kidnapping, and robbery, and after police interrogation, confessed to the crimes. Miranda had less than a high school education, had a history of mental illness, and had no legal counsel present at the time of interrogation. Given the circumstances, Miranda appealed to the Supreme Court, arguing that his confession had been acquired unconstitutionally. This ruling resulted in the "Miranda rights," which are read to all those arrested by the police.

Another critical Supreme Court ruling during this period comes from *Griswold v. Connecticut* (1965), which held that bans on contraceptives violate the privacy of marriage. Estelle Griswold was the executive director of the Planned Parenthood League of Connecticut and provided many women with contraception; a Connecticut court eventually convicted her for violating an 1879 law that prohibited the facilitation of contraceptives. The Supreme Court ruled that this was unconstitutional and eliminated the ban on contraceptive use. As these cases influenced the American population, conservative opponents of such legislation tried to restore the traditional values of the American family and pastime. Many argued against contraception and abortions, citing moral and religious concerns.

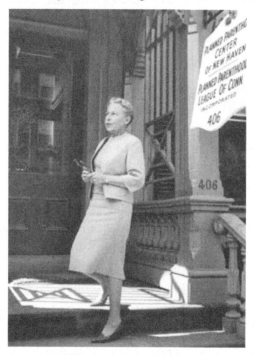

Estelle Griswold, c. 1965

These cases would drastically influence the future rights of the American public. Future legal battles would cite *Miranda v. Arizona, Griswold v. Connecticut,* and *Roe v. Wade* as examples of expanding judicial protection, freedoms, and controversial American rights. Other examples of the public divide during this period came from the legal proceedings of *Bakke v. The University of California* (1978), where the United States Supreme Court ruled it unconstitutional to use the basis of race for college admittance above merit or as the only determining factor.

The court ruled against using racial quotas but held that affirmative action was acceptable if it was used to promote greater diversity and used on a case-by-case basis. Some argued that such events highlighted a new problem of reverse discrimination and showed that while the attempt at creating an equal America was underway, it was far from over.

Demographic and societal shifts of the post-war years

During the postwar years, many Americans changed their perception of the American dream to one that included living in a Sun Belt state, California, Texas, or Florida, with many consumer amenities like radios and refrigerators. This ideal American life changed from those eager to work in industrial or manufacturing jobs while living in big northern cities to those interested in new sectors of work, such as the military installations or factories of the Sun Belt.

For the first time, Americans were less interested in living on the East Coast and focused their attention west into the southwestern states, propelling massive immigration into these regions and cementing the American transition out of the two world wars and into the Cold War era.

In addition to the formation and federal stimulation of the Sun Belt, the American population experienced an unprecedented surge that produced the baby boomer generation, quickly outnumbered any other demographic in the United States. Such numbers alone would allow this generation to influence American culture and the future of American society significantly, for example, the emergence of rock and roll music, suburbanites, and the explosion of the middle class.

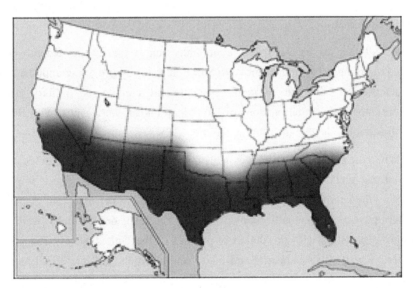

Sun Belt states

In this period, Americans were concerned with the state of American lands and natural resources. For the first time, legislatures could enact federal regulatory standards and establish governmental and non-governmental institutions to preserve and maintain the splendor of the United States. Examples were the formation of the *Environmental Protection Agency* (EPA) in 1970 and the first regulatory law of pollutants, the *Clean Air Act* (CAA), passed by Congress in 1970.

The long-term implications for this period can be seen in the transition of the American population away from staunch traditionalism to one supported by groups of revolution and social movements, such as the counterculture. The emergence of Sun Belt states also paved the way for millions of Americans to live their version of the American dream in new and various ways.

As Americans began to settle into the prosperous times of the 1950s and 1960s, the United States experienced an unprecedented explosion in the population, leading many to call this generation the baby boomers. The period that saw the most growth was from 1946 to 1964, with the highest rise in the population in 1957. This movement was unexpected but greatly influenced the culture and political landscape we see today, as this generation sparked the counterculture movement and expanded U.S. hegemony around the globe leading into the 21st century.

This population explosion, which saw the addition of nearly 50 million babies by the end of 1950, also catapulted the emergence of the Sun Belt as a political force. Following the postwar years, Americans settled in Sun Belt states such as California, Arizona, Texas, and Florida more rapidly than the northeastern industrial communities. This transition was partly due to the influx of investment and political influence stemming from these states but also the draw of living in states with better wealth distribution and climates more forgiving than the Midwest or Northeast.

In addition to an improved community and climate, the federal government encouraged thousands of people to move to Sun Belt states by providing abundant jobs using federal defense spending on weapons systems and completing military installations. Furthermore, more substantial portions of the federal budget were sent to Sun Belt states to finance infrastructure development in the region.

While the population shifted its focus to the Sun Belt states, former industrial sectors in the Midwest and Northeast, most notably in the Ohio Valley, were impacted very negatively by the boom and the expansion of other states. Former industrial giants and other manufacturing states (eventually known as the Frostbelt or Rustbelt) were becoming increasingly dissatisfied with the domestic policies of the United States. The policies now transitioned away from its industrial and manufacturing roots and intensified its focus on a service-based economy.

Small family farms also felt the pinch of the explosion of Sun Belt states, as larger agribusiness models were limiting and replacing small family-run farms. Such transitions between big and small businesses, East and West Coast perceptions and influences, and service versus industry set the stage for social tensions that would divide the country in the following years.

Immigration policies of the 60s

As Americans experienced enormous economic progress, their concerns regarding immigration quotas became less and less evident, pointing to the fact that America has been open to immigration during times of prosperity but opposed it during periods of economic crises or uncertainty. Many immigrants continued to view the United States as the land of opportunity and worked tirelessly to obtain passage to America and citizenship.

In October 1965, Congress, under the Presidency of Lyndon B. Johnson (1908-1973; 1963-1969), passed the *Immigration and Nationality Act,* also known as the *Hart-Celler Act,* which ended the immigration quotas of the early 20th century. Rather than enacting across-the-board quotas, immigration into the United States would now focus on skill sets and relationships with relatives who were already citizens or living in the country.

Restrictions were placed on visas, capping them at 170,000 per year with exceptions, including people born in "independent" nations in the Western Hemisphere—highlighting the age of the Cold War—and former citizens, ministers, and employees of the U.S. government. These laws reflected a change in the perception of Americans; formerly, many saw the influx of immigrants as troublesome and unproductive, but Americans were vastly more concerned with the spread of communism and the Soviet Union.

As immigrants came to the U.S. from Latin America and Asia, they tended to settle in less densely populated areas or where many of their compatriots already resided. This led to a new political climate in the southern and western parts of the country. Each immigrant group had a different culture and influenced the development of those areas differently.

By the early 1880s, the U.S. government was restricting the number of Asians allowed to immigrate to the country for work. Instead, they encouraged Mexicans to come and fill the jobs Asians were doing, like building the transcontinental railroad.

The American government also contacted Mexican laborers during the Second World War when it became apparent that the labor force was insufficient to meet demands. America promised the workers a fair wage, human rights protections, food, and housing.

In turn, the Mexican government signed the Emergency Farm Labor Agreement. This program lasted for two decades and had several unforeseen effects on immigration, as Mexican nationals could get accurate information from these migrant workers about labor conditions and decided, in ever-increasing numbers, to move north. It also started the illegal immigration movement, as many individuals did not want to wait for the legal channels and moved north illegally.

In 1960, Latinos accounted for less than 4 percent of the nation's population. In the last fifty-five years, that number has jumped to 16 percent, representing approximately 50 million people. A number of those Latinos are Mexican. The United States took much of its western territory from Mexico during the mid-1800s. Many people decided to stay at their homes and became Americans instead of relocating within the new Mexican boundaries. Many Mexicans crossed the border in the late 1800s in response to the California gold rush.

Although the programs meant to help workers legally enter and exit the country came to an end, Latinos continued immigrating to the United States. By 1965, the Immigration and Naturalization Service (INS) reported an apprehension rate of approximately 100,000. This was exacerbated by the 1965 *Immigration and Nationality Act*, which created the first-come, first-served basis for visas and put a quota on immigration from the Western Hemisphere.

Puerto Ricans, as citizens of a protectorate of the American government, enjoyed the same rights and privileges as American citizens when on the mainland. In 1948, Puerto Ricans could elect their governor. In 1952, the U.S. Congress approved a new Puerto Rican constitution that made the island an autonomous U.S. commonwealth, with its citizens retaining American citizenship. Puerto Rico formally adopted the constitution on July 25, 1952. This led to several waves of immigration from the island to the mainland as the people sought work and an escape from the island's endemic poverty. The U.S. government, in turn, tried to bring new industry and economy to Puerto Rico to reverse the flow of immigrants. This was relatively ineffective but did help those who remained on the island.

Fidel Castro (right) with fellow revolutionary Camilo Cienfuegos (left) in Havana, c. 1960

While Cubans had always lived in the United States, their population underwent a mass exodus from 1950 to 1960 as the Cuban Revolution occurred with the overthrow of dictator Fulgencio Batista. The Cuban population in America grew by almost 100,000 in a single decade. Fidel Castro (1926-2016) soon banned Cubans from attempting to leave the island, though he lifted the ban once to allow Cubans to reunite with their loved ones. Over 300,000 Cuban refugees came to America, and amnesty laws allowed the United States to welcome another 125,000 during the 1980s, as the federal government considered them refugees from communism.

The immigration of Asians to the United States was very different, primarily due to their location in relation to the United States and the anti-immigration laws of the 1800s. In the early 1800s, many Chinese immigrated to the United States to participate in the California gold rush and the building of the transcontinental railroad. Discrimination soon led to a ban on Chinese immigration, called the *Chinese Exclusion Act* (1882). This did not stop other Asians from entering the country, but America soon reached out to other countries to put an end to the immigration of unskilled laborers.

Toy vendor, Chinatown, San Francisco, c. 1900s

From 1917 to 1945, Asians were not allowed to enter the country at all due to the Asiatic Barred Zone. The exceptions were the Japanese and Filipinos, though this changed with the Japanese attack on Pearl Harbor. Due to discrimination and lack of connection to their home, immigrants already living in the United States tended to band together for mutual support, creating cultural enclaves like Chinatown.

The last discriminatory acts would be repealed in 1965, two years after the first Asian American man was elected as Senator for Hawaii. The end of these restrictive measures led to a surge of immigrants, especially after the wars turned many Asians into refugees, and several acts allowed the refugees special permission to enter the United States regardless of the quotas. In 1965, America passed the *Immigration and Nationality Act*, which allowed Asian immigrants to become citizens.

Environmental activism

As the Sun Belt gained prominence among Americans and politicians, many saw California and the Southwest's draws as desirable, causing massive population influxes to the regions. It became evident that the federal government planned to extract and use natural resources almost recklessly to feed the machine of postwar expansion.

The federal funding of the Sun Belt states caused many formerly prestigious industrial and manufacturing cities (e.g., Cleveland and other Rust Belt cities) to lose their draw. Instead, many Americans embraced the military installations and job opportunities being presented in the Sun Belt states. However, these states were less easily tamed by the American population, with extreme weather conditions, including the hot deserts of the Southwest and the lack of water necessary to sustain the population influx. As a result, many Americans began questioning the expansion of Sun Belt states at the expense of American natural resources, which were becoming more respected and protected. The depletion of resources and the declining Rust Belt states caused many Americans to view the expansion as risky and, at times, unnecessary.

Following the period of wartime industrial production, the U.S. government began to evaluate the environmental concerns raised by conservationists and the American public. Previously, the federal government had taken small steps towards maintaining the country's natural resources. However, it was not until the 1960s and 1970s that the American public became concerned with pollutants and the status of the environment.

One of the early advocates of conservation and environmentalism was Rachel Carson (1907-1964), a writer, social activist, and ecologist. Carson studied many subject areas relating to the environment and the sciences; she received a Master of Arts in Marine Biology from Woods Hole and undertook graduate studies in zoology at Johns Hopkins University.

In 1962, Carson released *The Silent Spring*, which raised concerns among the American public regarding the use of pesticides (particularly DDT) in the American agricultural system. In June 1963, Carson testified about the misuse of pesticides before the U.S. Senate Subcommittee on Government Operations.

Rachel Carson was one of the first conservators to speak out against the mistreatment of America's lands and natural resources during this period. She greatly influenced others to continue this same cause. Other notable activists of this period include Wisconsin Senator Gaylord Nelson, who championed the creation of Earth Day in 1969, mimicking the teach-in activists seen during the Vietnam War. Senator Nelson was like many other Americans who were influenced by the environmental concerns of the period and sought to use the federal government to regulate and protect the environment.

Rachel Carson and Robert Hines, c. 1960

Public perception during this period led to governmental responses, including the *Wilderness Protection Act*. Signed into law in 1964, this Act designated wilderness areas defined by the law as the most protected form of federal land. Under Republican President Nixon, the establishment of the Environmental Protection Agency (EPA) in 1970 and the passage of the *Clean Air Act* in the same year demonstrate the federal government's active attempts to regulate and protect the American public against the harms of pollution. The *Clean Air Act* allowed the federal government to control and regulate air pollutants considered hazardous to human health. Such legislative initiatives and social movements would set the stage for future generations to pursue conservation efforts.

Societal divisions over wars, policy, and moral values

As the middle class emerged following the boom of the 1950s, many Americans struggled to gain an identity in the new country. Some insisted upon maintaining the traditional values of the American family through hard work and faith; others argued this was a period of revolution and worked towards the civil rights and feminist movements.

During this period, the American public was divided on many things, including, but not limited to, the civil rights movement, desegregation, and the distinction and tensions experienced between conservatism and liberalism. Some Americans embraced the counterculture, while others saw it as an attack on the traditionalist views of the American public. Americans began to question the authority and leadership of the presidency as a result of expanded executive powers and the Watergate scandal, which engulfed President Richard Nixon. Additionally, many Americans wanted the federal government to regulate and conserve the natural resources and lands of the country, while others felt this was unnecessary.

The Korean and Vietnam Wars are two of the largest sources of contention among the American public, as many saw these conflicts as murderous and unwanted, and others believed the threat of communism was so significant that any action was necessary to impede Soviet expansion.

Marine Corps scaling wall during the Korean War

Debates regarding the sexual and reproductive rights of women during this period also caused considerable controversy. They left the American public with the task of deciding the morality of others, making many feel uncomfortable. These divisions show the transition America experienced in the postwar years. While it was prosperous and exciting to many baby boomers, others saw these polarizations as the context for future tensions in America.

The Vietnam War was a source of bitter contention in the United States during this period, as many of the older generations saw the need for stability in Southeast Asia without the influence of the Soviet Union, while the younger generations saw the conflict as unnecessary and sometimes even criminal. This sentiment was widely expressed in the counterculture and would dominate domestic politics during this period.

As affluent young Americans were afforded higher education opportunities, a division between the counterculture and its parent generation emerged and continued into the later years of the 20th century. Events like the Berkley free speech fight in 1964 caused many young Americans to view the college setting as one in which rebellion and revolution could be fostered, cultivating the historical "teach-ins" of the Vietnam era.

As the war continued, young Americans protested the use of napalm and other chemical weapons, massive aerial bombings—now commonplace in the war—and the killing of Vietnamese civilians at the hands of American military personnel. By 1968 and 1969, hundreds of antiwar protests had taken place and continued to be organized throughout the country. One such notable example took place on November 15, 1969, when as many as 250,000 protestors descended on Washington, D.C., and peacefully called for the withdrawal of American troops from the Vietnam War.

Many Americans, especially those who had fought in the two world wars, saw the protests as disrespectful, unpatriotic, and even treasonous. Other younger Americans who took part in the protests saw the actions of the American government in Vietnam as exercising unbridled authority, which many came to see as inappropriate in democratic states such as the United States. Forms of protest against the Vietnam War were seen in the military, where many who did not support the war or were tired of the endless campaign began speaking out against the policies of the Vietnam War. As American troops finally began to withdraw, many others waiting to leave the war actively spoke out against military leadership and the overall morale of the American forces.

Thousands of service members were dishonorably discharged for desertion, while close to 500,000 men dodged the draft from 1965 to 1973, many fleeing to Canada. This exemplified the domestic reaction to the occupation of Vietnam, the war itself, and the presidential administrations in the U.S. that perpetuated America's role in the conflict.

The role of the United States in the Vietnam War and the domestic challenges it presented indeed had lasting implications for the United States and the international system. In the future, Americans would be less confident of their military superiority, something they embraced following the two world wars. The conflict also brought financial strain to a nation experiencing enormous economic growth, eventually culminating in massive inflation and the oil crisis of 1973.

US Army spraying Agent Orange in Vietnam, C. 1971

Additionally, the American public harbored great division among each other and military service members following the conflict. Some saw the returning soldiers as murderers, and others saw them as the vanquished; neither was a comfortable perception for the American population. Medical issues later arose from the use of chemical weapons, such as Agent Orange, used against the Vietnamese and affecting many U.S. service people who were exposed to them. These types of policies would cause frustration and resentment on behalf of the military forces involved in the conflict toward the federal government, perpetuating the perception of a failed military offensive in Vietnam.

As Americans moved into the later years of the 21st century, many began seeing an intense polarization and divide among the American public and government officials. New social issues arose from this period, and many saw the need for reforms distinct from previous movements. Instead, Americans sought to embrace a new identity that would mold the international perception of the United States in the coming years.

Watergate rattled the American people's faith in the office of the President and the federal government. Several burglars were apprehended inside the Democratic National Committee (DNC), a federal building in Washington, D.C., while attempting to place wiretaps and illegally retrieve federal documents. While it was unclear if President Nixon ordered or had knowledge of such acts, it was immediately apparent that he had actively attempted to cover up the wiretap scandal.

President Nixon (1913-1994; 1969 to August 8, 1974) offered hush money to those initially questioned by law enforcement regarding the burglary and attempted to obstruct the investigation by the FBI. Nixon fired staff unwilling to support his position in the scandal and physically destroyed evidence of his administration's wrongdoing.

Watergate complex, c. 1974

In August 1974, President Richard Nixon resigned as the full extent of his involvement reached the American public. President Gerald Ford quickly and assertively pardoned President Nixon, removing any possibility of legal action. Such events greatly divided the American public, causing some to side with President Nixon and others to despise him and his presidency.

Economic and political crises of the 70s

As the 1970s ended, the U.S. government struggled to maintain the people's faith. Scandals and failures, in the eyes of many Americans, characterized the seventies. Nixon's Watergate scandal led to a drop in public opinion, as the American people questioned the morality and legality of their President's actions. President Nixon's eventual resignation left the people feeling betrayed and abandoned by their leader. It led to a lack of faith in the office of the President itself, a position that often offered hope and inspiration. Public trust in the President of the United States took years to recover from the blow dealt by the Nixon scandal.

The OPEC oil embargo caused a widespread economic recession and a wave of unemployment and inflation. Most people put the blame squarely at the feet of the American government. After the Iran hostage crisis' paralyzing effects on the Carter presidency, which once again weakened the American people's faith in their government and President, it was evident that the United States was ready for a change in leadership. Ronald Reagan harnessed the waves of religious fundamentalism and the neoconservative movements more than liberal President Jimmy Carter. Regan ushered in a new wave of conservative values and policies.

Political movements and changes are based on a hope for the future and a reaction to the past. Thus, many of the social and political changes that took place in the 1980s found their start in the tumultuous 1970s. While the fifties and sixties had been characterized by growth and national pride, the seventies were characterized by several perceived government failures. The economy, which thrived in the postwar years, was starting to settle. Several political scandals questioned the country's leadership and led to a sense of moral decay. Foreign policy was a constant source of embarrassment and chagrin for the federal government, as American political power seemed weak at home and abroad.

Economically, the issues in the 1970s were multi-dimensional. The United States produced as much oil as it could domestically, but demand continued to increase. To offset this demand, the United States purchased oil from abroad through OPEC, the Organization of the Petroleum Exporting Countries. This was a mutually beneficial agreement. The United States had one of the strongest economies in the world, and the American dollar was the international currency of choice.

However, this also meant that the OPEC nations had central control of a significant portion of the American economy because they controlled the means of energy production. As the United States bought more and more oil from OPEC, domestic production decreased accordingly. It was cheaper for businesses to purchase oil abroad than to produce it at home.

In 1973, several factors combined to severely impact the U.S. economy. First, the United States decided that the American dollar no longer had to have the backing of gold. This meant that the value of a dollar would be fluid and not depend on the amount of gold bullion in the Federal Reserve. While beneficial to Americans because it allowed the dollar's value to fluctuate in response to the market, this also affected the sale of oil.

OPEC sold oil by barrels based on the American dollar. As the dollar fluctuated, the price of oil fluctuated. In reaction to this discrepancy, OPEC decided to base the price of a barrel of oil on the gold standard instead. This instantly made oil more expensive.

In October of 1973, Egypt and Syria launched an attack on Israel in a conflict now known as the Yom Kippur War. Egypt and Syria wished to reclaim territory that they had lost to Israel during the Six-Day War of 1967. President Nixon recognized Israel as an asset to the United States after World War II and provided economic and military supplies to the country's aid. The OPEC nations were furious that the Americans would intercede on behalf of the Israelis and decided to issue an oil embargo. The terms of the embargo caused the price of oil to nearly double and sparked an international recession.

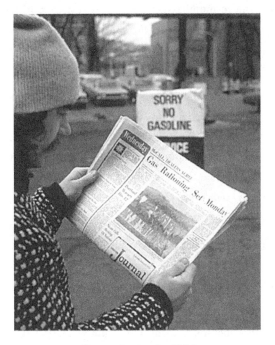

Gas rationing in 1974

The oil embargo caused a ripple effect throughout the economy. Increased oil prices meant a decrease in oil stores in the United States. This led to gasoline rationing to avoid rapid consumption. The rationing system was simple and based on license plates: an individual with a license plate that ended in an even number could only buy gas on even dates, and an individual with a license plate that ended in an odd number could only buy gas on odd dates. In theory, this would help avoid a run on the gas stations. Lines were long, and often, the station ran out of gas before it ran out of customers.

Petroleum is used for the industrial production of materials like plastic, which created its impact. Beyond the cost of gasoline, the demand for household products was starting to outpace the supply. This meant that price inflation rapidly became a problem.

As inflation rose, people needed increased wages to counteract the increased cost of living. As the cost to produce and transport products was skyrocketing, businesses could not provide the desired wage increases to their employees. Instead, Americans took other measures to stave off the increase in the cost of living. People became very conscious of their cars. Smaller models that consumed less gasoline became popular. People were also very considerate of how they drove. The national speed limit during the period was fifty-five miles per hour, the optimal speed for fuel conservation. Household energy consumption was also closely monitored as people tried to conserve energy.

Several other factors added to the economic downturn as the oil embargo rocked the American economy. Loss of faith in the economy meant the stock market began to drop. It lost 40 percent over eighteen months and took nearly a decade to regain the people's faith. With inflation on the rise, unemployment also rose. The percentage of unemployed Americans reached double digits over the decade. Interest rates hit 20 percent, meaning some items, like houses and cars, became unaffordable for Americans.

With the economy struggling throughout the nation, anger and resentment came to a head in the West over land. The federal government owned about 60 percent of the land west of the Rocky Mountains. This land was open for public usage to an extent, but the industries that utilized this land balked at the amount of government regulation and the expensive fees and fines. Ranchers, for instance, spent an inordinate amount of money on grazing permits and did not understand why they were charged for what was mostly a public service.

This led to many Westerners feeling that they were being exploited, as they cared for the land that the government-owned. They also complained that the government was unresponsive to the needs of the local population. Things like irrigation rights were established in Washington without any input from the local population. As tempers rose, the Sagebrush Rebellion ensued to fight federal control of the land.

The Sagebrush Rebellion gained momentum as the federal government enacted the *Federal Land Policy and Management Act* (FLPMA) in 1976, which stated that federal land would never be sold to private and public investors. The FLPMA also set aside land for federal parks. This meant that even though the land had previously been open to the public, it was no longer usable. Things like irrigation, which had formerly been allowed, were no longer options. This infuriated Westerners, who felt that their land was mostly stolen. President Reagan eased some anger when he appointed one of the Sagebrush leaders to his Department of the Interior. However, the resentment did not entirely fade until the 21st century.

Another event that had a significant impact on the way that Americans viewed their government during the 1970s was the Iran hostage crisis. The causes of the crisis go back to the 1950s when Iran's leader, Mohammad Mossadegh, decided that he wanted to nationalize Iran's petroleum reserves. The United States had a controlling interest in Iran's oil reserves and wanted to maintain its hold. Therefore, they planned a coup to replace Mossadegh with the more pro-Western Mohammed Reza Shah Pahlavi (1919-1980; 1941-1979).

Iran hostage crisis, c. 1979

In August 1953, the coup, code-named Operation TP-Ajax, was successfully implemented. While the Western world embraced Iran's new leader, the Iranian people were resentful. They felt that the Americans should not have a role in their sovereign nation, and as the Shah revealed himself to be a brutal dictator, anti-American sentiment grew. By 1970, the image of the Shah reached an all-time low, and some Iranian people were ready for a change in leadership. They turned to Ayatollah Ruhollah Khomeini, a radical Islamic cleric. The Shah fled to Egypt as the new regime took over in 1979.

Later that year, in October 1979, President Carter allowed the former Shah to enter the United States to seek medical treatment. The Shah was suffering from lymphoma and appealed to the President's moral conscience. The people of Iran were furious. A group of college students stormed the U.S. Embassy in Tehran and took sixty-six people hostage. The United States responded immediately with diplomatic overtures and economic sanctions. All Iranian holdings in the United States were seized. Still, they had little success.

Thirteen hostages were released soon after they were taken, but this was mainly because they were not Americans or were Americans who felt oppression themselves, like African Americans. Later, another would be released after developing medical problems. This added to the constant fear of the hostages. They did not know from one moment to the next whether they would live, die, or be tortured. Their captors often paraded them around, and several times, the watching American public feared for the lives of the hostages as they were presented to angry mobs.

President Carter wanted desperately to bring the hostages home. Morally, he felt that it was his duty as President to fight for his people, and the ineffectiveness of his actions frustrated him. Politically, this was compounded by the continual media coverage of the crisis and Carter's simultaneous running for reelection. In April 1980, Carter decided that the diplomatic route was not working. He gave the orders for Operation Eagle Claw, which would allow an elite team to enter Iran and free the hostages.

Two U.S. Navy aircraft parked on USS Nimitz for Operation Eagle Claw

The plan might have worked, but a sandstorm caused one of the planes to crash, killing the service members onboard. Carter looked desperate and ineffective to the American people, who had once again witnessed their leaders fail them. The American people did not trust a government that could not protect its citizens.

On Election Day in the fall of 1980, Ronald Reagan won by a landslide. Knowing that he had less than three months left as President, Carter redoubled efforts to bring the hostages home during his term. His efforts failed, however. The hostages were freed on Reagan's inauguration day after being held for 444 days.

Conservative revival of the 1980s

In reaction to the political failures and uncertainty of a disenchanted public, conservatives had a revival during the 1980s, which continued into the 1990s and the new century. The perception of the government shifted to a conservative viewpoint as people began to question and criticize their leaders openly. People lacked faith in the government and, therefore, wanted the government to control fewer vital industries and programs.

This drew people toward conservatives like Ronald Reagan, who stood as a staunch supporter of smaller government and deregulation of industries. While conservatism achieved gains and growth as a movement, conservatives were not entirely successful, as numerous liberal systems and programs were too complicated to change or defeat.

President Ronald Reagan, c. 1988

The 1980s gave rise to several fundamentalist and evangelical groups that opposed the more liberal social ideas of the 1970s. They saw a decrease in public opinion and felt that the best way to fix the government was back-to-basics fundamentalism that focused on religion and family values. These groups were surprisingly active, if sometimes short-lived. They played a definite role in the political sphere and opposed many of the new legislative initiatives of the time. The Moral Majority and Focus on the Family were two particularly popular groups.

The Moral Majority is often considered a fundamentalist Christian organization, and at its core, it is. However, the movement's founders, Richard Viguerie, Paul Weyrich, and Howard Phillips, quickly realized they needed to branch out and welcome all disenfranchised conservatives who could support the same goals. Ultimately, they wanted a group that could unite these factions and enact changes through political power—a fundamental conservative voting block to enhance and maintain the conservative morality of the nation.

Their political platform was very clear-cut but covered a wide range of issues. The Moral Majority was socially conservative; they opposed abortion and campaigned against the Equal Rights Amendment, which passed in Congress in 1972 and was making its way to the states for ratification but fell short.

They also opposed the idea of gay rights. Their ideas on sex, in general, tended toward the puritanical, and they opposed sex education and pornography. Instead, they wanted a strong national defense, which led to opposition to the *Strategic Arms Reduction Treaties* with the Soviets. They supported the stable nuclear family and family values. They wanted prayer in schools and what they described as "Bible morality." They were anti-communist and pro-Israel.

Their president, Jerry Falwell (1933-2007), led the Moral Majority and primarily used direct mail to spread their ideas. They published a circular called *The Moral Majority Report* and shipped it monthly to—according to Falwell—over 600,000 supporters. Falwell also claimed that almost the same targeted funding letters went out weekly. They claimed a supporting constituency of 50 million Americans and, especially in the 1980s election, focused on ensuring conservative leaders were elected.

Dr. Jerry Falwell, President of the Moral Majority and
the founder of Liberty University, c. 2006

The Moral Majority had a targeted political strategy for elections. In 1982, they crafted the "Top-Secret Battle Plan for 1982." They outlined a set of targeted objectives: the desire for a Human Life Amendment to fight abortion and support for the *Family Protection Act* (1981-1982), among others. In 1984, they pushed for the election of pro-Israel politicians and publicly supported Reagan's anti-communist Central American policies. In 1988, the *Civil Rights Restoration Act* became their focus, though they were criticized for some of their comments.

While the organization had much influence, it was not always the most political organization and was criticized for its actions. Splinter organizations like the Focus on the Family group emerged from differing opinions in the organization and decreased the power of the Moral Majority by separating its base. The Moral Majority was eventually disbanded in 1989, as Falwell redirected his attention to his Liberty University in Lynchburg, Virginia, and his work as an evangelical minister.

Focus on the Family was founded by psychologist James Dobson in 1977. Like the Moral Majority, Focus on the Family wanted to support fundamental Christian social conservatism. They created a family-centric political platform that blended fundamentalist ideals with family issues. They supported an education program that taught creationism and abstinence and supported public and school prayer.

The Focus on the Family also had a back-to-the-Bible approach to gender roles. They stood against anything that they felt would threaten the traditional family values they used as their bedrock, including rights for the LGBT community. They opposed abortion and pornography like their Moral Majority counterpart, but also addiction problems like gambling and substance abuse, which they felt might tear a family apart.

While the Moral Majority focused on targeted mailings, the Focus on the Family movement tried to branch out into other media types. They had a daily radio show hosted by the group's president, Jim Daly, published resources and a magazine for readers, and provided video and audio recordings of their programs. The organization continued spreading information in targeted programs, focusing on specific audiences they wanted to hold and those who were receptive to their message. Two popular radio broadcasts were *Adventures in Odyssey* for children and *Family Minute*.

Like their targeted radio shows and programs, Focus on the Family separated its work into different ministries, each with a separate focus. Love Won Out was a Focus on the Family ministry until it was sold to Exodus International, who later stopped all activities.

Jim Daly of Focus on the Family

Love Won Out was a primarily anti-gay ministry that focused on rehabilitation. Wait No More focused on adoption. They worked to get children adopted from foster care, but only by what they considered appropriate households. The program assists no same-sex couples or couples living together outside of wedlock.

Not all conservative initiatives were met with success. Many conservatives oppose abortion because they see it as an immoral action. Option Ultrasound is a program run by Focus on the Family that provides grants for pregnancy crisis centers. The goal of the program is to allow women considering aborting the fetus to "see" their child before they decide. The hope is that women change their minds when their baby is no longer abstract. To this end, the grants the group provides are used to purchase ultrasound machines that can show a mother her child.

Religious groups equated aborting a fetus with legalized murder and protested *Roe v. Wade* (1973). In 1992, conservatives were thwarted when *Casey v. Planned Parenthood*, which had its roots in the original *Roe v. Wade* decision, upheld and structured the abortion debate. Many states that disagreed with *Roe v. Wade* tried to limit abortions in their states by creating regulations or obstacles.

In 1982, Pennsylvania passed a law that included several obstacles to abortions. The *Abortion Control Act* required all women seeking an abortion to give informed consent and undergo a twenty-four-hour waiting period. Minors could not seek abortions without parental or judicial consent, and wives had to get consent from their husbands. The Act also mandated that abortion clinics report to the state.

Planned Parenthood quickly challenged the Act, claiming that it violated the holding in *Roe v. Wade*. The Supreme Court heard arguments in *Casey v. Planned Parenthood* (1992) and issued their decision. They ruled that many aspects of the Pennsylvania law were constitutional but that a woman's decision to receive an abortion is protected by the State. The Court ruled that the state could not regulate abortions before the viability point (not defined by the court) except to protect the health of the mother and that states could not interfere with an abortion if the mother's health were at risk.

They deemed that any "substantial obstacles" that prevented a woman from seeking an abortion violated the Constitution, but this did not include Pennsylvania's twenty-four-hour waiting period. The consent of the husband/father was deemed unconstitutional, as it impeded a woman's right to autonomy by requiring her to consider the wishes of the husband/father.

Immigration in the 80s and 90s

As the government and the economy changed, so did the composition of the American people. In the last several decades, the U.S. birthrate has started to decline. With an average of 1.9 children per family, Americans produce fewer children every year, leading to a slow decline in population. This means that if no immigration were allowed into the country, the population would decrease slowly. A birthrate of two children per family would create a sustained population as each family produced only enough children to replace them. With a birth rate under two, immigration accounts for all population increases in the United States. Most of these immigrants are people of color who come from vastly different backgrounds, particularly Asians and Latinos. This has encouraged Americans to consider their cultures and beliefs as the country moves forward.

Immigration to the United States after World War II increased significantly, as many people saw it as a place where they could achieve financial opportunities not available in their home countries. This was particularly true for those who lived in Latin American countries, where poverty was endemic, and in Asian countries that the Korean War and the Vietnam Wars impacted. As immigration increased, American citizens indicated their concerns about the new labor supply's impact on employment. The fear was that illegal immigrants would take jobs previously held by American citizens because they would be willing to work for lower wages.

As debates rage on about immigration and potential reform, it is essential to remember the social aspects of the demographic shift. While the issue goes beyond immigration, one of the most critical social bills affecting demographics does deal with immigration directly. The *Immigration Reform and Control Act* of 1986 was a landmark bill that analyzed the impacts of immigration into the United States, focusing on illegal immigration and how to control and contain it.

The *Immigration Control and Reform Act* was a way to assuage these fears. It required all employers with three or more employees to verify all employees' identities and their immigration status. Any employer who was found employing illegal immigrants would be fined. The Act granted amnesty for some 3 million illegal immigrants living in the country. While the *Immigration Control and Reform Act* has been considered mostly successful and is still in place today, there were loopholes.

For example, instead of hiring employees, a firm or business would hire a contractor to loan them (subcontractors) for jobs for a specific time. The subcontractors were then the responsibilities of the contractor and not the business. Therefore, the business could not be fined if these subcontractors were not legal citizens or legal foreigners using work visas. This loophole also meant that some of the subcontractor pay went to the business's contractor instead. Businesses that did not want to use subcontractors were still wary of hiring foreign citizens who might be in the country illegally.

While immigration has continued to be an important topic, and many presidents have pledged to continue immigration reform under their presidencies, the *Immigration Reform and Control Act* of 1986 is one of the few Acts that has been put into place to answer the question of immigration laws inside the United States.Many Central American immigrants traveled to America during the 1980s. While most of these immigrants came illegally, they came to escape violence, revolutions, and dictators in their home countries.

While most people assume that the immigrants were primarily working-age males, a significant number of females entered the country illegally in the 1980s and 1990s. Not all these immigrants were unskilled laborers, either. Many educated individuals fled their home countries for opportunities only available in America.

In total, Central Americans reached a population of 1.3 million people by 1990. The different groups traveled and settled in different places, establishing immigrant neighborhoods that became part of the local government. Guatemalans, for instance, tended to cluster in Texas and California, while Nicaraguans settled primarily in Miami.

While both Asians and Latinos served as vital additions to the labor force, they were also a central point for several cultural and political debates. These debates tend to focus on the perceived issue of illegal immigration and, therefore, tend more towards Latinos than Asians. Asian Americans do not experience the same cultural backlash as Latinos. This is primarily due to the significantly lower number of Asians who enter the country illegally, which allows them to be legally gainfully employed.

While many people fear that the number of immigrants is growing too large, it is essential to note that the economic slump of the early 2000s saw thousands of people voluntarily leaving the country as work becomes scarce. After the signing of the NAFTA and CAFTA agreements, the economic disparity between the countries lessened, and coming to America was no longer the only way to improve the quality of life.

This has not stopped some groups from speaking out against Latinos. Native First movements spread panic about the aging of the white population and tried to convince people to act against the Latinos. This is compounded by the lack of progress by the federal government to answer the illegal immigration question.

Some states have responded by taking matters into their own hands and enacting state laws that limit opportunities for those who cannot prove citizenship. The South and the West, particularly Arizona, passed over 300 regulations in 2010 alone, banning illegal immigrants from renting homes, procuring state driver's licenses, and even attending taxpayer-funded schools. As these measures are reviewed in court, the question remains as to what to do with the people living in America illegally.

Department of Homeland Security Secretary Janet Napolitano
swears in ten people as U.S. citizens under the Immigration and Nationality Act

While many people see immigration reform as a Latino issue, there are many illegal Asian immigrants as well who have been at the fringes of the immigration debate. In California alone, it is estimated that there are over 400,000 illegal Asian immigrants. Nationwide, the estimate is close to 1.3 million, making Asians the second-highest illegal group in the United States.

Typically, they have remained quiet, but as the possibility of real immigration reform is discussed, more Asians are speaking out and confessing to their illegal status. They point out that they, like Hispanics, have been productive members of society and deserve to have a role in the place where they live. By 2000, 4.2 percent of the U.S. population identified as Asian. In seven years, that number rose to almost 5 percent.

National security

The 21st century, marked by the ensuing Global War on Terror following 9/11, can be characterized as a period of social, economic, and demographic changes. Economically, the country attempted to adapt to the new global market and the associated problems. Demographically, waves of immigrants from Latin America and Asia changed the American landscape, politically and socially. Both new challenges meant that society could not stagnate and was forced to adapt as the people adapted.

The wars in Afghanistan and Iraq—as far as human lives are concerned—were not the costliest of wars, yet both wars eventually became unpopular. It was complicated for the United States to make any headway in countries where the terrorist organizations were so deeply embedded as to become part of the government or the ruling faction of the government. When it became clear that the reports of Weapons of Mass Destruction (WMD) in Iraq had been incorrect, public opinion for that war soured.

The war in Afghanistan was relatively well accepted. People felt that it was taking too long and that it was not as effective as it should be, but most people viewed the war in Afghanistan as necessary. The war in Iraq, however, made people nervous.

People were unsure of why the war had started, and many people were concerned that the war was a ploy to gain control of Iraq's oil resources. Some critics also raised the concern that President Bush was using the War on Terror as an excuse to finish what his father started during Desert Storm.

Americans were also concerned as to how these terrorists managed to infiltrate the country and plan these attacks without being identified by authorities. Americans were outraged by the fact that the attacks had been perpetrated under the oversight of some of the best investigative organizations in the world, particularly the FBI and the CIA.

In response, these organizations attempted to determine whether any Americans had held pre-knowledge of the attacks. They also wanted to know if another attack was imminent. The 9-11 Commission was created to answer these and other questions.

The result of these fears was the *Patriot Act*, passed just forty-five days after the September 11, 2001 attacks. The *Patriot Act* refers to a long history of warnings by former American Presidents after the American Revolution. They were worried that the American Revolution would encourage people to give away their liberties for the new government's security. They warned that those willing to give up their liberties for security are destined to lose both. A similar argument happened in response to the *Patriot Act* immediately after 9/11.

Americans were terrified that another attack was imminent and that the investigative agencies that failed to identify the first attack would fail again. This led to several measures being put into place that violated — according to many critics — civil liberties held by the American public.

The *Patriot Act* expanded the federal government's authority and allowed the newly created *National Security Agency* (NSA) to monitor domestic phone and email communications. It allowed the collection of financial records and metadata from an individual's cell phone and Internet history. The *Patriot Act* is controversial and has been accused of unconstitutionality several times. Public approval plummeted as citizens perceived the acts and unpopular wars as the government's attempt to aggregate power.

Transition of social norms

Another social law that indicated the considerable shift in public opinion and demographics as the United States reevaluated its social culture was Don't Ask, Don't Tell (DADT), which dealt with the public perception of sexuality and began one of the newest civil rights campaigns. Don't Ask, Don't Tell is the colloquial name given to efforts by Democratic President Clinton to end discrimination against homosexuals in the U.S. military.

Clinton's original intention was to create a bill that would immediately overturn the ban on gays in the U.S. military branches. However, this was met with immediate backlash from political contemporaries, including those in charge of military regulation committees. The argument was that by allowing gays to serve in the military openly, the functionality of the armed forces would be weakened. Ultimately, President Clinton reached a compromise called Don't Ask, Don't Tell.

The compromise allowed gays and lesbians to serve in the U.S. military, provided they did not disclose their sexual orientation and did not engage in any sexual practices. In turn, the bill would also protect gay soldiers against superior officers inquiring as to their sexual orientation and making decisions based on their answers. This compromise did not make either side particularly happy.

Those who felt that having gays openly serve in the military would affect military effectiveness were worried that the same effects would occur with gays serving in the military and keeping it secret. Similarly, gays were upset that Clinton's complete repeal of their military ban had been reduced to a secrecy agreement. Still, from 1993 to 2011, Don't Ask, Don't Tell illustrated the military's policies toward gays. This compromise did not stop homosexuals from being discharged from the military. Throughout the ban, many service people were discharged for refusing to hide their homosexuality.

When Barrack Obama (2009-2017) became President in 2009, one of his policy goals was the repeal of Don't Ask, Don't Tell. While he hoped to get DADT repealed immediately, it was felt that the impacts of the repeal needed to be examined beforehand. Therefore, the Pentagon studied how DADT's repeal would affect military effectiveness. They polled soldiers and commanding officers who overwhelmingly indicated that they were minimally or entirely unconcerned about the prospect of open homosexuality.

In the end, the ban on disclosure of one's sexual orientation was overturned when the study concluded that military operations would be minimally affected by any changes to the Don't Ask, Don't Tell policy. While this change was considered a significant victory for the LGBT community, the change in sexuality demographics is still a continuing issue. DADT symbolized a first step forward in one of the newest civil rights movements.

Chief of Naval Operations Adm. Gary Roughead (left) testifies about the comprehensive review working group report regarding "Don't Ask, Don't Tell"

Social history – summary of the period

In the late 1890s and the early years of the 20th century, journalists and progressive reformers—mostly urban and middle class, and often female—worked to reform existing social and political institutions at the local, state, and federal levels by creating new organizations aimed at addressing social problems associated with industrial society.

Progressive reformers responded to economic instability, social inequality, and political corruption by calling for government intervention in the economy, expanded democracy, greater social justice, and conservation of natural resources. Progressives promoted federal legislation to regulate the economy and environment, and many sought to expand democracy. National, state, and local reformers responded to economic upheavals, laissez-faire capitalism, and the Great Depression by transforming the United States into a limited welfare state.

Technological change, modernization, and changing demographics led to increased political and cultural conflict: tradition versus innovation, urban versus rural, fundamentalist Christianity versus scientific modernism, management versus labor, native-born versus new immigrants, white versus black, and idealism versus disillusionment.

Many Americans migrated during the Great Depression, often driven by economic difficulties, and during World Wars I and II due to the need for wartime production labor. Economic dislocations, social pressures, and the economic growth spurred by two world wars led to a higher degree of migration within the United States and the United States from elsewhere in the Western Hemisphere.

Although most African Americans remained in the South despite legalized segregation and racial violence, some began a "Great Migration" out of the South to pursue new economic opportunities offered by World War I. Many Mexicans were drawn to the United States by economic opportunities and ambivalent government policies of the 1930s and 1940s. Wartime experiences, such as the internment of Japanese Americans, challenges to civil liberties, debates over race and segregation, and the decision to drop the atomic bomb, raised questions about American values.

Seeking to fulfill Reconstruction-era promises, civil rights activists and political leaders achieved some legal and political successes in ending segregation, although progress toward equality was slow and halting. Following World War II, they utilized various strategies—legal challenges, direct action, and nonviolent protest tactics—to combat racial discrimination.

Decision-makers in each of the three branches of the federal government used measures including desegregation of the armed services, *Brown v. Board of Education*, and the *Civil Rights Act* of 1964 to promote greater racial justice. Continuing white resistance slowed efforts at desegregation, sparking a series of social and political crises across the nation. At the same time, tensions among civil rights activists over tactical and philosophical issues increased after 1965. Groups on the left also assailed liberals, claiming they did too little to transform the racial and economic status quo at home and pursued immoral policies abroad.

Latinos, American Indians, and Asian Americans began to demand social and economic equality and redress of past injustices. Stirred by a growing awareness of inequalities in American society and by the African American civil rights movement, activists also addressed issues of identity and social justice, such as gender, sexuality, and ethnicity.

Activists began to question society's assumptions about gender and to call for social and economic equality for women and sexual minorities. While the image of the traditional nuclear family dominated popular perceptions in the postwar era, the family structure of Americans underwent profound changes as the number of working women increased, and many social attitudes changed. Liberal ideas were realized in Supreme Court decisions that expanded democracy and individual freedoms, Great Society social programs and policies, and the federal government's power. However, these unintentionally helped energize a new conservative movement that mobilized to defend traditional visions of morality and the proper role of state authority.

Postwar economic, demographic, and technological changes impacted American society, politics, and the environment. A burgeoning private sector, continued federal spending, the baby boom, and technological developments helped spur economic growth, middle-class suburbanization, social mobility, a rapid expansion of higher education, and the rise of the "Sun Belt" as a political and economic force. Internal migrants, as well as migrants from around the world, sought access to the economic boom and other benefits of the United States, especially after the passage of new immigration laws in 1965.

After 1980, the political, economic, and cultural influences of the American South and West continued to increase as the population shifted to those areas, fueled in part by a surge in migration from regions that had not been heavily represented in earlier migrations, especially Latin America and Asia.

As federal programs expanded and economic growth reshaped American society, many sought greater access to prosperity, even as critics began questioning the increased use of natural resources. Responding to the abuse of natural resources and the alarming environmental problems, activists and legislators began to call for conservation measures and a fight against pollution. New demographic and social issues led to significant political and moral debates that sharply divided the nation. Conservatives and liberals clashed over many new social issues, the power of the presidency and the federal government, and movements for greater individual rights.

Although the Korean conflict produced some minor domestic opposition, the Vietnam War saw the rise of sizable, passionate, and sometimes violent antiwar protests that became more numerous as the war escalated. The public confidence and trust in the government declined in the 1970s due to economic challenges, political scandals, foreign policy "failures," and a sense of social and moral decay. This led to the growth of religious fundamentalism and the dissemination of neoconservative thought, all combined with invigorating conservatism.

A new conservatism grew to prominence in U.S. culture and politics, defending traditional social values and rejecting liberal views about the role of government. The rapid and substantial growth of evangelical and fundamentalist Christian churches and organizations, as well as increased political participation by some of those groups, encouraged significant opposition to liberal social and political trends.

Entering the 21st century, the nation continued to experience challenges stemming from social, economic, and demographic changes. The population continued significant demographic shifts with profound cultural and political consequences. The new migrants affected U.S. culture in many ways and supplied the economy with a substantial labor force. However, they became the focus of intense political, economic, and cultural debates.

The war on terrorism sought to improve security within the United States but raised questions about the protection of civil liberties and human rights. Demographic changes intensified debates about gender roles, family structures, and racial and national identity.

Notes for active learning

Intellectual & Cultural History: 1899 to Present

Cultural transitions brought about by technological development

The evolution of communication and transportation technology drove home the appeal many Americans found in the urbanization movement during the early 20th century. Improved roads, bridges, and automobiles allowed many upper- and middle-class workers to commute into big cities like New York and Philadelphia.

Indoor plumbing and electricity caused many immigrants to see New York and other booming cities as utopian versions of 20th-century dwellings. The explosion of the telegraph allowed Americans to communicate much faster, all while propelling the desire for bigger and more efficient urban cities, which Americans believed would be the key to success in the transitioning international system.

This population influx caused escalated tensions between native-born Americans and immigrants: the Populist movement and monopolies, conservatives and progressives, and isolationists and interventionists. Sources of contention in this period also included the transition of women away from the traditionalist mindset of the 19th century and the vilification of alcohol by the Prohibition movement. Significant tensions caused many Americans to rally against others and call for the expulsion of anything that might tarnish the perception of traditional America.

1888 Prohibition poster

The Prohibition movement was a period from 1920 to 1933, during which a nationwide constitutional law was enacted prohibiting the production, importation, transportation, and sale of alcoholic beverages. The movement peaked in 1919 with the ratification of the Eighteenth Amendment, which prohibited the manufacture, transportation, and sale of alcohol. The Eighteenth Amendment was repealed in 1933 with the ratification of the Twenty-First Amendment, which ended Prohibition.

The Prohibition era was associated with speakeasies (i.e., establishments that sold alcohol illegally), glamor, and gangsters. It was also a period when even the average citizen broke the law. Despite this legislation, millions of Americans drank liquor illegally, giving rise to bootlegging, speakeasies, and organized crime. Today, the Prohibition era is remembered as a time of social and political change in the United States.

Technological and economic advancements changed the perception of a happy life in America, including better wages and modern ideas and values. However, this new period was not free of conflict or tension. The lingering issues of racism, anti-immigration sentiments, and economic uncertainties caused many Americans to yearn for a more peaceful time. Examples of this change in perception can be seen most in the cultural movements of the period, including jazz, literature, flappers, and consumerism.

This would all be drastically altered following the onset of World War I when economic stresses, coupled with wartime policies, caused many Americans to doubt the prosperity of the early 20th century and turn to a pattern of isolationism. These concerns would only be reaffirmed with the outbreak of World War II, when Americans realized they would be engaged in conflict within the European theater, regardless of their isolationist mindset.

The new technologies of the early 20th century led to many social transitions, including the mass urbanization of the American population, which drastically changed the standard of living. Introducing electricity, indoor plumbing, and more reliable transportation gave many urban dwellers a higher quality of life within the city establishment. Shopping became a popular pastime for both women and men. Traditionalists favored America's past and were irritated by the mass wave of urbanization and industrialization. They argued for renewed investment in agriculture.

The accessibility of news also transformed the landscape of the early 20th century, allowing Americans to obtain information on more topics. Sensationalism and yellow journalism quickly emerged, using media spin and bias in hopes of forming public opinion, whether regarding the Spanish Civil War or the best car to buy. The *Saturday Evening Post* and *Ladies Home Journal* began reaching more women and rural readers, fostering a sense of American Nationalism and connectedness between the rural and urban populations.

Following the industrial and manufacturing boom in the first years of the 20th century, Henry Ford (1863-1947) revolutionized the American dream by making it possible for many to own an automobile. By 1913, Ford had perfected the assembly line and paid his workers five dollars per day, causing panic amongst others in the industry, as they did not want to pay their workers that much. Such high wages were not the industry standard but motivated many workers to seek better employment.

Model T Ford being used for fishing, c. 1913

By 1924, Ford was selling the Model T for less than $290, and with the industrial efficiency of the assembly line, a car was produced every ten seconds. The car's introduction also impacted the social norms of the period, and couples and families used the car to enjoy road trips and vacations, which later became an American pastime.

New forms of entertainment

Americans also loved the mass introduction of the radio. Initially, this technology was meant for navigation and scientific discoveries rather than consumerism. By the early 20th century, Americans had developed a love affair with their new source of information. However, it was cut short when many nations cut radio use upon entering World War I. Americans tuned in following the end of the conflict, and during World War II, they used the radio to gather and pass information. A notable example of the radio's popularity during this period is the "fireside chats" started by President Roosevelt during his term in office.

Americans began recognizing new heroes in American culture, such as Charles Lindbergh (1902-1974) and Babe Ruth (1895-1948), reflecting an improved standard of living that allowed time for leisure activities and research into popular sciences of the time. This was also the first time Americans became overwhelmingly interested in cinema and movie stars.

Poster for The Jazz Singer, c. 1927

The motion picture industry had been relatively unknown leading up to World War I, but popularity soon engulfed the industry and allowed for the release of *The Jazz Singer* in 1927. It was the first "talkie" film, marking the end of silent movies. Paramount, MGM, and Warner Brothers dominated the motion picture industry, arguably creating another monopoly that would greatly influence WWII's war efforts and Americans' consumer culture in the 20th century.

Other notable new ways to pass the time during the 20th century include introducing theme parks in major cities and offering vaudeville productions, which traveled the country, appealing to lower-class Americans as cheap entertainment. These improvements speak to the transition of the quality of life from the mid-19th century into the 20th century. Previously, families were preoccupied with the struggle of day-to-day life, with little time for leisure activities; by creating expanded job opportunities and encompassing a diverse workforce, industrialists, using technology, enabled many Americans to pursue dreams and ambitions previously unattainable.

Harlem Renaissance

The urbanization of the 20th century saw an influx of varied cultures in America. One such example is the Harlem Renaissance movement, where African Americans rebuffed the norms of Jim Crow laws with art, music, and literature. Following the Great Migration, many African Americans settled in the North and found new job opportunities and other oppressed minority groups to which they felt an association. Notable participants of the Harlem Renaissance movement include Langston Hughes (1902-1967), who wrote poetry and literature and worked as a social activist, and Marcus Garvey (1887-1940), who promoted black expressionism and racial pride.

Langston Hughes, c. 1963

Music and literature

Music and culture also played a substantial role in this period, with F. Scott Fitzgerald (1896-1940) calling this period the Jazz Age. Notable figures of the Jazz Age include Edward "Duke" Ellington (1899-1974)—who was an early pioneer of jazz and began his career playing at the Cotton Club, a hub of the Harlem Renaissance (1920 to c. 1935)—and Edward Hopper (1882-1967), known for his realist and watercolor paintings.

Other cultural innovators of the period (sometimes called the "lost generation" due to the disillusioning effect of World War I) were found in American literature, where they explored new writing styles and were interested in reaching new audiences.

Examples of American literature include *Three Lives* (1906) by Gertrude Stein (1874-1946), credited with giving popularity to the modernist writing style of the period. F. Scott Fitzgerald, in his novels *This Side of Paradise* (1920) and *The Great Gatsby* (1925), embodied the new consumer reading culture of the 20th century. Other notable authors of the "*Lost Generation*" included William Faulkner, T. S. Eliot, and Ernest Hemingway. These newly embraced writing styles caused many Americans to engage with literature in a previously unknown way and propelled some authors to great fame.

F. Scott Fitzgerald, c. 1940

Women during this period also experienced cultural transitions, including continued expansion into the workforce and the introduction of a more independent woman in the flapper. These women pushed the traditional envelope and embodied the rivalry between traditionalists and the new idea of women and feminism in the early 20th century.

Popular culture after World War II

As the U.S. economy exploded out of the postwar years, many Americans began experiencing a quality of life previously unknown to the middle and lower classes, and traditionalists were concerned with the social implications of this economic development. During the 1950s, most Americans experienced prolonged economic achievement, growth, and stability. Many Americans were earning more, causing the middle-class explosion, which included nearly 60 percent of the population. Middle-class earners in this period earned between $3,000 and $10,000 annually.

There was also rapid expansion into suburban living by the baby boomers, which also caused a new market of housing and financing to develop, propelling the American economy. Consumer amenities previously out of reach for the middle or lower classes enhanced this new life, including refrigerators, secondary automobiles, and washing machines. These consumer products were meant to show Americans how to live more comfortably. However, this new movement would spark a consumer culture that caused American rivalries. As the new generations took control of the economic and political spheres during this period, it became clear that a transition was underfoot from the traditionalist mindsets of their parents to a modern concept of the American dream and family. These new ideas greatly concerned many parents and conservatives, as they instead saw a deterioration of the social system they had so heartily embraced during the early 1950s.

These emerging tensions and rivalries within American society caused many to be concerned about the implications of economic expansion on the public. The lives of teenagers during this period were drastically different from those of their parents, inciting the counterculture movements of the late 20th century. As the baby boomers grew into young adulthood and responded to the Cold War pressures, new social movements often centered on nonconformity and individualism emerged.

The emergence of music as a social revolution was first introduced in the early 1950s, as many teenagers sought to find a music genre that embodied their interests and ambitions. This was a transition from early periods where music choice was typically decided by race, as Caucasians typically embraced country and gospel genres, and African Americans preferred rhythm and blues tracks.

In 1951, a Cleveland disc jockey named Alan Freed (1921-1965) coined "rock and roll" to characterize the young white population's interest in blues music. From this point, the movement exploded and would carry itself into contemporary periods.

Trading card photo of Alan Freed, c. 1955

In 1956, Elvis Presley (1935-1977) released his first radio sensation, "Heartbreak Hotel," which horrified many traditionalists and excited the younger populations. Examples can be seen in Elvis's appearances on the *Ed Sullivan Show* during the 1950s and 1960s, which was known across the country as a traditional family program. Original rock and roll music had a connotation of rebellion and sexuality, which would later be seen to a greater extent in the counterculture. Easy access to radios, Dick Clark's television program *American Bandstand* and 45-rpm records all propelled the music revolution to be a mainstay of this generation.

Elvis Presley, c. 1965

The Beat movement of the 1950s was a precursor to the counterculture movement, as many famous writers glorified wanderlust and free love in their novels. One such example comes from Jack Kerouac (1922-1969), who published *On the Road* (1957), which detailed two men's journeys across the United States, highlighted by drug experiences, free love, and what would later be described as the counterculture.

Other notable figures of the Beat movement included Allen Ginsberg (1926-1997) and William Burroughs (1914-1997). Another important literary work from this period is *The Affluent Society* (1958) by Harvard economist John Kenneth Galbraith (1908-2006), which detailed the rise of the middle class and economic growth following the war years, specifically World War II.

Counterculture

The young Americans who began the counterculture movement had an unknown ally amongst them—the sheer volume of participants following the years of the baby boom. The counterculture generation held the largest sector of the American population and, due to size alone, had a transformative influence over the American culture of the late 20th and early 21st centuries.

The counterculture embraced nonconformity and a transition away from traditional or parental values. Many were labeled as hippies who worked against everything their traditional parents had established during the prosperous years of the 1950s. As young Americans sought to find themselves away from suburban neighborhoods and the confines of traditional American family values, their parents worked to discredit the counterculture movement and bring back their conservative values. Instead, the counterculture movement embraced many social taboos, such as public nudity, free love, and the open use of recreational drugs (e.g., LSD, marijuana).

The counterculture embraced communal existence and saw the rise of couples living together outside of wedlock, something unheard of during the 1950s. In addition to testing social norms, the counterculture also provided Americans access to healthier foods such as granola, yogurt, and wheat germ, utterly alien to the American diet before this period. As young men and women sought to find their individuality, the explosion of tie-dyed shirts, afros, and long hair tied with wildflowers embodied the transformative idea of the counterculture. These frightened many traditionalists who thought the American family and core values had been tarnished.

The emergence of a sexual revolution was also seen during this period, which promoted free love and the use of birth control. While many initially saw this as the most expressive form of the counterculture movement, the downsides of such openness were quickly seen in terms of venereal diseases. The counterculture also embraced drug use, most notably LSD and marijuana, and notable academics such as Harvard professor Dr. Timothy Leary (1920-1996) advocated to support the open use of LSD. The federal Drug Enforcement Agency (DEA) arrested Leary in 1972.

However, drawbacks to such attitudes were quickly seen in drug addictions and "bad trips." The ramifications of the counterculture can still be seen today in dietary changes by the American public (towards both healthier and less healthy choices), acceptance of recreational drugs—notably marijuana use in recent years—and the continued perception of individuality as a key attribute.

Harvard professor Timothy Leary arrested by the DEA in 1972

Conservative resistance to popular culture

As the American political and military landscape changed during the Cold War, the American family experienced a significant transformation. As the "greatest" generation returned from war and settled back into American society, it was clear that the age of American prosperity was on the horizon, including domestic economic stability and growth, as well as the newly championed position as a global power.

However, not everyone saw the United States in this light during the 1960s and 1970s. The conservative school of thought saw these transitions as attacks against the traditional family structure and the American perception of the formal social structure.

Many conservatives spoke out against rock and roll music and the later counterculture movement to promote what they believed to be the best path for America. They reminded the American public of its traditional values, including stay-at-home mothers and obedient children. Many of these conservatives experienced considerable backlash and were marginalized by the 1970s movements.

Revolution in communication technologies

While the Internet has been around since the early 1970s as part of government technological research, the World Wide Web was invented in 1989 and did not become widely available until the 90s. Throughout this technological revolution, much has changed economically and socially.

The Internet has revolutionized communication, the job market, and social behaviors. The Internet and its associated technologies have vastly changed communication. Before the Internet, the only available options were letter writing, phone calls, and face-to-face interactions. Instead of letters, people could now send instant emails. This has drastically changed with the advent of computer technology and the birth of the World Wide Web.

Cell phones have moved beyond mere phone calling. Personal computers, tablets, and smartphones allow instant connection between people worldwide. Mass media has changed tactics; instead of continuous news coverage and newspapers alone, there are clips and articles online. The speed and frequency of our communications have also increased, as most forms of online communication happen in real-time and are instantaneous.

Social media sites receive traffic from around the world. It is estimated that about 4.2 billion people are online on any given day, and there are about 5.3 billion internet users globally as of 2023. This means that contact can be made worldwide. Networking sites allow personal and professional relationships between people who would never have met otherwise.

Twitter played an integral role in the Arab Spring rebellions in the Middle East by allowing protesters to coordinate online. This sharing of instantaneous news, knowledge, and culture has revolutionized how people see and interact with the world around them. It has changed how cultures are perceived, leading to connections and understanding between people of different backgrounds.

2011 uprising in Egypt

Business has been similarly affected by the technology revolution. Machines are making many humans obsolete in factories and production. The competition for jobs has also increased as sites allow web conferencing, and individuals can E-commute daily without being physically present. All files are digitized, allowing easy access, maintenance, and storage. This advent of technology puts them at risk from hackers who can access databases remotely. Colleges offer online courses and classes. However, some businesses are suffering. For instance, mom-and-pop bookstores find it harder and harder to compete with stores like Barnes & Noble and Amazon, which offer electronic books and printed copies for online purchasing from home.

The Internet has created many cultural and social changes, including novel words. An entire vocabulary has developed over the Internet. Individuals can email, tweet, or use social media (e.g., Facebook) with friends. The pound key (#) has now become the hashtag, and the art of the "selfie" is practiced by people worldwide. Entirely new language variations have emerged, such as leetspeak. Developed by computer hackers, leetspeak is a cipher version of English, where numbers and symbols substitute letters. Thus, "leet" might be spelled "1337" or "l33t."

There is also chatspeak, which is made from common texting acronyms. Chatspeak is designed for speed and shortening communication. LOL, for instance, means "laughing out loud" and has infiltrated even offline communication. Nude images and online rants live on the Internet forever and have become warnings to those who misbehave online. They have even given rise to entirely new industries that can be hired to clean up an individual's online image, which is essential as employers have begun investigating potential hires online.

Intellectual and cultural history – summary of the period

A revolution in communications and transportation technology helped to create a new mass culture. It spread "modern" values and ideas, even as cultural conflicts between groups increased under the pressure of migration, world wars, and economic distress.

New technologies led to social transformations that improved living standards for many, greater personal mobility, and better communication systems while contributing to increased political and cultural conflicts.

The rise of an urban, industrial society encouraged the development of a variety of cultural expressions for migrant, regional, and African American artists (expressed most notably in the Harlem Renaissance movement); it also contributed to national culture by making shared experiences more possible through art, cinema and the mass media.

Rapid economic and social changes in American society fostered a sense of optimism in the postwar years and underlying concerns about how these changes affected American values. Economic and social changes, in addition to the anxiety engendered by the Cold War, led to an increasingly homogeneous mass culture and challenges to conformity by artists, intellectuals, and rebellious youth.

Young people who participated in the counterculture of the 1960s rejected many of the social, economic, and political values of their parents' generation, initiated a sexual revolution, and introduced greater informality into U.S. culture. In response, conservatives, fearing juvenile delinquency, urban unrest, and challenges to the traditional family, increasingly promoted their values and ideology. The spread of computer technology and the Internet increased access to information and led to new social behaviors and networks.

Relationship matrix

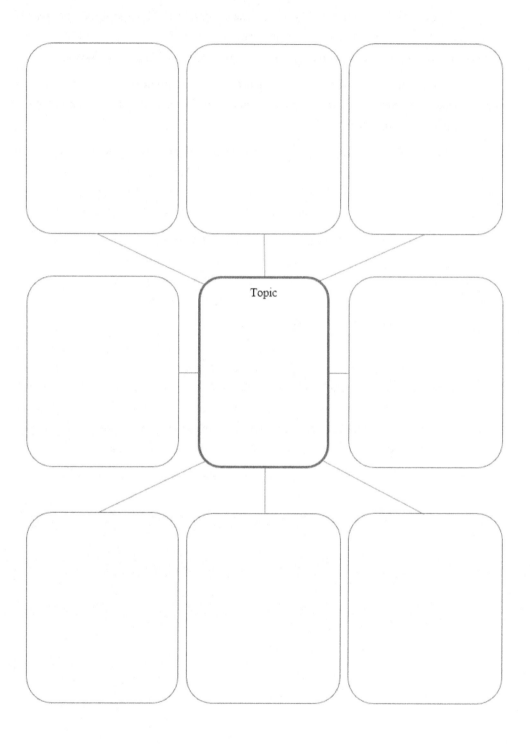

Notes for active learning

Notes for active learning

Appendix

AP US History Preparation and Test-Taking Strategies

Test preparation strategies

The best way to do well on AP US History is to know the subject well. There is no way around it and proper preparation is the key to success. Prepare for the test to answer with confidence as many questions as possible.

Study in advance

Devote 3 to 6 months to studying. The information is manageable by studying regularly during the weeks before the test.

Cramming is not a successful tactic. However, do not study too far in advance. Studying more than six months ahead is not advised and may result in fatigue and poor knowledge retention.

Develop a realistic study and practice schedule

Cramming eight hours a day is unfeasible and leads to burnout, detrimental to performance.

Commit to a realistic study and practice schedule.

Remove distractions

During this preparation period, temporarily eliminate distractions.

However, balance is key, and it is crucial not to neglect physical well-being and social or family life. Prepare with full intensity but do not jeopardize your health or emotional well-being.

Develop an understanding over memorization

When studying, devote time to each topic.

After a study session, write a short outline of the concept to clarify relationships and increase knowledge retention.

Make flashcards

Avoid commercial flashcards because making cards helps build and retain knowledge.

Consider using self-made flashcards to develop knowledge retention and quiz what you know.

Find a study partner

Occasionally studying with a friend preparing for the test can motivate and provide accountability.

Explaining concepts to another improves and fine-tunes your understanding, integrates knowledge, bolsters competence, and identifies deficiencies in comprehension.

Take practice tests

Do not take practice tests too early.

First, develop a broad and detailed understanding of concepts. In the last weeks, use practice tests to fine-tune your final preparation. If you are not scoring well on practice tests, you want time to improve without undue stress.

Alternate studying and practicing to increase knowledge retention and identify areas for further study. Taking practice tests accustoms you to the challenges of test-taking.

Test day strategies

Be well-rested and eat the right foods

Get a full night's sleep before the test for proper mental and physical capacity. If you are up late the night before, you will have difficulty concentrating and focusing on the test.

Avoid foods and drinks that lead to drowsiness (carbohydrates and protein). Avoid drinks high in sugar, causing glucose to spike and crash.

Pack in advance

Check what you are allowed to bring to the test. Pay attention to the required check-in items (e.g., printed confirmation, identification).

Pack the day before to avoid the stress of not frantically looking for things on test day.

Arrive at the testing center early

Starting off right is an advantage. Allow time to check in and remain calm before the test begins.

Map and test your route to the center in advance and determine parking locations, if applicable. If you are not familiar with the test location, visit before the test day to practice and avoid travel errors. Plan your route correctly to arrive at the center without additional challenges and unnecessary stress.

Maintain a positive attitude

Avoid falling into a mental spiral of negative emotions. Too much worry leads to underperformance.

If you become anxious, chances are higher for lower performance in preparation and during the test. Inner peace helps during preparation and the high-stakes test.

To do well on the test requires logical, systematic, and analytical thinking, so relax and remain calm.

Focus on your progress

Do not be concerned with other test-takers. Someone proceeding rapidly through the exam may be rushing or guessing on questions.

Take breaks and breathe deeply

Do not skip the available timed breaks. Refreshing breaks help you finish strong.

If time allows, eat a light snack to replenish your energy. Your mind and body will appreciate the available breaks.

The best approach to any test is *not* to keep your head down the whole session. While there is no time to waste, take a few seconds between questions to breathe deeply.

Momentarily clear your thoughts to relax your mind and muscles.

Time management

Timing

Besides good preparation, time management is the critical strategy for the exam.

Timed practice is not the objective at this stage. While practicing, note how many questions you would have completed in the allotted time.

Average time per question

In advance, determine the average time allotted for each question.

Use two different approaches depending on which preparation phase you are working on.

During the first preparation phase, acquire, fortify, and refine your knowledge.

During your final practice stage, use the time needed to develop analytical and thought processes related to specific questions.

Work systematically

Note your comprehension compared to the correct answers to learn the material and identify conceptual weaknesses. Do not overlook the value of explanations to questions; these can be a great source of content, analysis, and interdependent relationships.

During the second preparation phase, do not spend more than the average allotted time on each question when taking practice tests.

Pace your response time to develop a consistent pace and complete the test within the allotted time. If you are time-constrained during the final practice phase, work more efficiently, or your score will suffer.

Focus on the easy questions and skip the unfamiliar

Easy or difficult questions are worth the same points. Score more points for three quickly answered questions than one hard-earned victory.

Answer all familiar and easy questions to maximize points if time runs out.

Identify strengths and weaknesses

Skip unfamiliar questions on the first round as challenging questions require more than the average allotted time.

On the second review, questions that you cannot approach systematically or lack fundamental knowledge will likely not be answered through analysis.

Use the elimination and educated guessing strategy to select an answer and move on to another question.

Do not overinvest in any question

Some questions consume more time than the average and make you think of investing more time. Stop thinking that investing more time in challenging questions is productive.

Do not get entangled with questions while losing track of time. The test is timed, so you cannot spend too much time on any question.

Look at every question on the exam

It is unfortunate not to earn points for a question you could have quickly answered because you did not see it.

If you are in the first half of the test and spending more than the average on a question, select the best option, note the question number, and move on. You do not want to rush through the remaining questions, causing you to miss more answers.

If time allows, return to marked questions and take a fresh look. However, do not change the original answer unless you have a reason to change it. University studies show that hastily changing answers often replace correct and incorrect answers.

Answer all questions

How many questions are correct, not how much work went into selecting the answers matters. An educated guess earns the same points as an answer known with confidence.

On the test, you need to think and analyze information quickly. The skill of analyzing information quickly cannot be gained from a college course, prep course, or textbook. Working efficiently and effectively is a skill developed through focused effort and applied practice.

Multiple-choice questions

Strategic approach

There are strategies, approaches, and perspectives to answer multiple-choice questions and help maximize points.

Many strategies are known by you and seem like common sense. However, these helpful approaches might be overlooked under the pressure of a timed test.

While no strategy replaces comprehensive preparation, apply probability for success on unfamiliar questions.

Understand the question

Know what the question is asking before selecting an answer. It is surprising how many students do not read (and reread) carefully and rush selecting the wrong answer.

The test-makers anticipate these hasty mistakes, and many enticing answers include the specious choices. A successful student reads the question and understands it precisely before looking at the answers.

Focus on the answer

Separate the vital information from distracters and understand the design and thrust of the question.

Answer the question posed and not merely pick a factually accurate statement or answer a misconstrued question.

Rephrasing the question helps articulate what precisely the correct response requires. When rephrasing, do not change the meaning of the question; assume it is direct and to the point as written.

After selecting the answer, review the question and verify that the choice selected answers the question.

Answer the question before looking at choices

This valuable strategy is applicable if the question asks for generalized factual details. Form a thought response first, then look for the choice that matches your preordained answer.

Select the predetermined statement as it is likely correct.

Double-check the question

After selecting an answer, return to the question to ensure the selected choice answers the question as asked.

Make visual notes

Write, draw, or graph the question to determine the information provided, the objective, and the concept tested. Even if a question does not require a graphic answer, a chart or table often allows a solution to become apparent.

Experiments questions

Determine the purpose, methods, variables, and controls of the experiment. Understanding the presented information helps answer the question.

With multiple experiments, understand variations of the same experiment by focusing on the differences. For example, focus on the changes between the first and second experiments, second and third, and first and third. Direct comparison between experiments helps organize the information and apply it to the answer.

Factually correct, but wrong

Questions often have incorrect choices that are factually correct but do not answer the question.

Predetermine the answer and do not choose merely a factually correct statement. Verify that the choice answers the question.

Do not fall for the familiar

When in doubt, it is comforting to choose what is familiar. If you recognize a term or concept, you may be tempted to pick that choice impetuously.

However, do not go with familiar answers merely because they are familiar. Think through the answer and how it relates to the question before selecting it.

Words of caution

The words *"all," "none,"* and *"except"* require attention. Be alert with questions containing these words, as the answer may not be apparent on the first read of the question.

Fill the answers carefully

Many mistakes happen when filling in answers. Filling the answers correctly is simple but crucial. Be attentive to the question number and enter the answer accordingly. If you skip a question, skip it on the answer sheet.

Elimination strategies

If the correct answer is not immediately apparent, use the process of elimination.

Use the strategy of educated guessing by eliminating one or two answers. Usually, at least one answer choice is easily identified as wrong. Eliminating even one choice increases the odds of selecting the correct one.

Process of elimination

Eliminate choices:

- Use proportional estimations for quantitative questions to eliminate choices that are too high or low.

- Eliminate answers that are *almost right* or *half right*. Consider *half right* as *wrong* since these distractor choices are purposely included.

- If two answers are direct opposites, the correct answer is likely one of them. However, note if they are direct opposites or another reason to consider them correct. Therefore, eliminate the other choices and narrow the search for the correct one.

- For numerical questions, eliminate the smallest and largest numbers (unless for a reason).

Roman numeral questions

Roman numeral questions present several statements and ask which is/are correct. These questions are tricky for most test-takers because they present more than one potentially correct statement.

Roman numeral questions are often included in combinations with more than one answer. Eliminating a wrong Roman numeral statement eliminates all choices that include it.

Educated guessing

Correct ways to guess

Do not assume you must get every question right; this will add unnecessary stress during the exam. You will (most likely) need to guess some questions.

Answer as many questions correctly as possible without wasting time that should be used to maximize your score.

For challenging questions, random guessing does not help. Use educated guessing after eliminating one or two choices.

Playing the odds

Guessing is a form of "partial credit" because while you might not be sure of the correct answer, you have the relevant knowledge to identify some wrong choices.

There is a 25% chance of correctly guessing for random responses since questions have four choices. Therefore, the odds are guessing 1 question correctly to 3 incorrectly.

Guessing after elimination of answers

After eliminating one answer as wrong, you have a 33% chance for a lucky guess. Therefore, your odds move to 1 question right to 2 questions wrong.

While this may not seem like a dramatic increase, it can make an appreciable difference in your score.

Confidently eliminating two wrong choices increases the chances of guessing correctly to 50%!

When using elimination:

- Do not rely on gut feelings alone to answer questions quickly.

  Understand and recognize the difference between *knowing* and *gut feeling* about the answer. Gut feelings should sparingly be used after the process of elimination.

- Do not fall for answers that sound "clever," and choose "bizarre" answers.

  Choose them only with a reason to believe they may be correct.

Eliminating Roman numeral choices

A workable strategy for Roman numeral questions is to guess the wrong statement.

For example:

> A. I only
>
> B. III only
>
> C. I and II only
>
> D. I and III only

Notice that statement II does not have an answer dedicated to it. This indicates that statement II is likely wrong and eliminates choice C, narrowing your search to three choices. However, if you are confident that statement II is the answer, do not apply this strategy.

Free-response questions

Free-response questions typically require processing information into existing conceptual frameworks.

There are some personal choices for writing the desired response.

Free-response question skills

Be able to present and discuss relevant examples. Practice clarifying or evaluating principles.

Perform detailed analysis of relationships and respond to stimulus materials (e.g., charts, graphs).

Understand the question

As with the multiple-choice questions, understand what the question asks. Assume that the question, as written, is direct and to the point.

Mental rephrasing should not add or alter the meaning or essence of the question.

Answer the questions in order of competence

You are not bound to answer the questions according to their sequence. Survey questions and decide which require minimal effort or time.

Avoid getting entangled and frustrated to use time efficiently and maximize points.

Do not write more than needed

Additional work beyond the question's stated directives does not earn a higher score or result in extra credit.

For time management and keeping responses relevant, answer the question but avoid superfluous responses.

Organize thoughts

Before writing, brainstorm the questions' topics. Outline your thoughts on scratch paper during the composition process. Essential definitions, ideas, examples, or names are valid details when relevant.

Organized thoughts produce a coherent response. With practice, balance time between brainstorming and writing.

Follow the structure

Structure responses to match the order specified in the question for a grader-friendly answer.

The reader should not need to search for topics used in the grading criteria. A well-structured essay has complete sentences and paragraphs.

A formal introduction and conclusion are unnecessary; go directly into answering the question.

Answer questions in their entirety

It is essential to answer questions thoroughly, not just partially. For example, some questions ask to identify and explain. Performing only one step is inadequate and will be graded accordingly.

Task verbs

Below are *task verbs* common for free-response questions – underline these directives as you see them in practice questions and on the exam.

Refer to these tasks and verify when completed. Do not overlook them when writing a comprehensive response.

Compare – provide a description or explanation of similarities or differences.

Define – provide a specific meaning for a word or concept.

Identify – provide information about a specified topic without elaboration or explanation.

Describe – provide the relevant characteristics of a specified concept.

Develop an argument – articulate a claim and support it with evidence.

Explain – provide information about how or why a relationship, process, pattern, or outcome occurs, using evidence and reasoning.

Conclude – use available information to formulate an accurate statement demonstrating understanding based on evidence.

Explaining *how* typically requires analyzing the relationship, process, pattern, or outcome.

Explaining *why* typically requires analyzing motivations or reasons for the relationship, process, or outcome.

Write legibly

The reader must decipher your writing so the response can be scored appropriately, so write legibly. Practice writing under a time limit to produce a readable response. If this issue may exist, ask a friend to read a sample response to understand the words expressed.

Consider printing key phrases or highlighting them cleanly (e.g., asterisk, underline) in your response.

Use plain language

All claims should be directly stated. You do not want the graders to guess how something demonstrates a point.

Regardless of if they correctly guess your intentions, you will be graded critically for ambiguities. Present relevant information clearly and concisely to demonstrate the argument's primary points.

Use facts to bolster arguments

Written responses should include specific facts and avoid unsubstantiated claims. Do not use long, meandering responses filled with loosely-related facts regarding specific concepts. Avoid contradictions, circular definitions, and question restatements.

Review and correct answers

If questions are completed and time remains, review each response. These thoughtful revisions can earn crucial points.

Assess if anything is needed to be added or requires correction. Put a simple strikethrough through the error for a mistake, so the grader disregards that portion. If you add content, insert an asterisk (*) and refer the reader to the end of the essay.

Notes for active learning

Brief Chronology of Major Historical Events

Period 1: pre-Columbian period to 1789

1492	Columbus lands in the Bahamas
1520	Spanish explorers bring smallpox to the Mexican mainland
1521	Hernàn Cortés conquers the Aztec capital, Tenochtitlán
1598	New Mexico was founded by Juan de Oñate
1600	East India Company was founded
1602	Dutch East India Company was founded
1739	Stono Rebellion
1676-1677	the rebellion of Nathaniel Bacon
1744-1748	King George's War
1686	Dominion of New England
1730s-1740s	the Great Awakening
1732	Hat Act and Debt Recovery Act
1754-1763	French and Indian War
1754	Albany Congress
1763	Chief Pontiac's rebellion
1770	Boston Massacre
1773	Boston Tea Party
1775-1783	American Revolutionary War
1776	Colonies declare independence from Great Britain
1777	Articles of Confederation
1785-1795	Northwest Indian War (Little Turtle's War)
1787	Constitutional Convention
1787	The Northwest Ordinance is formed

Period 2: 1790 to 1898

1803	Lewis and Clark Expedition
1807	Embargo Act
1812	War of 1812
1819	Panic of 1819
1820	Missouri Compromise
1823	Monroe Doctrine was issued
1830	Indian Removal Act
1846	Wilmot Proviso
1846-1848	Mexican-American War
1848	Guadalupe Hidalgo treaty signed
1848	California gold rush
1848	Seneca Falls Convention
1854	Kansas-Nebraska Act
1861-1865	The Civil War
1862	Homestead Act
1863	Emancipation Proclamation
1864	Sand Creek Massacre
1865	The Thirteenth Amendment abolishes slavery
1876-1877	Sioux War
1876-1890	The Gilded Age
1890	National American Woman Suffrage Association
1890	Battle at Wounded Knee
1898	Spanish-American War

Period 3: 1899 to present

1903-1914	Construction of Panama Canal
1917-1918	World War I (American involvement)
1919-1920	Red Scare
1920	Nineteenth Amendment
1920-1933	Prohibition
1929-1939	Great Depression
1941	Attack on Pearl Harbor
1941-1945	World War II (American involvement)
1945	Atomic bombs dropped on Hiroshima and Nagasaki
1947	The Truman Doctrine is established
1947-1991	The Cold War
1948-1949	Berlin Airlift Crisis
1949	NATO was formed
1950-1953	Korean War
1954	*Brown v. Board of Education*
1954-1975	Vietnam War
1958	NASA is formed
1965	The Civil Rights Act outlawed segregation
1979	Iran hostage crisis
1986	Iran–Contra Scandal
1987	Reagan asks Gorbachev to tear down the Berlin Wall
1991	Operation Desert Storm
2001	September 11 terrorist attacks

Notes for active learning

Image Credits

Period 1 – Political History

The Landing of Columbus, Spencer, J. A. *History of the United States.* New York: Johnson, Fry, and Company, 1858.

Spanish explorers: thanksgiving before the image of the Virgin, Lossing, Benson J. *Our Country.* New York: Johnson and Bailey, 1895.

Spanish explorers are raising the memorial cross, Lossing, Benson J. *Our Country.* New York: Johnson and Bailey, 1895.

Cultivation of tobacco at Jamestown, Scott, David B. *A School History of the United States.* New York: Harper & Brothers, 1883.

Christopher Columbus, Baldwin, James. *Baldwin Reader: Fourth and Fifth Years Combined.* New York: American Book Company, 1897.

Mission Indians of Southern California, The World: Its Cities and People. London: Cassell & Company, Ltd., ca 1880.

Settlers in North Carolina, Lossing, Benson J. *Harper's Encyclopedia of United States History.* New York: Harper and Brothers Publishers, 1912.

The arrival of the Indian allies at the French camp, Stephens, Alex H. *A Comprehensive and Popular History of the United States.* Chattanooga: Hickman and Fowler, 1882.

Reading the Stamp Act, Markham, Richard. *Colonial Days: Being Stories and Ballads for Young Patriots.* New York: Dodd, Mead, & Company, 1881.

Boston Tea Party, throwing tea overboard, Stephens, Alex H. *A Comprehensive and Popular History of the United States.* Chattanooga: Hickman and Fowler, 1882.

Portrait of Mercy Otis Warren, Copley, John Singleton. *Portrait of Mercy Otis Warren.* 1763. Oil on Canvas. Museum of Fine Arts, Boston. Wikimedia Commons.

General George Washington, Ellis, Edward S. *The History of Our Country: From the Discovery of America to the Present Time.* Cincinnati: The Jones Brothers Publishing Company, 1910.

Period 1 – Economic History

Pueblo girl winnowing beans, Lummis, Charles F. "The Land of Poco Tiempo." *Scribner's.* Dec. 1891: 760-771.

Iroquois dwellings, Lossing, Benson J. *Our Country.* New York: Johnson and Bailey, 1895.

Algonquin Indian, Hutchinson, H. N. ed. *The Living Races of Mankind.* London: Hutchinson & Co., ca 1910.

Caravel with oars, De Oliveira, Brás. *Caravel with Oars.* 1894. *The History and Development of Caravels, Graduate Thesis.* By G. R. Schwarz. Texas A&M U, 2008. N. page. Print. Wikimedia Commons.

Portuguese galleons and carracks, João De Castro, D. *Portuguese Galleons and Naus (Carracks) Route map of the Red Sea Roteiro Do Mar Roxo 1540 Galleon Nau (Carrack).* 1540. Universidade De Coimbra, Portugal. *Wikimedia Commons.* Media Wiki, 3 Nov. 2013.

Henry Hudson, Drake, Francis. *Indian History for Young Folks.* New York: Harper and Brothers, 1912.

Typical Cayuse and his mount, Humfreville, J. Lee. Twenty Years Among Our Savage Indians. Hartford: The Hartford Publishing Company, 1897.

Trading with Indians, Drake, Francis. *Indian History for Young Folks.* New York: Harper and Brothers, 1912.

Introduction of slavery, Ellis, Edward S. *The Youth's History of the United States.* New York: The Cassell Publishing Company, 1887.

Depiction of a tobacco wharf in Colonial America, Depiction of a Tobacco Wharf in Colonial America. Digital image. *The Mariner's Museum and Park.* The Mariner's Museum. Wikimedia Commons.

Savannah, from a print of 1741, Bryant, William Cullen, and Sydney Howard Gay. *A Popular History of the United States.* New York: Charles Scribners' Sons, 1881.

Quaker woman preaching in New Amsterdam, Bryant, William Cullen, and Sydney Howard Gay. *A Popular History of the United States.* New York: Charles Scribners' Sons, 1881.

Colonial slave market in the 17th century, Lossing, Benson J. *Harper's Encyclopedia of United States History.* New York: Harper and Brothers Publishers, 1912.

Carolina Rice Field, Bryant, William Cullen, and Sydney Howard Gay. *A Popular History of the United States.* New York: Charles Scribners' Sons, 1881.

The scene on a plantation, Lossing, Benson J. *Harper's Encyclopedia of United States History.* New York: Harper and Brothers Publishers, 1912.

Sugar cane, Richardson, Abby Sage. *The History of Our Country.* Boston: Houghton, Mifflin, and Company, 1883.

Period 1 – Foreign Relations

Queen Isabella of Castile (left) and King Ferdinand V of Aragon (right), Ellis, Edward S., and Charles F. Horne. *The Story of the Greatest Nations.* New York: Francis Niglutsch, 1906.

Indians at a Hudson Bay Company trading post, Indians trade furs at a Hudson's Bay Company trading post in the 1800s. Digital image. *Hulton Archive.* Getty Images. Wikimedia Commons.

The Dutch trading with the Indians, Ellis, Edward S., and Charles F. Horne. *The Story of the Greatest Nations.* New York: Francis Niglutsch, 1906.

The first shot in the French and Indian War, Morris, Charles. *Pictorial History of the United States.* Philadelphia: John Winston Company, 1907.

Pontiac's attack on Fort Detroit, Drake, Francis. *Indian History for Young Folks.* New York: Harper and Brothers, 1912.

Thomas Jefferson (left), Jefferson: McMaster, John Bach. *A School History of the United States.* New York: American Book Company, 1897.

Alexander Hamilton (right), Hamilton: Richardson, Abby Sage. *The History of Our Country.* Boston: Houghton, Mifflin, and Company, 1883.

Period 1 – Social History

Spanish explorers: Cortés, Coligni, de Soto, and Verazzani, Lossing, Benson J. *Our Country.* New York: Johnson and Bailey, 1895.

Meeting of Cortés and Montezuma, Buel, J. W. *Around the World with Great Voyages.* Philadelphia: The Columbia Syndicate, 1892.

Heroic defence of Cuzco, Adams, Davenport W. H. *The Land of the Incas and the City of the Sun.* Boston: Dana Estes and Company, ca 1885.

King Philip, or Metacomet—Wampanoag chief, Wood, Norman B. *The Lives of Famous Indian Chiefs.* Aurora: American Indian Historical Publishing Company, 1906.

Domestic slave trade, Bryant, William Cullen, and Sydney Howard Gay. *A Popular History of the United States.* New York: Charles Scribners' Sons, 1881.

Dutch selling slaves to the Virginia planters, Mace, William H. *A School History of the United States.* Chicago: Rand, McNally, and Company, 1904.

Slave auction, Ellis, Edward S. *The Youth's History of the United States.* New York: The Cassell Publishing Company, 1887.

French Métis, Sellier, Charles-Auguste. *Metis Francais. La Nouvelle-France.* By Eugene Guenin. Paris: Hachette, 1900. 415. Print. Wikimedia Commons.

Engraving of George Washington, Ceracchi, Giuseppe. *Engraving of George Washington.* 1856. Stipple and line engraving. New York Public Library, New York. By Henry Bryan Hall. Wikimedia Commons.

Abigail Adams, Stuart, Gilbert. *Abigail Adams.* 1815. National Gallery of Art, Washington, DC. *Abigail Adams and Her Times*: D. Appleton, 1917. Print. Wikimedia Commons.

Period 1 – Intellectual & Cultural History

Spaniards are destroying Mexican idols, Lossing, Benson J. *Our Country.* New York: Johnson and Bailey, 1895.

Pueblo cart, Beadle, J.H. *Western Wilds, and the Men Who Redeem Them.* Washington, D.C.: Clark E. Ridpath, 1917.

Sugar plantation, Bryant, William Cullen, and Sydney Howard Gay. *A Popular History of the United States.* New York: Charles Scribners' Sons, 1881.

Roger Williams is building his house, Bryant, William Cullen, and Sydney Howard Gay. *A Popular History of the United States.* New York: Charles Scribners' Sons, 1881.

William Penn, Stephens, Alex H. A Comprehensive and Popular History of the United States. Chattanooga: Hickman and Fowler, 1882.

Portrait of John Locke, Kneller, Godfrey, Sir. *Portrait of John Locke.* 1697. Oil on Canvas. State Hermitage Museum, St. Petersburg, Russia. Wikimedia Commons.

Interior of Christ Church, Boston, Pratt, Mara L. *American's Story for America's Children: The Early Colonies.* Boston: D.C. Heath & Company, 1901.

Puritan, Lossing, Benson J. *Our Country.* New York: Johnson and Bailey, 1895.

Profile of Adam Smith, Cadell, and Davies. *Portrait of Adam Smith.* 1811. Vanderblue Collection.*Wikimedia Commons.* Media Wiki.

Period 2 – Political History

Postage with an image of the Founding Fathers drafting the Articles of Confederation, U.S. Post Office. U.S. Postage Featuring the Articles of Confederation. Digital image. Wikimedia Commons.

Shays' Rebellion, portraits of Daniel Shays and Job Shattuck, leaders of the Massachusetts Regulators. 1787. Cover of Bickerstaff's Boston Almanac. National Portrait Gallery, Smithsonian Institution, Washington, DC. Wikimedia Commons.

The Convention at Philadelphia, 1787, Juengling, Frederick, and Alfred Kappes. *The Convention at Philadelphia, 1787.* 19th Century. Engraving. *Teaching American History.* Ashland University. Wikimedia Commons.

James Madison, Bryant, William Cullen, and Sydney Howard Gay. *A Popular History of the United States.* New York: Charles Scribners' Sons, 1881.

The Bill of Rights 175th anniversary was celebrated on July 1, 1966, with a 5-cent stamp, Bureau of Printing and Engraving, U.S. Post Office [public domain]. Wikimedia Commons.

James Madison Bill of Rights $5 commemorative gold coin, United States Mint image [public domain]. Wikimedia Commons.

Surveying the Northwest Territory, Bagley, William, and Charles Beard. *The History of the American People.* Sacramento: California State Printing Department, 1920.

Paxton Boys' massacre of the Indians at Lancaster, Paxton Massacre. 1841. *Wikimedia Commons.* Media Wiki.

Drafting the Declaration of Independence, Pratt, Mara L. *American's Story for America's Children: The Early Colonies.* Boston: D.C. Heath & Company, 1901.

James Monroe's southern plantation, Lossing, Benson J. *Harper's Encyclopedia of United States History.* New York: Harper and Brothers Publishers, 1912.

Illustration of an execution, Revolution Square, France, Pierre-Antoine Demachy. *Place de la Révolution Exécution Capitale.* Gallicia. Wikimedia Commons.

John Jay, Lossing, Benson J. *Our Country.* New York: Johnson and Bailey, 1895.

Thomas Cooper, Thomas Cooper. Digital image. The University of Pennsylvania Library. Wikimedia Commons.

Missouri Compromise, 1820, Bagley, William, and Charles Beard. *The History of the American People.* Sacramento: California State Printing Department, 1920.

Map of the general route followed by Lewis and Clark, Henderson, Carrie. *The Lewis and Clark Expedition.* Chicago: McClung, 1904.

Seminole War: an attack upon Fort King by the Indian forces under Osceola, Barnes, A. S. *A Brief History of the United States.* New York: American Book Company, 1885.

David Wilmot, Carl Schurz, *Life of Henry Clay,* Boston: Houghton, Mifflin & Co., 1899, Vol. 2, facing p. 286. Wikimedia Commons.

Eyewitness's depiction of the Sand Creek Massacre, Howling Wolf. *At the Sand Creek Massacre.* Digital image. *Allen Memorial Art Museum.* Oberlin College and Conservatory. Wikimedia Commons.

John C. Calhoun, Goodrich, S. G. *A Pictorial History of the United States.* Philadelphia: E. H. Butler and Company, 1883.

Bleeding Kansas: slavery debate in Congress, Ellis, Edward S., and Charles F. Horne. *The Story of the Greatest Nations.* New York: Francis Niglutsch, 1906.

President Abraham Lincoln, Northrop, Henry Davenport. *American History for Young Folks: The Story of Our Great Country.* 1898.

Portrait of Lincoln surrounded by Civil War scenes, Ellis, Edward S. *The Youth's History of the United States.* New York: The Cassell Publishing Company, 1887.

Battle of Fort Sumter during the Civil War, Ellis, Edward S. *The Youth's History of the United States.* New York: The Cassell Publishing Company, 1887.

First Battle of Bull Run, stand of the Union troops at the Henry House, Ellis, Edward S. *The Youth's History of the United States.* New York: The Cassell Publishing Company, 1887.

General Robert E. Lee, Meredith, Roy. *The Face of Robert E. Lee: in Life and in Legend.* New York: Charles Scribner's Sons, 1947, p. 25. Wikimedia Commons.

Jefferson Davis, fist and only President of the Confederate States of America. Library of Congress.

President Andrew Johnson, Lillian C. Buttre, *American Portrait Gallery.* New York: J. C. Buttre, 1877.

Helen Hunt Jackson, Bolton, Sarah Knowles. *Lives of Girls Who Became Famous.* New York: Crowell, 1949. *Project Gutenberg.* Web. 22 Sept. 2015. Wikimedia Commons.

Period 2 – Economic History

Eli Whitney watching the cotton gin, Hubert, Philip G. *Men of Achievement: Inventors.* New York: Charles Scribner's Sons, 1893.

Gathering cotton in the field of a plantation, Montgomery, D. H. *The Beginner's American History.* Boston: Ginn and Company, 1902.

Benjamin Franklin, Butterworth, Hezekia, ed. *Young Folks History of America.* Boston: Estes and Lauriate, 1881.

Transporting cotton, One Hundred Years' Progress of the United States. Hartford, CT: L. Stebbins, 1871.

Samuel Morse is making the telegraph, Montgomery, D. H. *The Beginner's American History.* Boston: Ginn and Company, 1902.

Samuel Slater, Samuel Slater, Industrialist. 1881. *The Biographical Cyclopedia of Representative Men of Rhode Island.* National Biographical. Print. Wikimedia Commons.

Lowell women at the loom, Prints Division, New York Public Library, 1211 Ave. of the Americas, New York, NY 10036. In "The Life History of the United States," Time-Life Books, Vol. 3, 1974, p. 51.

Picking cotton, One Hundred Years' Progress of the United States. Hartford, CT: L. Stebbins, 1871.

Southern industry, Bryant, William Cullen, and Sydney Howard Gay. *A Popular History of the United States.* New York: Charles Scribner's Sons, 1881.

Mr. and Mrs. Goodhue Livingston and Mrs. Vanderbilt. 1890. *The First 400: Mrs. Astor's New York in the Gilded Age.* Rizzoli, 2000. Print. Wikimedia Commons.

Portrait of Alexander Graham Bell. c1914-1919. Moffett Studio, Canada. Wikimedia Commons.

John D. Rockefeller, Rockefeller, John D. *Random Reminiscences of Men and Events.* New York: Doubleday, Page, 1909. *Project Gutenberg.* Wikimedia Commons.

Andrew Carnegie, Carnegie, Andrew. *Autobiography of Andrew Carnegie.* Boston: Houghton Mifflin, 1920. *Project Gutenberg.* Wikimedia Commons.

Strikers at the Burlington Railroad shop yards, Strikers at the Burlington Railroad Shop Yards. 1922. *National Archives and Records Administration.* Wikimedia Commons.

Child labor in the textile mills, "Lawrence Strike of 1912: Photos." *Marxists Internet Archive.* David Walters. Wikimedia Commons.

Knights of Labor pentagram, "History: Knights of Labor." *Takver's Initiatives.* Wikimedia Commons.

Pullman strikers outside Arcade Building in Pullman, Chicago in 1894, "Pullman Strike." *Lincoln/Net.* Northern Illinois University Libraries. Wikimedia Commons.

East and West are shaking hands at the laying of the last rail of the Union Pacific Railroad, Russell, Andrew J. *East and West Shaking Hands at Laying Last Rail.* 1869. Yale Collection of Western Americana, Beinecke Rare Book and Manuscript Library, New Haven. *Beinecke Digital Collections.* Wikimedia Commons.

President Harrison, James Grant Wilson, ed., *The Presidents of the United States, 1789-1914,* v. 4, 1914, between pp. 4 and 5. Wikimedia Commons.

President Taft, Zorn, Anders. *President Taft.* 1911. *Mollbrink's Art Gallery.* Mollbrinks Konst. Wikimedia Commons.

Period 2 – Foreign Relations

The Battle of Fallen Timbers, Ellis, Edward S., and Charles F. Horne. *The Story of the Greatest Nations.* New York: Francis Niglutsch, 1906.

War of 1812, Battle of New Orleans, Goodrich, S. G. *A Pictorial History of the United States.* Philadelphia: E. H. Butler and Company, 1883.

President James Monroe, Spencer, J. A. *History of the United States.* New York: Johnson, Fry, and Co., 1858.

Mexican-American War, the battle of Palo Alto, Frost, John. *Pictorial History of the United States.* Connecticut: Case, Tiffany, and Company, 1846.

Commodore Oliver Hazard Perry, Bryant, William Cullen, and Sydney Howard Gay. *A Popular History of the United States.* New York: Charles Scribner's Sons, 1881.

Iron and steel company in Johnstown, Pennsylvania, Lossing, Benson John. *The American Centenary: A History of the Progress of the Republic of the United States during the First One Hundred Years of Its Existence.* Philadelphia: Porter & Coates, 1876. Print. Wikimedia Commons.

Period 2 – Social History

Nat Turner and his confederates in conference, Victor, Orville J. *History of American Conspiracies.* New York: James D. Torrey, 1863.

Frances Wright, John Chester Buttre, after J. Gorbitz. Wikimedia Commons.

Harriet Tubman, the Moses to her people, Siebert, Wilbur H. *The Underground Railroad from Slavery to Freedom.* New York: The MacMillan Company, 1898.

John Brown at Harper's Ferry raid, Lossing, Benson J. *Our Country.* New York: Johnson and Bailey, 1895.

Susan B. Anthony, Johnston, Francis Benjamin. "Miss Susan B. Anthony." *The World's Work: A History of Our Time.* Vol. 11. New York: Doubleday, Page, 1906. p.7362. *Internet Archive.* Wikimedia Commons.

Meriwether Lewis and William Clark, Henderson, Carrie. *The Lewis and Clark Expedition.* Chicago: McClung, 1904.

Map Route of the Trail of Tears, the forced relocation march of Native Americans in the 1830s, "Trail of Tears." *National Park Service.* U.S. Department of the Interior. Wikimedia Commons.

John O'Sullivan, Rafael De La Cova, Antonio, Dr. "John L. O'Sullivan." *Latin American Studies.* Dr. Antonio Rafael De La Cova, 15 Dec. 1997. Wikimedia Commons.

Emigrants to the West, Bryant, William Cullen, and Sydney Howard Gay. *A Popular History of the United States.* New York: Charles Scribner's Sons, 1881.

U.S. political poster for the Know-Nothing Party, Fillmore and Donelson 1856. Digital image. Wikimedia Commons.

Smith's first vision, Stenhouse, T. B. H. *The Rocky Mountains Saints.* New York: D. Appleton and Company, 1873.

Gold washing in California, Bright, Marshall H. *True Stories of American History for Our Young People.* 1898.

Certificate of the first homestead, according to the Homestead Act, "The Homestead Act of 1862." *National Archives and Records Administration.* National Archives and Records Administration. Wikimedia Commons.

Western Expansion: street in Abilene, Buel, J. W. *Heroes of the Plains.* St. Louis, MO: Historical Publishing Company, 1881.

Geronimo, Frank A. Rinehart. *Geronimo (Guiyatle) Apache.* 1898. Rinehart Indian Photographs, Lawrence, Kansas. *Lawrence Journal World.* Wikimedia Commons.

Adoption of the Thirteenth Amendment, "Adoption of the Thirteenth Amendment." *Harper's Weekly* 18 Feb. 1865: *The Institute of Museum and Library Services.* Wikimedia Commons.

Lucy Stone, Lucy Stone Wearing Bloomers. Digital image. *Kansas Historical Society.* Kansas Historical Society. Wikimedia Commons.

U.S. postage stamp honoring the Grange movement, United States. Post Office. *Stamp, National Grange.* 1967. Print. Wikimedia Commons.

Hauling coal locomotive, Hauling Coal. c. 1915-1925: Detroit. Print. Wikimedia Commons.

Horatio Alger, Whipple, John Adams. *Horation Alger, Jr.* 1852. *Harvard Library.* Wikimedia Commons.

Mary Greenleaf Clement, Willard, Frances E., and Mary A. Livermore. *American Women: Fifteen Hundred Biographies with Over 1,400 Portraits; a Comprehensive Encyclopedia of the Lives and Achievements of American Women during the Nineteenth Century.* Detroit: Gale Research, 1973. Print. Wikimedia Commons.

Booker T. Washington, Booker T. Washington. 1899. *Appleton's Popular Science Monthly.* Vol. 55. New York: D. Appleton, 1899. Print. Edited by William Jay Youmans. Wikimedia Commons.

Nathaniel Hawthorne, Matthews, Brander. *An Introduction to the Study of American Literature.* New York: American Book Company, 1896.

Period 2 – Intellectual & Cultural History

Frederick Douglass, Harper's New Monthly Magazine. Volume 50. New York: Harper and Brothers, 1875.

Harriet Beecher Stowe, Harris, Amanda B. *American Authors for Young Folks.* Boston: D. Lothrop and Co., 1887.

Charles Finney, Charles Grandison Finney. Digital image. Wikimedia Commons.

John James Audubon, Sarah K. Bolton, *Famous Men of Science.* New York: Thomas Y. Crowell & Co., 1889. Wikimedia Commons.

Passenger pigeon by John James Audubon, John James Audubon. Wikimedia Commons.

Ralph Waldo Emerson (left), Rowse, Sam W. Ralph Waldo Emerson. Harvard Square Library. Green Bird Media, 2007. Wikimedia Commons.

Henry David Thoreau (right), Lossing, Benson J. *Harper's Encyclopedia of United States History.* New York: Harper and Brothers Publishers, 1912.

Thomas Edison, Reich, Jacques. *Appleton's Cyclopaedia of American Biography.* Ed. James Grant Wilson and John Fiske. Vol. 2. New York: D. Appleton, 1887. Print. Wikimedia Commons.

Henry George, Beach, Chandler Belden, and Frank Morton McMurry. *The New Student's Reference Work.* Vol. 2. Chicago: F.E. Compton, 1914. Print. Wikimedia Commons.

Horace Mann, Mace, William H. *A School History of the United States.* Chicago: Rand, McNally and Co., 1904.

Mark Twain, "Mark Twain." *Appleton's Journal* (1874). Wikimedia Commons.

Period 3 – Political History

American Socialist Party Logo, Davenport, Tim. Socialist Party of America, 1915. Wikimedia Commons.

Protest to Save Sacco and Vanzetti, Postcard, London, England, in 1921. Digital image. Wikimedia Commons.

General Leslie Groves (left), military head of the Manhattan Project, with Professor Robert Oppenheimer (right), U.S. Department of Energy. *Groves Oppenheimer.* Wikimedia Commons.

Dwight D. Eisenhower, U.S. Army, 1947. *Naval History and Heritage Command.* Wikimedia Commons.

Thurgood Marshall. Okamoto, Yoichi Robert, 1967, *National Archives and Records Administration.* Wikimedia Commons.

President Lyndon B. Johnson, Shoumatoff, Elizabeth, 1968. White House Collection, Washington, D.C. *The White House Historical Association.* Wikimedia Commons.

Bill Clinton signing NAFTA. White House, 1993. *National Archives and Records Administration.* Wikimedia Commons.

Wind farm in Power County, Idaho. By Energy.gov (Flickr). Wikimedia Commons.

Period 3 – Economic History

President Franklin Delano Roosevelt, Executive Office of the President of the United States. 1933. Library of Congress, New York. Wikimedia Commons.

Huey Long on the cover of Time magazine, "Huey Long." *Time Magazine* 1 Apr. 1935. Wikimedia Commons.

Rosie the Riveter, United States. Westinghouse. War Production Coordinating Committee. *We Can Do It.* By J. Howard Miller. Virginia Historical Society. National Museum of American History, Smithsonian Institution.

John F. Kennedy, White House Photo Portrait, Looking Up. 1961. *JFK Library.* Wikimedia Commons.

General Motors headquarters in Detroit, Christian, Ralph. *National Parks Service.* Wikimedia Commons.

President Bill Clinton, United States. The United States Armed Forces. Executive Office of the President of the United States. *Wikimedia Commons.* By Bob McNeely. Media Wiki.

Newt Gingrich, United States. United States Congress. *Biographical Directory of the United States Congress.* Wikimedia Commons.

President George W. Bush, United States. U.S. Government Publishing Office. *U.S. Government Publishing Office.* U.S. Government. Wikimedia Commons.

President George W. Bush discusses strengthening Social Security at the Lake Nona YMCA Family Center in Orlando, 2005, United States. Executive Office of the President of the United States. *The White House: President George W. Bush.* By Eric Draper. Wikimedia Commons.

Period 3 – Foreign Relations

Alfred Thayer Mahan, Mahan, A. T. *The Story of the War in South Africa, 1899–1900.* New York: Greenwood, 1968. *Project Gutenberg.* Wikimedia Commons.

The Panama Canal in 1915, The Book of History: A History of All Nations from the Earliest Times to the Present, Volume XV: The United States, Flinders Petrie, W. M.; Holland Thompson; et al., New York: The Grolier Society, 1915. Wikimedia Commons.

President Wilson and French President Minister Poincaré, Strother, French, and Burton J. Hendrick, eds. *The World's Work: A History of Our Time.* Vol. 37. New York: Doubleday, Page, 1919. *Internet Archive.* Wikimedia Commons.

Henry Cabot Lodge, Everett, Marshall. *Famous Americans: Their Portraits, Biographies, and Thrilling Experiences.* Chicago, IL: Educational, 1901. *Internet Archive.* Wikimedia Commons.

USS California is sinking at Pearl Harbor, U.S. Navy. *USS California Sinking-Pearl Harbor.* 1941. National Archives and Records Administration, Still Pictures Unit, Archives II, College Park. Wikimedia Commons.

President Truman with Secretary of Defense George C. Marshall, Secretary of State Dean Acheson, and Secretary of the Treasury John Snyder, upon the President's Return from the Wake Island Conference. Rowe, Abbie, 1950. National Archives and Records Administration, Harry S. Truman Library, Independence, MO. Wikimedia Commons.

Marshall Plan Aid to France Included This Caterpillar Bulldozer Shown Here Arriving in 1949 to Help Rebuild That Country's Electric Power System. 1949. National Archives and Records Administration, Still Picture Records Section, Special Media Archives Services Division, College Park. *Wikimedia Commons.*

Edward Teller, McBride, Jacqueline. "Edward Teller." *Lawrence Livermore National Laboratory.* Lawrence Livermore National Security, LLC. Wikimedia Commons.

Robert R. Gilruth, responsible for Project Mercury, NASA. *Robert R. Gilruth-1958.* 1958. *Internet Archive.* Wikimedia Commons.

President Richard Nixon and Premier Alexei Kosygin sign the Cooperation in the Fields of Science and Technology Agreement between the United States and the Soviet Union. NASA, 1972. *NASA History Program Office.* Wikimedia Commons.

OPEC ministers, United States. Central Intelligence Agency. Executive Office of the President of the United States. *President Nixon and the Role of Intelligence in the 1973 Arab-Israeli War.* U.S. Federal Government, 1973. Print. Wikimedia Commons.

President Reagan and Soviet General Secretary Gorbachev in the White House Library, White House, 1987. Ronald Reagan Presidential Library and Museum, Simi Valley. The University of Texas. Wikimedia Commons.

Reagans are arriving in Moscow, May 29, 1988, by White House photographer. Wikimedia Commons.

Woman waving over the Berlin Wall, 1961, Budnik, Dan, 1961. Library of Congress, New York. Wikimedia Commons.

President Reagan Giving a Speech at the Berlin Wall, Brandenburg Gate, June 1987. Executive Office of the President of the United States,1987. Ronald Reagan Presidential Library. Wikimedia Commons.

Saddam Hussein, United States. Department of Defense. U.S. Air Force. American Forces Radio and Television Service. By D. Myles Cullen. *American Forces Network Online.* Wikimedia Commons.

Members of the coalition forces drive a tank during Operation Desert Storm, United States. Department of Defense. U.S. Air Force. Defense Imagery. By Dean M. Fox. *Defense Imagery Management Operations Center.* Wikimedia Commons.

World Trade Center on September 11, 2001, the National Park Service. Wikimedia Commons.

President Bush discusses the war on terror, Hewitt, Kimberlee, 2006. The White House. Wikimedia Commons.

Period 3 – Social History

Alice Paul, Edmonston. *Alice Paul, 1915.* 1915. Library of Congress, Washington, DC. Wikimedia Commons.

Hoover Dam site, United States. Geographical Survey. Department of the Interior. *River View of Boulder (Hoover) Dam Site.* By W. T. Lee. Mohave County, Arizona. 1904. Print. Wikimedia Commons.

Florence Kelley, Manuscripts and Archives Division, The New York Public Library. "Florence Kelley" *The New York Public Library Digital Collections.* Wikimedia Commons.

Hungarian immigrants are celebrating the sunflower harvest in Cleveland, Totya, Hu. *Hungarian Immigrants Cleveland.* 1913. Ellis Island Immigration Museum, New York. Wikimedia Commons.

The First Braceros Arriving in Los Angeles by Train in 1942, Lange, Dorothea, 1942. Oakland Museum of California, Oakland. *University of California, California Digital Library.* Wikimedia Commons.

Map of Japanese American Internment Camps in World War II, National Park Service. U.S. Department of the Interior. Wikimedia Commons.

The Ku Klux Klan on parade down Pennsylvania Avenue, U.S. Information Agency, 1928. National Archives and Records Administration, Still Picture Records Section, Special Media Archives Services Division, College Park. Wikimedia Commons.

Rosa Parks and Dr. Martin Luther King Jr., United States. U.S. Information Agency. U.S. Department of State. *Ebony Magazine*: John H, Johnson, 1955. *National Archives Records Administration.* U.S. Department of State, 8 July 2008. Wikimedia Commons.

Black students turned away in Little Rock, Arkansas 1957, Counts, I. Wilmer. *LTC Marion Johnson Turns Students Away.* 1957. *The National Guard.* Wikimedia Commons.

Cesar Chavez, United States. Environmental Protection Agency. *National Archives and Records Administration.* By Cornelius Michael Keyes. Wikimedia Commons.

Estelle Griswold, Lockwood, Lee, 1963. Time & Life Pictures. *Wikimedia Commons.*

Map of USA Highlighting Sun Belt. The University of Texas Libraries. Wikimedia Commons.

Fidel Castro and Camilo Cienfuegos in Havana. Korda, Luis,1959. Wikimedia Commons.

Toy vendor, Chinatown, San Francisco (c1900s), Genthe, Arnold. *Toy Vendor, Chinatown, San Francisco.* c. 1900s. Library of Congress, Washington, DC. Wikimedia Commons.

Rachel Carson and Robert Hines, United States. Department of the Interior. U.S. Fish and Wildlife Service. *U.S. Fish and Wildlife Service.* By Rex Gary Schmidt. NCTC Archives Museum, 1955. Wikimedia Commons.

Marine Corps is scaling a wall during the Korean War, U.S. Marine Corps. *Lopez Scaling Seawall.* 1950. *Naval History and Heritage Command.* Wikimedia Commons.

US Army is spraying Agent Orange in Vietnam, Photograph VA042083, Admiral Elmo R. Zumwalt, Jr. Collection: Agent Orange Subject Files, The Vietnam Center and Archive, Texas Tech University. Wikimedia Commons.

Watergate complex, U.S. Department of Justice. *Watergate Complex.* Gerald R. Ford Library & Museum "The Watergate Files" Exhibit. *National Archives and Records Administration.* Wikimedia Commons.

Gas rationing in 1974, Falconer, David. *No Gas 1974.* 1974. National Archives and Records Administration. *Wikimedia Commons.*

Iran Hostage Crisis, Enghelab Eslami Newspaper. *Banisadr Iran Hostage Crisis.* 1979. *Wikimedia Commons.*

Two U.S. Navy aircrafts parked on USS Nimitz for Operation Eagle Claw, Snyder. *F-14A VF-41 and VF-84 Operation Eagle Claw-1980.* 1980. U.S. Navy. *Defense Imagery Management Operations Center.* Wikimedia Commons.

Ronald Reagan Candid Black and White. Ronald Reagan Presidential Library, Simi Valley, CA. The *University of Washington.* Wikimedia Commons.

Dr. Jerry Falwell, By Liberty University. Wikimedia Commons.

Jim Daly of Focus on the Family, Jim Daly. 2010. *Focus on the Family.* Wikimedia Commons.

Department of Homeland Security Secretary Janet Napolitano swears in ten people as U.S. citizens under the Immigration and Nationality Act, United States. Department of Homeland Security. United States Coast Guard. *Defense Video and Imagery Distribution System.* By NyxoLyno Cangemi. U.S. Coast Guard. Wikimedia Commons.

Chief of Naval Operations Adm. Gary Roughead, Left, testifies before the Senate Armed Services Committee about the Comprehensive Review Working Group Report regarding the "Don't Ask, Don't Tell" Policy in 101203-N-FI224-113, Jones Vanderwyst, Tiffini M., 2010. *Defense Imagery Management Operations Center.* Wikimedia Commons.

Period 3 – Intellectual & Cultural History

1888 Prohibition poster, Principles of the Prohibition Party. 1888. Library of Congress Prints and Photographs Division, Washington, D.C.

Model T Ford being used for fishing, 1913, Model T Ford. 1913. *Grosse Pointe Public Schools.* Wikimedia Commons.

Poster for the jazz singer, Warner Brothers. *Blue Mouse Theatre* [Tacoma, Washington] 1928. Wikimedia Commons.

Langston Hughes, United States. U.S. Office of War Information. Gordon Parks. Wikimedia Commons.

F. Scott Fitzgerald, Bryant, Gordon. "F. Scott Fitzgerald, 1921." *Shadowland* 1921. Wikimedia Commons.

Trading card photo of Alan Freed, Topps Gum Cards, 1957. *Wikimedia Commons.*

Elvis Presley, United States. Executive Office of the Present of the United States. *The National Archives and Records Administration, Nixon Presidential Materials.* By Ollie Atkins. U.S. Federal Government. When Nixon Met Elvis Exhibit. Wikimedia Commons.

Timothy Leary arrested by the DEA in 1972, United States. Drug Enforcement Administration. U.S. Department of Justice. *U.S. Drug Enforcement Administration.* United States Department of Justice. Wikimedia Commons.

2011 uprising in Egypt, United States. *Voice of America.* Official External Radio and TV Broadcasting Service of the U.S. Federal Government. By Hamada Elrasam. U.S. Government. Wikimedia Commons.

Advanced Placement (AP) prep books by Sterling Test Prep

Biology Practice Questions

Biology Review

Physics 1 Practice Questions

Physics 1 Review

Physics 2 Practice Questions

Physics 2 Review

Environmental Science

Psychology

United States History

World History

European History

U.S. Government and Politics

Comparative Government and Politics

Human Geography

Visit our Amazon store

Made in the USA
Las Vegas, NV
07 May 2024

89643092R00249